This book, a celebration of the bimillennium of Horace's death and a successor to *Ovid Renewed* (Cambridge University Press 1988), explores, in as balanced and comprehensive a way as the editors could achieve, the presence of Horace in English letters and culture from the Renaissance onwards, in the form of a series of critical essays by different specialists, including two distinguished poets. The wide span of its coverage shows that there has been a continuous interest in Horace throughout the modern period, whereas it is often supposed that Horace's influence was only of central importance in the eighteenth century. Horace's 'autobiographical' mode was attractive to the humanists of the sixteenth century, and the lyric poetry inspired a richer response in the seventeenth than in the eighteenth. Horace indeed is a major (if often hidden) element in the English poetic tradition, both directly and as a result of the imitation and appropriation of his works by Wyatt, Jonson, Dryden, Pope and others. The book also casts fresh light on the character and interpretation of Horace, things intimately connected with the historical reception of his works, particularly by some of their most influential and sensitive readers, the great English poets.

The book is aimed at a wide and general readership: those interested in the classical heritage, the cultural importance of Horace, and issues of interpretation in comparative literature and cultural history.

HORACE MADE NEW

The title page of Richard Bentley's *Horace*, published by Cambridge University Press in 1711. *Photo*: Cambridge University Library.

HORACE MADE NEW

Horatian influences on British writing from
the Renaissance to the twentieth century

EDITED BY

CHARLES MARTINDALE
Professor of Latin,
University of Bristol

AND

DAVID HOPKINS
Senior Lecturer in English,
University of Bristol

Published by the Press Syndicate of the University of Cambridge
The Pitt Building, Trumpington Street, Cambridge CB2 1RP
40 West 20th Street, New York, NY 10011-4211, USA
10 Stamford Road, Oakleigh, Victoria 3166, Australia

© Cambridge University Press 1993

First published 1993

Printed in Great Britain at the University Press, Cambridge

A catalogue record for this book is available from the British Library

Library of Congress cataloguing in publication data applied for

ISBN 0 521 38019 7 hardback

The sources of the extracts printed in this book are as follows:

Extracts from 'The Lesson for Today' and 'Directive': *The Poetry of Robert Frost*, ed. Edward Connery Lathem (Jonathan Cape 1971); from 'Carmen Saeculare': C. H. Sisson, *In the Trojan Ditch* (Carcanet Press 1974); 'Wombwell on Strike': Donald Davie, *Collected Poems* (Carcanet Press 1990); the quotation from John Heath-Stubbs: *Artorius* (Enitharmon Press 1973); from 'The Return': Ezra Pound, *Collected Shorter Poems* (Faber & Faber 1968); from translations of Horace, *Odes* 1.11 and 1.31: *The Translations of Ezra Pound*, ed. Hugh Kenner (Faber & Faber 1970); from 'In Transit', 'The Horatians' and 'Ischia': W.H. Auden, *Collected Poems*, ed. Edward Mendelson (Faber & Faber 1976); from translations of Horace, *Odes* 1.13, 3.12 and 2.14: Basil Bunting, *Collected Poems* (Oxford University Press 1978); from Robert Pinsky; *An Explanation of America* (Princeton University Press 1979). Quotations from unpublished writings of Rudyard Kipling are reproduced by permission of The National Trust.

We offer this volume to
NIALL RUDD
Professor of Latin, University of Bristol (1973–1989)
Flaccus ille noster
as a retirement gift

CONTENTS

	List of illustrations	*page* xi
	Notes on contributors	xiii
	Note on abbreviations	xvi
	Preface	xvii
1	Introduction CHARLES MARTINDALE	1
2	Horace at home and abroad: Wyatt and sixteenth-century Horatianism COLIN BURROW	27
3	The best master of virtue and wisdom: the Horace of Ben Jonson and his heirs JOANNA MARTINDALE	50
4	Marvell and Horace: colour and translucency A. D. NUTTALL	86
5	Cowley's Horatian mice DAVID HOPKINS	103
6	Figures of Horace in Dryden's literary criticism PAUL HAMMOND	127
7	Horace's *Ode* 3.29: Dryden's 'Masterpiece in English' STUART GILLESPIE	148
8	Pope and Horace ROBIN SOWERBY	159
9	Good humour and the agelasts: Horace, Pope and Gray FELICITY ROSSLYN	184
10	Horace and the nineteenth century NORMAN VANCE	199

CONTENTS

11	Horace's Kipling STEPHEN MEDCALF	217
12	Some aspects of Horace in the twentieth century CHARLES TOMLINSON	240
13	Deniable evidence: translating Horace C. H. SISSON	258
	Postscript: images of Horace in twentieth-century scholarship DON FOWLER	268
	Notes	277
	Bibliography	313
	Index	317

ILLUSTRATIONS

PLATES

between pages 142 and 143

1 S. Botticelli, *Primavera* (Florence, Uffizi Gallery). Photo: Alinari.

FOUR IMAGES OF HORACE

2a Portrait of Horace from Lippert's collection of 'antique gems' (Mantua, Museo di Palazzo d'Arco, Gabinetto delle Stampe C-58). Engraving by J. C. Nabholz. Photo: Cavicchini.

2b Portrait of Horace: illustration from Holkham MS 318 fol. 35v. Reproduced by permission of Viscount Coke and the Trustees of the Holkham Estate. Photo: Coke Estates Ltd.

3a Portrait of Horace: illustration from Horace, *Opera* (J. Grüninger, Strasburg 1498): the first illustrated edition of Horace and the first published in Germany. Reproduced by Courtesy of the Master and Fellows of St John's College, Cambridge. Photo: Cambridge University Library.

3b Horace: detail from Raphael's *Parnassus* (Rome, Vatican), part of the section depicting Sappho and the lyric poets. Photo: Alinari.

HORATIAN EMBLEMS

4 *Agriculturae Beatitudo*, Otto Vaenius, *Emblemata* (Antwerp 1607) p. 89. Photo: University of London, Warburg Institute.

5a *In Medio Consistit Virtus, ibid.*, p. 19. Photo: University of London, Warburg Institute.

5b *Modum serva*, George Wither, *A Collection of Emblems Ancient and Modern* (1635), p. 169. Photo: Cambridge University Library.

EIGHTEENTH-CENTURY HORACE

6a Pope's grotto: sketch by William Kent (Devonshire Collection, Chatsworth). Reproduced by permission of the Chatsworth Settlement Trustees. Photo: University of London, Courtauld Institute of Art.

ILLUSTRATIONS

6b   Apotheosis of Horace: title page to André Dacier's edition of *Ars Poetica* (Paris 1691, volume 8 of his complete edition).
7   *Horace's Exclamation against his Tree* (also known as *A Landstorm*), by Philip James de Loutherbourg RA (1740–1812), commissioned 1771 (Plymouth, City Art Gallery). Lead, ink and wash. Photo: Robert Chapman.

TOWN AND COUNTRY MOUSE

8a   Thomas Bewick, *The Fables of Aesop and Others* (Newcastle 1818), p. 295. Photo: Bodleian Library.
8b   Beatrix Potter, illustration from *The Tale of Johnny Town-Mouse*, © Frederick Warne & Co. 1918, 1987.

DRAWINGS IN THE TEXT

Picture on page 28: Illustration to Horace *Ode* 1.1 from an edition published in Venice in 1505. Photo: University of London, The Warburg Institute.

Picture on page 49: Drawing from Caxton's *Aesop*, ed. R. T. Lenaghan (Cambridge, Mass., 1967). Photo: Cambridge University Library.

Picture on page 126: End-piece to the Story of the Country and the City Mouse, wood-engraving by Thomas Bewick, *The Fables of Aesop and Others* (Newcastle 1818) p. 294. Photo: Bodleian Library.

Picture on page 129: A page from *Q. Horatius Flaccus cum commentariis selectissimis variorum . . . Accurante Corn. Schrevelio* (Leiden, 1663), from the copy in the Brotherton Collection, Leeds University Library.

Picture on page 158: Title page from J. Baskerville, *Horace* (Birmingham 1762), vignette by Wale and Grignion. Photo: Cambridge University Library.

Pictures on pages 222 and 257: Sketches by Rudyard Kipling from an edition of Horace ('The Medici Press *Horace*', London 1910) owned by him. Sussex University Library. Reproduced by permission of the National Trust.

Picture on page 267: 'The Shepherd': illustration by Agostino Caracci in *De Laudibus Vitae Rusticae Ode Horati Epodon Secunda* (Aldus Manutius, Bologna 1586). Photo: University of London, Warburg Institute.

NOTES ON CONTRIBUTORS

COLIN BURROW is a Fellow of Gonville and Caius College, Cambridge and a University Assistant Lecturer in English. His book, *Epic Romance: Homer to Milton* will appear shortly. He wrote the chapter on Spenser in *Ovid Renewed* (1988).

DON FOWLER is Fellow and Tutor in Classics at Jesus College, Oxford and a University Lecturer in Greek and Latin Literature. He has written articles on Lucretius, Virgil and poetic closure, and regularly contributes a review of recent work on Latin literature to *Greece and Rome*. With his wife he is currently writing *Lucretius: A Companion*.

STUART GILLESPIE is a Lecturer in English at the University of Glasgow, and the General Editor of *Translation and Literature*. He is the editor of *The Poets on the Classics: An Anthology* (1988) and the author of several articles on seventeenth-century poetry and translation.

PAUL HAMMOND is a Senior Lecturer in English at the University of Leeds. His publications include *John Oldham and the Renewal of Classical Culture* (1983), *John Dryden: A Literary Life* (1991) and editions of *Selected Poems* by John Wilmot, Earl of Rochester (1982) and *Selected Prose* by Alexander Pope (1987). He is currently completing volume I of the Longman Annotated English Poets edition of Dryden.

DAVID HOPKINS is a Senior Lecturer in English at the University of Bristol. His publications include *John Dryden* (1986), *English Poetry: A Poetic Record* (1990) and a chapter on Ovid's witty depictions of violence in *Ovid Renewed*. He has recently completed, with Tom Mason, a book on the arts of poetry and poetry-reading, and is currently co-editing, with Paul Hammond, volumes II and III of the Longman Annotated English Poets edition of Dryden.

CHARLES MARTINDALE is Professor of Latin at the University of Bristol. His main research interests are concerned with the reception of classical texts.

NOTES ON CONTRIBUTORS

He is the editor of *Virgil and his Influence* (1984) and *Ovid Renewed*, author of *John Milton and the Transformation of Ancient Epic* (1986) and co-author of *Shakespeare and the Uses of Antiquity* (1990). He has contributed a chapter, 'Ovid, Horace and Others' to *The Legacy of Rome: A New Appraisal* (1992) and has recently completed a book on the importance of reception theory for classicists, entitled *Redeeming the Text: Latin Poetry and the Hermeneutics of Reception* (Cambridge University Press 1993).

JOANNA MARTINDALE is Librarian at Worcester College, Oxford. She wrote her D. Phil. thesis on 'The Response to Horace in the Seventeenth Century', and has edited the volume on *English Humanism: Wyatt to Cowley* (1985) in the Routledge Word and World series.

STEPHEN MEDCALF is Reader in English at the University of Sussex. He has published on a wide range of topics, from the Bible and the Classics (chapters in *Virgil and his Influence* and *Ovid Renewed*) via medieval literature to modern writers, including Chesterton, T. S. Eliot and William Golding. He is especially interested in the history of religious experience and consciousness.

A. D. NUTTALL is Professor of English and Fellow of New College, Oxford. He has written on Shakespeare, on the relationship of literature and philosophy and on the differences and continuities between antiquity and the post-classical world; in this last area his publications include contributions to *Virgil and his Influence* and *Ovid Renewed*, and a collection of essays entitled *The Stoic in Love* (1989). He has recently published a study of literary *Openings* (1992).

FELICITY ROSSLYN read English at Cambridge and subsequently studied Greek at Harvard. She is currently a Lecturer in English at the University of Leicester and an editor of *The Cambridge Quarterly*. Her doctoral thesis was a study of the diction of Pope's *Iliad*. Her publications include *Alexander Pope: A Literary Life* (1990) and articles on Milan Kundera, Ivo Andrić, and other post-war Eastern European writers.

C. H. SISSON's poems include translations from Heine, Catullus, Dante, Lucretius, Racine and Virgil, as well as versions of Horace's *Ars Poetica* and *Carmen Saeculare* and of *Odes* 1.11, 2.11 and 2.15 in *In the Trojan Ditch* (1974). His *Collected Poems* were published in 1984. His essays on translation are collected in *In Two Minds: Guesses at Other Writers* (1990).

NOTES ON CONTRIBUTORS

ROBIN SOWERBY read Classics and English at Cambridge and now lectures in English at the University of Stirling. His publications include student introductions to Virgil's *Aeneid*, Plato's *Republic* and Homer's *Iliad* and *Odyssey*, and a selection of Pope's poetry and prose for the Routledge English Texts (1988). He is currently working on a study of the classical genres in the Renaissance.

CHARLES TOMLINSON is Professor Emeritus of English at the University of Bristol. His *Collected Poems* were published in 1985 (expanded edition, 1987). His long-standing interest in the art of translation is reflected in *Poetry and Metamorphosis* (1983) and *The Oxford Book of Verse in English Translation* (1980).

NORMAN VANCE is Reader in English at the University of Sussex, and has written widely on nineteenth-century literature and society. His publications include *Irish Literature: A Social History* (1990) as well as contributions to *Virgil and his Influence* and *Ovid Renewed*. He is currently working on a study of *The Victorians and Ancient Rome*.

A NOTE ON ABBREVIATIONS

The following abbreviations are used for the various parts of Horace's *œuvre*:

Ars: Ars Poetica
Ep.: Epistles
Epod.: Epodes
S: Sermones
Saec.: Carmen Saeculare

PREFACE

THIS VOLUME COMPLETES a trilogy about aspects of the reception of the three great Latin poets of the Augustan period: its predecessors were *Virgil and his Influence* (Bristol Classical Press 1984) and *Ovid Renewed* (Cambridge University Press 1988). This volume has a slightly different focus from its predecessors', at once narrower and sharper. It restricts discussion to Horace's influence on British writers from the Renaissance onwards. In this way we have been able to secure a more complete coverage of a more limited area than was the subject of the two previous volumes. By ranging over the whole of post-Renaissance British literature in some detail the book corrects an imbalance in conventional thinking, according to which Horace's influence was only of central importance in the eighteenth century, and particularly for Pope. Without underestimating Pope's achievement, this book stresses that there was a continuous engagement with Horace throughout the modern period: Horace's 'autobiographical' mode was attractive to the early humanists, and it can be argued that the lyric poetry at least inspired a richer response in the seventeenth than in the eighteenth century. The volume has been compiled in the conviction that fresh light is cast on the character of Horace's own poetry by an exploration of its reception by some of its most persuasive and influential readers, the great English poets. The fascination exercised by Horace on later poets persists to this day, and we have accordingly enlisted two well-known contemporary poets among our contributors.

Like its predecessors, this book takes the form of a collection of critical essays by different hands, since, in our view, it is unlikely that any single scholar could write a history of British Horatianism at the appropriate level of engagement and knowledge. We have tried, in the choice of subjects and contributors, to secure a rounded treatment, and have discussed in detail, with all contributors, the nature of the enterprise and the contents of their chapters. On the other hand we have made no attempt to enforce uniformity of view, and differences of opinion and emphasis will be clearly visible to the reader. For example, CAM in the general Introduction sketches, as a starting-point for discussion, an approach to Horace (or rather 'Horace')

PREFACE

based on contemporary hermeneutics and on reception-theory. Other contributors take what some would think of as a more 'traditional' view of literary enquiry. All, however, share a common interest in the translation, imitation, appropriation, or (re-)fashioning of Horace's poems by later writers. *Horace Made New* is thus a unified project, not a miscellaneous set of essays, and each chapter has its part in the economy of the whole.

The volume is dedicated to Niall Rudd, whose distinguished career as a Latinist has centred on Horace and his influence. His publications in this area include, in addition to some twenty articles, *The Satires of Horace* (1966), the chapter on Horace in volume II of *The Cambridge History of Classical Literature* (1982) and an edition of *Epistles 2 and Ars Poetica* (1990), all published by Cambridge University Press, as well as the relevant portions of *Themes in Roman Satire* (1986). He has also published a widely used translation of Horace's *Satires and Epistles* (Penguin) and is currently editing a volume for Bristol Classical Press, entitled *Two Thousand Years Alive: Essays for Horace's Bimillennium*. He will not agree with all the opinions expressed in this book, but he will, we trust, see the project as a useful supplement to his own work.

Horace Made New also reflects the collaborative work now being done by the Departments of English and of Classics and Archaeology at the University of Bristol which has centred on an open English–Classics seminar designed to explore issues associated with reception, translation and intertextuality. Earlier versions of a number of the chapters in the book were first given as papers to this seminar.

Because the book is designed to appeal to a wide and general readership, we have asked contributors to employ, in citations of English poetry, modernized spelling and punctuation, even where the edition which they are following (and which is cited accordingly in the notes) retains the original. Contributors were also asked to cite Horace from the new Teubner text (ed. D. R. Shackleton Bailey), unless they specify otherwise.

A final preliminary note. At the time of writing this Preface, it is impossible to tell whether the book will actually appear in 1992 or 1993. Horace died in 8 BC. Our hope is, nevertheless, that the volume might be considered, in spirit if not perhaps, in the event, strictly in letter, as a contribution to the celebrations of Horace's bimillennium of posthumous life.

CAM   DWH
UNIVERSITY OF BRISTOL

September 1991

I

INTRODUCTION
Charles Martindale

I

MANY WRITERS, INCLUDING most of those discussed in this book, and a great many readers, have had a friend – in Quintus Horatius Flaccus. More, perhaps, than any other ancient poet his writings have encouraged, and continue to encourage, reading in terms of what is now sometimes called 'the poetics of presence', the belief that literature makes present to us the consciousness and mind of the author behind or beyond the text. But which Horace are we talking about? – 'Fat, beery, beefy Horace', as one English scholar called him,[1] or the more elegant courtier and lover preferred by several French critics. Horace has done duty as a quasi-Christian moralist, as a hedonistic enthusiast for 'a generous bottle and a lovesome she', as an English landowner and country-gentleman. To Ezra Pound Horace 'baldheaded, pot-bellied, underbred, sychophantic' . . . 'sensuous only in so far as he is a gourmet of food and of language', had 'but the clubman's poise and no stronger emotion than might move one toward a particularly luscious oyster';[2] but to the impulsive Ben Jonson he was rather 'the best master both of virtue and wisdom, an excellent and true judge upon cause and reason' (*Discoveries*, 3204). We might conclude that there are, and always have been, many Horaces, not one Horace. 'Horace', it could be argued, is a construction, by readers and reading communities, in terms of specific reading practices, and there are no final grounds, no ultimate courts of appeal, to which we can have recourse to establish the 'true' or the 'real' Horace among the various images. On this view the history of Horace's 'reception' assumes great hermeneutical importance: whether we like it or not, indeed whether we know it or not, our current images of Horace, our current readings of his poems, are shaped by that history – even to reject a past reading or a past image is, in a sense, to acknowledge its authority, to become enmeshed in its traces. The various poets and writers treated in this volume offer readings of Horace at least as searching as those of modern scholars; but, equally importantly, those readings, widely influential, have also been, directly or obliquely, constitutive of ours.

It is probably true that some images of Horace have tended to predominate over others, as his works have regularly been appropriated for certain interests and for certain sets of values. Horace is commonly regarded as a 'classic' writer (in several senses of that highly charged term), as an apostle of Reason, moderation, common sense, balance, good taste, as the poet of the middle way, of ordinary decencies, as the praiser of friendship, country life, retirement, privacy, simplicity (it is worth observing how value-laden is every one of these words, how open their meanings to contestation). For example in the 'The Horatians' (1968) W. H. Auden finds Horace's natural modern successors among groups like clergymen –

> Among those I really know, the
> British branch of the family, how many have
> found in the Anglican Church
> your Maecenas who enabled
> a life without cumber, as pastors adjective
> to rustic flocks

– or 'organists in trollopish / cathedral towns', or museum curators, and he identifies himself with their ordinariness:

> We can only
> do what it seems to us we were made for, look at
> this world with a happy eye
> but from a sober perspective.

In more hostile vein, in John Heath-Stubbs' *Artorius* (1973), the critic Phyllidulus (a thinly disguised Dr Leavis) offers this account of Horace as an Augustan poet:

> It was said that Augustus found Rome brick and left it marble – and something analogous occurred to poetry in the same generation. One may happen to prefer brick. Marmoreal is a term that has been applied to the Odes of Horace. If this style be marble, it is a veneer which does not serve to conceal the writer's essential commonplaces of mind – a commonplaceness which infuses likewise the whole corpus of his epistles.[3]

Portraits like Auden's or Phyllidulus' can be defended, but – like all others – they not only accept, or reproduce, certain values, but also depend on foregrounding some elements and downplaying, even erasing, others. Passages from different poems which can support this picture are selected and interpreted in particular ways, and then provide a core around which the other writings are organized. (In the Renaissance the process was facilitated by the existence of *florilegia* and other collections of favourite excerpts from the Latin poets, usually arranged by topic.) Poems, or parts of poems, which fit the picture can then be termed 'typically' or 'characteristically' Horatian;

Introduction

at such moments Horace is 'most himself'. Many modern studies of Horace will illustrate these and other tropes of the rhetoric of authenticity used to validate particular images of the poet.

It is possible to construct – again, of course, by judicious selection – a very different image from the one just sketched. Let us look at some of the key elements, and first at the way in which Horace is regarded as a classic writer. Of course his poetry rapidly became part of a dominant canon, and in that sense a 'classic', but the word is often taken to imply the possession of a style which is, in some sense, normative and free from eccentricity and excessive idiosyncrasy. This may be defensible, to an extent, of the hexameter poems (where we can encounter a relaxed *sermo purus*); but what of the *Odes*? It is possible that some of Horace's original readers at least may have found them weirdly experimental.[4] In them we meet a style which combines the arty and the prosaic, along with a highly artificial, mannered word order and a structural wilfulness which can require a reader to strain in the attempt, taxing or vain, to apprehend (e.g. *Odes* 1.7). Some of this can be well illustrated by the end of 2.11 (a *carpe diem* poem, full of evocative images of flux), where Horace uses *scortum*, an 'unpoetic' word for prostitute, to describe the flute-girl Lyde in a passage which concludes with an artfully tangential and intricately wrought description of the woman's hair-style:

> quis devium scortum eliciet domo
> Lyden? eburna dic, age, cum lyra
>   maturet incomptam Lacaenae
>   more comam religata nodo.

Who will entice the shy tart Lyde from her house? Come, tell her to hurry with her ivory lyre, binding her uncombed hair back in a knot, Spartan-fashion.

There is also a tension between the 'modern' subject-matter and the 'archaic' lyric structures and procedures which Horace adapted from Sappho, Alcaeus, Pindar and other early Greek *lyrici*. This process of adaptation was something different from (say) Virgil's use of the hexameter, since there had been a continuous tradition of epic writing in Latin since Ennius. For Horace's *Odes* the main surviving precedents are two Sapphic poems by Catullus. Poem 11 (*Furi et Aureli, comites Catulli*), echoed twice in the *Odes* (1.22; 2.6), anticipates Horace (it can be argued) in the use of contrasted registers and tones, the contrived structural asymmetry, the unexpected turns in the argument, the plangent dying fall.

Partly for reasons such as these it has often been argued that the *Odes* resist adequate translation, since most translators prettify the originals and assimilate them to more ordinary lyric models. A sense of the possible strangeness of Horace's lyric style can be encountered only here and there in translations and imitations: for example, in Milton's metaphrastic rendering of the Pyrrha *Ode* (1.5) or Ben Jonson's of 4.1; in Pound's version of 1.11, the Leuconoe *Ode* ('Ask not ungainly askings of the end'); in the stiff, convoluted idioms and arch conjunctions of vocabulary in some of Auden's Horatian pieces –

> Dearest to each his birthplace; but to recall a green
> valley where mushrooms fatten in the summer nights
>   and silvered willows copy
>   the circumflexions of the stream
>
> is not my gladness today: I am presently moved
> by sun-drenched Parthenopea, my thanks are for you,
>   Ischia, to whom a fair wind has
>   brought me rejoicing with dear friends
>
> from soiled productive cities.   (from 'Ischia')

or in Kipling's parody of *Odes* 1.1 ('There are whose study is of smells': 'Horace, Bk.v. Ode 3'). Kipling starts by reproducing the alien movement of the rhetorical organization which scholars call the priamel, while in the first line the omission of the antecedent is likewise a Latinism (= *sunt quorum*). The combination of prosaic vocabulary in lines 3–4 ('How something mixed with something else / Makes something worse') with the artificial 'increasing without Venus', the presence of such polar contrasts as 'cure, or cause disease' or 'farthest roll and fastest turn', and the deft understatement of the final picture of the poet by his fireside, all reveal an alert understanding of the nuts and bolts of Horace's style.[5]

Or let us consider the question of restraint, balance and propriety. The Cleopatra *Ode* (1.37) may be balanced in its structure (we could analyse the poem as an introductory stanza, followed by approximately three stanzas each for events up to and after Actium, divided by a pair of pivotal similes in stanza 5). But, despite any dialectical character, the *Ode* hardly offers us a moderate account of Cleopatra or a middle way between positive and negative assessments of her; rather Cleopatra is first abused, without any mitigation or remorse of voice, as sexually immoral, drunk, madly elated by success, with her retinue of diseased eunuchs (men unmanned), and then, in an extraordinary tergiversation, which has received various different explanations, she is given the 'male' characteristics of courage, philosophical equanimity and regal stature in the hour of her defeat and death. The partial regendering – *nec muliebriter / expavit ensem* ('nor did she fear the sword like a woman') – is the more surprising because, in one of the similes, the doves figuring her are called *mollis* (a word regularly implying effeminacy). The *Ode*, with its excited rhythms, its grand Pindaric sweep and massive final sentence, offers us (on this view) not so much balance or detachment as two bizarrely juxtaposed and opposing stances.[6]

Introduction

Certainly Horace's general treatment of women does not always seem marked by 'restraint'. Two *Epodes* (8 and 12) abuse old women by dwelling, with powerful particularity, on their decaying bodily characteristics, repulsive to the male lover.⁷ The reference to fellatio (represented in numerous Latin texts as degrading for the performer), at the end of 8, still has some power to shock; the artistic texture of the verse with assonance of the open vowels can enforce on the reader a sensuous collusion: *quod ut superbo provoces ab inguine, / ore allaborandum est tibi* ('to arouse my prick from its proud crotch, you have to work hard with your mouth'). Scholars have various strategies for not incorporating such writing in the category of 'typically Horatian'. Poems like these are called 'exercises' as opposed to 'true (i.e. sincere) poems' (all poems both are and are not in some sense exercises). Their character is assigned to the genre, not to the poet (as though matters of genre were not operative in all Horace's works). Of course the sentiments of these *Epodes* need not be put down to any personal idiosyncrasy of the writer; they can be paralleled elsewhere in Roman invective, in the *Priapea*, for example, in Martial, or in graffiti. But they nevertheless reflect, and helped to perpetuate, dominant images that were part of a discourse about sexuality, something which we might not wish to evade by a merely formalist ruse. More generally (with the exception of 13 which is felt to be closest in manner to an *Ode*) the *Epodes* are treated as immature, an argument not normally used about the *Eclogues*, written by Virgil at a similar stage; anyway Horace continued to abuse ageing flames in powerful verse in the *Odes* (1.23; 4.13). Scholars look round carefully for signs of such 'immaturity'. Fraenkel finds them in *Epode* 6 in the 'lack of discretion and the sense of consistency which distinguish the mature works of Horace',⁸ which leads the poet to present himself first as a dog ('of good breed') and then as a bull. Fraenkel seems to have forgotten that in *Odes* 2.5 Lalage is figured as a heifer in the green meadow, and then as an unripe grape. Indeed discontinuous imagery of this kind (perhaps in imitation of Callimachus) is characteristic of much of Horace's most admired poetry. At the end of the Dellius *Ode* (2.3) we have a particularly striking example – destined all to die, we are like sheep gathered into the same fold: our lots will sooner or later be shaken out of the urn; we are bound for the eternal exile on Charon's skiff:

> omnes eodem cogimur, omnium
> versatur urna serius ocius
> sors exitura et nos in aeternum
> exsilium impositura cumbae.

Gordon Williams sees a transition from the *Epodes* and *Sermones* where 'anger, contempt, and amusement are the fundamental emotions (though he often transcends these emotions in both works)' to the maturity of the *Odes* and *Epistles* which 'express a more meditative, more philosophical, more humane attitude'.⁹ It would take long to unpack all the unexamined assumptions in these judgements; suffice it to say that in both Dante and Milton anger and contempt fuelled some of their greatest writing, or that denunciation of human wickedness, by Swift (say) or Pope, could be seen as having its own 'humanity'.

Or again let us take the matter of 'good taste'. Here there is a distinct danger of constructing a discrete and mystified notion of taste outside historical and cultural contingency and above competing ideologies, something which literary theorists call 'the fetishization of the aesthetic'. In the poems in which he directly discusses literary matters, Horace in general subscribes to Aristotelian notions of propriety and decorum. But it is not difficult to find fissures in the system. Women are expected to adhere to the decorum of time, and thus, as we have seen, are excoriated for continuing the life of love beyond the years 'appropriate' to it. But when the male lover finds that Venus is no respecter of age (*Odes* 4.1), he apparently treats the matter in a very different tone, with wit, sympathy and sentimental pathos. As with 'life', so with art. In the *Ars Poetica* Horace criticizes the bad poet who incongruously 'paints the dolphin in the woods, the boar in the waves of the sea' (29f). But, in one of the sprightliest of his political *Odes* (1.2), he disregards such advice with a striking picture of the great Flood, when 'the race of fishes clung to the tops of elm-trees which had once been the well-known haunts of pigeons, and terrified deer swam on the rising flood'.¹⁰ We tend to associate such fantasies more with Ovid and the poets of the 'Silver Age', and indeed Ovid describes the Flood in similar terms in *Metamorphoses* Book 1 (293ff). The passage reminds us yet again that Horace can be a more varied writer than he is often given credit for, and that there are many passages in his poems which may not conform to narrower notions of literary propriety. In *Odes* 3.3.12 we read that Augustus will drink nectar 'with crimson lips' (*purpureo ore*); in 2.5 Lalage is figured as a heifer unable to bear the weight of the bull rushing into Venus; in 2.20 Horace details his metamorphosis into a swan in grotesque (if humorous) detail. Whatever one thinks of such flourishes (bad taste?), they hardly conform to conventional notions of tasteful writing. A. E. Housman issued a stern warning about the difficulty of using 'taste' as a criterion for resolving disputed matters of text:

When Horace is reported to have said *seu mobilibus veris inhorruit adventus foliis*, and when pedants like Bentley ... object that the phrase is unsuitable to its context, of what avail is it to be assured by persons of taste ... that these are exquisite lines? Exquisite to whom? Consider the mutations of opinion, the reversals of literary judgement, which this one small island has witnessed in the last 150 years: what is the likelihood that your notions ... of the exquisite are those of a foreigner who wrote for

Introduction

foreigners two millenniums ago? And for what foreigners? For the Romans, for men whose religion you disbelieve, whose chief institution you abominate, whose manners you do not like to talk about, but whose literary tastes, you flatter yourself, were identical with yours ... It is not to be supposed that this age, because it happens to be ours, has been specially endowed with a gift denied to all other modern ages; that we, by nature or by miracle, have mental affinity with the ancients, or that we can lightly acquire it, or that we can even acquire it at all. Communion with the ancients is purchasable at no cheaper rate than the kingdom of heaven; we must be born again. But to be born again is a process exceedingly repugnant to all right-minded Englishmen. I believe they think it improper, and they have a strong and well-grounded suspicion that it is arduous. They would much rather retain the prevalent opinion that the secret of the classical spirit is open to anyone who has a fervent admiration for the second-best parts of Tennyson.[11]

From such a perspective the appreciation of ancient poetry becomes a more difficult matter than we normally care to acknowledge. A possible response is a hermeneutic approach which concedes that, just as there is no simple return to an originary meaning, so we cannot, indeed should not, abandon our fore-understandings and sensibilities, accepting that Horace has only remained available to us by that long process of mediation and appropriation which constitutes his reception and which is none the less always open and contestable, always capable of further modification, yet in such a way that the new descriptions will contain the traces of previous descriptions.[12] That is indeed what living in 'history' means; we are both constrained and enabled by that complex textual weave we call the 'past'.

Then there is the matter of moderation, of the mean. The phrase *aurea mediocritas*, 'golden mean', from the *central* poem of Book 2 (10.5), has become so familiar that we are apt to forget that it is another Horatian oxymoron, something paradoxical. The mean's meaning is somewhat slippery. When in *Sermones* 1.2 Horace proposes sex with freedwomen and slaves as the Aristotelian mean between sex with married women and sex with low prostitutes, it is hard for us to take the doctrine at its face value. If the extremes were known and fixed, it would be easy to locate the central point, but this way of thinking might sit uneasily with Horace's emphasis on flux. So the mean may rather be a way of finding something to hold on to as a centre in a turning world, of fashioning a life which makes some sort of sense amidst the gyrations and contradictions of experience. The mean would not then be a position of stasis, but would involve movement within an unstable world, as the individual accommodates herself or himself to present conditions (a version of Rorty's 'soft pragmatism'?). As such it need not evince the complacency of some eighteenth-century versions (see e.g. Addison in *Spectator* 464: 'The middle condition seems to be the most advantageously situated for the gaining of wisdom.'[13]) When Charles Jennens (librettist of

Messiah) prepared excerpts from 'L'Allegro' and 'Il Penseroso' for Handel to set to music, he added a third part, 'Il Moderato', to resolve Milton's passionate dichotomies. (Handel, who set Milton's words to some of his most expressive music, found less to inspire him in the banalities of this synthesis, and the final section of the oratorio is frequently omitted in modern performances.) The new text includes the words:

> Keep, as of old, the middle way,
> Nor deeply sad, nor idly gay,
> But still the same in look and gait,
> Easy, cheerful and sedate.

That this is offered as specifically 'Horatian' wisdom is confirmed by a subsequent couplet:

> Who safely steer two rocks between,
> And prudent keep the golden mean.

This is one way in which the Horatian mean has been appropriated. Fortunately there are others. Following Harold Bloom, who argues that all readings can be regarded as misreadings (strong or weak), we might designate the Jennens version a 'weak misreading'. But even the static view of the mean can be made thrilling, when it is accompanied by a sense of what threatens its stability.

The widespread eighteenth-century view of Horace as a classic and measured writer finds embodiment in the frontispiece to Bentley's famous edition of Horace, which appeared in 1711 (cover and frontispiece).[14] The design, by the Dutchman Jan Goeree (1670–1731), the son of an antiquary, is set in a wooded grove below Mount Helicon, where, under a laurel tree, a pedestal supporting a bust of Horace forms a shrine which is visited by Apollo with his lyre, while a female figure, probably the lyric Muse Euterpe (or perhaps Minerva, the goddess of wisdom), assisted by winged Genii, decorates the shrine with a garland. A satyr is directed towards Apollo's action, while in the background we can discern a herm. The whole design must be an allegory of Horace's inspiration, artistry and fame, but the details admit of various readings. The evergreen laurel presumably signifies eternity and poetic prowess. The satyr perhaps hints at the story of Apollo and Marsyas, frequently interpreted as the victory of intellect over passion. Horace, poet of the middle way, is placed in a mean position between the herm in its dark background and the excessive dazzle at the top of Helicon where the horse Pegasus strikes out the spring Hippocrene with his hoof. It is mildly ironical that this conventional representation of Horace should appear in Bentley's brilliantly iconoclastic edition. The great scholar's choice of author was probably pointed: again and again he would show how the received text of Horace, so beloved by the mob of gentlemen-amateurs who wrote at ease, was corrupt or misunderstood.

Introduction

It is perhaps easier to justify the dominant image of Horace from the *Sermones*. It is here that the longer passages of 'autobiography' – including the more extended descriptions of the Sabine farm – are to be found. Yet even here, in writings about them, a certain selectiveness is evident. *Sermones* 1.2 concerns sex. According to Niall Rudd 'the main theme... is folly opposed to good sense in sexual relations',[15] and the anodyne word 'bawdy' is apt to put in an appearance in accounts of it. Pope, perhaps, was not so sure. He issued, anonymously ('in the manner of Mr Pope'), an imitation entitled 'Sober Advice from Horace' (together with the Latin text and notes by himself attributed to Bentley, which criticize the 'mistakes' of the imitator), a work which a leading Pope scholar finds (in contradistinction, in his view, to the original) 'fairly nasty' and 'in the notes if not in the text, pornographic'.[16] On the words *mirator* CUNNI CUPIENNIUS ALBI (so printed), 'Cupiennius admirer of a white cunt' (i.e. the cunt of a woman wearing the white *stola* of the *matrona*), translated 'hoary shrine', 'Bentley' comments: 'Here the imitator grievously errs, *cunnus albus* by no means signifying a white or grey garment, but a thing under a white or grey garment, which thing may be either black, brown, red, or particoloured.' As usual Pope's ironies ricochet. Bentley is mocked for his pedantry and humourlessness, but nonetheless his interpretation of Horace is a persuasive one; Horace's obscenities are frequently glossed over by readers over-concerned with propriety and 'morality', and dishonest in repudiating a fascination with sex.[17] Horace's 'unromantic' attitude to women is often described as typically Roman, and compared to Lucretius'. The comparison is unconvincing. Lucretius' suspicion of sexuality is fuelled by a fierce philosophical commitment; by contrast when in *Sermones* 1.3.107–8 Horace writes *nam fuit ante Helenam cunnus taeterrima belli / causa* ('for before Helen a cunt was the most terrible cause of war'), the voice seems rather that of Shakespeare's Thersites. *Cunnus* functions as a metonymy for woman, who is thereby reduced to this single orifice.

Nevertheless Horatian *causerie*, and in particular the *Epistles*, could provide a model for that eighteenth-century culture-hero, the Man of Sense. In *Spectator* 618 the *Epistles* are characterized as follows (I have italicized some of the words and phrases which carry a particularly strong – if unexamined – ideological charge):

The qualifications requisite for writing epistles, after the model given us by Horace, are of a quite different nature. He that would excel in this kind must have a good fund of *strong masculine sense*. To this there must be joined a *thorough knowledge of mankind* . . . and the *prevailing humours* of the age. Our author must have his mind well seasoned with the *finest precepts of morality*, and be filled with *nice reflections* upon the bright and dark sides of *human life*. He must be a master of *refined raillery*, and understand the *delicacies*, as well as the *absurdities*, of *conversation*. He must have a lively *turn of wit*, with an *easy and concise* manner of expression . . . He must . . . appear a *man of the world* throughout.[18]

This number is attributed to Ambrose Philips, but the sentiments are Addisonian enough. The *Spectator* and *Tatler* (along with other periodicals) were busy civilizing, and uniting, the nation after the political disasters of the previous century. Tags of Horatian wisdom were frequently quoted, and their 'flexible, homogeneous forms' could be seen as the modern prose equivalent of Horatian *sermo*. The manner has been described as 'eirenic and urbane', as 'blandly homogenizing', operating in the 'emulsive space of the public sphere', whose hallmark is 'its consensual character'.[19] Addison is too anodyne a writer for many moderns, although he has been defended skilfully, and in strikingly 'Horatian' terms, by C. S. Lewis as affording 'some tranquil middle ground of quiet sentiments and pleasing melancholies and gentle humour to come in between our restless idealism and our equally restless dissipations'.[20] What one may miss, perhaps, are the flashes of a deeper melancholy which so attracted Dr Johnson to Horace; thus on 7 August 1777, he wrote to Mrs Thrale: 'At Birmingham I heard of the death of an old friend, and at Lichfield of the death of another. *Anni praedantur euntes*' (*Ep.* 2.2.55).[21] Again in the essayists the key words seem 'fixed', their meanings wholly given; in Horace their ideological equivalents (it can be argued) are subjected openly to play, mobility, exploration and a sense of discovery. Horace obviously played an important role in the development of the English essay (Swift's *A Tritical Essay*, a parody of the form, contains several citations from his writings). Cowley's influential masterpiece, the *Essays*, combines verses both original and translated (including some of Horace's) and relaxed, ruminative prose: his themes include the shortness and obscurity of life, the joys of solitude and the small of scale, love of the countryside, the nature of contentment – and praise of Horace.

Even the ordinariness of Horace's life can be challenged. The son of an ex-slave, he rose to become familiar with many of the greatest among Rome's elite. In his youth he had favoured the Republican cause and fought at Philippi, commonly regarded as one of the decisive battles in world history. He witnessed other events of importance. He may have been with Maecenas at Actium. He apparently accompanied him on a delicate diplomatic mission to negotiate with Antony (*Sermones* 1.5). Chosen by the *princeps* to compose the hymn for the Secular Games of 17 BC, he became virtually poet laureate, a celebrity pointed out in his perambulations through Rome (*Odes* 4.3). Augustus offered him the post of private secretary (*ab epistulis*), which Horace was able to refuse, to the applause of later ages.[22] Such is not the story of Everyman.

This revised portrait of Horace has been offered, not to give a 'true' likeness, still less a definitive one, but as a rhetorical ploy, to make the point that poems, like people and the world in general, are endlessly redescribable. And so we may return again, with this presumption in mind, to the problem of Horace's self-representation.

Introduction

2

In retrospect even the bitterest antagonists of an age can seem to hold a surprising amount in common. So it may prove with out present contest of faculties. New Critics, Post-structuralists, even many Historicists (old and New) share a hostility to traditional forms of biographical criticism and to what Roland Barthes called 'the author function'. Texts, not authors, are to be the focus of attention, and critics exercise care not to appear entrapped by the 'biographical fallacy'. All this makes it difficult to get a purchase on one of Horace's most distinctive achievements as it appears from the history of his reception. Against the current critical consensus we must set the reports of so many readers over the centuries that in Horace's poems they have encountered a unique individual, even a kind of friend. This is not simply a matter of general reading practices, for similar reports are not made for all ancient poets. So striking an inscribing of the self is not found commonly in literature; indeed it was hardly found again on such a scale until Petrarch's more morbidly, obsessively introspective self-fashionings in the fourteenth century.[23] In Horace it is achieved in part by the fragments of what appear to be an autobiography (however fictive and rhetorically contrived, partly as validation of his poetic calling), but more by a sense of play of personality (however elusive) over the material, which makes his whole corpus more than simply the sum of its parts, constituting a compelling *imago vitae*. That this play of personality is largely, or even wholly, a matter of style – and thus a linguistic construct – is no objection; such differences of style are precisely what differentiate people in 'life' also. The difference in the reception of the three major Augustan poets is, in that sense, instructive. Ovid helped to sustain an interest in female sexuality and a sceptical view of the world, and provided a mass of mythological material as subject matter for art and literature. Virgil's *Aeneid* could underpin a commitment to Empire (with England as a second Rome) and easily be appropriated to a Christian view of a heaven-directed *telos* and the sacrifice of individual human happiness in the pursuit of 'higher' goals. Horace, however, rather supplied a texture of life, a lived aesthetic (repeatedly in his work we encounter discussions of his artistic views alongside a concern with ethics and 'proper living'). Hence his life on the Sabine farm became the inspiration for Jonson (for example in 'To Penshurst', the first in a sub-genre of English country-house poems); for Herrick in a Devonshire vicarage; for Pope at Twickenham; for Tennyson on the Isle of Wight; for Kipling in 'Sussex by the sea'; and many another.

The dangers and excesses of biographical criticism can be illustrated from Eduard Fraenkel's influential *Horace*, which was published in 1957, but which, in terms of its methodology, could easily have been written fifty years earlier. 'Horace ... never lies', Fraenkel declares at one memorable moment. (We may recall Syme's dry rejoinder: 'Horace, so weighty authority avers, "never lies". Quite so, he is too crafty for that. And this epistle [2.1] will be found to disclose craft of a high calibre, in both senses of the term.'[24] Fraenkel indeed has few doubts about the transparent truthfulness of his hero's self-representation. Dismissing a supposed deficiency in Suetonius' account in the *Vita Horati*, he writes: 'That need not worry us since for the history of Horace's friendship with Maecenas and with Augustus we are provided with the most reliable and detailed evidence'[25] (i.e. that of Horace himself). Suetonius had written 'and working himself into the favour (*insinuatus*) of first Maecenas and a little later Augustus he held a not inconsiderable place in the friendship (*amicitia*) of both'. By writing *insinuatus*, Fraenkel claims, Suetonius 'puts on the facts his own interpretation, the interpretation of a man living at the court of Hadrian'. The assumption that a modern scholar is better placed to judge the nature of social relationships in the ancient world than Suetonius is itself interesting. And Fraenkel does not consider the possibility that it is precisely the writings of Horace (and other Augustan poets) which have created the picture that the court of Augustus was so different from that of Hadrian (less decadent? – one might recall Augustus' friendship with the 'unspeakable' Vedius Pollio, rumoured to throw his slaves to the lampreys.[26]) 'Facts' are anyway always 'under description', not least those found in the writings of sophisticated poets. Fraenkel rejects, brusquely, the suggestion in the 'Life' that Horace was 'somewhat intemperate in sexual matters' (and used to disport himself with prostitutes in a room full of mirrors – 'the filthy detail was presumably a *locus communis*'). Of course ancient biographies are notoriously untrustworthy, but Fraenkel's willingness to accept or reject particular items depends rather evidently on whether or not they fit his idea of Horace. Fortunately, in the case of Horace's sexual habits, we again have 'the most reliable evidence': in *Sermones* 2.3.325 we are told of Horace's passion for 'a thousand girls, a thousand boys'. Fraenkel's insights into the mind of Horace leads at times to a virtual fusion of identities. One may instance his paraphrase at the end of *Odes* 4.11:

> The poet does all he can to make his invitation [to Phyllis] attractive. It is as if he said in a quiet voice: 'My dear girl, I am an old man, really no company for a pretty girl like yourself, though I do care a great deal for you. You need not pretend to be in love with me. I know all about your affair with Telephus and how it came to an end. What a pity! But you remember what happened to men and women in the old stories when they overreached themselves, and you know the saying of Pittacus . . . [Greek text omitted]. But let us not moralize. You are a fine musician, and I think I know something about music myself. Here I have a new tune; I should very much like to hear you sing it with your lovely voice. Shall we try and practise it and, perhaps, forget our worries for while?'[27]

Is this a convincing recreation of the voice of Horace? Or could the accents rather be those of an elderly academic addressing a favourite young graduate

Introduction

student? Fraenkel must have known, better than most, that the function of *psaltriae* at a symposium was to provide entertainment, including sex, for the men, and that *amor* in Horace cannot be equated, unproblematically, with one particular form of the twentieth-century language of sentiment. All sense of alterity, of otherness, has been lost in a moment of romantic – and self-indulgent – identification.

Partly, perhaps, in opposition to such writing, and reflecting too the preoccupation with patronage and power which currently fuels the 'New Historicism', a fresh orthodoxy may now be emergent. Horace is, on this view, an adroit careerist, constructing for himself through his poetry an advantageous position among the Roman elite. David Armstrong, who compares Horace to George Osborne in *Vanity Fair*, sees him as concerned, primarily, with 'self-positioning', and the construction of a 'gentlemanly status as an *amicus* of the great'. Horace's 'Epicurean day' (S 1.6.110ff) is 'a leisure class' topos; he mouths the clichés of the governing classes, thereby ensuring his acceptability among them. Armstrong, like many others, is sceptical of Horace's claim that poverty (*paupertas audax*, Ep. 2.2.51) originally drove him to write. Only a moneyed man, he argues, is likely to have secured the post of *scriba quaestorius*, and Horace was probably already a member of the equestrian class.[28] Similarly Ian DuQuesnay sees the *Sermones* as a clever piece of self-fashioning and oblique support for the regime, consequent on Horace's entry into the circle of Maecenas and the gift of the Sabine 'farm' (*aliter* a small villa estate): 'His basic strategy is to present an attractive image of himself and his friends as sophisticated, cultured and intelligent men who are humane in their attitudes to others and mindful of the *mos maiorum*'[29] (one may compare some modern views of Pope). This new portrait, it should be noticed, no more escapes the 'poetics of presence' than did older and more positive ones; indeed it simply inverts them, while still concerned with the motives of an essentially extra-textual Horace.

The elusiveness of Horace is increased by the contradictions and inconsistencies that we (and he) find in the attitudes expressed in his poems, the sense of a personality divided. *Nil admirari*, 'to marvel at nothing', he assures Numicius (*Ep*.1.6.1–2), is the best course to keep one's happiness, but in *Odes* 3.25, to convey a sense of his inspiration, he had figured himself as a Bacchante, alone and at night, amazed at the snow-clad landscape of Thrace, a hauntingly visionary picture:

>   non secus in iugis
>   exsomnis stupet Euhias,   (Edonis, Shackleton Bailey)
>   Hebrum prospiciens et nive candidam
>   Thracem ac pede barbaro
>   lustratam Rhodopen, ut mihi devio
>   ripas et vacuum nemus
>   mirari libet.   (8–14)

> Just as on the mountain ridges a sleepless Bacchante is amazed as she looks out at the [river] Hebrus and Thrace white with snow and [Mount] Rhodope traversed by wild feet, so as I wander it is my pleasure to marvel at the banks and empty grove.

Horace himself constantly draws attention to such self-divisions, though more with the wry interest of Montaigne than the desperate soul-searchings of Petrarch. Is he a poet of the town or the country? Almost always he is considered the latter, yet he can give impressively vivid descriptions of town life (e.g. *S* 1.6.111ff; *Ep*.1.7.46ff), and Davus his slave criticizes him for his divided loyalties on this score (*S* 2.7.28ff). Of course a sense of division may well have played an important part in the history of introspection and constructions of the self (cf. e.g. the *Medea* of Euripides and Seneca, St Augustine's *Confessions*). In *Epistles* 120.21–2 Seneca, starting from Horace *Sermones* 1.3.11–17, argues that virtue requires consistency: 'Magnam rem puta unum hominem agere. Praeter sapientem autem nemo unum agit, ceteri multiformes sumus... mutamus subinde personam et contrariam ei sumimus quam exuimus' ('Think it a great matter to play one man. Apart from the Stoic philosopher no one plays one man; the rest of us have many characters. We constantly change our masks and put on a different mask from the one we take off.') Seneca includes himself among the inconstant many, which compels him to continuous self-examination. A strong sense of the vicissitudes of the self seems to encourage a search – however fruitless – for the 'true I'.[30]

It is the same with irony, perhaps the favourite Horatian figure. Irony is strictly unprovable and impossible to quantify. As any student of Swift or Jane Austen knows, it never *merely* inverts the sentiments ostensibly expressed, but complicates them in ways which cannot be wholly controlled (one is reminded of the Derridean 'supplement' and 'trace'). There is a form of irony, prevalent among English writers (Betjeman would be a good example), which can be read as highly collusive. Horace's taste for irony is epitomized in his fondness for what scholars term the *recusatio*, the poem of refusal, a format which has the effect of undermining generic stabilities, since the poet perfoms the very task for which he expresses inadequacy. In *Odes* 4.2, for example, Horace describes, with finely wrought detail, the calf he is going to sacrifice, in contrast to the grand hecatombs of Iullus Antonius; similarly he recommends Pindarizing to Antonius, while he himself will imitate the bee in careful but laboured art. In both poetry and 'life' Horace favours simplicity, but here he does so in a poem which starts by imitating Pindar's grand sweep and which is itself Pindaric in scope and complexity. In *Odes* 1.6 he assigns the task of praising Augustus' general Agrippa to the epic writer Varius who can do so *digne*, 'worthily' (i.e. in proper epic style); yet

Introduction

this *Ode* remains itself a panegyric of the great man. Are the reductive phrases used to describe the Homeric themes in stanza two (*gravem / Pelidae stomachum; duplicis Ulixei*) a disparagement of epic, or a sign of Horace's incapacity to sustain epic flight? In such poems is Horace rejecting the higher forms of art, or rather slyly incorporating them within his own lyric mode, or both? In *Odes* 4.1 he begins by declaring himself too old for love (and thus to write lyric poetry) and ends with a supremely eloquent expression of his supposedly tongue-tied passion for the beautiful boy Ligurinus, in an artfully self-deconstructing gesture.

The presence, or possible presence, of irony makes any attempt to assign precise meanings to Horace's poems unusually problematical. *Epode* 2 ends with a surprising turn when the praise of country life is assigned to the usurer Alfius. At whom is any irony directed? The materialistic businessman like Alfius? The poet himself (also to be a part-time country-dweller?)? The sentimental reader? Anyone who shared the vogue for 'simple' country living? And in what ways (if any) should the irony modify our reading of the first sixty-six lines? Does it mean that the details of the *laudes ruris* are not to be taken at face value? C. H. Sisson, whose sprightly version ends his contribution to this volume, reads the whole *Epode* back through its final lines; the majority of the poem's numerous imitators solved the problem in the opposite way — by suppressing the closing stanza altogether. Again in *Odes* 1.34 Horace announces his conversion from Epicurean materialism to theism consequent on his seeing lightning in a clear sky. Some have taken this *Ode* as the record of a genuine religious 'conversion', but, in view of the heightened diction used of the 'miracle' (mock-heroic?), many would today agree with Dr Johnson's comment: 'Sir, he was not in earnest: this was merely poetical.' Nisbet–Hubbard detect a change of tone, towards a greater seriousness, in the final section which sceptically underlines the vicissitudes of life,[31] but the image of fortune as a bird, which, with a shrill scream, snatches a crown from one person's head to place it on another's, could itself be humorous or grotesque. Horace cannot easily be tied down to a single philosophical system (*Ep.*1.1.14 *nullius addictus iurare in verba magistri*). Or take *Odes* 3.9, the amorous dialogue *donec gratus eram tibi*. There seems a surprising agreement among critics that the piece is charming, or vapid (according to taste). Gordon Williams calls it 'a blithe Mozartian duet'[32] (Susanna and Count Almaviva?). But might not the poem rather be taken as (decadently?) *faux-naïf* (more like 'là ci darem la mano'), a reading conformed to the character of its sophisticated and slippery creator as often conceived? But whatever problems of interpretation it brings with it, irony, on whatever scale, is an important part of the *texture* of Horace's writing, in most readers' view of it.

Is to talk about Horace, or to find a sense of personality in his writings, necessarily to commit oneself to the 'biographical fallacy' or the 'poetics of presence'? It can be argued that it need not do so; indeed, that deconstruction (at least in its Derridean form) can help to explain in what way it makes sense to talk of an encounter with 'Horace'.[33] Under the influence of the New Criticism more sophisticated scholars often had recourse to the notion of a persona: what we call 'Horace' should be seen simply as a mask, or series of masks, adopted to afford a particular rhetorical stance. The idea was not new. Howard Weinbrot has shown how, in the English Augustan period, there was considerable debate about whether poets expressed their own opinions ('sincerely') or filtered them, obliquely, through masks, and that most of the positions adopted in the twentieth century can be paralleled for the eighteenth.[34] However, the concept of persona does not solve the underlying problem, it simply pushes it back a stage. For there still has to be a 'real' Horace who adopts the masks we meet in his poems and who is thus, theoretically, distinguishable from them. Moreover, it ignores the fact that in 'life' too we adopt personae, that there is no easy distinction to be made between a real 'I' and the varied stances (connected to specific contexts) that I present to the world (or to myself). Of course 'Horace' is a construction in words, whose relationship to the 'Horace' whom his contemporaries knew (all quite differently of course) cannot be determined,[35] not least since we have virtually no access to him beyond the poems he wrote. But equally our sense of our own personalities, and those of others, is always, at least to an extent, of this kind. Any sense of the self, or of another, could be described as a 'fiction' discursively constructed; or better as a 'counter-factual', like the meaning of a work of literature, and one likewise subject to *différance*, as a short digression will show.

Différance is Derrida's neologism which combines the idea of difference (meaning is an effect of the contrast between signs) and deferral (meaning always resists 'closure', a final – or originary – meaning, because signs never stand still). Derrida has, provocatively, called authors themselves 'an effect of *différance*', and his writings can help us with our problem. Derrida rightly insists that texts continue to mean, to remain readable, in the *absence*, the non-presence, of the author, who becomes 'an idiom which constructs itself' in language; otherwise they would not be 'iterable', and their projection (through history) would become impossible. His notorious slogan 'there is no "outside-text"' ('Il n'y a pas d'hors-texte') does not imply that authors do not write books, or that there is no physical world, or that events do not occur in history; but rather that meaning is always elaborated within language, that there is no escape from textuality. When Barthes, writing about the 'reality effect', warns us against taking fictional and written people as 'real', because we interpret them according to reading practices and the ideologies they

Introduction

encode,[36] we may retort that we 'read' the people we meet in a similar fashion. Barthes' over-confident, over-absolute distinction between text and world, life and literature, invites deconstruction. Thus a marriage, a meeting, a building, a poem – history itself – are all, in this sense, 'texts'; 'facts' or events are 'always already' written, always already under description. In Bernard Harrison's elegant formulation, 'the text itself is the bearer of all the Reality that inheres in meaning'.[37]

To talk of a textual Horace is not to deny that there was an individual Quintus Horatius Flaccus who, at a particular time and place, wrote the poems, or to say that this point is of no significance; rather it is to affirm two things, first that Horace is wholly *in* his writings, not outside them, above or beyond them, and secondly that people, like the Horace whom Maecenas knew, are themselves 'written'; none of us is separable from the texts we weave. People are like books because we read them, according to certain cultural conventions, in the light of their words, actions and gestures, with no ready access to a fully present consciousness. In the sense that others have of us, we are all – and not merely authors – effects of *différance*. So no reading of a person is ever final. As we have seen, each reader can be said to construct her or his own 'Horace', just as each one of us has a different sense of the people she or he encounters (though of course we can modify, or change, our readings of book or person by discussing them with others); it does not follow that either Horace, or our acquaintance, have no separate existence from those individual readings of them. Reading a book and getting to know a person thus become analogous activities. With both people and books there is the possibility, if we can attain some transcendence of our existing views, of an extension of our potentialities brought about by the 'alterity' of the other party. (Auden apparently once asked: 'Have you been read by any good books lately?') Any language which implies that to read is *simply* to decode, or to demystify, is as arrogant as it is 'hegemonic', an implicit claim to that mastery over the text, that commitment to a final, closed meaning, which is precisely the 'logocentrism' condemned by Derrida. Seeing through books, like seeing through people, may make it impossible to see, for neither people nor books nor the world are ours wholly to command. Like people, books have their reticences, their partial disclosures, their resistances to complete appropriation. Indeed, as I have implied, 'good' reading may be reading which tries to respect the book's otherness. But this does not entail an attempt to empty yourself of your own values and experience (let alone to internalize all an author's views, as read), or a failure to try to unpack the hidden assumptions of the work. An approach like Fraenkel's resembles hagiography, or sentimental fantasy, more than criticism or dialogue.

Personalities are not fixed, but in a constant state of coming into existence. There is a sense in which in reading a book, as in many other occupations, we are engaged in a process of finding, or making, a self for ourselves, though that self will always be provisional. This may be the special value of a poet like Horace, and could help to explain his influence and popularity. The reader is performing an activity mirrored within the poems themselves in which 'Horace' too is engaged in just such an act of self-fashioning. This is why it does not greatly matter whether or not Horace's account of the events of his life (like the role of his father, or his introduction to Maecenas) are accurate or not (whatever we take that to mean): their main value, both to Horace and to us, is not as reconstruction of the past but as part of a construction of the present. It is what Horace is and has become, not what happened to him, which gives these events their status as authentic autobiography. Most of the Horatian poets in this book used Horace to help define themselves to themselves, even if often the results were (to us) less interesting and simpler than the model. But we can watch the process of fashioning and being fashioned, with particular excitement, when Pope reads Horace, Pope who, in famous words from Johnson's *Life*, 'hardly drank tea without a stratagem'. Frank Stack concludes his study of Pope and Horace with these words:

In so many ways these are poets of 'self-portraiture' . . . and yet both Horace's poetry and Pope's seem to question the very idea of 'self' while they assert or imply it. Focusing so intently on human inconsistency and contradiction both Pope and Horace hint that 'self' is an ideal to be achieved and rarely attained, that desires and passions have 'identities' of their own, and that the energies of the whole self – conscious and unconscious – cannot be contained in the fixed ideals of morality, the received forms of poetry, or rigid conceptions of personal identity. Looking at the parallel texts of Pope's *Imitation of Horace* it is difficult to say if 'self' is the origin of poetry, or its goal, or rather, as Eliot would say, that from which the poet is attempting to escape.[38]

3

Horace lived in an age of great image-makers. But his own image (*monumentum*, something which *shows*) was the most successful construction of all, truly more lasting than bronze, beyond even his declared aspirations (*Odes* 3.30). However, it was in the field of politics (in a more restricted sense) that Horatian equanimity was most difficult to sustain and where his stance has proved most controversial. Recently, as we have seen, it has become fashionable for scholars to seek to unmask the ideologies encoded within texts and the reading practices which sustain them (though from what lofty position of an 'outside-ideology' is not usually made clear). And here the presiding genius is no longer Derrida but his austere compatriot

Introduction

and opponent Michel Foucault, with his doctrine that power is always everywhere (a doctrine which should disconcert only sentimentalists and liberals). Hostility to Horace's support of Augustus is, of course, nothing new. Dr Johnson, quoting *Odes* 3.5.2–3, observed that 'no modern flattery... is so gross as that of the Augustan age'.[39] Eighteenth-century writers, some under the influence of Tacitus, argued that the bright image of Augustus would look more tarnished were it not for his poets.[40] Dryden had earlier called Horace 'a temporizing poet, a well-mannered court slave, and a man who is ... ever decent, because he is naturally servile'. Wicksted wrote:

> Their harps with flattering sounds repaid
> The imperial patron's skilful cost;
> But whilst th'applauded artists played,
> The Roman liberty was lost.

Shaftesbury, more sympathetic, saw property and patronage as a cage in which Horace was entrapped, while seeking his freedom.[41] Likewise a realization of the role that the Classics have played in sustaining a class hegemony is also no recent insight. Dr Johnson defended the practice of classical quotation, from the strictures of the radical John Wilkes, on the grounds that 'there is a community of mind in it'.[42] But one of the speakers in Ronald Knox's *Let Dons Delight* (admittedly the one with whom Knox ostensibly has least sympathy) observes acutely: 'God knows why it should be so, but as a matter of observation it seems to me quite certain that the whole legend of the "English Gentleman" has been built upon Latin and Greek. A meets B on the steps of his club and says, "Well, old man, *eheu fugaces*, what?" and B says "*Dulce et decorum est pro patria mori*", and the crossing-sweeper falls on his knees in adoration of the two men who can talk as learnedly as that.'[43]

When R. G. M. Nisbet writes that, after receiving his Sabine estate, 'Horace now finally renounced the angry convictions of his youth to become the ingratiating ironist the world loves so much',[44] the ancestry is clear. Behind him stands the dominant figure of Sir Ronald Syme, whose *Roman Revolution* was written during the rise of Fascism and published in 1939. Horace is the object of many barbs: '"Nunc est bibendum" sang the poet Horace, safe and subsidized in Rome'; 'Catullus ... could not have been domesticated, tamely to chant the regeneration of high society, the reiterated nuptials of Julia or the frugal virtues of upstarts enriched by the Civil Wars ... That did not matter. The New State had its lyric poet, technically superb'.[45] To write as Syme does can seem oddly like bad manners, another achievement of Horatian tact. Might the feline Horace have been more impressed by the delicate insinuations of the Neronian satirist Persius?

> Unlike in method, with concealed design,
> Did crafty Horace his low numbers join;
> And, with a sly insinuating grace,
> Laughed at his friend and looked him in the face,
> Would raise a blush, where secret vice he found,
> And tickle while he gently probed the wound.
>
> (1.116–18 trs. Dryden)

Syme, however, needed to disparage Augustan literature in order to establish his view that Augustus was a ruthless war-lord. But, ironically enough, his book only serves to reinforce the position, fostered by Augustan ideology, that the age was a nodal-point in world history.

The Foucauldian approach concentrates on the key terms out of which Augustan ideology was created and sustained. Categories like 'public' and 'private', 'art', 'morality', 'politics' and so forth, and their Roman 'equivalents', are not, on this model, given in nature but established in discourse; and the ways in which the boundaries of such 'mobile signifiers' are fixed reflects prevailing interests and structures of power. Horace's stance of quietude, compromise and common sense is often characterized as 'unpolitical'. Yet, it can be maintained, these were the very positions best calculated to promote harmony and consensus and thus to help cement the position of the *princeps*. Colin Macleod, in an admired series of articles,[46] depoliticizes Horace and thus occludes an important part of the significance of his writing. Even in Horace's own terms there was a political element to *otium*,[47] the peace and prosperity established by Augustus (clearest in *Odes* 4.5 and 15), together with a philosophical one of Epicurean colouring, and indeed a social one – Horace now knew his place after youthful years of living dangerously. Of course *otium* could also be appropriated to other ends, as by Horace's friend, the elegist Tibullus, who, like his patron Messalla, remained uncommitted to the regime. Terry Eagleton has argued that the periodical writers (themselves, as we have seen, inspired by Horace) effected something comparable in eighteenth-century England. He suggests that they achieved

> a codifying of the norms and regulating of the practices whereby the English bourgeoisie may negotiate an historic alliance with its social superiors. When Macaulay remarks that Joseph Addison 'knew how to use ridicule without abusing it', he means in effect that Addison knew how to upbraid the traditional ruling class while keeping in with it, avoiding the divisive vituperation of a Pope or Swift.

On their stress on Reason, Eagleton comments:

> The public sphere ... acknowledges no given rational identity beyond its own bounds, for what counts as rationality is precisely the capacity to articulate within its constraints; the rational are those capable of a certain mode of discourse, but this cannot be judged other than in the act of deploying it.[48]

Introduction

The relevance of all this to Horace will be obvious. In earlier times these things were well enough understood. So Cowley in his *Essays* notes the connection betwen quietude, country life and political acquiescence (seen by him, of course, as a sovereign good);

> The innocence of this life is the next thing for which I commend it ... for no men are so free from the temptations of iniquity ... They are without dispute of all men the most quiet and least apt to be inflamed to the disturbance of the commonwealth ... In our late mad and miserable civil wars ... I do not remember the name of any one husbandman who had so considerable a share in the twenty years ruin of his country as to deserve the curses of his countrymen.[49]

So too with the distinction between public and private, where we might be justified in talking of Horace's espousal of 'the politics of privacy'. Paul Zanker alleges, in connection with the supposed emergence of a private sphere in Rome during the late Republic, that 'there is no doubt that the private life of luxury and aesthetic pleasures in country villas enabled an already enfeebled aristocracy to accept more easily the transition to one-man rule'.[50] Certainly claims for the separateness of the two spheres sits uneasily with the realization that the central plank of Augustus' reforms concerned the regulation of relationships inside the bedroom; but ideology can precisely help to efface contradictions of this kind. Horace's poetry in general promotes such a separation: politics are the prerogative of great men, and only the *Odes* on affairs of state are categorized among τὰ πολιτικά. Indeed even here Horace has ways of modifying a purely 'public' stance, for example by the sportive concluding stanza of *Odes* 3.3, or the personal incorporations into the programme of the Pindaric epinician (*Odes* 3.4). *Odes* 3.14 offers contrasting pictures of the public celebration of Augustus' return from Spain and a private symposium organized by the poet. The middle stanza makes clear the link (while Augustus rules, Horace is safe). Augustus guarantees Horace's jealously guarded privacy and is in turn guaranteed by it. On the occasions when Horace erases the distinction, the result can seem a disagreeable pre-echo of totalitarianism. In *Odes* 4.5.9ff (a poem in praise of the Augustan peace) a simile paints a moving picture of a mother on the curved shore, looking out in longing for her son; this is used to figure the desire of the *patria* for the *princeps*. Family and state have become one, united in love (*dux bone, il duce?*).

Horace's skilful accommodation of himself to the existing order (though, in his case, used to support a 'revolutionary' leader) is usually seen as a 'conservative' stance, and certainly he has been popular with writers who would see themselves as having a conservative disposition (including, for example, C. H. Sisson or the older Auden). But characteristic Horatian stances can be, and have been, appropriated for more than one political position. During the Renaissance, for courtiers and men of affairs (like Wyatt) faced with the vicissitudes of fortune and the frown of princes Horatian topoi assumed urgent and practical life. Even more obviously oppositional is the pointed quietude of Royalist writers during the Interregnum. The difficulty of sustaining an Horatian poise can give especial power to their productions. The divide between public and private need not efface political structures, but can bring challenge or comfort. (Thus it can be argued that Dryden's turning to Horatian self-possession as a still point in the flux of life was a movement of hard-won *defiance*.) Faced with a Royalist appropriation of Horace as covert opposition, Marvell reclaimed him from retirement and submission to authority for 'radical' political *action* in his 'Horatian Ode' for Cromwell (1650). The classicizing, Horatian colour both conceals and discloses a gap between ancient and modern, with a consequent traffic of meaning between the two areas. For example, in a singular slippage, Caesar is used of *both* Charles and Cromwell. And what is the relationship between the gods of the poem and the Christian God? Is Marvell using the Horatian form to imply what would otherwise be unsayable, that God is indifferent to ancient right and even to virtue, that God is a Hobbesian? In general, it may be, Horace is likely to appeal most to those able to reconcile themselves to their sense of the present order of things. Northrop Frye suggests that he shows us 'the virtue of being able to live in a civilisation'.[51] This may well strike a chord with many, but we should also remember Walter Benjamin's powerful saying: 'There is no document of civilisation which is not at the same time a document of barbarism.'[52]

4

But *non hoc iocosae conveniet lyrae. quo, Musa, tendis?* The tone of this last section has been abrasive, one-sidedly polemical, in short – 'unHoratian'. The very word ideology has, to the pragmatic British ear, a somewhat foreign and menacing sound. The proper note, in a work such as this, should be one of praise; and, if we would speak true, much to the man is due. Yet, despite the bimillennium, this may not be the most favourable time to be writing the introduction to a book in celebration of Horace. In the 1960s and 1970s, for a complex of reasons, Horace was a focus for significant discussion within the classical departments of British universities; he was, for example, the central presence in Gordon Williams' *Tradition and Originality in Roman Poetry*, published in 1968, to wide acclaim. Today Horatian scholarship seems largely content to mark time, and fashion has shifted to other authors – Ovid in particular. Such are the tides of fortune, as 'Horace' would have been the first to acknowledge.

Introduction

On one commonly evoked criterion, the test of time, Horace has no difficulty in making good his claim to be a major poet. Like Virgil and Ovid he is one of those who, through their centrality in the education of the elite, have helped to shape what T. S. Eliot called 'the mind of Europe', as this book demonstrates for 500 years of British history. But can the claim for his greatness still be made actual for today's readers? The possible charges against him are formidable. His poetry moves almost exclusively in a 'male' ambience, lessening its appeal to many women (perhaps the only powerful image of a woman in his entire work is the Cleopatra of the last three stanzas of *Odes* 1.37, and even that is at the price of the partial erasure of her 'femininity'). Horace's 'girls' mainly serve to provide glamour and various services. He can be pictured as the clever, devious, strategic defender of coterie values and upholder of an unattractive autocracy. His themes can be represented as the stalest of commonplaces. Many of his traditional virtues can be made to seem vices. Scholars often respond to such charges by stressing the technical skill with which Horace deploys his topoi, his irony and so forth. As a result criticism has reached a similar impasse to that of the later works of Pope, where again we find an excessive concern with technique and a neglect of larger meanings. Admittedly a formalist defence is not wholly to be despised. In one way it is curious how much we seem to expect poets to be in some way sages, when what primarily differentiates them from non-poets is their particular skill with words. Horace's poems, especially his *Odes*, are usually skilfully crafted. Brigid Brophy talks about poems 'held in shape by excellently hard bony forms' by an 'adroit word-tactician'.[53] More than that there is the dance of the structure (involving deliberate disproportion and unpredictable turns, as well as arguments by juxtaposed images, as in *Odes* 2.5), which indeed is not merely a matter of form: 'The meaning lay in the transitions themselves, in a certain balance of sensibility, a nice adjustment between imagery and statement which met the insoluble problems of life with a controlled use of distraction and irrelevance' (this of the Soracte *Ode*, 1.9).[54] In other words we find the play of a textual 'Horace' over the material which establishes its special 'texture'; and this texture transforms what otherwise might seem a set of rather trite topoi into something more rich and strange. Even if we thoroughly dislike what we take to be Horace's politics, we may be moved by his expressions of joy (Dryden thought his principal characteristic was his 'good humour'[55]) and sadness, or rather often joy and sadness together, which makes the joy seem more vulnerable. It may be felt that few have expressed the emotion of nostalgia for lost youth more poignantly: *age iam, meorum / finis amorum / (non enim posthac alia calebo / femina)* (*Odes* 4.11.31–4, 'come last of my loves – I will not burn for any other woman after this').

This texture could be seen partly in terms of the kind of 'wit' which involves seeing the world from more than one angle, in this like the wit praised by Eliot and other modern critics, something which suggests that Horace may still be recuperable for our time. In his hugely influential essay of 1921 Eliot praised Andrew Marvell for his 'tough reasonableness', for the 'succession of concentrated images', for the 'alliance of levity and seriousness (by which the seriousness is intensified) . . . a quality of sophisticated literature'.[56] There follows his famous definition of 'wit':

> Wit is not erudition . . . It is not cynicism, though it has a kind of toughness which may be confused with cynicism by the tenderminded . . . It involves, probably, a recognition, implicit in the expression of every experience, of other kinds of experience which are possible.

This definition can be made to fit well with Horace's 'wit'. For example, Horace's critique of the elegists (*Odes* 1.33; 2.9) seems based on their narrowness of vision, their one-sided self-absorption. Perhaps then it is along these lines that a defence of Horace today might be mounted (though Marvell differs from Horace in that his extraordinarily acute, even weird, sensibility often seems to lack any corresponding emotion or potential moral weight).

Let us take a single, short, well-known poem by Horace to test this thesis:

> O fons Bandusiae, splendidior vitro,
> dulci digne mero non sine floribus,
>   cras donaberis haedo,
>   cui frons turgida cornibus
> primis et Venerem et proelia destinat,
> frustra: nam gelidos inficiet tibi
>   rubro sanguine rivos
>   lascivi suboles gregis.
> te flagrantis atrox hora Caniculae
> nescit tangere, tu frigus amabile
>   fessis vomere tauris
>   praebes et pecori vago.
> fies nobilium tu quoque fontium,
> me dicente cauis impositam ilicem
>   saxis, unde loquaces
>   lymphae desiliunt tuae.

O spring of Bandusia, more shimmering than glass, worthy of sweet wine not without flowers, tomorrow you will be given a kid, whose forehead swelling with its first horns marks it out for both Venus and battles. In vain – for this scion of a playful flock will stain your cold waters with red blood. Thee the fierce hour of the burning Dog knows not how to touch, thou a lovely coolness for bulls wearied by the share providest and for the wandering flock. Thou too shalt be among the

Introduction

fountains famous in song, when I tell of the ilex-tree positioned above your hollow rocks, whence your talking liquids leap down.

This poem (*Odes* 3.13) was apparently taken by Wordsworth partly as a sort of pre-emptive Romantic nature poem (see 'Liberty', 100–5). Let us see how well it responds to a more 'Eliotic' reading. The internal logic of the poem seems to suggest that Bandusia is an actual spring, known to the poet, though otherwise unfamiliar, to which he promises a fame like that of the fountains celebrated in Greek literature. Gordon Williams' insistence, in best New Critical fashion, that it does not matter whether or not Bandusia existed could thus be misleading.[57] For if Bandusia is taken as imaginary, then the poem advances a more Ovidian thesis, that the poet can give to airy nothings a local habitation and a name. The smallness of the spring suggests that it can also be taken as a Callimachean symbol of the well-wrought poem (for water imagery of poetry cf. Callimachus *Hymn* 2, to Apollo, 108–12), and the *Ode* certainly offers a concentrated display of poetic art. But this does not prevent the fountain's (textual) actuality, its appearance and sounds, from being vividly evoked. The rhetorical flourish in *frustra* and the elaborately periphrastic language about the kid could be read as pathos or malicious mock-pathos; from one angle the kid may not be able to sustain epic treatment, but then 'the ant's a centaur in his dragon world'. The mingling of blood and water almost inevitably suggests, in a post-Symbolist world, a Yeatsian tension between life and art. A. Y. Campbell asked, not unreasonably, 'who wants a drink out of the fountain of Bandusia after that?' for which he is rebuked, roundly, by David West: 'So modern taste does not like blood in running water . . . The critic must shed his local prejudices . . . what is described is a complex stimulus, the life blood spurting from an animal's jugular, an ancient religious observance of your race.'[58] West's argument is dangerously circular. Can we know how the poem's presentation of sacrifice would have struck contemporary readers? We deduce a context of feeling and then use that context to interpret the text which provided it. Anyway there is something evidently, even nastily twentieth-century about West's formulation. Reading is a dialogue of sensibilities; readers should not strip theirs away to offer as a sacrifice on the altar of Historicism. Perhaps the mingling of the (warm) red blood and the cool (transparent) water could have disturbed some readers even in antiquity: certainly the description is a miniature artistic *tour de force*, a double antithesis achieved by the juxtaposition of two adjectives, each implying its opposite. Formally the poem is a hymn, and thus carries a charge of quasi-religious emotion which, however, is modified in complex ways, in tension with a purer aestheticism. There is also a clash between any humility implicit in the prayer form and the proud implication that Horace can confer immortality on an unknown spring through the power of his poetry. The *Ode* is perhaps less immediately likeable than at first sight appears, but rather more interesting, with the sense that it is the product of a complex 'sensibility'. And it is not to yield to any doctrine of the 'typically Horatian' to say that only 'Horace' could have written it.

5

(with apologies to Sir Ronald Syme . . .)

In 8 BC Quintus Horatius Flaccus died, wealthy and successful. Having no children he named as heir the *princeps* he had served so loyally. Since his return to Italy after Philippi he had, by ceaseless effort, achieved 'perfection of the art'. What personal price, if any, he had paid for that achievement, the world will never know. Like the Pollio of his *Ode* (2.1) he had trodden through fires hidden beneath treacherous ash, but without burning his feet. It was almost certainly during the Protectorate that the Royalist Richard Lovelace, student of Horace, wrote one of his finest lyrics, 'The Grasshopper', to his friend, another amiable admirer of Horace, Charles Cotton. During these dark times the two companions (forced by circumstances to be at once radical and reactionary) could find, in the values Horace had so often expounded, shelter from the storm (see pp. 73–4). Imprisoned twice for his fruitless services to his king, Lovelace died, broken and destitute, in 1657. He received a pauper's funeral. Such are the ironies of history and of reception, ironies which our sceptical poet might have relished:

> Fortune that with malicious joy
>   Does man her slave oppress,
> Proud of her office to destroy,
>   Is seldom pleased to bless;
>   Still various and unconstant still,
> But with an inclination to be ill,
>   Promotes, degrades, delights in strife,
>   And makes a lottery of life.[59]

2

HORACE AT HOME AND ABROAD: WYATT AND SIXTEENTH-CENTURY HORATIANISM

Colin Burrow

IF ONE COULD ask a mid-seventeenth-century poet, 'Would you like to be Horatian?' most would leap at the offer. They would probably think one was offering them the chance to write sober meditations on the value of country life. Put the same question to a mid-*six*teenth-century English poet, however, and the chances are the answer would be 'What's that?' Horace – his *Sermones* and *Epistles* at any rate – may well have been widely read in the sixteenth century (by 1530 there were plenty of editions of his complete works with simple glosses to enable those with the precursor of Loeb Latin to make out what the words meant); but there was little sense in England of what it might mean to be 'Horatian'. This sounds no bad thing, since it might indicate that Horace was fresh, unsullied and awaiting assimilation. But writers who have no recognized identity and no familiar, characterizing epithets tend to remain unread, or, if they are read, their influence remains shadowy and unformed.

This was certainly the case with Horace before the sixteenth century. Dante's brief vision of 'Orazio satiro'[1] in Limbo is a paradigm of the way an unassimilated author enters the work of someone alert to classical influence: Horace has a vague defining adjective, drawn from one genre in which he is known to be important, and he looms through the dark like something major. But he is not present in the text of the *Divine Comedy* except as a wraith glimpsed once in a while by a commentator. Most imitators begin by noticing and replicating what critical traditions have said is distinctive about their originals. If the relationship works, they end up being enabled to say unlikely things because they come to notice aspects of their predecessors which weren't part of the received wisdom. But preconceived notions and clichés kick-start the whole process, and clichés for Horace were in short supply before the seventeenth century. As a result, sixteenth-century readers found him more or less incomprehensible. Thomas Drant's preface to his translations of Horace's *Sermones* (the first into English in 1566) makes no reference to Horace as a poet who versifies retreat from public life, nor to any of the more obvious features of 'Horatianism' as it came to be understood. Instead there is a strikingly honest account of what he is like to read:

The poet is thus: sometimes he wadeth very far in fetching out his matter, and sometimes he is brittle, and soon broken from his matter. So that thou must be deep witted to begin with him and well witted to take him with thee. Thou must (gentle reader) bring in thy self help to the understanding of him, and will likewise to thine own amendment.[2]

This passage places remarkable emphasis on the reader. Drant's requirement that 'thou must be . . . well witted to take him with thee', taken with his appeal at the end of the extract to 'bring in thy self help' to the reading of Horace, implies that he regards Horace as a kind of Do It Yourself poet, whom you have to make for yourself, and in the process, perhaps, make a bit of yourself. Because Drant can't draw on a stockpile of epithets, he has to invent his own Horace, and so turns the process of reading the *Sermones* into a companionable dialogue between author and reader.

Drant's account of reading Horace also has a weird accuracy. Because he has no distracting notion of 'Horatianism', he is well able to recognize that Horace's *Sermones* are deliberately fashioned to resist the extraction of dogma. Horace emerges more from the jumps and jolts, the implicit links and unspoken coherences which unsettle the flow of his satires, than through direct statement. The 'Satires' are not called *Satirae* but *Sermones*, conversa-

tions; and, as the collection proceeds, Horace blends more and more into the endless chatter of people around him, until by the last poem in the collection, 2.7, he is reduced to little more than a questioning stooge.[3] Attitudes which it is tempting to attribute to Horace often do emerge through these other voices, but they remain latent and in need of energetically reconstructive reading in order to be extracted. *Sermones* 2.1, a dialogue between Horace and the lawyer Trebatius, sets the tone of the second book, and points the direction in which the whole collection is tending. The conversation is underpinned by a lurking unease, jovially shuffled off, about the relation of satire to the Roman libel laws. Horace wonders whether, in the face of criticism, he should give up poetry altogether:

> sunt quibus in satira videar nimis acer et ultra
> legem tendere opus, sine nervis altera quidquid
> composui pars esse putat similisque meorum
> mille die versus deduci posse.   (2.1.1–4)

> There are those to whom I seem in my satire too biting and to go beyond the law. Another group thinks that whatever I compose is nerveless, and that they could turn out a thousand verses a day like mine.

The things other people say about Horace are irreconcilable, but this extract manages to imply a measure of sympathy for both the views it introduces. That he transgresses the law (either the formal limits of the genre or the Roman law against libel) is given a nod of agreement by audaciously ending the line with *ultra*. It might also seem a fair point that he is nervelessly slack and infinitely imitable, since the lines do have an underwritten, demotic fluidity. Horace appears at first to have accepted his critics' notions of what's Horatian about him. But a closer look reveals rough edges. He composes, whereas his rivals churn out poems which are perhaps no more than derivative fakes (*similisque meorum*). The passage seems to speak with other, non-Horatian voices, but these are made to carry a secret low voice of hostility to their own cause. By a kind of ventriloquism Horace makes his critics reveal just what's unique about Horace: his satire is at once spicily suggestive of illegality or indecorum *and* conversational. This combination is its main resource. He is not a poet who presents a myth, a topos or a notion which could be labelled and easily transferred to other works. But he operates by just flirting with this sort of pre-defined poetic identity, and then unsettling it by suggesting it is someone else's image of him, from which he is as intimately distant as a ventriloquist and his dummy.

The paradigm of this technique – and Horace's most imitated poem – is the *beatus ille* Epode (1.2), which lists the pleasures of country life with what has seemed to many to be Horatian warmth, and then concludes by undercutting the whole screed with 'Thus spoke the usurer Alphius.' The final about-turn is a pretty crude device to make a simple sentiment appear sophisticated, and the whole *Epode* lacks the ability Horace learnt in writing the *Sermones* to weave a voice of detachment into voices of zealous simplicity.[4] But it does show how committedly anti-Horatian Horace is: as he seems on the edge of producing 'Horatian themes' he will shrink away from them, with something which could be seen as either timidity, or a determination to be free from the constrictions of having an image. This is a deep-seated instinct in the *Sermones*. In 2.6 he produced two sighs of contented homeliness which seem to fix him as a poet for whom country living is the final resting place of desire: *hoc erat in votis* (This was in my prayers, line 1), he says while at his farm, and *o rus, quando ego te aspiciam* (O countryside, when shall I see you again? line 60) he says while missing it. Both phrases seem to rise like emotions – and were often used by later writiers to capture either release from town or imprisonment in it. But, in the next *Sermo*, 2.7, Horace has a conversation with Davus, his town slave, in which this longing for the country, described from another viewpoint, becomes little more than a sophisticated man's version of discontent. As Davus (whose voice dominates the *Sermo*) says

>   Romae rus optas, absentem rusticus urbem
>   tollis ad astras levis.   (2.7.28–9)

At Rome you long for the country; in the country you praise the city to the skies, you fickle creature.

Davus makes it look as though the previous *Sermo* could have begun *hoc erat in votis* if Horace had just arrived at Rome from the country. Horace often insinuates human desires and moral attitudes into locations, and it often looks as though his Sabine farm is the ultimate place of valuable repose. But there's something – it's almost a species of embarrassment, a fear of acquiring definable attitudes and of the publicity which a straight expression of longing brings – which cuts off his meditations on the country from becoming ideals. He needs the *possibility* of idealism, abstraction, of becoming a poet with a fixed identity and stable preoccupations, in order to show that he is *not* that kind of poet. He needs to be almost, but not quite, Horatian in order to establish his freedom.[5] This is why 'Horatianism' and Horace are always fighting with each other in writers who imitate Horace. Construct an ethos from the poems and they become impossible to imitate: their tendency to turn paeans on country life into dramatic monologues at the last minute seems merely irritating. Cowley, for example – who often falls prey to a kind of 'Horatianism' which straightforwardly sanctions retreat from public affairs – overlooked the inconveniently ironical final lines in his translation of the

Wyatt and sixteenth-century Horatianism

beatus ille Epode.⁶ But, on the other hand, if one has no notion at all of what Horace might be about, he seems just jumpy and brittle, a fit inhabitant of a poetic limbo of ill-defined shapes.

Something of a distinctly Horatian shape, however, first began to emerge through the gloom when sixteenth-century poets were drawn to the firm but oblique manner adopted by Horace towards his patron Maecenas in *Epistles* 1.7, a verse letter apologizing for his long absence from Rome. The *Epistle* turns Horace's farm into a complex of values: it was given to him by Maecenas, so traces of obligation cling to it; but it is also identified with health and freedom from Rome, to which Maecenas wants Horace to return. This makes the place of writing a spot in which to cultivate a lifestyle, something like an ideal 'Horatian' rusticity. But most of the *Epistle* is taken up with short and funny stories, which explore apparently abstract questions about moderation and the giving of gifts:

> forte per angustam tenuis volpecula⁷ rimam
> repserat in cumeram frumenti pastaque rursus
> ire foras pleno tendebat corpore frustra,
> cui mustela procul 'si vis' ait 'effugere istinc,
> macra cavum repetes artum, quem macra subisti.'
> hac ego si compellar imagine, cuncta resigno,
> nec somnum plebis laudo satur altilium nec
> otia divitiis Arabum liberrima muto.   (*Ep.* 1.7.29–36)

By chance a skinny little fox had crept through a narrow chink into a grain bin, and, after feeding, was vainly trying to get out again with its body stuffed. A weasel from a little distance said to him, 'If you want to escape from there, you must go back skinny into the narrow gap which you came through skinny.' If challenged by this fable, I give everything up. I don't praise the peasant's sleep while I am sated with fowl, nor do I change my total leisure for the riches of Arabia.

The inset dialogues and snippets of fable in Horace's *Epistles* seem at first far simpler, more univocal, than the manipulation of other voices in the *Sermones*; but there is a latent dialogue going on here too. Horace's *Epistles* have a recipient, and often give a reader the sense of overhearing a private communication where things dark or helpful are being implied. What we know Maecenas knows Horace must be wanting to say charges an old fable with tension, and allows a muted and sly version of Horace's opinions to emerge through what others think about him. Maecenas would read this unimpeachably general anecdote with its final comment and hear a quiet voice saying, 'My eyes were too big for my stomach: take it all back.' The very privateness of this way of addressing the question implies an intimacy between poet and recipient which neutralizes any hurt or offence. The reader, as Drant implied, has to tease out the sense.

Horace in the Maecenas *Epistle* is solidly fixed in one place, with a muted but independent voice; but at the same time he hides behind a politely abstract manner whatever resentment he might want to convey to his patron. This combination was exactly what a very specific class of early Renaissance poets needed. A member of a Renaissance court, compelled to move around Europe on diplomatic missions at the will of his prince or patron, repeating scrupulously false messages from one ruler to another as he went, would accumulate in the course of his travels a powerful head of resentment against his employer. As he endured yet another lumpy bed, smoky chimney, bad glass of wine, or another calculatedly perfunctory reception by some foreign ruler, Horace's combination of vehemence and privacy would seem the only way to write. These people needed a poet who identified places with values, since home was where they wanted to be; and they needed a poet who could mutedly express hostility to someone to whom he owed everything. This accidental coincidence of needs created sixteenth-century Horatianism.

In 1517 Ippolito d'Este planned to take his entourage to Hungary. One of his followers, Ludovico Ariosto, dug his heels in and refused to go. He wrote a verse epistle to the uprooted court which deploys Horace's *Epistle* to Maecenas in order to articulate a vehement desire to be free of courtly servitude. It concludes with a version of the fox in the grain-pit story, in which a more appropriate animal, an ass, devours the contents of a granary:

> Temendo poi che gli sien péste l'ossa
> si sforza di tornar dove entrato era,
> ma par che 'l buco più capir nol possa.
> Mentre s'affanna, e uscire indarno spera,
> gli disse un topolino: – Se vuoi quinci
> uscir, tràtti, compar, quella panciera:
> a vomitar bisogna che cominci
> ció c'hai nel corpo, e che ritorni macro,
> altrimenti quel buco mai non vinci. –
> Or, conchiudendo, dico che, se 'l sacro
> Cardinal comperato avermi stima
> con li sui doni non mi é acerbo et acro
> renderli, e tòr la libertà mia prima.[8]

Fearing then that his bones would be beaten to a pulp, he forced himself to turn round to where he'd got in. But he could no longer get through the hole. While he sweated away, and hoped in vain to squeeze through, a tiny mouse said to him, 'If you want to get out of there, get rid of that belly padding, my friend. You'll have to begin puking up what you have in your body, and go back to being thin, or else you'll never get out of that hole.' Now, in conclusion, I say that if the reverend cardinal thinks he has bought me with his gifts, it's not hard or bitter for me to give them him back, and take my original liberty.

Wyatt and sixteenth-century Horatianism

This is Horace with the dampers off; but Ariosto manages to imply that the grotesque details he adds to the scrupulously spare tale of his original are actually latent in it. The fox in Horace's fable could not decently have talked about spewing up Maecenas' gifts, but Ariosto makes the soberly literalistic point that this is the only practical option he has if he is to get thin quickly. He makes Horace's fable sound like a protracted euphemism, which conceals bodily muck – the reality of a fat, squirming, imprisoned animal – and powerful resentment behind immaculately legal vocabulary: Horace's carefully exact *cuncta resigno*[9] becomes a retch.

Ariosto has heard and amplified what Horace's *Epistle* means to its recipient, and since his Satire is addressed not directly to his patron, but to his brother Alessandro and another member of the mobile court, he can afford to make the latent patent. The price of this insight is the loss of Horace's flexible evasiveness, and the growth of something which turns, at the end of his poem, into near dogma. Ariosto's rousing intention to seize his *libertà prima* must be a version of Horace's muted longing for *otia liberrima*. This *libertà* (to which Ariosto returns repeatedly in the *Satire*) means freedom not to do what a *signor* wants, not to scuttle around the world in search of preferment, but to stay at home instead. The widespread insistence in Renaissance editions that Horace is refusing *servitium* to Maecenas may have prompted Ariosto to see in the *Epistle* what is virtually a politics of place.[10] But he creates from these hints the idea that freedom is stillness, where you want to be: home. This identification of home and something like a political value lends itself very well to the epistolary form. Ariosto either writes from home to the exiled court, or, in the later more pained and dislocated Satires, from a place of exile to someone who is where the poet wants to be. In each case a place or the loss of it provides the grounds for an attack on the *mores* of those who are not there. The distance of place implicit in the epistolary form enables writers to explore disparities in value between where they are and where they want to be. Renaissance commentators often remarked that Horace's *Sermones* and his *Epistles* were similar, and that both were directed to an addressee: *Epistolis enim absentibus loquimur, sermone praesentibus* ('we speak in epistles to absent people, in conversation to those present').[11] Ariosto was the first writer to recognize that there was a much deeper affinity between satire and epistle. While he was attempting to impose Ferrarese rule on the province of Garfagnana in 1522 he used the epistolary form to deplore the place he was in, and to long for the place of his addressee:

> Già mi fur dolci inviti a empir le carte
> li luoghi ameni di che il nostro Reggio,
> il natio nido mio, n'ha la sua parte.   (4.115–17)

Those delightful places, where our Reggio, my native nest, is situated, were once to me sweet invitations to fill pages.

Once lost, Reggio becomes a *locus amoenus*, a place to write to and long for. Ariosto creates a nostalgia of location through Horace's vocabulary (*natio nido* derives from Horace's reference to the absent Rome as *nidus*),[12] and makes a place become the embodiment of a poetic lifestyle. This does not just enable him to create a firmly centred persona, rooted in a locale; it also fills a major gap in the lexicon of most sixteenth-century languages. There was an acute shortage of terms in both Italian and English by which to describe differences between national forms of life. In a period which could not use abstract nouns like 'culture' to describe how places differ in their timbre, epistolary satire was a vital way of asserting values through descriptions of a location imbued with the spirit one wants. And after Ariosto this association of Horace with the values of place became instinctive. Thomas Drant did not translate Horace's satire about travel, the Journey to Brundisium (1.5), but replaced it with a satire of his own, directed against the religious practices of the ultimate alien place: Rome.[13] Loss of place translates into loss of values for Du Bellay too, since many of the *Regrets* are epistles from a French exile in Rome to the home which he identifies with true religion and with poetic creation.[14] The association of Horace and exile persists right through to Sir Henry Wotton, the English Ambassador to Venice on and off between 1610 and 1623, who left in his personal papers a collection of poems which include a meditation on the happy life and a translation of one of Horace's *Odes*, together with a number of other poems which delineate many of the central concerns of seventeenth-century 'Horatianism'.[15] Horace was eagerly adopted as a model for articulating what courtier-diplomats felt but lacked the words to say: that places hold ethical significance. This is the outline of Horace which gradually forms from Dante's dim shape.

And this is the form in which Horace first came to England. Sir Thomas Wyatt was almost a full-time ambassador from Henry VIII to the Emperor Charles V between 1537 and 1540. He died in 1542 of a cold contracted on a heated gallop to meet a Spanish envoy. He did not like the job: his letters to Thomas Cromwell ask for leave to go home with increasing plangency and desperation. He was strip-searched in Spain, bruised his shins trying to catch a minor traitor called Brancetour in France, was briefed to murder Cardinal Pole (which he failed to do), and was shouted at by Charles V in the course of relaying a message from his Prince.[16] He probably spent less than six months in England in the three years of his most intensive diplomatic activity, 1537–40. He had the classic career profile of someone who badly needed Horace. But he probably first encountered a version of the *Sermones* which had been refashioned in the image of Ariosto's Horatianism, rather than

Wyatt and sixteenth-century Horatianism

Horace's own poems. Wyatt read and imitated the epistolary Satires of Luigi Alamanni, who read Ariosto, and through him Horace.[17] Through this chain of reception, Italian 'Horatianism' was toughening up from Horace's flexibility into dogma. And the final link was particularly steely. Alamanni was, like most sixteenth-century Horatians, an exile, who had left Florence in 1522 after a failed coup against what he had decided was a tyrannical government.[18] From the French court he wrote epistles which extended Ariosto's longing for *libertà* into a republican asssault on monarchy (with careful riders to the effect of 'I hate all kings – except you, your Majesty'). Ariosto's *libertà*, sprung from the humble origins of Horace's *otia liberrima*, becomes a zealous desire for republican freedom. Horace ceases to be a poet who toys with identities: he becomes vigorously polemical. Alamanni's version of the *beatus ille Epode*, for example, loses its concluding uncertainty and ends instead with a vigorous political hit:

> Cotal (quasi cangiar volesse sorte)
> cantò 'l Tyranno, che Sicilia oppresse,
> Ma l'altro giorno poi condusse a morte
> I due miglior che Syracusa havesse.[19]

So said – as if *he* would want to change his lot – the Tyrant who oppressed Sicily, although the next day he condemned to death the two best men in Syracuse.

In the process of a literary game of Chinese whispers Horace's latent discontent with Maecenas has turned into a vehement political animosity: Ariosto amplifies; Alamanni broadcasts through a loudhailer.

The next in the line was Wyatt, who whispers indeed by comparison with his immediate predecessors. His imitation of Alamanni in his first Satire softens the contours of the Italian Horatian idiom. Something muted but full of latent suggestion emerges:

> Non di loda honorar chiara immortale
> Cesare e Sylla, condannando a torto
> Bruto, e la schiera che più d' altra vale.[20]

[I cannot] honour with bright immortal praise Caesar and Sulla, condemning Brutus to be wronged, and the band who are worth more than the others.

> I am not he that can allow the state
> Of him Caesar and damn Cato to die,
> That with his death did 'scape out of the gate
> From Caesar's hands, if Livy doth not lie,
> And would not live where liberty was lost,
> So did his heart the common wealth apply. (37–42)[21]

Alamanni blazes about Brutus, and the defenders of republican liberty, while Wyatt chooses a famous regulator of appetite to admire. The effect is of a careful self-censorship, a clipped preference for the uncontroversial. This restraint, though, issues in some revealingly tangled syntax and some complicatedly suggestive thoughts. Cato's death is the consequence of his laudable love of liberty in a setting of political domination. In such a setting 'Not damning Cato to die' does not just mean refusing to punish the innocent rather than the powerful; there's just a trace suggestion that it means not giving assent to the whole form of government which leads Catos to feel they need to die. This strain of covert unease about tyranny is also picked up in 'And would not live where liberty was lost', which floats looking for a subject somewhere between Cato and Wyatt. 'So did his heart the common wealth apply' also suggests a checked unease: it means both 'He loved the republic so much as to die for it' and 'By doing so, by dying, he devoted himself to the republic.' These uneasily ambiguous phrases create a shady suggestion that dying is what serving the state amounts to, and that Cato is perhaps not the only one who would not live where liberty was lost. The passage is made thrilling by what it seems to have repressed, but which it is on the edge of saying: that passive resistance to tyranny is something necessary in Tudor England. It may be that the whole sentence simply goes wrong a bit – as early Tudor sentences tend to. But it may be that strategically going wrong a bit is Wyatt's replacement for Alamanni's stridency. Sixteenth-century editions of the *Sermones* very often have an introduction on the nature of satire, which often quote the accusation levelled by Horace against Horace in 2.1 that *ultra legem tende[t] opus*.[22] This phrase is often introduced in a manner which implies that the defining quality of satire is a continual brinkmanship with the law. Wyatt's version of Alamanni has just this quality of skirting around the outer limits of what can safely be said about liberty and overpowerful rulers. It also has just the quality of imminent offence which rises through Horace's *Epistle* to Maecenas. Nothing is being said explicitly against his royal employer, but something is being got across.

It's possible that a direct confrontation with Horace made Wyatt rewrite Alamanni. But Wyatt had very good practical reasons for making Alamanni's outspoken hostility to kings revert to a more Horatian latency, since in 1534 Henry VIII had passed a revised version of the Treason Act, which brought expressing or wishing to encompass the death of the King – words and thoughts – within the definition of treason. People had in the past been executed for verbal treason; but after 1534 this was official, explicit policy.[23] No writers are known to have suffered directly for publishing treasonable works of literature, and G. R. Elton has egregiously argued that it was simply another phase in the Cromwellian enlightenment, aimed at turning the English law into a bureaucratically exact system.[24] It is not likely to have

Wyatt and sixteenth-century Horatianism

seemed that way to a poet translating an explicitly republican author in the immediate aftermath of the Act. The Treason Act forces Wyatt to push Alamanni's discontent underground, since after 1534 writers had to be careful what they said about Brutus and Caesar, and what the one did to the other.

As the poem progresses it takes on more and more of Horace's repressed resilience. Alamanni's poem is set against an unspecified backdrop of Provençal exile, but Wyatt's gradually centres on the core values latent in the Maecenas *Epistle*: personal liberty, stasis at home. After exhausting the corruptions of court life, Wyatt heaves a sigh of relief:

> This maketh me at home to hunt and hawk
> And in foul weather at my book to sit;
> In frost and snow then with my bow to stalk.
> No man doth mark whereso I ride or go;
> In lusty leas in liberty I walk. (80–4)

This feels like autobiography, partly because it makes its verbs feel like nouns and its nouns feel so solid: 'book', 'hunt', 'hawk', 'bow', sit like bulwarks against the dangerous and abstract corruptions of the court which they follow. But reading in bad weather has bookish Horatian prototypes too. In the *Epistle* to Maecenas, in which Horace presses his claim for *liberrima otia*, he also describes himself tucked up reading as a retreat from the diseases of Rome into which his patron wishes him to venture:

> quod si bruma nives Albanis illinet agris,
> ad mare descendet vates tuus et sibi parcet
> contractusque leget. (1.7.10–12)

If winter coats the Alban fields with snow, your poet will go down to the sea and, taking care of himself, will curl up with a book.

And Alamanni continued the topos in Satire VIII (which takes most of its detail from the Maecenas *Epistle*):

> Qui canto ogni hor con le mie Muse, quale
> Mi sforza il tempo rio, l'usanza antica,
> Ch'altro rimedio non mi giova e vale.[25]

Here I sing each hour with my Muses, as bad weather and ancient custom compels me to do, since I have no other remedy to cheer or sustain me.

Wyatt may have ingrafted this musing, home-centred aspect of Italian Horatianism into his version of Satire X in order to give it a less dangerous centre of gravity than Alamanni's political vehemence. Wyatt goes on to say – with all the satisfaction of a Horatian diplomat who has finally left the alien unpleasantness of the outside world beyond his familiar walls – that he is no longer in France, Spain, Flanders or Rome sampling their sundry coruptions:

> But here I am in Kent and Christendom
> among the Muses where I read and rhyme,
> Where if thou list, My Poyntz, for to come,
> Thou shalt be judge how I do spend my time.   (100–3)[26]

By 1540 Wyatt had been to all the places that he lists, on a variety of diplomatic missions, and, after a protracted period of enforced exile, being at home could have meant enough to him to make him relocate his original in Kent and Christendom. The Satire manages to recreate something of Horace's centred homeliness without acknowledging the presence of its predecessor: it all seems to come from Wyatt's own circumstances, to be made by and about *him*. He has, as Drant suggested, brought himself to his reading, and so makes Horace converge, as it were by accident, with his own manner of writing.

There was a strong pressure from contemporary interpretations of Horace to associate Horatian forms with personal attitudes in this way. Renaissance editors believed that many of Horace's *Epistles* were private communications between friends, tailored to the interests of their addressees. This belief was so strong that *Epistles* 1.18 and 19 were thought to be directed to the same man, an invented composite called Lollius Scaeva, simply because they touch on similar issues.[27] Wyatt's poem opens with a very firm assertion that his work is also caught up in his own experience: '*Mine own* John Pointz' insists that this is not an imitation of a stale literary prototype, but a letter to a real person. Wyatt's Satire (to use his own awful pun) may well be as pointed as Horace's *Epistles* were believed to be. John Pointz is usually, though unhelpfully, described by editors as 'a courtier'. He was also Commissioner of the Peace for Essex from 1536 (which is probably why Wyatt ends up by saying 'Thou shalt be judge . . . '), and there are strong indications that in the late 1530s he was becoming more involved in the tangles of Henrician government. In 1535 he proffered a defence of Tyndale (who was about to be strangled and burnt) to Cromwell. Three years later he entered the muck of government in earnest to serve on the Commission of Sewers. And in 1539 a John Pointz joined in Cromwell's information game, and reported a man called John Plommer as saying 'there shall be a new world or midsummer day'. This sounds seditious and perhaps dimly millenarian, but it might have constituted encompassing in word or thought the death of the king, and so could have been the end of Plommer. On investigation, the accused ingeniously protested that he'd actually said 'he hoped there should be a new order or midsummer day; meaning that the King at his Parliament would make some order of punishment for those who neither fast nor pray'.[28] A

Wyatt and sixteenth-century Horatianism

careful reinterpretation of 'order' turns sedition into law-enforcement. It was a standard and frequently deployed defence against the Treason Act to claim that one had been misinterpreted or misheard, and that one had in fact only uttered some harmlessly general remark or proverb: Tudor courtiers – and local agents of government like Pointz – knew how to interpret, apply and hide behind general or apparently pious statements. 'Mine own John Pointz' may well be just such a piece of privy communication. In the very late 1530s, when deadly court games of reportage and misrepresentation were at their height, and when Pointz was participating more actively in Tudor government, the piously general language of Wyatt's epistle has a real bite:

> I cannot with my words complain and moan
> And suffer naught, nor smart without complaint,
> Nor turn the word that from my mouth is gone
> . . .
> I cannot wrest the law to fill the coffer,
> With innocent blood to feed myself fat. (28–35)

The lines about turning words and wresting the law are Wyatt's additions to his source. Pointz was busily moving into an environment where he needed to turn the sense of words from others' and, perhaps, his own lips, while he drew a fat stipend; Wyatt is just safely at home, distanced from the dangerous corruptions at court, delivering a carefully calculated jibe at his friend:

> None of these points would ever frame in *me*. (56)

That is, 'in *you*, yes; but not in *me*.' The poem is often criticized because most of its lines follow Alamanni in beginning 'I cannot . . . I cannot'. This does drag on the ear; but imagine a sarcastic stress on the 'I', directed by a homely Wyatt against a John Pointz rapidly losing his newly acquired gloss of courtly sophistication, and the whole poem comes to resemble the prevalent view among Renaissance editors of a Horatian *Epistle*: a conversation between absent people. It also has the kind of latent bite which Ariosto extracted from Horace – which one of Wyatt's other additions makes toothsome enough:

> *I* cannot, *I*; No, no, it will not be! (76)

Whether or not Pointz took the point will never be known. But it was there to be taken.

Wyatt took a second shot at Pointz in the next Satire, which begins with a familiar Horatian fable:

> My mother's maids when they did sew and spin,
> They sang sometime a song of the field mouse
> That, for because her livelood was but thin,
> Would needs go seek her townish sister's house. (1–4)

This transformation of *Sermones* 2.6 into folk memory again makes Horace seem to have arrived by coincidental overlap with personal circumstances. Some critics have believed that Wyatt's nurses actually did croon Aesopian rhymes to him, and that Horace is represented in the second Satire through such a blur of tradition that he cannot be said to have influenced the poem.[29] These critics have in all probability been taken in. The medium through which classical authors reached their Renaissance imitators often creates an apparent distance between poems and their originals, which can make – and can even be used to make – Renaissance poets appear to be creators rather than imitators of the classical source. Texts, notes, glosses and prefatory bumf of sixteenth-century scholarship make up much of the medium through which texts are transmitted, but another vital constituent in the accretion of meanings around classical texts is the way they had been selectively filtered by their early imitators. If one adds to this medium the mass of more or less accidental verbal, legal and social pressures brought to bear on the mind of the imitator, then the whole process of imitation becomes decidedly tangled. An author is only going to write like an ancient poet by a fantastically improbable coalescence of accidents. Wyatt *uses* the circumstances pressing down on his text in the second Satire to create something that appears to be a contemporary revision of his predecessor. The poem is an epistle (once more to Pointz) derived from Horace, which is trimmed to fit its addressee; and the trimming makes Horace seem a long way away. Wyatt cuts the first part of Horace's fable in which the town mouse comes to the country, because Pointz the country mouse, seeking some gain or grain at Court, would not be interested in that part of the story. Wyatt is also writing in the atmosphere created by the Treason Act: indirect speech, allusive speech, speech received from folklore, was *safe*. And this permeates every aspect of his writing. His physical survival depended on his ability to make his language appear to be traditional and nothing to do with him. In 1541 he was imprisoned for, among other things, allegedly saying that the King should be 'thrown out of a cart's arse'. Since this was a common (and sometimes fatal) punishment for criminals, and since after 1534 imagining or wishing for the death of the King was Treason, it was not a clever thing to say. Wyatt's defence, though, was a classic defence against the Treason Act: 'it is a common proverb, "I am left out of the cart's arse"', meaning something is 'evil taken heed to, or negligently, slips out of the cart and is lost'.[30] He claimed he had meant to express only the impeccably ambassadorial sentiment that Henry VIII was in danger of being left out of European negotiations. He doesn't say 'As my mother's maids always used to say, your honour . . .', but the habit of mind is the same: this is safe folk-lore, impersonal, undirected – with just the hint of a hit at a person in power.

This hint of a hit at a person in power is what makes the tale of the mice far more than *just* safe folk-lore. It feeds on a repressed current of feeling about the damage which a word in the wrong place could do to a courtier. And this undercurrent turns Horace into something nightmarish:

> And to the door now is she come by stealth
> And with her foot anon she scrapeth full fast.
> Th'other for fear durst not well scarce appear,
> Of every noise so was the wretch aghast.
> At last she asked softly who was there.
> And in her language as well as she could
> 'Peep', quod the other, 'sister, I am here.'
> 'Peace', quod the town mouse, 'why speakest thou so loud?' (36–43)

The way the country mouse speaks 'in her language as well as she could' catches both Wyatt's bashfulness about making mice speak, and the mouse's effort to make her own language sound as slick as she can for urban sophisticates. She is a foreigner out of place, and this leads the folk tale to blend into dystopia. An innocent little sprightly mousey 'Peep' in this alien place turns into a command for silence. Wyatt's interest in mousespeak and terror is far more pronounced than that of Horace. And little in Horace prepares for the horrid dim fear of Wyatt's conclusion to the tale:

> She cheered her with 'How sister, what cheer!'
> Amidst this joy befell a sorry chance
> That, wellaway, the stranger bought full dear
> The fare she had. For as she looked askance
> Under a stool she spied two steaming eyes
> In a round head with sharp ears. (49–54)

Horace's mice have their feasts rudely interrupted by a pack of Molossian hounds, who suddenly and vigorously enter. The terrifying inspecificity that Wyatt's mouse sees is quite different. It's a child's eye view of a decidedly non-Cheshirish cat, all circles and triangles, drawn by someone who doesn't have the concept of a cat, but who knows they can convey terror. Quite apart from being the best bit of mouse-psychology in the language, Wyatt's cat is a terrifying projection of ill-defined, almost extra-linguistic yet overwhelmingly powerful fears which grow in the Henrician court. A thing without words is *always there* (unlike Horace's dogs), always hiding under a chair to get you. One doesn't need to force the shape of Henry VIII or Cromwell's informers into that round head with sharp ears to feel the covert message to Pointz rising through the Horatian tale: there are nameless or unnameable things here which can kill you. Horace is indeed out of focus in Wyatt's second Satire, but things take shape from the alarming blurs, personal things, which make it seem that the poem just happens to converge from Wyatt's and Pointz's experience.

Things begin to take on perhaps too clear a shape after line 70, however:

> Alas, my Poyntz, how men do seek the best
> And find the worst by error as they stray . . .

The fable is left behind as Wyatt moves into a more abstract mode of delivery and lectures Pointz on the dangers of desires, and the importance of regulating the mind. Several critics have objected to this shift of tone;[31] but, successful or not, it derives again from the medium through which Wyatt saw Horace. Most sixteenth-century editions of the *Sermones* and *Epistles* said that the two genres follow each other naturally, like ploughing and sowing:

In prioribus enim duobus libellis quos sermonum inscripsit vitia persequitur. In reliquis duobus quos epistolarum nomine nuncupavit, virtutem et honestatem fere praecepit. In qua re agricolam solertem imitatur, qui primum radices et herbas nocivas ex agro suo avellitque sementem concerat.[32]

> In the first two books which are called *Sermones* he attacks vice. In the other two, which have the name of *Epistles*, he usually teaches virtue and honesty. In this he imitates a skilled farmer, who first ploughs up roots and noxious plants from his field and then sows seed.

Wyatt truncates this Georgic of the mind into a single poem. He attacks his friend's beliefs about the benefits of court life with a tale drawn from Horace's *Sermones*, then adds a meditative epistle to instruct him in how he should behave. 'My mother's maids' is a deliberate attempt to fuse Horace's *Sermones* together with his *Epistles*. But there is a continual danger in its more abstract and epistolary phase that generalities will become simple-minded abstractions, and that Wyatt will lose touch with the uneasy, guided imprecision of his idiom. This comes out in the way towards the end of the poem pronouns of address oscillate unstably between singular and plural:

> None of ye all there is that is so mad
> To seek grapes upon brambles or briers,
> Nor none, I trow, that hath his wit so bad
> To set his hay for conies over rivers;
> Ne ye set not a drag-net for a hare.
> And yet the thing that most is your desire
> Ye do mis-seek with more travail and care.
> Make plain thine heart that it be not knotted
> With hope or dread, and see thy will be bare
> From all affects whom vice hath ever spotted. (85–94)

The proverbial lore about not fishing for rabbits is not, like the tale of the mice, obliquely charged with meaning for its addressee: it is just trying to be generally applicable to Wyatt's plural audience. He is here, perhaps, beginning to think that he can become 'Horatian' by reducing his voice to one of sober generality. This is one of the perils of imitating Horace's *Epistles*: the addressee slips away, and one is left (as Horace is so often so nearly left) pushing doctrines for the good life which have no immediate purchase on their readers or recipient. Wyatt does not succumb to Horace's influence, or to the weight of his authority: he succumbs, perhaps, to an over-rigid, over-simple notion of what is Horatian about him.

But, towards the end of the extract just quoted, he narrowly manages to escape from inventing and imprisoning himself within a new and rigid version of Horatianism. The swoop into the singular from 'Ye do' to 'make plain thine heart' creates an intimacy which goes beyond general piety; it makes us and Pointz fuse for a moment, as we are intimately asked to do the one thing we all must do, but which we all must do singularly and for ourselves: sort out our minds. This momentary intimacy takes Wyatt back, both to his directedly abstract idiom and to the homely values of the early part of the Satire. Homeliness becomes a metaphor for inner tranquillity, a repose of the mind on itself:

> Thyself content with that is thee assigned
> And use it well that is to thee allotted.
> Then seek no more out of thyself to find
> The thing that thou hast sought so long before,
> For thou shalt feel it sitting in thy mind. (95–9)

These lines sound like total Wyatt: apparently general, yet replete with a private inner significance which is not fully revealed. But they are also almost a cento of notions from Horace. Satisfaction with one's lot is an idea Horace hammers out relentlessly,[33] and the view that the mind is its own place frequently comes into his letters from the country to men who move around the world. The *Epistle* to Bullatius, who has scudded around the Empire in pursuit of unspecified official business, hating wherever he went, concludes by locating satisfaction in the mind: *quod petis hic est, / est Ulubris, animus si te non deficit aequus.* ('What you seek is here, it is Ulubria, if you do not lack a contented mind', *Ep.*1.11.29–30.[34]) And in the setting of a debate between country and town, Horace states a preference for being a country mouse. The mind is to blame for its restless longing:

> rure ego viventem, tu dicis in urbe beatum:
> cui placet alterius, sua nimirum est odio sors.
> stultus uterque locum immeritum causatur inique:
> in culpa est animus, qui se non effugit umquam. (1.14.10–13)

I say that living in the country is the good life, you say living in town is. Let each of us please ourselves, provided there's no discontent with our own lot. We're both stupid to accuse the places, which aren't to blame at all: the guilty party is the mind, which never escapes itself.

As Wyatt circles back to thoughts from the real Horace he abandons his posture of 'Horatian' abstraction and creates something which feels totally his own. His domesticated generality, the 'thing' somehow felt sitting in the mind, fuses tags from Horace with his own habitual refusal to specify what it is he wants or fears. That magical phrase 'Thou shalt feel it sitting in thy mind' holds a weight of contentment: it manages to imply that the mind is at once the bottom and the armchair beneath it, each comfortably supporting the other. But what the 'thing' might be is deliberately left uncertain, kept safely free from the intrusive eyes of courtly misinterpreters. Horace is almost censored: the chief contentment in life is occluded by the need for privacy. But nonetheless it seems desperately important, desperately to do with Wyatt's self.

The force exerted by Horace on Wyatt's Satires only becomes apparent if one follows the lines of association (and repression) which tangle the mind of the imitator. Wyatt is true and wants to be true, not to Horace, but to what lies between himself and Horace. This is why he so often sounds so very like Wyatt when he approaches most closely to the *Sermones* and the *Epistles*: as he gets closer to his sources, so the pressures of his own circumstances become stronger. His last Satire, addressed to Sir Francis Brian, is the most powerful example of this paradox. It is an energetically personal account of a row between Wyatt and his addressee, which seems closer to Wyatt's life and further from Horace that any of the other Satires. But Nott, Wyatt's greatest editor, proposed that the poem was in some way derived from *Sermones* 2.5, in which, by way of an unorthodox coda to the *Odyssey*, Teiresias instructs Odysseus how to make money by hunting legacies. 2.5 is one of the most unsettling late *Sermones*, in which a figure of literary and prophetic authority is used to preach such wholesome practices as courting sickly rich folk and handing over one's wife to a wealthy patron. Horace himself is entirely absent from the authoritative immorality of the poem, and this has prompted Niall Rudd to call the poem 'un-Horatian'.[35] In a way though, the poem is the culminating moment of Horace's programmatic anti-Horatianism. Its reduction of all dogma to dialogue is where all Horace tends:

> hoc quoque, Teresia, praeter narrata petenti
> responde, quibus amissas reparare queam res
> artibus atque modis. quid rides?'
>   'iamne doloso
> non satis est Ithacam revehi patriosque Penates
> adspicere?   (1–5)

'Tell your questioner this, Teiresias, as well as what you have already said: how should I seek to win back my lost wealth? Why do you laugh?' 'Now, isn't it enough for the wily Odysseus to get back to Ithaca and to see his homeland and household gods?'

Wyatt and sixteenth-century Horatianism

This is meant to sound all wrong. Odysseus is the archetype of the man who just wants to go home; here he is made to want more money. Teiresias ruthlessly goes on to assault the ideals of Odysseus (who plaintively cries out that Penelope is true when he is told to hire her out), and to attack the practices of Rome from a location distant in space and time. The *Sermo* is an experiment in perspective, in which Homer's hero and Roman modes of behaviour are seen from odd and deliberately alienating angles. Its setting abroad, and its apparently total instability of outlook, brings it close to the concerns which form Ariosto's Satires: exile and loss of values fuse. For a sixteenth-century Horatian poet, *Sermones* 2.5 would seem central to Horace's output, since several writers in the period associated Odysseus with diplomatic exiles and voyagers to alien places: Du Bellay in his epistolary laments aligns himself with Odysseus' longings for home, and educational manuals identify Homer's hero with travellers abroad on political and educational missions.[36] Horace's bewildered Odysseus would seem a perfect vehicle for exploring the displaced moral hunger of a diplomatic exile.

This network of associations – with what is almost a ruthless imitative logic – turns Horace's poem into Wyatt's last Satire. The addressee of the poem, Francis Brian, was a resident ambassador to Francis I in 1538, while he and Wyatt were severally engaged in breaking down the imminent alliance between France and the Habsburg Empire. Like Wyatt, Brian spent most of his time trotting up and down at the behest of Henry VIII.[37] Why not give all this up, says Wyatt

> And mightst at home sleep in thy bed of down
> And drink good ale so nappy for the nonce,   (strong and frothy
> Feed thyself fat and heap up pound by pound?   for the occasion)
> Likest thou not this? 'No' Why? 'For swine so groins
> In sty and chaw the turds moulded on the ground,
> And drivel on pearls, the head still in the manger.
> . . .
> Though I seem lean and dry without moisture,
> Yet will I serve my prince, my lord and thine,
> And let them live to feed the paunch that list,
> So I may feed to live, both me and mine.'
> By God, well said, but what and if thou wist
> How to bring in as fast as thou dost spend?
> 'That would I learn.' And it shall not be missed
> To tell thee how.   (15–31)

This is something extremely rare in early sixteenth-century imitations of Horace: a fully blown *sermo*, a conversation, with a quickfire rattiness on either side, in which neither party seems to have access to truth. Horace's late *Sermones* unsettle any sense that there might be a single posture emerging through the talk; Wyatt here arrives at a rapprochement with this idiom by undermining the stable certainties of his own 'Horatian' ideals. For Brian, Wyatt's insistence on the value of staying at home – which underlies the 'Horatianism' of his Satires to Pointz – is no more than the desire of a sluggish fatty to sit and munch. (Wyatt was indeed full in the face.) The dialogue form uproots Wyatt's own network of Horatian values, and systematically strips away comforting reference points from its readers, miming the psychological effects of exile from a valued place. The opening of the poem resounds with reassuring certainties which sound very like – rather too like – the flatly proverbial section of the previous Satire, in which Wyatt lectured Pointz with Horatian authority:

> 'A spending hand that always poureth out
> Had need to have a bringer-in as fast';
> And 'On the stone that still doth turn about
> There groweth no moss' – these proverbs yet do last.
> Reason hath set them in so sure a place
> That length of years their force can never waste.   (1–6)

But the next lines pull these stable certainties out from under our feet. The poem is not just a string of proverbs, but an epistle, in which the apparently objective remarks of a figure of authority are unsettled by their dramatic and epistolary setting:

> When I remember this and eke the case   (also)
> Wherein thou stands, I thought forthwith to write,
> Brian, to thee, who knows how great a grace
> In writing is to counsel man the right.
> To thee, therefore, that trots still up and down
> And never rests, but running day and night
> From realm to realm, from city, street, and town . . .   (7–13)

The opening, apparently inert and preachily flat allusion to 'a spending hand', when directed to Brian, has a vicious edge: at Nice in 1538 Wyatt lent £200 to Brian, who was as hard up as Horace's Odysseus, and in some danger of prosecution, since personal debt was specifically excluded from diplomatic immunity in this period.[38] Brian wrote strings of proverbs and called them poems. These facts taken together make the opening of this Satire anything but inertly sententious: it is positively bitchy. It pulls from the drab generality of Brian's verse the sharp directedness of Wyatt's Horace, in which a privy conversation emerges from apparently neutral, toneless sayings. It magnificently discards 'Horatian' certainty in favour of Horace's ability to bite at a person's preoccupations through flatly received phrases.

This is of course just what diplomats have to be able to do. Hiding his identity and yet asserting opinion is Horace's main method in the *Sermones*; and this was exactly what Wyatt's life and diplomatic livelihood depended on. In 1539 Henry VIII ordered him to call Charles V an 'ingrate', so as to provoke a conflagration which could be used to draw the Emperor away from the imminent alliance with France. Wyatt did his job: he relayed the insult to the most powerful man in Europe. The Emperor, as planned, blew up. Wyatt wrote a vigorously conversational report of the exchange:

'For I would you knew I am not ingrate, and if the king your master hath done me a good turn, I have done him as good or better. And I take it so that I can not be toward him ingrate. The inferior may be ingrate to the greater, and the term is scant sufferable between like. But peradventure because the language is not your natural tongue you may mistake the term.' 'Sir', quod I, 'I do not know that I misdo in using the term that I am commanded.'[39]

Wyatt, trembling in his boots, is careful to point out both that the word is not his, and that it is indeed what he has been asked to say. And massive international forces hung on the responses to and interpretation of this second-hand, diplomatic insult: Cromwell reported the Emperor's words to the French king as indicating a 'fantasy that he should be peerless which must needs partly appear by his words to Mr Wyatt, though they be never so gently interpreted'.[40] Francis I's warmth towards the Emperor was temporarily cooled by Wyatt's skill in diplomatic insults. For Wyatt, the 'urbanity' of Horace, the sly digs of the *Sermones* and the privy nips of the *Epistles* were not ornaments of politeness: they were a necessary diplomatic skill, the means of surviving whilst managing to say what you thought. And, in his last Satire, this diplomatic power to abuse, fused with Horatian snideness, is directed against Brian. He speaks through Horace, with crooked directness, about the effects of diplomatic servility on one's ability to talk straight. 'Wyatt' the speaker adopts the tone of authority, but preaches corruption:

> Thou know'st well, first, whoso can seek to please
> Shall purchase friends where truth shall but offend.
> Flee therefore truth: it is both wealth and ease.
> For though that truth of every man hath praise,
> Full near the wind goeth truth in great misease.
> Use virtue as it goeth now-a-days,
> In word alone to make thy language sweet.   (32–8)

The tone of stable assertion that marred the closing stages of the epistle to Pointz is revived again to preach corruption. This is uncannily redolent of the kind of corrupt but authoritatively stated advice which Horace's Teiresias offers to his wandering pupil; but this juxtaposition of a certain tone with a slithery content is also the result of a diplomat's life. When Henry Wotton jokingly defined an ambassador as 'an honest man sent to lie abroad for the good of his country'[41] he was not too far from the truth. After negotiating with Brian, the French ambassador to Henry VIII wrote to his King 'I find so little stability in the English with their subtleties and their proneness to suspicion that I cannot tell how far you may depend on [their word].'[42] In the shiftless, uncertain environment of Tudor diplomacy Wyatt is actually offering good advice, which Brian put into practice: lying *is* how ambassadors earn their bread. Poems deriving from Horace in this period are usually about dislocation; this Satire turns the experience of being abroad into a total uncertainty about who or what to believe. It grows from the 'anti-Horatian' stance of *Sermones* 2.5 into a bewilderingly brilliant account of what it feels like to inhabit an ethical nowhere-land. And the poem itself occupies a kind of nowhere-land: Wyatt had, in 'My mother's maids', tried to fuse *Sermo* and *Epistle* sequentially; but the Satire to Brian is *simultaneously* a *sermo*, a conversation between people who are present, and an epistle to an absent friend. This makes it exist in two places at once: its argument echoes through the corridors of an ambassadorial lodging, and simultaneously smoulders in a diplomatic bag in transit across the ocean. And this locationlessness permeates its argument, dissolving any certainty, any trace of 'Horatian' dogma. The poem is far from suggesting – as some critics have argued[43] – that Brian is right to pursue outspoken honesty in the service of his Prince. It insinuates, rather, that honest virtue and success in civil service can never coexist. Either you lie or your fail. The implicit didactic point emerging from the poem has nothing to do with the protestations of either party: it is a species of moral unlocatedness. Wyatt does not advocate simple quietism, a Horatian withdrawal from public affairs; rather, all dogma dissolves into the irreconcilable antagonism of two speakers caught in the dislocating spaces of sixteenth-century diplomacy. Even the poem's final, apparently dogmatic exhortation 'Content thee then with honest poverty' is another final stab of elegant savagery against Brian, masked as 'Horatian' sententiousness: after 1538 Brian fell catastrophically from court favour and so was *compelled* to settle for an honest poverty he neither wished for nor enjoyed. No simple assertion is simply true in this poem, which is at once total Horace and a complete response to the pressures of exile which created sixteenth-century Horatianism.

At least one later poet responded to the complexities of the dialogue. When Sir John Harington (a member of the family which preserved two major manuscripts of Wyatt's verse for posterity, and who sighed, with Horace *o rus, quando ego te aspiciam* while at court longing for Kelston) wrote an epigram about leaving home to go to war abroad in Ireland in the 1590s, his language naturally gravitated towards Wyatt's Satires:

> At home Canary wines and Greek grow loathsome:
> Here milk is Nectar, water tasteth toothsome.

Wyatt and sixteenth-century Horatianism

> There without bak't, rost, boyld, it is no cheer.
> Bisket we like, and Bonny Clabo here.   (curdled milk)
> . . .
> At home on silken sparvers, beds of Down,   (bed canopies)
> We scant can rest, but still toss up and Down:
> Here I can sleep, a saddle to my pillow,
> A Hedge the Curtain, Canopy a Willow.⁴⁴

'Bak't, rost, boyld' recalls the longings of Wyatt's country mouse in 'My mother's maids' for the urban sophistication of her sister, who, in Harington's family manuscript, 'feedes on boiled meat, bake meat, and on roast'.⁴⁵ The 'beds of down / toss up and down' rhyme is drawn from the Satire to Brian. Harington's joke description of the horrors of home grounds itself on Wyatt's Horatian epistles and their implicit valuation of liberty at home above all other demands. But Harington's view of Wyatt also recognizes, in its swirlingly uncentred yet affectionate criticism of home, the other side of Wyatt's Horace: that Wyatt was, by the time he wrote the Satire to Brian, so attuned to the instabilities of Horace that he had discarded any simple 'Horatian' doctrine. He'd become so locationless that he could help a subsequent writer to make something like a Horatian poem.

3

THE BEST MASTER OF VIRTUE AND WISDOM: THE HORACE OF BEN JONSON AND HIS HEIRS

Joanna Martindale

IN MARVELL'S POEM 'Tom May's Death', Ben Jonson's shade admonishes the turncoat Tom May in the Underworld:

> When the sword glitters o'er the judge's head,
> And fear has coward churchmen silencèd,
> Then is the poet's time, 'tis then he draws,
> And single fights forsaken virtue's cause.
> He, when the wheel of empire whirleth back,
> And though the world's disjointed axle crack,
> Sings still of ancient rights and better times,
> Seeks wretched good, arraigns successful crimes.
> But thou, base man, first prostituted hast
> Our spotless knowledge and the studies chaste,
> Apostatizing from our arts and us,
> To turn the chronicler to Spartacus.   (63–74)

These lines are a clever parody of Jonson's Horatian role, which he first adopted in *Poetaster* and later developed in his non-dramatic poems. Marvell is surely recalling Jonson's adaptation in *Poetaster* of the opening lines of *Odes* 3.3:

> iustum et tenacem propositi virum
> non civium ardor prava iubentium,
>   non vultus instantis tyranni
>   mente quatit solida neque Auster,
> dux inquieti turbidus Hadriae,
> nec fulminantis magna manus Iovis:
>   si fractus illabatur orbis,
>   impavidum ferient ruinae.   (1–8)

The man who is just and fixed in his purpose, not the zeal of citizens issuing wrong orders, not the face of the threatening tyrant disturbs in his firm intention, nor the

The Horace of Ben Jonson and his heirs

South Wind, the turbulent ruler of the unquiet Adriatic, nor the mighty hand of thundering Jove; if the world should break and fall in, the ruins will strike him untrembling.

In Jonson's adaptation, Horace's picture of the man who is unperturbed amid political turmoil and natural disasters[1] is redrawn as the poet beset by informers, state tyranny and censorship (the tyrant's threatening face becomes an 'ear'); Horace–Jonson is being arraigned before Augustus by the tribune, Lupus:

> A just man cannot fear, thou foolish tribune;
> Not though the malice of traducing tongues,
> The open vastness of a tyrant's ear,
> The senseless rigour of the wrested laws,
> Or the red eyes of strained authority
> Should, in a point, meet all to take his life.
> His innocence is armour 'gainst all these.   (V.iii.61–7)[2]

Marvell's lines are also concerned with poetic integrity, but the setting is altered to suggest the political turmoil of the mid-century. His line 'And though the world's disjointed axle crack' goes back directly to the Horatian original (line 7). It may also recall Jonson's version of Horace's lines in *Catiline* (see his use of the word 'crack'):

> But to just men,
> Though Heaven should speak with all his wrath at once,
> That with his breath the hinges of the world
> Did crack, we should stand upright and unfeared.   (IV.29–32)

As I shall seek to demonstrate below, Jonson had made the lines from Horace a keystone of his Horatian persona, and they had been taken up after him by many of his sons to formulate an ideal of constancy: Herrick has no less than six epigrams basing a definition of the good man on Horace's figure.[3] Horace's images could be adapted to a variety of different settings; in some of the mid-century versions, the storm imagery becomes the storm of Civil War.[4] A witty adaptation of Horace's lines to a judicial context, which Marvell may also be remembering, occurs in Denham's 'Elegy on the Death of Judge Croke'. Sir George Croke was one of the judges in the notorious ship-money case, when Charles I tried to levy inland counties for the maintenance of the navy without consulting Parliament and John Hampden was prosecuted for non-payment; at risk of royal displeasure, Croke found against the tax. The poem celebrates this modern instance of the resolved man unmoved by the *vultus instantis tyranni*, or as Denham, Royalist as he was, cleverly puts it, the pressure of the *primum mobile*; by an ingenious development of the imagery of *Odes* 3.3.7–8, Croke is said to be the axis on which the moving world turns (perhaps the source for Marvell's metaphors of 'wheel' and 'axle'):

51

> Him nor respect nor disrespect could move;
> He knew no anger, nor his place no love.
> So mixed the stream of all his actions ran,
> So much a judge, so much a gentleman;
> Who durst be just when justice was a crime,
> Yet durst no more ev'n in too just a time;
> Not hurried by the highest mover's force
> Against his proper and resolvèd course;
> But when our world did turn, so kept his ground
> He seemed the axe on which the wheel went round.
> No ague in religion e'er inclined
> To this or that extreme his fixèd mind,
> Whose zeal was warm when all to ice did turn,
> Yet was but warm when all the world did burn.[5] (23–36)

In his lines in 'Tom May's Death', Marvell thus picks up, with his accustomed literary acuity, a whole tradition of earlier seventeenth-century poetry begun by Jonson. In Jonson's speech, he demonstrates his understanding of Jonson's Horatian role as embodied for example in the opening of the 'Epistle. To Katherine, Lady Aubigny' (*Forest* 13): his embattled stance alone against the world as defender of virtue and his indignant scorn at poetasters and profaners of the poetic art who write for profit not truth, 'Sworn enemy to all that do pretend'. Marvell perhaps imitates too something of the Jonsonian–Horatian manner (though the end-stopped couplets are not Jonsonian): its clarity and vigour, the brief concrete images and the absence of elaborate conceits.

But Marvell should not be identified with Jonson. If the poem was written in 1650, he was after all, if not for the reasons ascribed to May in the poem, himself in the process of making a change in political allegiance. He admired the ability to change: his Cromwell both in 'An Horatian Ode' and in 'The First Anniversary' is not the Stoic man of *Odes* 3.3, unchangeable, but is heroic through Machiavellian powers of adaptability.[6] In a vivid passage in 'The First Anniversary', he was to adapt Horace's famous lines on the golden mean in *Odes* 2.10, which had frequently been combined by earlier seventeenth-century poets with celebrations of constancy, to praise Cromwell's opportunism:

> rectius vives, Licini, neque altum
> semper urgendo neque, dum procellas
> cautus horrescis, nimium premendo
>   litus iniquum. (1–4)

You will live better, Licinius, by neither always pushing into the deep, nor, while you shudder frightened at storm winds, pressing too close to the dangerous shore.

The Horace of Ben Jonson and his heirs

> So have I seen at sea, when *whirling winds*
> Hurry the bark but more the *seamen's minds*,
> Who with mistaken course salute the sand,
> And threat'ning rocks misapprehend for land;
> While baleful Tritons to the shipwreck guide,
> And corposants along the tacklings slide,   (St Elmo's fire)
> The passengers all wearied out before,
> Giddy, and wishing for the *fatal shore*,
> Some lusty mate, who with more careful eye
> Counted the hours and every star did spy,
> The helm does from the artless steersman strain
> And doubles back unto the *safer main*.   (265–76, my italics)

John M. Wallace showed how the figure of the 'lusty mate' is drawn from a popular contemporary political analogy, justifying revolutionary measures in a disturbed state.[7] But the setting so concretely evoked in Marvell's lines comes straight from Horace's poem: the crew ignore the latter part of Horace's advice not to press into the shore through fear of winds, while Cromwell seizes the *right* moment (Horace's *neque semper* implies that it is sometimes right) to press into the deep. (In Wallace's analogues the situation is vaguer and more obvious: the pilot and crew are drunk or asleep and the ship is near the rocks.)

When we are considering how Marvell came to write 'Tom May's Death' after 'An Horatian Ode', which is at least partially sympathetic to Cromwell, the fact that the poem is a dramatic monologue should be borne in mind. The conservatism and scorn for republicanism expressed in Jonson's speech is part of the Jonsonian pastiche, like the praise of constancy. 'Tom May's Death' was probably written either in 1650, when May died, or in 1661, when his body was removed from Westminster Abbey. At either time, despite the affectionate character of the parody, Jonson's ghost would have been sounding an old-fashioned note.[8]

Indeed, in the Restoration, the Jonsonian–Horatian model was to lose its dominance. Contrast Jonson's picture of Horace, after Daniel Heinsius, 'the best master both of virtue and wisdom' (*Discoveries* 2592) with Dryden's confident characterization in the preface to *Sylvae* (1685) (perhaps influenced by André Dacier's commentary, which stressed Horace's humour and anti-Stoic attitudes):

His morals are uniform, and run through all of them [his works]; for let his Dutch commentators say what they will, his philosophy was Epicurean; and he made use of gods and providence only to serve a turn in poetry... The most distinguishing part of all his character seems to me to be his briskness, his jollity, and his good humour.

In place of Stoic sage, Horace was often to become Epicurean bon viveur or libertine – 'loose Horace whose verses have almost as many nudities as his closet' (Creech):

> But when to give our minds a feast indeed,
> Horace, best known and loved by thee, we read,
> Who can our transports or our longings tell,
> To taste of pleasures, praised by him so well?
> With thoughts of love and wine by him we're fired,
> Two things in sweet retirement much desired;
> A generous bottle and a lovesome she
> Are the'only joys in nature, next to thee.[9]   (Otway)

But in the first part of the century, the Jonsonian–Horatian model was immensely influential; we can hear it in the poetry of Carew, Herrick, Vaughan and Lovelace, and it was indeed to persist into the Restoration period in Cowley's *Essays in Verse and Prose*.

How justifiable is it to speak of Jonson's Horatian role or a Jonsonian–Horatian model? Would a better approach be to look at the influence of the group of Latin writers who influenced him most, rather than pick out Horace?[10] Horace was certainly not the only poet imitated by Ben Jonson, who was interested in a wide range of Latin authors, especially the Roman moralists, satirists and historians: Seneca, Martial, Persius, Juvenal, Cicero and Tacitus. His characteristic method of imitation, exemplified in 'To Penshurst' and 'To Sir Robert Wroth', is to combine reminiscences of several poets into a new whole; the ability to range over the corpus of Latin literature and make connections between passages from different authors which fit in with his own concerns is an impressive feature of his classicism.[11] When we say that Horace inspired a certain idea, it may often be possible to point to other Roman sources. Jonson's formulation of the idea of the Stoic man, for example, often combines reminiscences from Seneca with Horace.

Nevertheless, the association with Horace is particularly strong and was frequently made by both Jonson himself and his contemporaries.[12] From the time of *Poetaster* on, Jonson's use of Horace was not just a question of imitating particular themes and stylistic elements; through allusion to Horace, he defines his poetic role. Jonson gave his imitation of Horace a strong personal flavour: it is a recreation, not a pastiche – in his own terms it is well-digested. It was something he passed on to his sons. Thus, Herrick's 'A Country Life, to his Brother, Master Thomas Herrick' reworks a tissue of Horatian allusions in a Jonsonian style, with Herrickian touches. Such a poem may fairly be described not merely as classical or Roman but as Jonsonian–Horatian.

Poetaster, in which Jonson first adopted a Horatian persona, was first

The Horace of Ben Jonson and his heirs

acted in 1601 and published in 1602 as a blow in the feud Jonson was waging with Marston and Dekker, the so-called War of the Theatres. Jonson's strategy in the play was to project the literary quarrels of his own day back into the world of Augustan Rome. The characters and the action of the part of the plot which concerns Horace were built up from Horace's *Sermones*, especially the literary *Sermones*, 1.4 and 10. While Jonson is cast as Horace, the two names given to Dekker, Demetrius Fannius, come from a passage in *Sermones* 1.10.78–91 where Horace speaks of the envious and incompetent artists whom he scorns and the audience of the few whose admiration he seeks (the speech is adapted in v.iii.456–62). Marston appears as Crispinus who in the *Sermones* is both the foolish Stoic (1.1.120, 1.3.139, 2.7.45) and more importantly the poet who challenges Horace to a poetic contest on the criterion of length (1.4.13–16). By the brilliant stoke of identifying the famous bore of *Sermones* 1.9 as Crispinus and dramatizing the *Sermo* in a *tour de force* at the beginning of Act III, Jonson fills out the picture of Marston as the foolish poet: he is an envious braggart, who thinks writing quickly is a virtue and who cannot tell the difference between the art of poetry and trivial accomplishments:

> I protest to thee, Horace (do but taste me once), if I do know myself and mine own virtues truly, thou wilt not make that esteem of Varius or Virgil or Tibullus, or any of 'em indeed, as now in thy ignorance thou dost – which I am content to forgive. I would fain see which of these could pen more verses in a day or with more facility than I, or that could court his mistress, kiss her hand, make better sport with her fan or her dog . . .   (III.i.161–8)

(If this identification was indeed Jonson's own – and neither the Scholia nor Horace's chief sixteenth-century editor Lambinus identify the bore – Dryden must be thinking of *Poetaster* when he makes the same identification in the preface to *All for Love* with a similar aim of deflating his modern opponents – evidence that Dryden had studied the Jonsonian Horace.)

In the literary *Sermones*, Horace speaks of the attacks made on him, and in *Poetaster* Jonson builds up a plot in which the envious poetasters attempt to overthrow the virtuous poet Horace and are exposed and punished. Satire, distrusted in Elizabethan England and banned by order of the bishops in 1599, is vindicated in the figure of Horace–Jonson: the satirist's sharpness is claimed to be 'forced out of a suffering virtue / oppressèd with the license of the time' (v.iii.369–70) and it is malicious interpretation which 'hurts or wounds the body of a state' (v.iii.139). Jonson utilizes Horace's own words to present his defence of satire. Horace–Jonson is attacked by the braggart, Captain Tucca, for his malice, in a lively rendering of *Sermones* 1.4.34–8:

> A sharp thorny-toothed satirical rascal – fly him. He carries hay in his horn. He will sooner lose his best friend than his least jest. What he once drops upon paper, against a

man, lives eternally to upbraid him in the mouth of every slave tankard-bearer or waterman; not a bawd or a boy that comes from the bakehouse but shall point at him. 'Tis all dog and scorpion. He carries poison in his teeth and a sting in his tale.

(IV.iii.109–16).

Later on, Horace–Jonson defends himself with a version of Horace's reply in the same *Sermo*. He is quite different from the backbiter, the truly malicious man:

>   absentem qui rodit, amicum
> qui non defendit alio culpante, solutos
> qui captat risus hominum famamque dicacis,
> fingere qui non visa potest, commissa tacere
> qui nequit, hic niger est, hunc tu, Romane, caveto.   (81–5)

The man who slanders one who is absent, who doesn't defend a friend when another blames him, who seeks for the loose laughter of men and the reputation of a wit, who can invent things not seen, who cannot keep quiet what's entrusted to him, this is the black-hearted man, him, Roman, beware.

>   Such as will bite
> And gnaw their absent friends, not cure their fame,
> Catch at the loosest laughters, and affect
> To be thought jesters, such as can devise
> Things never seen or heard, to'impair men's names
> And gratify their credulous adversaries,
> Will carry tales, do basest offices,
> Cherish divided fires, and still increase
> New flames out of old embers, will reveal
> Each secret that's committed to their trust. –
> These be black slaves; Romans, take heed of these.   (v.iii.329–39)

I quote in Latin and English because this is an important passage which becomes part of the Jonsonian mythology. Jonson reinforces his picture of the embattled but undaunted satirist with the passage from *Odes* 3.3. quoted above.

Jonson's device of dramatizing Horace's *Sermones* was thus a clever way of ridiculing his literary opponents while putting his own behaviour in the best possible light, and at the same time addressing themes of importance to him. As E. W. Talbert demonstrated,[13] *Poetaster* is a Renaissance defence of poetry, like Sidney's *Defense of Poesy*, a stage representation of the humanist theme of the conflict between the Muses and barbarism. More specifically it develops a defence of satire begun in earlier plays: Horace-Jonson is the third in a series of portraits of the satirist starting with Asper in *Every Man out of his Humour* and Crites in *Cynthia's Revels*. Jonson relates Horace's

The Horace of Ben Jonson and his heirs

Sermones to his own interests, and his reading of them is characteristic. Modern scholars have seen Horace's three literary *Sermones* as playful pieces of 'shadow-boxing',[14] but Jonson took them straight. The right to attack was a less direct issue for Horace, since his *Sermones* do not contain a large element of invective (his claim in *Sermones* 1.4 that he has been criticized for venom may well be fictional). *Sermones* 2.1 ends with a joke: when Trebatius the lawyer reminds him of the threat of the law:

> 'si mala condiderit in quem quis carmina, ius est
> iudiciumque.' (82–3)

'If someone compose bad poems against another, there is justice and legal process.'

Horace laughs this off with a pun – *mala carmina* may mean either libellous poems or poorly written poems – though also hinting at his support by Augustus:

> 'esto, si quis mala; sed bona si quis
> iudice condiderit laudatus Caesare?' (83–4)

'Very well, if they are bad; but if anyone writes good poetry and is praised with Caesar for judge?'

Art, *bona carmina*, is what Horace cares about, and is the true theme of his literary *Sermones*. Jonson cares about art too; elsewhere he often borrows from Horace on the theme of the need for toil in art.[15] But he was also deeply in earnest in his defence of satire. For one thing, unlike Horace, who was in no danger from the authorities by the time of *Sermones* 2.1, Jonson was in real danger from the law; he had been imprisoned in 1597 for his share in *The Isle of Dogs* and was to be imprisoned again in 1605 for his share in *Eastward Ho!*. *Poetaster* itself brought its author into trouble; in the dedication of the play to Richard Martin, Jonson says that he saved the play for posterity 'which so much ignorance and malice of the times then conspired to have suppressed'. The importance given to the role of Lupus, the foolish magistrate who seeks to imprison Horace (the name comes from *Sermones* 2.1.68, but the character is Jonson's own invention) reflects the real threat of the law to Jonson. Secondly, Jonson was strongly committed to a moral and corrective theory of satire. In his translation of *Sermones* 2.1 inserted at the end of Act III in the Folio text of 1616, he upholds the moral ideal of Lucilian satire with great fervour (III.v.103-112); and for Horace's pun at the end of the poem he substitutes a careful definition of the permissible liberty of the satirist, drawing a distinction between lewd libels and moral satire, and working in Martial's claim in *Epigrams* 10.33.9-10 that he mentions no names:

> Aye, with lewd verses, such as libels be,
> And aimed at persons of good quality.
> I reverence and adore that just decree.
> But if they shall be sharp, yet modest, rhymes
> That spare men's persons and but tax their crimes,
> Such shall in open court find current pass. (III.v.130–5)

In *Satiromastix*, his reply to *Poetaster*, Dekker was quick to jeer at Jonson's identification of himself with Horace, fastening on Jonson's social insecurity 'the fortunes and conditions of his life'.[16] At the beginning of the play (I.ii), he gives an amusing picture of Horace–Jonson desperately searching for rhymes in his efforts to write the 'flowing measures' of an ode, and at the end the discrepancies between Horace and Jonson are detailed (V.ii.254–63), 'Horace loved poets well and gave coxcombs to none but fools, but thou lov'st none, neither wise men nor fools but thyself', and so on.[17] But though Dekker's play had the last word in the War of the Theatres, Jonson was after all to have the last laugh: his identification with Horace became a commonplace with his contemporaries.

Jonson carried over the Horatian role he had created for himself in *Poetaster* into his poems. We can see this from a comparison between the 'Apologetical Dialogue' to the play and the three odes to himself, where Jonson makes major poetry out of the theme of *bona carmina* – the need for industry and artistic standards. According to Jonson, the 'Apologetical Dialogue' was 'only once spoken upon the stage', and it did not appear in print until the Folio text of 1616. In it, the author appears and defends his play to two callers. Jonson develops further both his defence of satire (using ideas from Martial) and his Horatian role. He presents himself as untouched by fortune and the malice of his enemies (the 'tongues of slaves' come from Juvenal *Satires* 9.118–20), like the Stoic wise man of *Sermones* 2.7 (quoted below page 60):

> The Fates have not spun him the coarsest thread
> That, free from knots of perturbation,
> Doth yet so live, although but to himself,
> As he can safely scorn the tongues of slaves,
> And neglect Fortune more than she can him. (23–7)

Jonson also develops, with the assistance of Juvenal *Satires* 7.27–9, the picture of himself as a learned and laborious artist, burning the midnight oil 'to come forth worth the ivy or the bays', scorning and scorned by the multitude (see lines 209–15, 233–5). Two of the three odes to himself – 'Where dost thou careless lie?' (*Underwood* 23) and 'If men and times were now' – contain identical lines to some in the 'Apologetical Dialogue' and a similar portrayal of the poet, and may have been written about the same time. In the

The Horace of Ben Jonson and his heirs

Jonson rejects popular applause and turns into himself for his 'proper strain', rising above fortune:

> Minds that are great and free
> Should not on fortune pause;
> 'Tis crown enough to virtue still, her own applause, (16–18)

and thus triumphing over both envy and ignorance, 'Safe from the wolf's black jaw, and the dull ass's hoof'. (This line comes from the 'Apologetical Dialogue'.) In the second of the two odes, Jonson mourns the past when poetry was valued for its immortalizing powers (another Horatian topic) and laments the present age of barbarism. He goes on to give a picture similar to that in the 'Apologetical Dialogue', again echoing Juvenal 7, of the poet's hard labour for his art and the unappreciativeness of his audience:

> Break then thy quills, blot out
> Thy long-watched verse,
> And rather to the fire than to the rout
> Their laboured tunes rehearse,
> Whose air will sooner hell than their dull senses pierce:
> Thou that dost spend thy days
> To get thee a lean face
> And come forth worthy ivy or the bays,
> And, in this age, canst hope no other grace. (19–27)

(These lines directly echo the 'Apologetical Dialogue'.) The poem ends with an appeal to Minerva to triumph over the forces of barbarism as in *Poetaster*, adding 'Gorgon Envy' to the ranks of the giants from *Odes* 3.4.53–8.

It is interesting to find the same themes and the same picture of the poet in the famous ode written many years later after the failure of *The New Inn*, in 1629, demonstrating the consistency of theme in Jonson's work. The poem is full of bitter scorn for the ignorance of the theatre audiences of Jonson's day, and once again, Jonson turns to himself and his own powers, resolving to emulate the ancient lyric poets, including 'thine own Horace'. These three poems are often seen just as expressions of spleen on Jonson's part for his dramatic failures. But they also express, through an adaptation of Horace's Callimachean pose of spurning the vulgar herd and writing for the few, Jonson's belief in the value of art and his Horatian conviction of the need for effort in writing good poetry – ideas which can be paralleled in *Discoveries*, a similar product of Jonson's humanism.

Another mature poem, written in 1623, 'An Epistle Answering to One that Asked to be Sealed of the Tribe of Ben' (*Underwood* 47), is closely linked to the Horatian themes of *Poetaster*. Writing at a different point in his career, annoyed by his exclusion from the preparations for the return of Prince

Charles from Spain with the Infanta, and with a new enemy in Inigo Jones, Jonson turns to the same passages from Horace which he had employed before. He gives a fine evocation of himself as the man of integrity despite the ignorance and malice of the world:

> Well, with mine own frail pitcher, what to do
> I have decreed: keep it from waves and press,   (crowd, crush)
> Lest it be jostled, cracked, made nought or less;
> Live to that point I will for which I'am man,
> And dwell as in my centre as I can . . .   (56–60)

Behind this passage lie the two descriptions of the just man from *Odes* 3.3. (already quoted) and the Stoic *sapiens* in *Sermones* 2.7:[18]

> 'Quisne igitur liber?' 'sapiens, sibi qui imperiosus,
> quem neque pauperies neque mors neque vincula terrent,
> responsare cupidinibus, contemnere honores
> fortis et in se ipso totus, teres atque rotundus,
> externi ne quid valeat per leve morari,
> in quem manca ruit semper Fortuna'.   (83–8)

'Who therefore is free?' 'The wise man, who has command over himself, whom neither poverty nor death nor chains frighten, brave to resist desires and to despise honours, and all self-contained, smooth and round, so that nothing external can stay on his smoothness, against whom Fortune always rushes crippled.'

These lines too were favourites with Jonson, who translates them more directly in Epigram 98, 'To Sir Thomas Roe' (lines 3–6). In the 'Epistle', Jonson also draws a picture of the vicious antithesis of the virtuous man, which is derived from the portrait of the backbiter in *Sermones* 1.4, quoted above:

>   that will jest
> On all souls that are absent, ev'n the dead,
> Like flies or worms which man's corrupt parts fed;
> That to speak well, think it above all sin,
> Of any company but that they'are in;
> Call every night to supper in these fits,
> And are received for the covey of wits;   (party)
> That censure all the town, and all the'affairs,
> And know whose ignorance is more than theirs . . .   (16–24)

(This draws on the continuation of the Horace passage, in lines 86–91.) This passage came to be associated in Jonson's mind with Inigo Jones; he uses it again in 'On the Town's Honest Man', (*Epigrams* 115) (see lines 13–17, 27–8).

In the three odes to himself and the 'Epistle', Jonson has developed and refined the Horatian voice first adopted in *Poetaster*. He has softened its shrillness and made it an eloquent, persuasive and flexible instrument. Dekker in *Satiromastix* parodied quite well Jonson's self-righteous and hectoring tone in *Poetaster*:

> To see my fate, that when I dip my pen
> In distilled roses and do strive to drain
> Out of mine ink all gall; that when I weigh
> Each syllable I write or speak, because
> Mine enemies with sharp and searching eyes
> Look through and through me, carving my poor labours
> Like an anatomy; Oh heavens, to see
> That when my lines are measured out as straight
> As even parallels, 'tis strange that still,
> Still, some imagine they are drawn awry!
> This error is not mine but in their eye,
> That cannot take proportions. (I.ii.192–203)

In the poems, however, Jonson achieves both greater dignity and a more relaxed intimacy; he both deepens and lightens his tone. In the three odes to himself, Jonson presents an intimate portrait of the artist, expressing other emotions than the scorn which predominates in the 'Apologetical Dialogue'. 'If men and times were now' expresses as movingly as *Lycidas* the isolation and disappointments of the artist's vocation. In 'Where dost thou careless lie?', we see Jonson haranguing himself rather than his enemies, and feel a strong sense of his commitment to his art. *The New Inn* ode contains painful personal reference to his old age and physical decrepitude (Jonson suffered a stroke in 1628 which left him bedridden for the rest of his life): 'And though thy nerves be shrunk and blood be cold / . . . no palsy's in thy brain.'

The Horace of *Poetaster* was drawn from the *Sermones*; although he is seen composing an ode at the beginning of Act III, this seems to take its form from ideas about poetic inspiration rather than from close imitation of the particularities of Horace's style in the *Odes*. Only one passage from the *Odes* was incorporated. In his poems, Jonson makes fuller use of various aspects of the *Odes*, including elements of style, mixtures of tone, irony, tactful address and methods of self-portraiture. Horace provided a model for inserting personal colour in both lyric and epistle, and in such poems as 'Inviting a Friend to Supper', Jonson matches the geniality of Horace's invitation poems; like Horace's, his poetry is often most attractive when he is talking about himself. Jonson draws on Horace for the wider range of tone and the more varied self-portraiture of the poems. Though his voice is still often sterner and more harshly satiric than Horace's generally is[19] – contrast Horace's lines on the backbiter with their slight touch of mock-heroic – *hic niger est, hunc tu Romane caveto* – with Jonson's darker rendering in 'An Epistle' with its characteristic imagery, 'like flies or worms which man's corrupt parts fed' – it has other tones. In such a poem as 'An Ode', 'High-spirited friend' (*Underwood* 26), he combines ethical weight of utterance with a Horatian tact and delicacy. The combination of ethics and personal address, the delicate blend of compliment – congratulation for the friend's recovery and recognition of his achievement – with advice, and the employment of medical imagery appropriate to the friend's situation, are close to one of Horace's characteristic formulations in the *Odes*. Like Horace in the *Odes*, in his poems to his friends, Camden, Selden and others, Jonson creates an ideal world of friendship and cultivation, modifying his embattled stance. In other poems, he employs the Horatian device of humorous self-portraiture and physical description.[20] In 'My Answer. The Poet to the Painter' (*Underwood* 52) and 'Epistle. To My Lady Covell' (*Underwood* 56), he jests about his figure and his age in a way reminiscent of Horace's references to his personal appearance in *Epistles* 1.4 and 20. Following Horace, he carried this picture of himself into his love poems. Jonson translated *Odes* 4.1 (*Underwood* 86), where Horace presented a detached picture of himself as the middle-aged lover *circa lustra decem*, with a blend of self-mockery and nostalgia which Jonson captured better than Pope, whose version verges on the coy. In the Charis sequence (*Underwood* 2) and 'My Picture Left in Scotland' (*Underwood* 9), he adopted a similar persona.

In such poems, we see a more courtly and accommodating Jonson. Nevertheless, I believe it is correct to give primacy to the ethical in Jonson's interpretation of Horace. As we have seen, Jonson is attracted to passages in Horace to do with integrity. Another example is the famous opening of 'To Penshurst' (*Forest* 2):

> Thou art not, Penshurst, built to envious show
> Of touch or marble; nor canst boast a row   (black stone)
> Of polished pillars, or a roof of gold;
> Thou hast no lantern whereof tales are told,
> Or stair, or courts; but stand'st an ancient pile,
> And, these grudged at, art reverenced the while.
> Thou joy'st in better marks, of soil, of air,
> Of wood, of water; therein thou art fair . . .   (1–8)

This is derived from the opening of *Odes* 2.18, where Horace contrasts wealth with inner riches, with a similar rhetorical pattern:

> non ebur neque aureum
>   mea renidet in domo lacunar,
> non trabes Hymettiae
>   premunt columnas ultima recisas
> Africa, neque Attali
>   ignotus heres regiam occupavi,

The Horace of Ben Jonson and his heirs

>   nec Laconicas mihi
>   trahunt honestae purpuras clientae.
>
>   at fides et ingeni
>   benigna vena est . . .   (1–10)

Neither ivory nor golden ceiling are resplendent in my house, nor do Hymettian beams weigh down columns quarried in furthest Africa, nor have I gained a palace, the unknown heir of Attalus, nor do well-born clients drag along Laconian purple for me. But I have honesty and a rich vein of talent . . .

Jonson adopts the Horatian scheme[21] to express the difference between real and apparent greatness, outer show and inner worth, a theme which is everywhere present in his work, along with the related themes of the difference between the appearance of virtue and true virtue, and the difference between title and virtue, 'great' and 'good'.

It is characteristic of Jonson's imitation to relate the Horatian passage to his own moral vision. If we look at the original contexts of the pictures of the just man from *Odes* 3.3. and the *sapiens* from *Sermones* 2.7, we find that neither has an application to the poet himself, and that ironies surround the second. The former is a compliment to Augustus, in which Horace manipulates the Augustan propagandizing mythology: the virtue of constancy associates Augustus with heroes who gained heaven through effort and virtue, Pollux, Hercules, Bacchus and Romulus, associations which were an established part of the Augustan mythology. The second is spoken by a *doctor ineptus* figure, the slave Davus. That the Stoic ideal was impossible was a standard charge, and the notion that the circle was the perfect figure was also mocked. Horace does not usually adopt the Stoic point of view, and elsewhere laughs at the inhumanity and immoderateness of the figure of the *sapiens*. He does give us pictures of personal poise, but these two passages are not among them.[22]

In emphasizing Jonson's ethical approach to Horace, I differ from the interpretation offered by David Norbrook in his important book *Poetry and Politics in the English Renaissance*, where he argues that Ben Jonson saw Horace as a pragmatist in political affairs, accepting the *status quo*, with a low view of the poet's calling and a cynicism about human nature:

> It was appropriate, then, that he should model himself on Horace, in whom the austerity of some earlier Latin writers had given way to delicate irony with a courtly tone. Jonson found Horace 'the best master, both of vertue, and wisdome'. He was such a good judge of causes and reasons 'not because he thought so; but because he knew so, out of use and experience.' Horace had no time for utopian speculation, he concentrated on what was concretely possible. He gently satirised poets who had high vatic pretensions, representing himself as a plain man who preferred to cultivate his rural estate. But he was also, as Jonson recalled, 'in high favour with the Emperour', and his poetry celebrated the peace which the imperial regime had brought to a countryside formerly ravaged by civil war.[23]

Norbrook points out that Ben Jonson was willing to collaborate with people whose behaviour scarcely harmonized with his ethical theories, for example the shady financier Sir William Cockayne, and makes much of Jonson's admiration for Machiavelli.

Of course, it does not do to sentimentalize Jonson. He was an ambitious self-made man who established himself as court poet. As such – and he admits it himself in 'To My Muse' (*Epigrams* 65) and 'An Epistle to Master John Selden' (*Underwood* 14) – he often praised disreputable individuals such as Frances Howard, for whose first and second marriages he wrote masques. But this does not necessarily mean that he was a cynical admirer of Machiavellian *realpolitik* or a hypocrite in his many praises of integrity. Indeed, his constant worrying over the themes of friendship, patronage, benefits, flattery and praise suggests unease rather than cynicism.[24] It seems odd to portray as a time-serving accommodater a man who was constantly in trouble with the authorities, not only in his rumbustious youth under Queen Elizabeth, but also under James I, who patronized him, and Charles I, who passed him over: *The Isle of Dogs, Poetaster, Sejanus, Eastward Ho!, Epicoene, Time Vindicated, Neptune's Triumph, The Devil is an Ass, A Tale of a Tub* all got their author into difficulties, as well as various episodes in his private life, including his impolitic quarrel with Inigo Jones. It seems more likely to me that Jonson looked to Horace as a model who offered both a high appraisal of the poet's role and his memorializing powers (*pace* Norbrook, Horace sometimes assumes a vatic role and constantly asserts the immortality of his poetry), and an example of a man of low birth who consorted with the great and yet maintained his integrity; as Howard Erskine-Hill points out, Horace rebukes Augustus in *Poetaster* for reproaching him with his poverty and is praised for his free-speaking (v.i.77–99).[25]

Jonson's imitation of Horace ranges from the creation of a moral tone and persona to a close interest in verbal details. Two editions of Horace's complete works owned by Ben Jonson survive: the first, with commentary on the *Odes* and *Epodes* by Bernardino Partenio (Venice 1584), in the University Library Cambridge, the second, printed in Basle in 1580, in the library of Magdalene College Cambridge. Both contain underlinings in the text and commentary which may be Ben Jonson's, since they appear to reflect his opinions and interests.[26] If they are his, they show Jonson responding to Horace at the level of phrases and motifs, perhaps with a view to redeployment. Jonson's translations also show him working at this intimate level with the text of Horace. In his translation of *Odes* 4.1 (*Underwood* 86), he imitates some of the verbal features of the original. Perhaps aided by Partenio who comments on the feature,[27] he translates the twin antitheses of the lines:

The Horace of Ben Jonson and his heirs

> desine, dulcium
> mater saeva Cupidinum,
>   circa lustra decem flectere mollibus   (4–7)
> iam durum imperiis

>   Refrain,
> Sour mother of sweet loves, forbear
> To bend a man, now at his fiftieth year
>   Too stubborn for commands so slack.   (4–7)

This seems to me the most successful of Jonson's translations from Horace; he conveys something of the complex blend of tones, including the lyrical pathos of the conclusion:

>   Me now, nor wench, nor wanton boy
> Delights, nor credulous hope of mutual joy,
>   Nor care I now healths to propound,
> Or with fresh flowers to girt my temple round.
>   But why, oh why, my Ligurine,
> Flow my thin tears down these pale cheeks of mine?
>   Or why, my well-graced words among,
> With an uncomely silence fails my tongue?
>   Hard-hearted, I dream every night
> I hold thee fast! but fled hence with the light,
>   Whether in Mars his field thou be,
> Or Tiber's winding streams, I follow thee.   (29–40)

In his own poems, Jonson generally incorporates his reminiscences of Horace's *Odes* into his couplet style. This, with its caesural flexibility and varied rhythm which reflect the movement of thought and feeling, may owe something to Jonson's study of Horace's hexameter poems. Jonson did learn something too from the style of the *Odes*, though he does not normally imitate Horace's more extreme collocations of words as Milton was to do in his translation of the Pyrrha *Ode*. In 'Where dost thou careless lie?' he imitates some features of the style and structure of the *Odes*. Unlike the more logical seventeenth-century lyric, an *Ode* by Horace characteristically avoids abstract discussion and proceeds by a series of concrete images and exempla, drawn from myth, history, contemporary life, or Horace's own lifestyle, without connecting links to point the stages of the argument.[28] A common feature is the blending of related themes without clear distinctions being drawn; this is often done so deceptively that the reader does not notice that Horace has moved on to something different. Jonson imitates this characteristic structure in his ode. He eschews the ethical pointers and ethical discriminations which are the hallmark of his couplet style, as in the opening of 'To Penshurst' quoted above:

> Thou art not, Penshurst, built *to envious show*
>
> And these *grudged at* art *reverenced* the while
>
> Thou joy'st in *better* marks . . .

(In *Odes* 2.18, by contrast, Horace does not bring in a conceptual word until *beatus* in line 14). The ode proceeds with a series of questions and images, without connecting links. Jonson expresses his depression at the state of poetry in concrete terms, thus:

> Are all the'Aonian springs
>   Dried up? Lies Thespia waste?
> Doth Clarius' harp want strings,   (Apollo)
>   That not a nymph now sings?
>   Or droop they as disgraced,
> To see their seats and bowers by chatt'ring pies defaced?   (7–12)

The questions are very typical of Horace's *Odes*. Jonson also imitates the expressive brevity of allusion in the *Odes*, witness his lines on Prometheus:

> Then take in hand thy lyre,
>   Strike in thy proper strain,
> With Japhet's line aspire   (Prometheus)
> Sol's chariot for new fire,
>   To give the world again;
> Who aided him, will thee, the issue of Jove's brain.   (Athena)
>   (25–30)

Here, although the phrase 'Japhet's line'[29] comes from *Odes* 1.3, Jonson changes the force of the myth to fit in with his theme of the triumph of knowledge over ignorance. In Horace's poem Prometheus is an *exemplum* of human impiety – *audax omnia perpeti / gens humana ruit per vetitum nefas* ('Bold to endure everything, the human race rushes through forbidden crime') (25–6). Jonson makes him a humanist discoverer of knowledge, and he alludes to the help given Prometheus by Athena, goddess of wisdom, 'the issue of Jove's brain.' The suggestion might have come from Partenio, who in his note on *Iapeti genus* mentions Athena and explains that Prometheus' fire had been interpreted as *philosophia* and *intellectualis vita*. The point here is the compression of the allusion. Jonson's stanza does not recall any of Horace's, but it is handled with equivalent force and control in the disposition of sense and line units; the run-on line in the opening of stanza two quoted above is characteristic of Horace. Jonson manages by his energetic handling of the phrase to give about the right weight of language for an imitation of a Horatian ode; one might contrast Randolph's charming 'An Ode to Master Anthony Stafford', which is too light in language and rhythm for Horace.

The Horace of Ben Jonson and his heirs

What Jonson seems to be aiming at is the full brevity of the style of the *Odes*. Recent discussions of Ben Jonson have rejected the idea of him as a poet of the exclusively plain style: 'Jonson's style is plain in a manner fully compatible with rich allusion, delicate suggestion and complex wit'.[30] Horace was one model for this allusiveness.

Jonson's imitation of Horace is selective. He redeploys what can be fitted in with his own preoccupations. Consequently, there are important sides of Horace which he neglected. Though he writes about natural limits (adapting Ofellus' lines on mortality and the limits of ownership from *Sermones* 2.2.129–35 in *The Devil is an Ass* (II.iv.29–39) to expose Fitzdottrell's dreams of wealth and property),[31] we do not often find in him Horace's sense of the sadness of the passage of time (his translation of *Odes* 4.1. is an exception), nor does he employ Horace's characteristic *carpe diem* argument for symposiac purposes, against the background of flux and death. Jonson's echo of *Odes* 1.11 comes in a speech in *The Devil is an Ass*, where Wittipol is attempting to seduce Fitzdottrell's wife:

> Let not the sign o' the husband fright you, lady,
> But ere your spring be gone, enjoy it. Flowers,
> Though fair, are oft but of one morning. Think,
> All beauty doth not last until the autumn.
> You grow old while I tell you this. And such
> As cannot use the present are not wise.   (I.vi.127–32)

(The penultimate line translates Horace's *dum loquimur, fugerit invida / aetas*, 'While we speak, jealous time has fled', 7–8.) The context makes the argument a dubious one, and the resonances of Horace's *carpe diem* argument are not exploited to the full. This gave Jonson's sons an opportunity to follow into territory where Father Ben had led and bring back new discoveries; Herrick and Lovelace both latch on to the transience–*carpe diem* association. But Jonson's ethical interpretation kept his sons from transforming Horace into the light-hearted boozer which he too often became in the Restoration.

What Jonson bequeathed to his sons above all was the confidence with which he imitated Horace and other classical authors. Thomas M. Greene writes:

> Jonson occupies his preeminent place in the history of English classicism because in a real sense he invented a classical idiom for his language, just as more broadly he invented a classical temper, a moral style or set of styles, both recognizably native and recognizably derivative from Latin. Once the thing was done, the achievement became transparent, but it was nonetheless momentous ... To be an English poet after he wrote was to command a finer, more various and sophisticated power.[32]

As Greene demonstrates in his subtle account of Jonson's classicism, Jonson's relation with ancient authors is not the aggressive theft it is sometimes portrayed as but a nourishing exchange: 'Has anyone ever *given* more to Martial, enhanced his achievement more, than Jonson in his imitations?' In imitating ancient authors, Jonson could be both other and himself (see Greene's analysis of 'Inviting a Friend to Supper').[33]

Jonson showed his sons ways of assimilating classical ideas to native ideas and to their own preoccupations; of fusing classical features of style with English idiom. He showed them how to select a passage from the classics which harmonized with an English subject, as Martial's epigram to Licinianus (*Epigrams* 1.49) is adapted to compliment Sir Robert Wroth and his love of hunting. Through his imitation of Horace, he demonstrated how to convert an ancient author to modern use, while doing justice to the qualities and ethos of the original. His sons were to show a similar boldness in recreating Horace — sometimes indeed with less urbanity and more quaintness, but often also with equal passion and conviction.

I shall look at three poems in some detail as illustrations of the confident assimilation of Horace after Jonson. My first is Carew's elegant poem 'The Spring':

> Now that the winter's gone, the earth hath lost
> Her snow-white robes, and now no more the frost
> Candies the grass, or casts an icy cream
> Upon the silver lake or crystal stream;
> 5 But the warm sun thaws the benumbèd earth,
> And makes it tender, gives a second birth
> To the dead swallow; wakes in hollow tree
> The drowsy cuckoo, and the humble-bee.
> Now do a choir of chirping minstrels bring
> 10 In triumph to the world the youthful spring.
> The valleys, hills and woods, in rich array,
> Welcome the coming of the longed-for May.
> Now all things smile; only my love doth lour;
> Nor hath the scalding noon-day sun the power
> 15 To melt that marble ice which still doth hold
> Her heart congealed, and makes her pity cold.
> The ox which lately did for shelter fly
> Into the stall, doth now securely lie
> In open fields; and love no more is made
> 20 By the fireside; but in the cooler shade
> Amintas now doth with his Chloris sleep
> Under a sycamore, and all things keep
> Time with the season — only she doth carry
> June in her eyes, in her heart January.

The Horace of Ben Jonson and his heirs

Here Carew recalls Horace's spring description at the beginning of *Odes* 1.4:

> solvitur acris hiems grata vice veris et Favoni,
>   trahuntque siccas machinae carinas,
> ac neque iam stabulis gaudet pecus aut arator igni,
>   nec prata canis albicant pruinis.   (1–4)

> Biting winter is loosed with the pleasant succession of Spring and the Zephyr, and machines draw the dry keels [to water]; no longer does the flock rejoice in the stalls nor the ploughman in the fire, nor are the fields white with hoary frosts.

(Note the ox of line 17 and the *neque iam* motif[34] of lines 2–4, 17–20.) But he has recast it into a modern idiom and turned it to that most popular form of European lyric, the love complaint, combining Horace with Ronsard, especially the sonnet 'Vous mésprisez nature' (*Le Second Livre des Amours*). Carew abandons the idea of the antithesis between man's life and the seasons on which Horace's *Ode* hinged and utilizes instead a variation of the stock topic of the contrast between the spring world of love and the sad lover: winter has changed to spring, but his mistress remains wintry (the theme of Ronsard's sonnet). In contrast to the obliquity of the Horatian structure, with its characteristic submerged logic (a picture of the change from winter to spring starts off an argument that as we are going to die we should enjoy ourselves now) Carew's poem makes its logic explicit and is neatly symmetrical: the first contrast drawn between the mistress and the season is in the centre of the poem (l.13); and the second is in the final line, with its elegant chiasmus and graceful wit; in each case there is a strong caesural pause. The stylized language of the natural description – 'snow-white robes', 'candies', 'icy cream', 'silver lake or crystal stream' – is in a seventeenth-century mode: that popularized by Joshua Sylvester in his translation of Du Bartas' *La Semaine*, where natural objects are compared to art objects and in particular landscape is seen in terms of clothes ('candies' is one of Sylvester's favourite words.)[35]

Carew does not attempt here in the Jonsonian manner to invest his poem with a Horatian ethos, but rather plays with a range of traditional ideas (there is an allusion to Virgilian pastoral in lines 19–22 *ante focum, si frigus erit, si messis, in umbra*, 'before the fire if it is cold, if harvest-time in the shade' *Eclogues* 5.70), combining them into a new whole. The confidence with which he does so is Jonsonian.

An example of a naturalization of Horace which probes the ethos of the original more deeply is Lovelace's 'Advice to my Best Brother'. This is a kind of meditation on *Odes* 2.10, using each of Horace's stanzas as a starting point for further thoughts. The setting of the poem is unclear: we do not know what circumstances Frank Lovelace was in when it was written. The advice is metaphorical and we cannot infer that the addressee was about to embark on a sea voyage. The first twenty-eight lines are a reworking of Horace's first stanza[36] (quoted above on page 52), with its advice to steer a middle course, avoiding the deep sea and the shore:

> Frank, wilt live handsomely? trust not too far
> Thyself to waving seas, for what thy star
> Calculated by sure event must be
> Look in the glassy-epithet and see.   (Icarian Sea?)
> 5   Yet settle here your rest and take your state,
> And in calm halcyon's nest ev'n build your fate;
> Prithee lie down securely, Frank, and keep
> With as much no noise the inconstant deep
> As its inhabitants; nay steadfast stand
> 10 As if discovered were a Newfoundland
> Fit for plantation here; dream, dream still,
> Lulled in Dione's cradle, dream, until   (Venus, born out of the sea)
> Horror awake your sense, and you now find
> Yourself a bubbled pastime for the wind,
> 15 And in loose Thetis' blankets torn and tossed;   (sea nymph, mother of Achilles)
> Frank to undo thyself why art at cost?
>   Nor be too confident fixed on the shore,
> For even that too borrows from the store
> Of her rich neighbour, since now wisest know
> 20 (And this to Galileo's judgement owe)
> The palsy earth itself is every jot
> As frail, inconstant, waving as that blot   (imputation of disgrace)
> We lay upon the deep, that sometimes lies
> Changed, you would think, with'his bottom's properties;
> 25 But this eternal strange Ixion's wheel
> Of giddy earth ne'er whirling leaves to reel
> Till all things are inverted, till they are
> Turned to that antic confused state they were.   (1–28)

Here, lines 1–16 are an expansion of Horace's advice not always to sail out to deep sea into an attack on the sea (it is important to realize that the advice 'yet settle here your rest' is ironic; if Frank deludes himself that this is possible, he will be rudely awakened), and lines 17–28 are an expansion of Horace's advice not to go too near the shore into an attack on the land.

How different is this poem, with its engaged and urgent tone, from the cool elegance of Carew's 'The Spring'! Lovelace has followed Jonson in making the element of address a key factor in his imitation of Horace, giving emotional force to moral platitudes. He has looked at Horace's poem – where the setting is rather obscure[37] – and applied it to modern circumstances; it speaks from the aftermath of Civil War. Horace's urbane address to Licinius, with its neat series of epigrams, has been transformed into something less

The Horace of Ben Jonson and his heirs

balanced and more pessimistic. The focus is *rebus angustis*, 'strictest things': in his lengthy expansion of Horace's imagery, Lovelace puts across a strong sense of life's insecurity and dangerousness: no course of life is safe. In fact he has altered the tenor of Horace's allegoria from, 'steer a middle course' to 'do not be too confident in any course of life'. We note that he expands the imagery in a curiously literal way: Frank is to mistrust the shore because Galileo has proved that it is 'inconstant'. The language of the passage is violent (e.g. 13–15) and it ends with a picture of chaos. Against this hostile environment Lovelace offers Stoic resistance in a fine translation of Horace:

> A breast of proof defies all shocks of fate. (47)

But the last stanza returns to the contemplation of uncertainty:

> For tell me how they differ, tell me, pray,
> A cloudy tempest and a too fair day? (65–6)

As with Carew's poem, the language, with its string of conceits and allusions, is in a seventeenth-century mode – lacking, indeed, the control and clarity of Horace (I have never seen a satisfactory explanation of the expression 'glassy-epithet'), but with some striking images and phrases.

My third poem is Vaughan's 'To his Retired Friend, an Invitation to Brecknock', from his early collection *Olor Iscanus* ('The Swan of Usk'). This is a good example of the seventeenth-century Horatian epistolary manner, opening with some fifty lines of intimate banter, which also serve to set the Civil War background and the Puritan takeover of the town from which the friends must escape though revelry. A more intense passage at the end recalls the symposiac Odes, with its picture of the wintry weather outside (Vaughan imitated the Socrate Ode directly in another poem in the collection 'To my Worthy Friend Master T. Lewes') and the fire within:

> Come then! and while the slow icicle hangs
> At the stiff thatch, and winter's frosty pangs
> Benumb the year, blithe, as of old, let us,
> 'Midst noise and war, of peace and mirth discuss.
> This portion thou wert born for; why should we
> Vex at the time's ridiculous misery?
> An age that thus hath fooled itself, and will
> (Spite of thy teeth and mine) persist so still.
> Let's sit then at this fire, and while we steal
> A revel in the town, let others seal,   (make legal agreements)
> Purchase or cheat, and who can, let them pay,
> Till those black deeds bring on the darksome day;
> Innocent spenders we! a better use
> Shall wear out our short lease, and leave the'obtuse
> Rout to their husks; they and their bags at best
> Have cares in earnest, we care for a jest. (73–88)

Here the Horatian *carpe diem* rationale for feasting has been given a contemporary slant: Vaughan and his friend cannot do anything about the Civil War,[38] so their best use of 'our short lease' is in innocent revelry rather than Puritan acquisitiveness. Note that Vaughan looks back to Horace through Jonson. The indignation and confident scorn, and the element of satire here are Jonsonian; Vaughan imitates the satiric use of the 'let others' topic, as in 'To Sir Robert Wroth', 'Let this man sweat and wrangle at the bar' ... The lines also contain an echo of *The New Inn* ode, 'No, give them grains their fill, / Husks, draff to drink and swill.' Jonsonian too are the antitheses between a 'stealing' and 'spending' which are innocent and the dark 'sealing' and 'cheating' of other men (here, the Puritans) and the punning antitheses of the final line. In 'An Invitation', one of the best of his secular poems, Vaughan achieves a fine evocation of the Jonsonian–Horatian mode, with a slant of his own.[39]

All three poems achieve a translation of Horace into contemporary idiom and style. It was partly because of this stylistic assimilation that the frequency of imitation of Horace in the early seventeenth century used to be overlooked. Unlike the post-Restoration poets, who often signalled their modernizations of Horace as 'an imitation of Horace', the earlier seventeenth-century poets do not always alert us to the source of their inspiration. But the early seventeenth century, as Howard Erskine-Hill has argued,[40] may lay claim to be called the Horatian period of English literature, because, following the example of Ben Jonson, imitations compass both the *Odes* and the hexameter poems. Although the age of Dryden and Pope used to be thought of as the 'Augustan' period, for the post-Restoration poets it was Horace's hexameter poems which were the main source of inspiration. There were some fine responses to the *Odes* in the later period: Dryden's translation of 3.29, Sedley's of 2.8 and Otway's of 2.16; Sedley's 'Love still has Something of the Sea' which captures the tonal complexity of Horace's erotic mode; some late passages of Dryden where he responds to the tempered affirmation of such poems as *Odes* 3.29; and some charming poetry by a group of poets who followed Abraham Cowley's lead in his Horatian *Essays in Prose and Verse*.[41] Nevertheless, I think it is true to say that the *Odes* became a less fertile source of inspiration for lyric poetry, and there was a tendency to trivialize their tone and simplify their structure in translation and imitation.

The early seventeenth century made a rich response to the *Odes*, which it 'discovered'. Jonson's translations of *Odes* 3.9 and 4.1 and *Epode* 2 (*Underwood* 87, 86, 85) (though not printed until 1640) inaugurated a series of more complete translations from the *Odes*, starting with John Ashmore in 1621. The most sensitive was that of Sir Richard Fanshawe in *Selected Parts of Horace, Prince of Lyrics* 1651, where he responds to both the humour and the pathos of his originals and experiments with lyric metres to represent Sapphics and Alcaics. There are several splendid recreations of Horace's

The Horace of Ben Jonson and his heirs

Odes in original poems: for example Herrick's 'His Age', Fanshawe's 'An Ode upon Occasion of His Majesty's Proclamation in the Year 1630', Marvell's 'Horatian Ode', Milton's sonnet to Lawrence and Lovelace's 'The Grasshopper. To my Noble Friend Mr Charles Cotton'.[42] I shall look at this last in some detail and I quote it here in full:

> Oh thou that swing'st upon the waving hair
>   Of some well-fillèd oaten beard,
> Drunk every night with a delicious tear
>   Dropped thee from Heaven, where now thou'art reared,
>
> The joys of earth and air are thine entire,
>   That with thy feet and wings dost hop and fly;
> And when thy poppy works, thou dost retire
>   To thy carved acorn bed to lie.
>
> Up with the day, the sun thou welcoms't then,
>   Sport'st in the gilt plats of his beams,   (braids or patches)
> And all these merry days mak'st merry men,
>   Thyself and melancholy streams.
>
> But ah, the sickle! golden ears are cropped;
>   Ceres and Bacchus bid goodnight;
> Sharp frosty fingers all your flowers have topped,
>   And what scythes spared winds shave off quite.
>
> Poor verdant fool! and now green ice! thy joys,
>   Large and as lasting as thy perch of grass,
> Bid us lay in 'gainst winter, rain, and poise
>   Their floods with an o'erflowing glass.
>
> Thou best of men and friends! we will create
>   A genuine summer in each other's breast;
> And spite of this cold time and frozen fate
>   Thaw us a warm seat to our rest.
>
> Our sacred hearths shall burn eternally
>   As vestal flames; the North wind, he
> Shall strike his frost-stretched wings, dissolve and fly
>   This Etna in epitome.
>
> Dropping December shall come weeping in,
>   Bewail the'usurping of his reign;   (Parliament banned the
> But when in showers of old Greek we begin,   celebration of Christmas
>   Shall cry he hath his crown again!   in 1644)

> Night as clear Hesper shall our tapers whip
>   From the light casements where we play,
> And the dark hag from her black mantle strip,
>   And stick there everlasting day.
>
> Thus richer than untempted kings are we
>   That asking nothing, nothing need:
> Though lord of all what seas embrace, yet he
>   That wants himself is poor indeed.

Like the three poems looked at above, 'The Grasshopper' employs seventeenth-century procedures. Behind it we sense the presence of the Soracte *Ode*; it is based on the same idea of cold weather outside 'dissolved' by fire and wine and cheer within, and has the same movement of thought. But the structure of the poem is, apparently at least, that of a post-classical form: the emblem poem. Lovelace begins with a description of the grasshopper which in a surprising series of shifts and turns combines the Anacreontic and Aesopian traditions. In the former, the grasshopper is the epitome of the happy life, doing nothing but drinking and singing, nourished by nature and escaping the pressures of time and winter;[43] in the latter, more familiar to us today but not more prevalent in the seventeenth century, the insect fails to provide for winter and dies. Lovelace captures the Anacreontic gaiety very charmingly in his opening three stanzas; such an insect might well be used as an argument for drinking. But Lovelace's grasshopper looks back to an ode by Casimir Sarbiewski (1595–1640), the neo-Latin imitator of Horace celebrated in his day as the 'Polish Horace': *O quae populea summa sedens coma* (*Odes* 4.23). And perhaps the intrusion of the Aesopian winter in the fourth stanza of Lovelace's poem came as less of a shock to those who recalled the elegiac end of Casimir's poem:

> ut se quaeque dies attulit optima,
> sic se quaeque rapit; nulla fuit satis
>   umquam longa voluptas
>   longus saepius est dolor.[44]   (9–12)

As each best day arrives, so each departs; no pleasure has ever been long enough; grief is more often long.

(Earl Miner in his commentary on 'The Grasshopper' notes that each of Lovelace's first three stanzas ends with a dying fall; 'in retrospect we observe how the grasshopper's fall in the structural movement of the first half of the poem is enacted within the general downward movement of imagery in each stanza'.[45]) The message Lovelace draws from the death of his grasshopper is not the traditional prudential Aesopian one, but the Horatian *carpe diem*

The Horace of Ben Jonson and his heirs

argument, and this too is sprung as a surprise: in stanza five, the friends are to lay in – not the grain we might expect, but as it turns out at the end of the sentence, 'an o'erflowing glass'. Lovelace is following the Horatian logic of the Soracte *Ode*, where reminders of winter lead similarly to injunctions to make full use of the present; Lovelace has made more explicit the submerged connection between winter and old age and death which exists in Horace's ode. In the final stanzas of the poem, Lovelace uses the same elements as Horace in *Odes* 1.9 to combat winter weather: fire, wine, company and an act of the mind to abandon care, but he expresses them in a conceited seventeenth-century manner, with metaphoric play on ideas of warmth, thawing (*dissolve frigus*, *Odes* 1.9.5), summer and winter. The poem is rounded off in stanza ten with a moral statement in the Jonsonian–Horatian manner.[46]

Despite its unHoratian features – the fancifulness of the description of the grasshopper, the conceits – Lovelace's poem has the quintessential blend of elements for an imitation of Horace's symposiac Odes. Without achieving Horace's compression and control, it has something of the right intensity and ornateness of language, and also the right mixture of formal and colloquial – expressions such as 'poor verdant fool' and 'green ice' have the witty piquancy of such phrases as *simplex munditiis* (*Odes* 1.5.5) or *splendet . . . salinum* (2.16.14). We may apply to Lovelace's poem the contrast made by J. B. Leishman between the style of Prior in 'To Miss Margaret Pulteney in the Nursery' and Marvell in 'The Picture of Little T. C. in a Prospect of Flowers':

While Prior's poem is a unique achievement within the limits of that kind of familiar style practised by some of the best poets of his time, Marvell, like other seventeenth-century poets, like Horace in some of his Odes, and perhaps unlike any post-seventeenth-century poet before Yeats, has been able to combine a kind of familiarity with a kind of splendour.[47]

'The Grasshopper' has too the element of intimate personal address, which welds the poem together. It has the complex progression of thought with structural turns. And it has the Horatian blend of tones, with its mingling of elegiac pathos, asperity even – 'poor verdant fool' – with tempered gaiety and affirmation. (The tone is of course not identical with Horace; arguably it is less sceptical and level-headed. Can the friends really achieve 'everlasting day' or is this just defiance?)

'The Grasshopper' looks at an aspect of Horace which Jonson had not responded to. *Carpe diem* has here its full Horatian resonance. In Horace's poetry, *carpe diem* is not usually employed as a seduction argument in the context of a love poem, like the seventeenth-century persuasions to enjoy, 'To His Coy Mistress', 'Go Lovely Rose' and others. (An exception is *Odes* 4.10 to Ligurinus; and there is perhaps a hint of seduction in 1.11, the poem from which the famous phrase comes.) Generally, in Horace *carpe diem* is a symposiac topic: a drinking companion is urged to enjoy the present. The erotic is only part of the invitation to pleasure, a philosophical attitude of mind is implied rather than total immersion in pleasure (see *Odes* 3.29.41–8) and a sense of the sadness of transience tempers the gaiety. Herrick's 'Gather ye Rosebuds' derives from pseudo-Ausonius, not from Horace, for whom the best parallels are Lucretius' exhortations to enjoy the banquet of life or passages from Epicurus. Whether he understood Epicurus or not – and Epicurus' pleasure doctrine was finding exponents in the middle of the seventeenth century – Lovelace has captured the refinement of the Horatian *carpe diem*.[48] A contrast may be drawn here with the Restoration translations of Horace's invitation poems, many of which heighten the libertine element, for example the translation of *Odes* 1.4 in Dryden's first miscellany, sometimes misattributed to Rochester, in which Horace's *Ode* becomes an erotic fantasy, or the versions of 1.9 by Congreve or Tom Brown:

> We'll have no more of business, but, friend, as you love us,
> Leave it all to the care of the good folks above us.
> Whilst your appetite's strong and good humour remains,
> And active, brisk blood does enliven your veins,
> Improve the sweet minutes in scenes of delight,
> Let your friend have the day and your mistress the night.[49]

One of Jonson's sons follows him in making a more sustained allusion to Horace: Herrick, in *Hesperides*, where he does not just produce imitations of individual poems but investigates a series of Horatian themes over the body of the work and builds up a Horatian persona.

Many recent studies,[50] mostly by American scholars – like Jonson, Herrick is better appreciated outside his native country – have demonstrated that Herrick is a poet of a much wider range than is displayed in the standard selections in anthologies, which focus on the poems inspired by the Greek Anthology, epitomized by the famous 'To the Virgins, to Make Much of Time'. Scattered throughout *Hesperides* is a series of poems in which Herrick meditates on Horatian themes. One of Ben's most devoted sons (he wrote five poems to his master), he studied the Jonsonian–Horatian manner and imitated it in several of his poems, for example 'A Country Life, to his Brother Master Thomas Herrick' and 'A Panegyric to Sir Lewis Pemberton'. The former is a tissue of Horatian echoes, and looks back to *Epode* 2 through Jonson's reworking of it in 'To Sir Robert Wroth'.[51] In the following passage, Herrick incorporates the Jonsonian–Horatian vision of the Stoic *sapiens*:

> But thou liv'st fearless; and thy face ne'er shows
>   Fortune when she comes or goes,
> But with thy equal thoughts prepared dost stand,
>   To take her by the either hand;

The Horace of Ben Jonson and his heirs

> Nor car'st which comes the first, the foul or fair;
>   A wise man every way lies square,
> And like a surly oak with storms perplexed,
>   Grows still the stronger, strongly vexed.
> Be so, bold spirit; stand centre-like, unmoved;
>   And be not only thought but proved
> To be what I report thee, and inure
>   Thyself, if want comes, to endure.[52]   (93–104)

Here, Herrick employs the metre of 'To Sir Robert Wroth' which is designed to recall the iambic distich of *Epode* 2,[53] and also imitates Jonson's heroic tone, his characteristic moral discriminations ('thought' and 'proved') and the movement of his verse. As critics have noted,[54] other passages establish a more distinctively Herrickian note, quieter and less heroic:

> Yet can thy humble roof maintain a choir
>   Of singing crickets by thy fire;
> And the brisk mouse may feast herself with crumbs,
>   Till that the green-eyed kitling comes.   (kitten)
> Then to her cabin, blessed, she can escape
>   The sudden danger of a rape.
> And thus thy little-well-kept stock doth prove
>   Wealth cannot make a life, but love.   (121–8)

This scene of domestic comfort and cheer, with its stress on humble pleasures and its eye for small details, may remind us of the vignettes in the fable of the town and country mouse in *Sermones* 2.6. or the picture of the simple but philosophical meal in the same satire, and sounds a characteristic Herrickian–Horatian note. In 'A Panegyric to Sir Lewis Pemberton', Herrick performs a splendidly genial and exuberant variation on 'To Penshurst', in the Jonsonian–Horatian vein. There are other Jonsonian–Horatian poems in the collection, too: poems of heroic exhortation and address, such as 'To his Worthy Friend, Master Thomas Falconbridge', and a series of epigrams on the *sapiens*, some put into a contemporary setting (e.g. 'His Cavalier').

There are also several poems in which Herrick meditates on Horatian themes ignored by Jonson: *carpe diem* and *non semper*. 'His Age, Dedicated to his Peculiar Friend Master John Weekes, under the Name of Posthumus' is an ambitious attempt to write a Horatian ode, combining a characteristic Horatian complex of ideas and sliding from one to another in Horace's manner; the poem is full of reminiscences of Horace, especially the *Odes* on transience, 2.14, 1.4 and 4.7:

> Ah Posthumus! our years hence fly,
>   And leave no sound; nor piety,
>   Or prayers, or vow

>   Can keep the wrinkle from the brow;
>   But we must on,
>   As fate does lead or draw us; none,
>   None, Posthumus, could e'er decline
>   The doom of cruel Proserpine.
>
>   The pleasing wife, the house, the ground
>   Must all be left, no one plant found
>   To follow thee,
>   Save only the cursed cypress tree;
>   A merry mind
>   Looks forward, scorns what's left behind;
>   Let's live, my Weekes, then, while we may,
>   And here enjoy our holiday.
>
>   We'have seen the past-best times, and these
>   Will ne'er return; we see the seas
>   And moons to wane;
>   But they fill up their ebbs again;
>   But vanished man,
>   Like to a lily lost, ne'er can,
>   Ne'er can repullulate, or bring   (bud again)
>   His days to see a second spring.
>
>   But on we must, and thither tend
>   Where Ancus and rich Tullus blend
>   Their sacred seed;
>   Thus has infernal Jove decreed;
>   We must be made
>   Ere long a song, ere long a shade.
>   Why then, since life to us is short,
>   Let's make it full up by our sport.[55]   (1–32)

The elaborate stanza, like Jonson's stanza in 'Where dost thou careless lie?' though not based on one of Horace's own stanza forms, is associated with the genre of ode; and though Herrick does not achieve the Horatian weight of language but substitutes his own fluid grace, the complex elegiac rhythm of the first stanza, with its disposition of phrases, pauses and rhymes coming to a firm close with 'The doom of cruel Proserpine', is inspired by the Postumus *Ode* with its striking enjambement:

>   Eheu fugaces, Postume, Postume,
>   Labuntur anni.   (1–2)

Herrick here treats death and *carpe diem* less in the jaunty manner of 'Gather ye rosebuds while ye may' and more with a Horatian austerity and melancholy, tempering the hedonism of the invitation to mirth. The poem

The Horace of Ben Jonson and his heirs

moves on to introduce the Epicurean Horatian theme of content in simple pleasures, a favourite with Herrick:

>   We are not poor, although we have
>   No roofs of cedar, nor our brave
>   Baiae, nor keep
>   Account of such a flock of sheep;
>   Nor bullocks fed
>   To lard the shambles, barbels bred   (fishes like carp)
>   To kiss our hands, nor do we wish   (Vedius Pollio ordered
>   For Pollio's lampreys in our dish.   a slave to be thrown
>   to lampreys)
>
>   If we can meet and so confer
>   Both by a shining salt-cellar;
>   And have our roof,
>   Although not arched, yet weather-proof,
>   And ceiling free
>   From that cheap candle bawdry,   (dirt, pronounced bawdery)
>   We'll eat our bean with that full mirth
>   As we were lords of all the earth.   (41–56)

Here Herrick and Weekes are cast as the innocent Horatian country dwellers, vegetarians (the bean comes from *Sermones* 2.6.63), rejecting luxurious pleasures and as blest as kings (*licet sub paupere tecto / reges et regum vita praecurrere amicos* 'under a poor man's roof, you may surpass in life kings and the friends of kings' *Epistles* 1.10.32–3). Herrick alludes to both *Odes* 2.18, with its rejection of ivory and gold ceilings and the rich man's marble house at the fashionable Roman resort of Baiae, and *Odes* 2.16, with its contrast between the rich Grosphus with his *greges centum* (hundred flocks) and Horace:

>   vivitur parvo bene, cui paternum
>   splendet in mensa tenui salinum   (13–14)

He lives well on little, whose ancestral salt-cellar shines on a small table.

Herrick's poem continues with stanzas about constancy and friendship, and ends with a long portrayal of his old age, where he fuses his comic Anacreontic role of lustful old man with a portrayal of the nostalgia of old age, which is both humorous and pathetic. The poem comes to the quiet close and concrete image characteristic of the Horatian ode:

>   Thus, till we see the fire less shine
>   From the'embers than the kitling's eyne,
>   We'll still sit up

> Sphering about the wassail cup,   (sending round in a circle)
> To all those times
> Which gave me honour for my rhymes;
> The coal once spent, we'll then to bed
> Far more than night bewearièd.   (145–52)

'His Age' shows that Herrick understood the Epicurean pleasure doctrine behind the Horatian *carpe diem* as advocating not total immersion in sensual pleasure but a proper use of time, involving an attitude of mind. Another poem which revolves around the same theme is 'A Paranaetical or Advisive Verse, to his Friend, Master John Weekes'. Again, this is a poem based on themes and images from the *Odes*, but it is less of a tissue of Horatian phrases and Herrick has chosen to write it in octosyllabics. We find the same mingling of related themes and the same variety of tones from grave to gay. Herrick starts from the idea that life should not be spent in the acquisition of wealth but in modest pleasures; then a reminder of time is insinuated:

> Time steals away like to a stream,
> And we glide hence away with them.
> No sound recalls the hours once fled,
> Or roses being witherèd;
> Nor us, my friend, when we are lost,
> Like to a dew or melted frost.   (22–7)

Here we have two Horatian images for the passage of time – the river (*Odes* 3.29 *cetera fluminis ritu feruntur*, and 2.14 *labuntur anni*) and the rose (2.3 *nimium brevis flores . . . amoenae rosae*). After urging Weekes once more to mirth and full living, the poem ends with a final quiet reminder of death, with the urn image of *Odes* 2.3.26 and 3.1.16:

> And that we'll do, as men who know,
> Some few sands spent, we hence must go,
> Both to be blended in the urn,
> From whence there's never a return.   (36–9)

Another theme which Herrick often adopts from Horace is that of *non semper*, where a natural analogy is employed to show that things do not always stay the same. Horace uses this as an argument against incessant mourning in *Odes* 2.9; to mix joy with mirth in 1.7; for hope for better times in 2.10:

> sperat infestis, metuit secundis
> alteram sortem bene praeparatum
> pectus. informis hiemes reducit
>   Iuppiter, idem

The Horace of Ben Jonson and his heirs

> summovet. non, si male nunc, et olim
> sic erit. quondam cithara tacentem
> suscitat Musam neque semper arcum
>   tendit Apollo. (13–20)

The well-prepared breast hopes in bad, fears in favourable times the other lot: Jupiter brings back ugly winters and also removes them; if it is bad now, it will not always be; Apollo sometimes arouses the Muse from her silence with his lyre and does not always bend his bow.

Herrick in turn uses *non semper* in a variety of ways: making it an argument for hope for better times in 'Good Precepts or Counsel' and for ceasing to weep in 'Comfort to a Lady upon the Death of her Husband'. The most original and interesting poem based on the Horatian *non semper* is 'Farewell Frost or Welcome the Spring', where Herrick uses it as a ground for hope in a political context. The poem opens with the seasonal theme of *Odes* 2.10.15–17, which Herrick has expanded into a picture of the coming of spring based on the spring descriptions in *Odes* 1.4 and 4.7 but redeployed as a *non semper* argument, not a *carpe diem* one: seasonal change expresses change for the better, not worse:

> Fled are the frosts, and now the fields appear
> Reclothed in fresh and verdant diaper.
> Thawed are the snows, and now the lusty spring
> Gives to each mead a neat enamelling.
> The palms put forth their gems, and every tree
> Now swaggers in her leafy gallantry.
> The while the Daulian minstrel sweetly sings,   (the nightingale,
> With warbling notes, her Terean sufferings.   Philomela, raped
> What gentle winds perspire! As if here   by Tereus)
> Never had been the Northern plunderer   (Boreas, the North
> To strip the trees and fields, to their distress,   Wind, a reference to
> Leaving them to a pitied nakedness.   the Scots invasion)
>   (1–12)

The picture of Spring is a composite one: lines 1 and 2 recall *Odes* 4.7.1–2, lines 3 and 4 *Odes* 1.4.1 and 4, and there are echoes of Ovid and Virgil in the next two. The line about the Northern plunderer stripping the trees recalls 2.9.6–8. Like Carew in 'The Spring', Herrick has adorned the description with Sylvesterian language – 'verdant diaper', 'enamelling', 'swaggers' 'leafy gallantry'. A political meaning has been insinuated: the pitied nakedness of the trees and fields suggests the depredations of the Civil War, so that the Sylvesterian anthropomorphism is not just decorative but has the effect of pathos. Herrick then continues with another *non semper* analogy, that of

81

calm succeeding to storm, echoing *Odes* 2.9, and draws a political application: peace will follow the storm of Civil War. The poem ends with a final image of consolation drawn from the Bible, the dove of Noah's Ark:

> And look how when a frantic storm doth tear
> A stubborn oak or holm long growing there,
> But lulled to calmness, then succeeds a breeze
> That scarcely stirs the nodding leaves of trees;
> So when this war, which tempest-like doth spoil
> Our salt, our corn, our honey, wine, and oil,
> Falls to a temper, and doth mildly cast (calmness)
> His inconsiderate frenzy off, at last,
> The gentle dove may, when these turmoils cease,
> Bring in her bill, once more, the branch of peace. (13–22)

'Farewell Frost' demonstrates Herrick's ability to fuse a variety of disparate sources into a new unity, here a poem infused with feeling about the political events of the time – not ignoring the contexts of the original motifs but harnessing them to an appropriate new use.

As well as meditating on *carpe diem* and *non semper* themes, Herrick has a series of poems in which he expresses his lifestyle in Horatian terms, following the Horatian method of making autobiographical details into poetic material.[56] In a number of poems, he builds up a picture of himself as the retiring and modest country dweller, living alone with his maid Prue and his dog, which is clearly indebted to Horace, as well as to Martial in his Horatian vein (e.g. *Epigrams* 3.58). In 'His Content in the Country', Prue and Herrick are seen as Horatians, innocent country dwellers:

> Here, here I live with what my board
> Can with the smallest cost afford.
> Though ne'er so mean the viands be,
> They well content my Prue and me.
> Or pea, or bean, or wort, or beet,
> Whatever comes, content makes sweet;
> Here we rejoice because no rent
> We pay for our poor tenement;
> Wherein we rest, and never fear
> The landlord or the usurer.
> The quarter-day does ne'er affright
> Our peaceful slumbers in the night.
> We eat our own, and batten more
> Because we feed on no man's score;
> But pity those whose flanks grow great
> Swelled with the lard of others' meat.
> We bless our fortunes when we see

The Horace of Ben Jonson and his heirs

> Our own beloved privacy;
> And like our living, where we'are known
> To very few, or else to none.

Here we find many Horatian details: vegetarian diet, sound sleep, self-sufficiency and avoidance of rack-renting.[57] The concluding lines on solitude recall Horace's praise of the man *qui natus moriensque fefellit* ('who living and dying escapes notice') and the *fallentis semita vitae* ('the path of life which escapes notice') (*Epistles* 1.17.10, 18.103). The Horatian gestures are made lightly and easily, so that one might mistake their sophistication for simplicity. Another such poem is 'His Grange or Private Wealth', where Herrick lists his property following the *non ebur aut aureum . . . at* scheme of *Odes* 2.18 – though the detail is more characteristic of the *Epistles*, or indeed of Martial, than the *Odes*. Once again the Horatian gestures are made so lightly that we hardly notice that the picture of 'rural privacy' draws on literature as well as life, but the light emphasis on innocence, smallness and content – 'Where care / None is, slight things do lightly please' – takes us back to the Sabine farm and the *modus agri non ita magnus* ('the piece of land not very large') (*S* 2.6.1): like Horace, Herrick makes his lifestyle a symbol of a moral preference. Here Herrick is imitating Horace's pose of the small man:

> parvum parva decent. mihi iam non regia Roma,
> sed vacuum Tibur placet aut imbelle Tarentum.   (*Ep*.1.7.44–5)

> Small things suit the small man: me now not royal Rome but empty Tibur or unwarlike Tarentum pleases.

There is mock modesty in this pose, which suits the often tongue-in-cheek Herrick. Such a tone had been too unheroic for Jonson, but is favoured by Herrick – 'as my small pipe best fits my little note' ('A Ternary of Littles'). It suits the epigrammatic mode, where any subject, however large, may be fitted into small compass (see the opening sonnet).[58] Herrick enjoys making larger forms into epigrams: e.g. recasting the themes of the Horatian ode into epigram, as in 'His Content in the Country' or 'Content not Cates'. The unheroic tiny note of 'His Grange', with its slight ironic exaggeration, is thus a literary gesture, a feigned naïvety, not to be mistaken for the real thing (though it often has been: 'Herrick is a poet of a charmingly fanciful but simple sensibility').[59] Both 'His Grange' and 'His Content in the Country' have a very quiet irony, or in T. S. Eliot's famous phrase 'a recognition, implicit in the expression of every experience, of other kinds of experience which are possible'. Indeed in other poems, Herrick expresses his distaste for country living.

The presence of this series of Horatian poems complicates the picture that Anne Baynes Coiro has presented in her sympathetic study of Herrick. She sees Herrick moving during the course of *Hesperides* from an Anacreontic epigrammatic role, 'pastoral', inebriated and escapist, to Martial's 'realistic', urban mode, adviser of princes, confronting death and failure; the book moves from country to town, from gaiety to gloom. There is much that is attractive in her picture: in particular, the emphasis on the sombre sides to Herrick's poetry and the recognition of his shifting self-presentation.[60] However, the presence of the Horatian poems throughout *Hesperides* disrupts what seems to me an over-schematic pattern: happy to sad, country to town – there are several Horatian poems in the seventh century where the crucial change is said to take place, e.g. nos. H–642, H–662, H–670, H–674 in J. Max Patrick's numeration,[61] and there is a sequence as late as the eighth century, nos. H–723–5. There are dark poems throughout the book; the first Civil War poem is in the first century (H–77); the first poem about loss of inspiration, 'To his Friend, on the Untuneable Times', is at no. 210. Herrick seems purposely to disrupt any clear autobiographical sequence: why does 'To Dean Bourn' come at the beginning of the book (H–86), before Herrick is evicted to London? Why are the two poems to the Lares back to front, the first (H–333) telling of dispossession from his country living, the second (H–674) of contented possession? Herrick did not number the poems; it is only in the edition of J. Max Patrick that they are so numbered, and the reader of the original edition had no way of telling how far through the book he was. Herrick was certainly concerned with the shape of his book as a whole, witness the opening and closing sequences; he was concerned to present it as a collection, like Horace's *Odes*, the work of one man, Robert Herrick, the embodiment of a unique sensibility. But I think that, instead of a progression, Herrick saw his book more as a mosaic or tapestry, in which various strands are blended (the first poem suggests as much). One important strand is the Horatian one, which deepens the picture and extends the emotional range – mediates between Anacreon and Martial. Here the jaunty *carpe diem* of the Greek Anthology is made more sober and philosophical, and Herrick comes to terms with the country he elsewhere spurns.

Coiro gives a much better account of Herrick's classicism than Gordon Braden, who claims that, with some exceptions, Herrick only imitates phrases from classical authors and takes no account of the contexts in which they appear 'the heft or timbre of his authors' voices but none of their specific intentions', 'moments of verbal grace rather than structures of meaning'.[62] Coiro provides many examples which go against Braden's contention and shows that Herrick transmutes Anacreon and Martial. Of course, there are many borrowings that are purely verbal, but equally there are poems which borrow attitudes more than phrases, e.g. 'A Paraenetical or Advisive Verse' or 'His Content in the Country'.

In *Hesperides*, Herrick succeeds in establishing a distinct voice, recalling

The Horace of Ben Jonson and his heirs

Horace and Jonson but not identical with either. Less of a dogmatist and idealist than Jonson, a great lover of ceremony and festival, he is able to respond more to the sadness of Horace's treatment of transience and to his Epicurean hedonism. His style does not have the chiselled solidity of the *Odes* or the energy of Jonson, but is an elegant, fluid and delicate instrument; in the careful placing of long words he sometimes recalls Horace:

> Whenas in silks my Julia goes,
> Then, then, methinks, how sweetly flows
> That *liquefaction* of her clothes.
>
> Next, when I cast mine eyes and see
> That brave *vibration* each way free,
> Oh, how that glittering taketh me!

Herrick's classicism, influenced by Jonson, is at its best a delicate and sophisticated assimilation.

4

MARVELL AND HORACE: COLOUR AND TRANSLUCENCY

A. D. Nuttall

THIS ESSAY IS not a study in influence. Rather, with a free use of evaluative terms which may seem scandalous to some, it sets two supreme lyric poets side by side and searches, not in the manner of F. R. Leavis for unnoticed, disabling weaknesses, but for distinctive strengths. The secret and wholly impracticable purpose of the exercise is to see – as a child might put it – 'which poet wins'.

> How vainly men themselves amaze
> To win the palm, the oak, or bays;[1]   ('The Garden')

Is this nature poetry? It is written by Marvell, who is famous for a certain, seventeenth-century kind of nature poetry, for an obsession with greenness, even perhaps for an occasional fantastic phytophilia. Yet the answer to the question is clearly 'No'. These plants are not noticeably green. Commentaries sedulously explain that the palm is the meed of victory in athletic contests or in war, that the oak is the civil crown and the bays are the reward of poetry and, for once, this official gloss is wholly – is strangely – adequate. These plants are not rooted in the soil; they have become their public meanings. The poetry is therefore virtually co-extensive with the paraphrasable, conceptual significance.

The coldness of the verse in this opening stanza is, to be sure, strategic. It figures the unnatural character of the competitive, public existence it formally reprehends. The ambitious reader is schooled and reproved, for the moment, in his own language. Moreover that language is even allowed a temporary victory by appropriation; it is permitted to petrify things naturally green – but not for long. All is done in order that the subsequent almost erotic encounter with real plants may surprise with an unlooked for vivacity. That which we thought we had domesticated proves to be wild, still.

> The luscious clusters of the vine
> Upon my mouth do crush their wine;
> The nectarine and curious peach,

Marvell and Horace

> Into my hands themselves do reach;
> Stumbling on melons, as I pass,
> Insnared with flowers, I fall on grass.

A. J. N. Wilson has written persuasively of Marvell's use of a *color Romanus*,[2] a 'Roman colouring', derived from ancient poets. Yet in 'The Garden' the Roman character of the gravely censorious opening seems to draw all colour from the plants named. As I have written elsewhere, they seem to have been carved in marble.[3] We have therefore not so much a *color Romanus* as an *albitudo Romana*, 'a Roman whiteness', a blank pallor in the august verbal sequence.

There is no explicit reference to monuments or statuary at the beginning of 'The Garden', but in 'The Mower against Gardens' (another poem about artifice, plants and sexuality but with the garden figuring, this time, on the side of artifice as a place of horticultural violation) we have the lines,

> And fauns and fairies do the meadows till,
>   More by their presence than their skill.
> Their statues polished by some ancient hand,
>   May to adorn the gardens stand:
> But howso'ere the figures do excel,
>   The gods themselves with us do dwell.

The mysterious voice which utters these lines comes from outside the garden wall, from the sweet, forgotten fields. The thought is nevertheless like the thought in the second stanza of 'The Garden', which moves by a false tautology from the emblematic, conceptually translated plants of Quiet and Innocence to the plants themselves.

Since we have identified the cool, anti-natural style with Rome, the subsequent lyric explosion or rupture is by implication wholly un-Roman in character. It would therefore seem to be a waste of time to look for similar tensions within the work of a Latin poet.

Consider, nevertheless, Horace, *Odes* 4.8:

> non incisa notis marmora publicis,
> per quae spiritus et vita redit bonis
> post mortem ducibus, non celeres fugae
> reiectaeque retrorsum Hannibalis minae,
> non incendia Carthaginis impiae
> eius, qui domita nomen ab Africa
> lucratus rediit clarius indicant
> laudes quam Calabrae Pierides . . .

Not marble tablets graven with public memorials, through which breath and life return after death to great captains, not the rapid flights of Hannibal and the threats flung behind him, nor the burning of impious Carthage declare with more glory the praises of him who came home having made his name by conquering Africa than do the Muses of Calabria . . .

'The Muses of Calabria' are a reference to the Calabrian poet, Ennius. There seems at first reading to be some sort of contrast between the public carved memorial and the vivid life which follows. But there are problems. Orellius (John Gaspar Orelli) in his nineteenth-century commentary and excursus on this poem is perhaps more honest in the registration of difficulty than some more recent commentators.

First, he resists the translation of *reiectaeque retrorsum . . . minae* as 'threats recoiling on *his own head*', pointing out obstinately, *in poetae verbis ipsis certe non inest*, 'it plainly is not there, in the actual words of the poet'.[4] That some such idea of an ultimate poetic justice may be triggered by the word *retrorsum* in the mind of a reader who knows the story of Hannibal is wholly probable. But such subauditions are to be distinguished from poetically enforced secondary senses. Orellius was right to insist first on the bare meaning as primary. To do so – to confine the imagination for the moment to the spatial sense – assists indeed the strange and powerful transition from the stillness of incised marble to the wild instability of flight. But this very transition creates further problems, also noticed by Orellius. Horace seems to set out with the idea that poetry confers a more splendid and lasting fame than marble monuments, but then to allow his sentence to be invaded, incongruously, by *the deeds themselves*. It is all very well to say poetry is better than sculpture for conferring glory on heroic deeds. But it is very odd to say that it is better than the glorious deeds themselves. It is the kind of thought which might appear, suitably ironized, in an epigram by Martial. It can hardly be offered (even if deeds without poets fall into oblivion) with a straight face. The matter is complicated to the point of absurdity by the fact that *this* poet has in any case partly forgotten the story (Horace confuses the elder and the younger Scipio).[5] Orellius wonders whether the absurdity might be removed if we assume that Horace intended the scenes of flight and fire to have been in fact sculpted on the monument.

If Horace were indeed describing some sort of triumphal frieze, we would have here a strangely contracted *ecphrasis*, that is a poem describing (another) work of art. If we admit this thought we shall find that the puzzling transition-without-overt-contrast from incised stone to life and motion is indeed accounted for. *Ecphrasis* from the earliest times delighted in just this transformation; the glittering shield of Achilles with its carved scenes of rural life blackens where the ploughshare has passed (*Iliad*, 18.548) and centuries later Keats' Grecian Urn will hold in its white stillness pipes, timbrels and wild ecstasy; the altar to which the mysterious priest leads the heifer will be, though carved in marble, green.

If all this is correct, Horace's thought is, contrary to expectation, more intricate than Marvell's. The English poet contrasts the civic emblem with the green reality, cold statuary with the rural deities themselves. The Roman poet, like the English, first conveys the idea of incised marble and then at once counters with images of turbulent life. This contrast, however, in accordance with the ancient law of *ecphrasis*, is *internal* to the description of the monument. Marble is not simply the livery of death. Wrought by art it can convey movement, life and flight. But even now we have not finished, for poetry, says Horace, can do even more. Though marble may quicken the slain hero, verse can shed a yet greater glory on him. Yet all of this depends on an interpretation which Orellius admits with his usual honesty we hold *precario*, 'on sufferance', 'precariously'.[6]

May Horace, nevertheless, have beaten Marvell, a thousand years before, at his own game of dexterous intelligence fused with lyric force? Twentieth-century criticism has in general preferred complexity to simplicity. I, a true son of the century, have in general shared this preference. Yet I suspect that in the present case the passages cited from Marvell are better both as poetry and as thought, because they are simpler. Horace's rhetorically transcended *ecphrasis* passes too swiftly to engage either the imagination or the intelligence (it is a little like what happens when a story is boring because too rapidly told). In Marvell the elementary contrast between the conceptual and the natural is allowed to give an unimpeded power to the whole. Indeed, in 'The Garden' its gradual unfolding composes a poem which, astonishingly, prefigures one central project of a later Romanticism. It enacts the death of its own too-rational conceits in deference to a greenness which 'means' only itself. Horace is, as it were, too smart for the primary problem – that poetry is art and is therefore radically separate from the artless nature it reveres – ever to show. But, note, we are comparing on-form Marvell with off-form Horace (some, indeed, have considered these lines so bad that they cannot have been written by Horace). It might be said that the Marvellian contrast is present in Horace *in extenso*, since everyone feels in the *Odes* a tension between Rome and the social privacy of the Sabine farm, between the stony rhetorical Alcaics which open the third book and the sweet especial rural scene of 3.13. There, in the description of the spring at Bandusia, colour breaks in with a force which, amid the innocence, can shock us, as the kid's blood reddens the clear water; meanwhile the swelling horns of the sacrificial victim promise both violence and sexuality. Most powerfully of all, Horace's great poem of heroic horror, *Odes* 3.5, ends with Regulus moving through his Roman friends, returning to the Carthaginian torture chamber:

> . . . non aliter . . .
> quam si clientum longa negotia
> diiudicata lite relinqueret
>   tendens Venefranos in agros
>   aut Lacedaemonium Tarentum.

... Just as if, some case in court having been decided, he were leaving the lengthy business of his clients behind him, making his way [the best I can do for *tendens* which Kipling called untranslatable][7] to Venefran fields or Lacedaemonian Tarentum.

It is important to understand that the places named at the end are the familiar weekend resorts of the Roman man of affairs, anxious to escape the rat-race of the capital for at least a few days. The poet achieves an extraordinary effect by reversing the usual emotional order of similes. Instead of seeking intensification by comparing the action with some still more violent analogue, he can (because of the unostentatious courage of Regulus) compare horror with its opposite, with the ordinary sweetness of holiday. This principle was understood by Dante, when he likened Brunetto Latini in hell with 'those that run for the green cloth at Verona' (*Inferno*, 15.122).

The moment in the Regulus Ode has great power, but it is not philosophic power. The primary contrast between reality and mere conception, so strong in Marvell, is still wholly absent from the Latin poem. Meanwhile, it might be said, Marvell can in any case match the Latin poet's turning-inside-out of the intensifying simile. Charles I on the scaffold, submitting to the executioner's axe, Marvell tells us,

> ... bowed his comely head
> Down, as upon a bed.
> ('An Horatian Ode upon Cromwell's Return from Ireland', 63–4).

At first, indeed, Charles is exalted in language which, as Joanna Martindale has pointed out,[8] directly recalls Horace's exaltation of Cleopatra at the end of *Odes* 1.37: '*He* nothing common did or mean'; *non humilis mulier*, 'no abject woman, this'. But then Marvell swiftly opposes humility, after all, to grandeur. The lines about Charles come from a poem which Marvell explicitly described as Horatian. Indeed this poem seems strangely suspended between Latin and English. It has long been noticed that the lines

> with his keener eye
> The axe's edge did try   (59–60)

seem somehow to promise an epigram which is not complete until one thinks in Latin: *acies* means both 'edge' and 'the glance of an eye'. The placing of the comparative adjective 'keener' seems to require a pun in the noun, but this is available only in the dead language. Latin-less readers may well complain that they are ill-used. A parallel difficulty, this time cross-cultural rather than cross-linguistic, lurks perhaps in

> Nor in the shadows sing
> His numbers languishing.   (3–4)

Marvell and Horace

The unlearned reader will intuit readily enough a contrast between obscurity and the blaze of public action, but the factor which may elude the Northern reader is that for one living under a fierce Mediterranean sun shadows connote not only obscurity but comfortable ease – the *vita umbratilis* ('life in the shade'). In Euripides' *Bacchae* the ostentatiously manly Pentheus (half-attracted, against his will, by the epicene Dionysus) scorns the god's complexion, never exposed to the rays of the sun (458). In England boys who 'hugged the fireside' used to be – perhaps still are – condemned in a similar way.

By almost universal consent[9] the central achievement of Marvell's ode is its political balance – a balance attained not through the extinction of feeling but through generous, intelligent emotion. Cromwell's greatness is undoubted; England will never be the same again. But we cannot forget the bloody hands of the soldiers as they clapped and the dignity of the dying King. Moreover, although this is a poem about historical transformation, its central actor is in the end more a replicator than a true revolutionary: Cromwell the Caesaricide becomes himself a second Caesar in the last lines of the poem.

This combination of balance with strong feeling is matched, it is often said, in Horace's Ode on Cleopatra (1.37). Here (somewhat as in Marvell's 'The Garden') there is a great distance in tone between the opening lines – a jovial call to drink and dance to celebrate the defeat of the mad Egyptian woman – and the conclusion:

> . . . deliberata morte ferocior,
> saevis Liburnis scilicet invidens
>   privata deduci superbo
>   non humilis mulier triumpho.

> . . . Her spirit greater as she resolved to die; scorning – do you not see? – to be brought back uncrowned on barbaric galleys to grace an arrogant triumph, no abject woman, this.

The transition from Cleopatra as the wine-maddened ruler of a sexually debilitated court to the proud figure at the end is sudden but not absolutely abrupt. We see her first in power, and then as a hunted victim, the dove pursued by the hawk. At this stage (for courage comes to her only with the certainty of death) she is presented as terrified. But then, strangely, having begun to build sympathy for Cleopatra, Horace allows the language of hatred (*fatale monstrum*, 'deadly monster') back into his verse, at the point of her capture. But we are perhaps underestimating the poet's subtlety. By this stage, *fatale monstrum*, 'deadly monster', applied to a hunted dove, must carry virtual inverted commas – not fully ironical, indeed, but moving in that direction; this is what the Romans *call* her. Then comes the *volta*:

> . . . fatale monstrum; quae generosius
> perire quaerens nec muliebriter
> expavit ensem . . .

> . . . the deadly monster – who, seeking death, showed no womanish fear of the sword . . .

The Loeb translator inserts the word 'yet' as a mark of reversal. But there is no *tamen* or *atqui* in the Latin. Instead we have the inexorable continuity of *quae*, 'who', the feminine gender reasserting the sex of Cleopatra against the neuter, *monstrum*, 'monster'. The detested freak and the woman who rose above terror are one and the same; Horace refuses to help us with an adversative conjunction.

Yet, once more, philosophic force, and this time we may add, political force, are virtually absent from Horace's poem. David Norbrook has argued that the 'Ode upon Cromwell's Return' is part of a more general Republican appropriation of Horace (formerly the favourite of the Monarchists); behind the complex troping of the poem he discerns the influence of Machiavelli.[10] In one way it may be that Marvell's thought is actually more fundamental than Machiavelli's. As he engages with the mystery of historical change, he seems almost to stumble on the modern dispute between those who believe history is changed by great individuals and those who think that larger, impersonal movements are always the true agents of change. Cromwell, to be sure, is in Marvell's poem unequivocally effective, as an individual: 'So much one man can do' (75). Yet there is for Marvell an element of extreme historical paradox in his very effectiveness. When Marvell describes the way Cromwell cut violently through his own party the thought 'In normal history the party should have produced *him*, the phenomenon', seems not very far away. Cromwell's effectiveness seems somehow to figure in antithesis to history itself:

> . . . Could by industrious valour climb
> To ruine the great work of time,
>   And cast the kingdom old
>   Into another mould.   (33–6)

Meanwhile a surviving sense that Cromwell is somehow both the agent and still in some way the product of change can be seen in the extraordinary image, 'Urged his active star' (12). It is as if Cromwell were whipping and spurring a mount which is in any case bearing – or driving ('active') – him into the future.

Christopher Ricks has written of Marvell's skill in tying a kind of 'teasing knot' in which clarity and unclarity are combined. When the poet says in 'A Dialogue between the Soul and the Body' that the soutl 'fettered stands / In feet, and manacled in hands', we hear the Latin *manus* in 'manacled'; the effect is a little like that in Escher's famous picture of a hand drawing itself.¹¹ John Donne had written earlier, in his Third Meditation, the words, 'strange fetters to the feet, strange manacles to the hands,'¹² but here, because manacles and hands are not identified, the knot is still untied. The Latin poem *Pia Desideria* (1628) by the Continental Jesuit Hermann Hugo comes much closer with

> Ipsa loco caveae membra fuere meae,
> Pes compes, manicaeque manus, nervique catenae.

> My very limbs were a prison to me; the foot a fetter, manacles the hands and the sinews chains.¹³

The opportunity for a glancing, interlinguistic slippage (as from 'manacled' to 'hands') is of course not available to Hugo. But with the phrase, 'Urged his active star' Marvell gives to what might otherwise seem a mere decorative ingenuity of late metaphysical verse real historiographical force.

Marvell is indeed drawing on Latin sources for his politically expert portrait of Cromwell, but rather from Tacitus and Lucan, whose *Pharsalia* fuelled Republican feeling in seventeenth-century England. Not that Cromwell is an unambiguous hero of Republicanism. R. H. Syfret showed exactly how Marvell drew on Lucan, making an amalgam of the Lucanian Caesar and the antithetical Lucanian Pompey.¹⁴ Tacitus especially, whether impelled by a purely formal love of asymmetry in his anti-Ciceronian sentences or from acute political insight, liked to describe historical figures as *loci* of an uncomfortably disjunct motivation. We may take as an example his notoriously disorienting picture of Petronius Arbiter, the exquisite contemporary of Nero:

utque alios industria, ita hunc ignavia ad famam protulerat, habebaturque non ganeo et profligator . . . sed erudito luxu.   (*Annals*, 16.18)¹⁵

> As others are thrust into the limelight by hard work, so Petronius got there by indolence, but he was not looked upon as a mere glutton or conspicuous spender – rather as one who made a science of pleasure.

It could be said that the whole of Marvell's Cromwell ode is a turning inside out of a more famous observation of Tacitus (with reference to Galba): *capax imperii, nisi imperasset*, 'Capable of rule – had he never ruled' (*Histories*, 1.49).¹⁶ Cromwell was a simple gardener – had he not overturned the state.

Yet such paradoxes of motivation or effect fall short of the historiographical mystery glimpsed by Marvell. Horace, meanwhile, writing a hundred years before Tacitus, remains amazingly 'unpolitical'. This may have been a matter of evasive design; James Michie has called him 'the master of the graceful sidestep'.[17] It may be pointed out that in the sense in which all statements are political (that is, by commission or omission) Horace's poem is notably 'safe' in its sentiments. Cleopatra can be admired when she is certain to die because from this point she poses no threat. The generosity can be easily afforded by a nation made rich by conquest. The incipient irony in *fatale monstrum*, 'deadly monster', is the only hint of Roman self-criticism and it is faint indeed.

It may be thought that one feature of Marvell's genius, his power of writing 'interlinguistic' poetry, is necessarily unavailable to the Latin poet; for him there can be no interplay of ancient and modern since he is himself unequivocally ancient. Oddly enough however, there is a loosely equivalent tension in Horace. Roughly speaking, the Greek lyric poets are to him as he is to Marvell. He was aware, as the Greeks themselves in the nature of things could not be, that his *Odes* were a feat of transposition.

> dicar . . .
> . . . ex humili potens
> princeps Aeolium carmen ad Italos
> deduxisse modos. (*Odes* 3.30)

> I, grown to power from a low origin, will be talked about . . . for having married Aeolian poetry to Italian metre.

The reader is slightly surprised by the form of the sentence. One expects Horace to say that he joined Italian poetry to Greek metre, since that is what he in fact did (the Alcaics, Sapphics and Asclepiads employed by Horace are not native to Latin but taken by him from Greek sources). Of course Horace borrowed not only metres but themes, and it is possible that by *Italos modos* he really means, not 'Italian metres' but 'Latinised metres', 'metres now rendered Italian'. Nevertheless the more stiff-necked sort of reader may well get a certain feeling he or she has had before, when confronted by fairly intricate Latin verse: that the lines are a sort of jig-saw puzzle into which all the necessary components of the sentence have been fitted, under metrical necessity, and that the reader is tacitly left free to rearrange them – to glean, in fact, the meaning I first suggested, 'famous for having married Italian poetry to Greek metres'. The very first words of Ovid's *Metamorphoses*

> in nova fert animus mutatas dicere formas
> corpora . . .

are rendered by the Loeb translator, presumably on precisely this principle of 'occasional licence to re-arrange', as 'My mind is bent to tell of bodies changed into new forms'[18] (Ovid, it will be noticed, actually says, 'of forms changed into new bodies').

Marvell and Horace

The present example, *Odes* 3.30, is certainly disputable, but the more general suggestion that a Horatian *Ode* can have the character of a laboured puzzle, into which the different elements are laboriously fitted, would, I believe, be accepted by most of his readers. And this 'jigsaw' quality is not Greek. Take *Odes* 3.14:

> dic et argutae properet Neaerae
> murreum nodo cohibere crinem;
> si per invisum mora ianitorem
> fiet, abito.
>
> lenit albescens animos capillus
> litium et rixae cupidos protervae;
> non ego hoc ferrem calidus iuventa
> consule Planco.

And tell the bright Neaera to hurry and knot her scented hair. If the detested doorman causes a delay, just leave. My whitening hair weakens the desire for quarrelling and wanton conflict. I would never have put up with this in my hot youth, when Plancus was consul.

It will be apparent from my translation that I am not persuaded that *argutae*, the adjective applied to Neaera, necessarily means 'clear-voiced' here. A more general sense, 'clear', 'crisp', 'bright' seems entirely appropriate, for nothing else in the passage specifies sound as particularly important. 'Bright', admittedly, is weak for so assertive a word (I thought of 'sharp' and even 'snazzy'). The language in general in these verses is not especially learned or, by the standards of surviving Latin literature, remarkably remote from speech. The use of the jussive subjunctive without *ut* (*dic properet*, 'tell hurry') seems to have been a useful telescoped form, widely employed.[19] But a peculiar effect is achieved by building this idiomatic language, these less than noble sentiments into an alien metrical form of challenging difficulty. We may take for comparison some surviving lines of Anacreon on the incongruity of love and white hairs:

> Σφαίρῃ δηὖτέ με πορφυρέῃ
> βάλλων χρυσοκόμης Ἔρως
> νήνι ποικιλοσαμβάλῳ
> συμπαίζειν προκαλεῖται.
> ἡ δ᾽, ἐστὶν γὰρ ἀπ᾽ εὐκτίτου
> Λέσβου, τὴν μὲν ἐμὴν κόμην,
> λευκὴ γάρ, καταμέμφεται,
> πρὸς δ᾽ ἄλλην τινὰ χάσκει.[20]

Golden-haired Love, hitting me yet again with a crimson ball, challenges me to play with the young creature in embroidered sandals. But she (coming as she does from fair Lesbos) finds fault with my hair for being white and is off, in open-mouthed pursuit of another girl.

I have tried to translate both the Horace and the Anacreon literally, but the point I wish to make eludes the closest translation. Because of the alien metre Horace's poem, for all its idiomatic lightness, is laboured as the Greek poem is not. No doubt the easy availability in Greek of particles, δή (here joined by elision to αὖτε), γάρ, μέν – little words of fugitive meaning, 'you see', 'for', 'on the one hand', makes everything easier for Anacreon. Horace meanwhile must plug in his adjectives where he can, often at some distance from the nouns they qualify. It may be said that πορφυρέη, 'crimson', is as far from Σφαίρῃ ('ball') as *argutae*, 'bright', is from *Neaerae*, but thereafter all Anacreon's adjectives are contiguous to the relevant nouns, whereas in Horace *murreum*, 'scented', is far from *crinem*, 'hair', as is *invisum*, 'detested' from *ianitorem*, 'doorman', *albescens*, 'whitening', from *capillus*, 'hair', *rixae*, 'conflict', from *protervae*, 'wanton' and *animos* from *cupidos* ('spirits', 'desiring', telescoped in my translation as 'desire'). This is the kind of poetry made to wrinkle the smooth brow of the child with the dictionary and grammar to hand: 'Oh, I see, *argutae* isn't a nominative plural; it must go with *Neaerae*' and so on. It is partly because of this running cross-cultural awkwardness that the lyric or humorous resolutions of Horace convey so strong a feeling of release, as in the last two lines quoted.

The effect was tellingly imitated by Kipling in a piece of light verse discussed elsewhere in this volume, 'Horace, Bk.v, Ode 3',[21] 'There are whose study is of smells'. Kipling's usual method in this marvellous *jeu d'esprit* is to employ a species of *grammatical* calque; that is, the transposition into the nearest equivalent English elements not of a single sense confined to a single word, but of whole arrangements of words. The first line, 'There are whose study is of smells', is grammatically elliptical in a way which is natural to Latin but unnatural to English (which would normally give 'There are people who like to study smells'). Kipling, too, can plant within his alien framework the deliberately idiomatic, the so to speak 'super-ordinary' English phrase:

> Me, in whose breast no flame hath burned
> Life-long, save that by Pindar lit,
> Such lore leaves cold: I am not turned
> Aside to it . . .

Here 'leaves cold' is common speech, while the harshly separated 'me' is Latin; it imitates a similar separation in *Odes* 1.1, *me doctarum hederae praemia frontium / dis miscent superis*, 'me the ivy, the reward of brows schooled in poetry, links to the gods on high'.

It would appear that in our general comparison of Marvell and Horace the Roman poet is, so far, the loser. Surprisingly, he can match and perhaps exceed the 'interlinguistic' effects essayed by the English poet, but Marvell's philosophic depth and political resonance lie quite beyond his reach. Yet Horace can cause us to catch our breath, can shake us, as Marvell never does. How – when – does he do this?

> Diffugere nives, redeunt iam gramina campis
> arboribusque comae;
> mutat terra vices et decrescentia ripas
> flumina praetereunt.
> Gratia cum Nymphis geminisque sororibus audet
> ducere nuda choros.
> immortalia ne speres, monet annus et almum
> quae rapit hora diem. (*Odes* 4.7)

The snows are fled away, grasses return to the fields, leaves to the trees, Earth's cycle changes, and rivers flow lower in their channels. The Grace together with the Nymphs and her sisters two dares to lead the dance naked. The year and the hour which ravishes the sweet day warn you not to hope for things immortal.

The last two lines are the ones which strike home. Compare the opening of a drinking song, also about the futility of hoping for immortality, by Alcaeus:

> Πῶνε καὶ μέθυ', ὦ Μελάνιππ', ἄμ' ἐμοι. τί φαῖς,
> δινάεντ' ὅτ' ἀμείψεαι Ἀχέροντα μέγαν πόρον
>
> ζάβαις, ἀελίω κόθαρον φάος ἄψερον
> ὄψεσθ'; ἀλλ' ἄγι μὴ μεγάλων ἐπιβάλλεο.[22]

In *The Oxford Book of Greek Verse in Translation* this poem is given the title 'Immortalia ne speres', 'not to hope for things immortal', Horace's words in *Odes* 4.7. I am not sure whether the title was chosen by C. M. Bowra, but his translation follows, and I give it here:

> Drink, Melanippus, and be drunk with me.
> How can you think that you will ever see,
> Once over Acheron, the pure bright day
> Again? Come throw such proud desires away.[23]

Alcaeus goes on, as does Horace, to speak of great figures from the past who show how death cannot be defeated. What he does not do is to affirm, before he proceeds to mythology, that the sweetness of the air on an April day warns us that we cannot have immortality. Yet Horace does just that. It may be that this is sheer incompetence on Horace's part: he meant to write about Autumn and to show how the death of the year pointed to our own extinction – and somehow wrote about Spring instead. Or else these lines are something very strange indeed: the discovery of despair in the very heart of bliss.

This was the poem which so moved A. E. Housman that he was unable to finish his lecture.[24] It moves not because of any grand philosophic design but because of a piercing truth to experience. Of course the thought can be smoothed if we paraphrase, 'The rapid succession of the seasons reminds the poet that he must himself change and die.' But this sentence builds exclusively on *rapit*, 'ravishes', 'seizes', 'hurries away' and entirely represses the sharp encounter of *ne speres* 'hope not' and *almum diem*, 'the sweet day'. I do not say (for who can?) that no Greek poet ever did this before, but I do say that in Horace's hand this effect has an over-spilling power, is more than formal (Simonides' fr. 61 is barely relevant).

Marvell writes about the onset of death in 'To his Coy Mistress'.

> But at my back I always hear
> Times wingèd chariot hurrying near:
> And yonder all before us lie
> Deserts of vast eternity.

The sheer grandeur of this is not easily equalled in English lyric poetry. The thought is – majestically and successfully – conventional. Only the appropriation of 'eternity' – normally the property of Christian optimists – to a featureless futility supplies an element of surprise. We are not now, as earlier, comparing bad Horace with good Marvell, but good with good. And Horace, I submit, wins – not by stronger colour, but by a sudden translucency, an unexpected truth which is simultaneously strange and familiar.

It begins to look as if Horace's greatest strength may lie in an unexpected quarter. Both our poets can modulate tone, astonishingly, from an initial gravity to other modes. Both can contrive within a single poem remarkable shifts of sympathy. Horace alone can arrest the reader with a sudden emotional involution which is intelligible only because, at the most intimate level, it is already known. It is a quality which had traditionally been called 'personal' and it is a little surprising to find it in the supplier of *color Romanus*, 'Roman colour' (or 'Roman whiteness') to English literature for, like glass, it can have no hue; it can, however, dazzle even as it yields to our penetrative gaze.

In 'To his Coy Mistress' Marvell writes,

> I by the tide
> Of Humber would complain,

and the commentaries refer us to Marvell's personal history (he left Hull Grammar School to go up to Cambridge in 1633 and finally became a Member of Parliament for Hull from 1659 to 1678). But the self-referring humour, though certainly present, remains somehow less important than the majestic cadence of the lines, marked as they are by 'strong' (often monosyllabic) rhymes. Even a personal reference becomes in Marvell grandly supra-personal. In Horace it is otherwise. The brief rueful self-descriptions in the *Epistles* are fascinating: *pinguem . . . / Epicuri de grege porcum*, 'a well-fed pig from Epicurus' herd' (1.4.15–16) and the oddly precise picture of a short, prematurely grey man, fond of the sun, irascible but quick to recover his temper (1.20.24–5). To read these lines gives a faint version of the excitement one would feel if one came across – what we know we can never have – a photograph of Horace.

But such isolated self-presentation cannot be crucial to Horace's status as a poet. If Marvell does not do this, Donne after all does, though *his* self-imaginings may be tainted by an element of macho self-advertisement.[25] For the quality of personal surprise to be truly important poetically it must be integrated in a larger whole – must be integrated in such a way that the surprise is not destroyed. This is done in the first Ode of the fourth book:

> intermissa, Venus, diu
>   rursus bella moves? parce precor, precor.
> non sum qualis eram bonae
>   sub regno Cinarae. desine, dulcium
>
> mater saeva Cupidinum,
>   circa lustra decem flectere mollibus
> iam durum imperiis: abi
>   quo blandae iuvenum te revocant preces.
>
> tempestivius in domum
>   Pauli purpureis ales oloribus
> commissabere Maximi,
>   si torrere iecur quaeris idoneum.
>
> namque et nobilis et decens
>   et pro sollicitis non tacitus reis
> et centum puer artium
>   late signa feret militiae tuae,
>
> et, quandoque potentior
>   largi muneribus riserit aemuli,
> Albanos prope te lacus
>   ponet marmoream sub trabe citrea.
>
> illic plurima naribus
>   duces tura, lyraque et Berecyntia
> delectabere tibia
>   mixtis carminibus non sine fistula;

illic bis pueri die
> numen cum teneris virginibus tuum
laudantes pede candido
> in morem Salium ter quatient humum.

me nec femina nec puer
> iam nec spes animi credula mutui
nec certare iuvat mero
> nec vincire novis tempora floribus.

sed cur heu, Ligurine, cur
> manat rara meas lacrima per genas?
cur facunda parum decoro
> inter verba cadit lingua silentio?

nocturnis ego somniis
> iam captum teneo, iam volucrem sequor
te per gramina Martii
> Campi, te per aquas, dure, volubilis.

Will you set in motion, Venus, wars long suspended? Please, please spare me. I am not the man I was when good queen Cinara ruled me. Hard mother of sweet love-gods, don't try any more, now that fifty years have passed, to guide with the reins an old horse whose mouth is too hard to respond to your soft commands. Be on your way, where you are called by the heart-pleasing prayers of the young. More properly to the house of Paulus Maximus will you be borne on shimmering swan-wings, if you are looking for a suitable heart to scorch. *He* is upper class and good looking, a far from tongue-tied defender of anxious clients; a boy of a hundred accomplishments, he will bear the banner of your service far afield. And when, having outdone the presents of some generous rival he shall have his laugh, he'll have you done in marble, at the lakeside, under a canopy of citron wood. There you will fill your nostrils with plentiful incense, and enjoy the mingled music of lyre and Berecyntian flutes, nor will the pipe be missing. There twice a day boys and tender maidens will make the earth shake with snowy feet in triple time, in the Salian dance. As for me, neither woman nor boy can please me now, nor credulous hope which trusts in love returned, nor competitive drinking sessions, nor garlands of fresh flowers. But why, oh Ligurinus, why, every now and then does a tear wet my cheek? Why does my eloquent tongue falter, inelegantly, in the middle of a sentence? In my dreams at night, now I catch and hold you, now I pursue you flying, you through the grasses of the Campus Martius, you, hard-hearted, through the rolling waters.

It is a poem which gets better as it goes on. After the measured ironic scorn of the first part of the poem the tears are almost embarrassing – but that, indeed, is the point. *Facunda*, 'eloquent', is a stroke of genius. The Loeb translator unforgivably weakens the effect with 'once eloquent'. There is no word for

Marvell and Horace

'once' in the Latin. Once again a deliberate collision is being loosened and rationalized by an explicator. Horace, here and now, is a good talker at dinner parties. That is why it is so shocking, so strange ('why, Ligurinus, why . . ?') that he should lose track of his sentence as the tears well in his eyes. I alluded earlier to photographs. The notion is applicable to a certain place in English poetry where Horace's lines are truly matched, to W. B. Yeats' 'Among School Children'.

> I walk through the long schoolroom questioning;
> A kind old nun in a white hood replies;
>   . . . the children's eyes
> In momentary wonder stare upon
> A sixty-year-old smiling public man . . .
> I look upon one child or t'other there
> And wonder if she stood so at that age . . .
> And thereupon my heart is driven wild . . . [26]

Yeats' stroke of genius is the word 'public'. This, indeed, we may say without reservation for we are now in the twentieth century has the effect of a photograph – a snapshot in a newspaper. One can almost see the glint of light on the spectacles, obscuring the print. The seemingly robust, inwardly frail public image invaded by disabling passion is common to both Horace and Yeats. Elsewhere true analogues (as distinct from 'sources') are hard to find.

Pope who picked up the trick of self-presentation from Horace ('I cough like Horace, and tho' lean, am short', *Epistle to Dr. Arbuthnot*, 116) is one poet who is ready to essay the larger task of integrating such moments in a more complex field, a field which accommodates both the public and the private self. His 'Epistle to Miss Blount, on her Leaving the Town, after the Coronation' is a subtle balancing of carefully separated *pictures* – figures seen from the outside – and sympathetic identification. Miss Blount is shown in her boring country house and Pope himself appears at the end in the London streets. But the mind of the urbane poet is invaded, with disorienting force, by Miss Blount, who is herself imagining – not the poet, indeed, but London life. The poem flirts, like a fan opening and closing, over what may be love. The whole is perhaps too clever or too pusillanimous to be great. In Pope's poem it is the roaring city which occludes all else at the end (except tantalizingly, for the last four words).

> Gay pats my shoulder, and you vanish quite;
> Streets, chairs, and coxcombs rush upon my sight;
> Vexed to be still in town, I knit my brow,
> Look sour, and hum a tune – as you may now.[27]

Horace ends instead with the dream pursuit of the loved person and with unsubdued pain. The words 'hard' and 'rolling' (*dure, volubilis*) are set for ever in an unappeasable contiguity. The completeness of the passion and its intensity are simultaneously conveyed with a limpid lyric intensity, now unimpeded by irony, humour or trivial self-regard. *Rursus bella moves* remains, as a whole, unequalled.

The disappointing secret result of my secret project is, I suppose, some sort of draw (Marvell ahead at first, Horace drawing level at the end). I have written from a consciousness that such exercises in comparative evaluation are absurd: the fluid complexity of the material, the variety of criteria, the multiplicity of responses make this an argument which, we all know, can never be concluded. Yet I have written also from an entirely naïve involvement in the whole exercise. If criticism – by etymology, 'judging' – never so much as tries to weigh one poet against another, has it, perhaps, died?

5

COWLEY'S HORATIAN MICE
David Hopkins

Belinda: Oh gad, I have a great passion for Cowley! Don't you admire him?
Sharper: Oh madam, he was our English Horace!
                                William Congreve, *The Old Bachelor*

    At the large foot of a fair hollow tree –
    Close to ploughed ground, seated commodiously,
    His ancient and hereditary house –
    There dwelt a good, substantial country mouse;
5   Frugal and grave, and careful of the main,   (studious in pursuit of food)
    Yet one who once did nobly entertain
    A city mouse, well-coated, sleek and gay,
    A mouse of high degree, which lost his way,
    Wantonly walking forth to take the air,
10 And arrived early, and belighted, there   (trapped in the daylight)
    For a day's lodging.
                   The good hearty host
    (The ancient plenty of his Hall to boast)
    Did all the stores produce that might excite,
    With various tastes, the courtier's appetite:
15 Fitches and beans, peason, and oats and wheat,   (wild, wayside peas; peas)
    And a large chestnut, the delicious meat
    Which Jove himself (were he a mouse) would eat.
    And for a *hautgoust* there was mixed with these   (strong flavoured relish)
    The swerd of bacon and the coat of cheese: (rind)
20 The precious relics, which at harvest he
    Had gathered from the reapers' luxury.
    'Freely', said he, 'fall on, and never spare!
    The bounteous gods will for tomorrow care!'
    And thus at ease on beds of straw they lay,
25 And to their Genius sacrificed the day.   (guardian spirit)
        Yet the nice guest's Epicurean mind
    (Thought breeding made him civil seem, and kind)
    Despised this country feast, and still his thought
    Upon the cakes and pies of London wrought.
30 'Your bounty and civility,' said he,

'Which I'm surprised in these rude parts to see,
Shows that the gods have given you a mind
Too noble for the fate which here you find.
Why should a soul so virtuous and so great
35 Lose itself thus in an obscure retreat?
Let savage beast lodge in a country den;
You should see towns, and manners know, and men,
And taste the generous luxury of the Court,
Where all the mice of quality resort;
40 Where thousand beauteous shes about you move,
And by high fare are pliant made to love.
We all ere long must render up our breath;
No cave or hole can shelter us from death.
Since life is so uncertain and so short,
45 Let's spend it all in feasting and in sport;
Come, worthy sir, come with me, and partake
All the great things that mortals happy make!'
    Alas, what virtue hath sufficient arms
T' oppose bright Honour and soft Pleasure's charms?
50 What wisdom can their magic force repel?
It draws the reverend hermit from his cell.
    It was the time when witty poets tell
'That Phoebus into Thetis' bosom fell;   (a sea-nymph)
She blushed at first, and then put out the light,
55 And drew the modest curtains of the night.'
Plainly the truth to tell, the sun was set,
When to the town our wearied travelleers get.
To a lord's house, as lordly as can be,
Made for the use of Pride and Luxury,
60 They come; the gentle courtier at the door
Stops, and will hardly enter in before –
'But 'tis, sir, your command, and, being so,
I'm sworn t' obedience' – and so, in they go.
    Behind a hanging in a spacious room
65 (The richest work of Mortlake's noble loom)   (a famous tapestry works)
They wait a while their wearied limbs to rest
Till silence should invite them to their feast;
'About the hour that Cynthia's silver light   (Diana's (i.e. the moon's))
Had touched the pale meridies of the night.'   (midnight)
70   At last, the various supper being done,
It happened that the company was gone
Into a room remote, servants and all,
To please their nobles' fancies with a ball.
Our host leads forth his stranger, and does find
75 All fitted to the bounties of his mind.
Still on the table half-filled dishes stood,

     And with delicious bits the floor was strewed.
     The courteous mouse presents him with the best,
     And both with fat varieties are blessed.
80 Th' industrious peasant everywhere does range,
     And thanks the gods for his life's happy change.
       Lo! in the midst of a well-freighted pie
     They both at last glutted and wanton lie;
     When see the sad reverse of prosperous Fate,
85 And what sad storms on mortal glories wait!
     With hideous noise down the rude servants come;
     Six dogs before run barking into th' room;
     The wretched gluttons fly with wild affright,
     And hate the fullness which retards their flight.
90 Our trembling peasant wishes now in vain
     That rocks and mountains covered him again.
     Oh, how the change of his poor life he cursed:
     'This, of all lives,' said he, 'is sure the worst!
     Give me again, ye gods, my cave and wood;
95 With peace, let tares and acorns be my food!'   (wild peas, growing as weeds)

Abraham Cowley's 'The Country Mouse: a Paraphrase upon Horace, 2 Book, Satire 6' – first published in *Verses upon Several Occasions* (1663) and subsequently reprinted as part of the essay 'Of Agriculture' in *Several Discourses by way of Essays, in Verse and Prose* (1668) – is not well known today, by readers of either classical or English literature. Modern classicists have, with a few notable exceptions, neglected the rich sources of appreciative insight into ancient literature that are locked up in the work of the English translator-poets. And for most students of English poetry, Cowley has become a virtually forgotten figure. Twentieth-century literary historians have effectively 'marginalized' him by affording him that most unappetizing of all literary labels, 'transitional figure' – characterizing him as a 'decadent metaphysical' who employed Donneian extravagance without Donne's intellectual energy or emotional commitment and/or as a 'precursor of Augustanism', whose later work can be seen to anticipate the 'public' and 'polite' verse-forms and manner of the Age of Reason.[1]

    But things have not always been thus. Contrary to common belief, Cowley was no mere seven-days' wonder, whose work enjoyed a short-lived vogue in his own lifetime and then rapidly fell out of favour. His verse and prose were, in fact, frequently reprinted and read long after his death. The *Essays* in particular were continuously available in popular editons until well into the present century.[2] Cowley's work, moreover, was widely felt to possess qualities and virtues which were distinctively its own. From the beginning, to be sure, many of the poet's admirers had tempered their enthusiasm with serious reservations about his habitual excesses and extravagances. But the praise nevertheless persisted, and frequently came from weighty, and sometimes unexpected, sources.

Milton, for example, is even reported to have ranked Cowley with Spenser and Shakespeare as the third great English poet.[3] Dryden affirmed that nothing could 'appear more beautiful' to him than the 'strength' of the imagery in Cowley's Odes.[4] Pope told Joseph Spence that Cowley was 'a fine poet, in spite of all his faults', praised 'the language of his heart' – he was referring, perhaps, both to the autobiographical writing of the *Essays* and to Cowley's movingly affectionate poems on friends and contemporaries – and drew on the poet's phrasing and rhythms on many occasions in his own verse.[5] William Cowper paid eloquent testimony to the way in which Cowley, having retired from Court life, found 'rich amends / For a lost world in solitude and verse'.[6] Samuel Johnson, whose 'Life of Cowley' is often thought of as an attack on the poet and on the 'metaphysical' tradition as a whole, in fact praises Cowley's best work in the strongest possible terms, noting with emphatic approval Cowley's 'agility', 'gaiety of fancy' and 'facility of expression' and judging that, when writing at his best, his 'volatility is not the flutter of a light, but the bound of an elastic mind'.[7] Perhaps the most surprising of all Cowley's admirers (given the apparently vast temperamental and aesthetic gulf between the two men) was Wordsworth, who referred to Cowley as an 'able writer and amiable man' and advised a correspondent to 'read all Cowley; he is very valuable to a collector of English sound sense'.[8]

Written between 1660 and 1667, and published posthumously in 1668, Cowley's *Essays* contain the reflections of the poet's final years. Having been disappointed in his hopes of Court preferment at the Restoration, Cowley obtained a favourable lease of some royal lands, and went into retirement, first at Barn Elms near Putney and then, from 1665, at Chertsey, where he lived until his death in 1667. The *Essays* reflect, in part, Cowley's personal sense of regret and sadness at having (as he now saw it) squandered so much of his earlier life in his career as a courtier and public servant.

The first piece in the volume, 'Of Liberty', sets the agenda for the collection as a whole. In this essay, Cowley announces that he intends to discourse on 'the liberty of a private man in being master of his own time and actions, as far as may consist with the laws of God and of his country' and to 'enquire what estate of life does best seat us in the possession of it'.[9] Liberty, he suggests, consists in the individual's capacity to free himself from the domination of ambition, covetousness and voluptuousness. The truly happy man, he argues, in this essay and in the collection as a whole, is he who has achieved the ability to put aside vain desires, and to live in full possession of the 'cheap plenty' and 'substantial blessedness'[10] which life can offer.

Cowley's *Essays* are frankly eclectic in form and spirit, and, like the *Essais* of Montaigne on which they are in some ways modelled, treat their subject from a variety of perspectives and in a variety of tones, manners and voices. Verse is mingled with prose, and 'original' writing with translation, paraphrase and imitation (from Horace, Martial, Seneca, Virgil and other classical poets), to form a continuing conversation-piece about the nature of contentment and the happy life. The happy man is seen, at various points in the volume, as a wise Stoic, fortified by inner calm and self-possession against the buffets of life, as a happy husbandman relishing the simple pleasures and beautiful scenery of the countryside, as a Lucretian philosopher contemplating the causes of things, as a gentleman-farmer participating in good conversation among choice friends in congenial surroundings, and as a pre-lapsarian Adam, enjoying the delights of a Golden Age innocence.[11] Cowley's version of Horace's tale of 'The Country Mouse' was incorporated in this larger pattern, and to see it in its setting in the *Essays* as a whole is to become conscious of both the daring and the surprising aptness of the poet's decision to excerpt Horace's fable from the *Sermo* of which it was originally an integral part.

The sixth *Sermo* of Horace's second book offers a set of reflections on the farm in the Sabine hills which has been obtained for Horace by his patron, Maecenas. This farm, Horace says, has provided him with all he could ever have desired. It is true that the presence of his beloved Maecenas gives Rome, in theory, advantages over the country. But when in Rome, Horace reflects, he can scarcely enjoy Maecenas' company. Life in the city is a perpetual jostle and bustle. Others envy the poet's intimacy with his patron, or try to exploit it for their own ends, badgering him with requests, or trying to pry out of him the state secrets which, as Maecenas' confidant, they are sure he must possess. (When he is not forthcoming, they think he is being strategically cagey.) It is not surprising, therefore, that, whenever he is in the city, Horace longs ardently for his farm, where life is, at one and the same time, more relaxed and more serious. The verse translation of this part of the *Sermo* by Francis Fawkes (1720–77) is both close to the prose-sense of the Latin, and also usefully conveys, for the English reader, something of the affectionate warmth of Horace's tone:

> When shall I see my peaceful country farm,
> My fancy when with ancient authors charm?
> Or, lulled to sleep, the cares of life elude
> In sweet oblivion of solicitude?
> Oh, for those beans which my own fields provide,
> Deemed by Pythagoras to man allied;
> The savoury pulse served up in platters nice,
> And herbs high-relished with the bacon slice!
> Oh, tranquil nights, in pleasing converse spent;

> Ambrosial suppers that might gods content!
> When with my chosen friends (delicious treat!)
> Before the household deities we eat,
> The slaves themselves regale on choicest meat.
> Free from mad laws, we sit reclined at ease,
> And drink as much, or little, as we please.
> Some quaff large bumpers that expand the soul,
> And some grow mellow with a moderate bowl.
> We never talk of this man's house or vill',   (villa)
> Or whether Lepos dances well or ill;
> But of those duties which ourselves we owe,
> And which 'tis quite a scandal not to know:
> As whether wealth or virtue can impart
> The truest pleasure to the human heart;
> What should direct us in our choice of friends,
> Their own pure merit, or our private ends;
> What we may deem, if rightly understood,
> Man's sov'reign bliss, his chief, his only Good.[12]

After such a passage, the tale of the town and country mouse is clearly intended to come as a surprise. For Horace's *Sermo* is made to culminate not, as one might have expected, in a report of the poet's earnest philosophical conversations with his well-read peers, but in a nursery fable told (as a riposte to one of the company who has spoken enviously of a rich miser) by a rustic neighbour who, we are wryly told, *garrit anilis / ex re fabellas* ('rattles off old wives' tales that fit the case'). Horace is obviously taking a considerable risk, which will tax his celebrated urbanity and deft mastery of transitions to the full, if the ending of his poem is not to appear the grossest anti-climax.

Cowley, by including his retelling of the country mouse story in the *Essays*, immediately after his renderings of two of the most famous ancient encomia of rural happiness (the *O fortunatos nimium* passage from Virgil's second *Georgic*, and Horace's second *Epode*)[13] can be seen to be taking a risk which is in some ways analogous to that taken by Horace in *Sermones* 2.6. The subject of rural content is one in which, as we have seen, Cowley had a considerable personal investment, and on which, throughout the *Essays*, he sees his own thoughts overlapping with the weighty reflections of a number of his favourite writers, ancient and modern. Indeed, it might be argued that the risk taken by Cowley was in some respects even greater than that taken by Horace. For Horace's treatment of his own concerns throughout *Sermo* 6 and, indeed, throughout the *Sermones* as a whole, is, famously, shot through with a playful irony and self-mockery that frequently leave us slightly unsure how seriously we are to take him, and how seriously he is taking himself. (The joke about Pythagorean beans included in the praise of the Sabine farm, quoted above, provides a good example of this effect.) The surprise which is sprung on the reader at the end of the sixth *Sermo* is, therefore, one of a succession of daring shifts and transitions of tone and manner which the attentive reader of the *Sermones* has come to expect, and to see as characteristically Horatian. In contrast, Cowley's treatment of weighty matters in the *Essays* is, for all his occasional lightness of touch, generally several notches higher up the scale of earnestness and solemnity from that of Horace. His decision to reprint 'The Country Mouse' without apology among more obviously 'serious' treatments of rural happiness suggests his confidence that the poem was nothing short of a *tour de force* of witty poise.

Cowley's title describes his method of translation in 'The Country Mouse' as 'paraphrase', and Horace's text is, indeed, freely expanded and extensively reworked in the English version. Cowley relocates the Roman fable in an English setting, and discovers in his original a set of oppositions and contrasts which take on a distinctive edge in their new context. For the sentiments and characters of Cowley's mice embody the contrasts not only of country versus town, and of retirement versus the life of business and affairs, but also of traditional English rural life versus that of the post-Restoration Court, and of hearty hospitality in the English shires versus the refinement and social luxury of London. But in relocating Horace's fable in his own seventeenth-century England, Cowley was, as we shall see, at the same time responding to important dimensions of the tale in its original Latin. For the humour and point of Horace's fable, Cowley had evidently decided, turned on the Roman poet's decision to bestow upon the tiniest of mammals a series of susceptibilities, attributes and virtues which come into play whenever human beings begin to ponder seriously questions of pleasure, friendship, society and the good life. And there was, Cowley clearly thought, a particular felicity in Horace's location and dramatization of such matters in the setting of a convivial meal.

When Cowley's town mouse visits the country mouse in his rural retreat he is described as having an 'Epicurean mind'. This was a phrase which the poet clearly expected to have immediate resonance for contemporary readers, and it is, indeed, a key phrase in the poem. For, as Cowley realized, the significance of Horace's fable is closely bound up with the fact that it debates questions about the good life and true happiness in terms which derive ultimately from the teachings of a thinker to whom Horace was greatly indebted throughout his work: the Greek philosopher Epicurus (341–270 BC). It is therefore necessary, before proceeding further, to consider the important 'Epicurean' dimension of both Cowley's poem and its Horatian original.[14]

The doctrines of Epicurus centred on the need for human beings to achieve *ataraxia*, the state of freedom from mental and physical anxiety which alone can guarantee happiness and lasting pleasure – the true goals of all worthwhile human activity. The study of philosophy, Epicurus taught, can help men to achieve *ataraxia* by removing all those distracting and irrelevant cares which customarily afflict their lives. Human bodies and souls, like everything else in the world, consist of atomic particles in combination. The soul's mortality is certain, and there is, therefore, nothing to be feared in death. The gods live in perfect contentment in a remote realm, and play no part in the operations of our world. There is thus no need for men to live in hope of divine rewards or in dread of divine retribution. Our cosmos came into being by a chance combination of atoms and is merely one of an indefinite number of worlds, past, present and future. It is therefore vain to seek after any supernatural explanation of change and causation. Ambition and competition afflict men with the agonies of jealousy and failure. Public life should therefore be rejected in favour of an existence of serene retirement, in which, freed from those turmoils of hope and fear which result from the wrong kinds of intense emotional involvement, men can lay hold on life's solid pleasures and relish their existence with complete and untrammelled fullness.

It is easy enough to see how such a philosophy, centring as it does on doctrines of mortalism and hedonism, would be open to misconstruction and vilification. Indeed, from antiquity onwards, Epicureanism became frequently associated in the popular imagination with a particularly mindless form of gluttony and atheism, and Epicurus' Garden (the eponymous headquarters of his school of philosophy at Athens) was often thought of merely as a 'front' for profligate debauchery. His philosophy was, consequently, widely misunderstood and substantially neglected for much of the Middle Ages and the early modern era.[15]

Though a few earlier English writers had displayed some first-hand knowledge of Epicurus,[16] it was the substantial revaluation of Epicureanism in the 1640s by the French philosopher and mathematician Pierre Gassendi (1592–1655) that was to prove crucially influential on this side of the Channel. Two books have been recognized as having played a crucial role in mediating Gassendi's re-appraisal of the moral and ethical parts of Epicurus' philosophy to the English general reader. The year 1656 saw the publication of *Epicurus' Morals: Collected and Faithfully Englished*, the first popular exposition in any vernacular of Epicurus' moral teaching, prefaced by 'An Apology for Epicurus' by Walter Charleton (1619–1707), a physician who had probably known Cowley in the 1640s.[17] Four years later, in 1660, the poet and classical scholar Thomas Stanley (1625–78) published, in vol. III of his encyclopaedic *History of Philosophy*,[18] a comprehensive account, drawing substantially on Gassendi, of both the physical and moral aspects of the Epicurean system.

Cowley's Horatian mice

The English exponents of Epicurus were, like Gassendi, anxious to emphasize those aspects of Epicurean moral teaching which are closest to Christianity, and to palliate those parts of Epicurean doctrine which could not easily be squared with Christian belief. Both *Epicurus' Morals* and Stanley's *History* distinguish clearly between the pleasure which forms the *summum bonum* in the Epicurean system and the less desirable forms of pleasure which were the goal of other groups of hedonistic philosophers with which Epicureanism had, over the centuries, become popularly confused. Stanley makes a particularly sharp distinction in this respect between the Epicureans and the Cyrenaics, the sect founded by Aristippus of Cyrene, probably in the third century BC. The Cyrenaics, Stanley explains, asserted 'corporeal pleasure to be our ultimate end . . . not catastematic, permanent pleasure, which consisteth in privation of grief and a quiet, void of all disturbance, which Epicurus held'.[19] For them, pleasure was an intrinsic good 'though proceeding from the most sordid, dishonest thing'.[20] The only real pleasure, they believed, was to be found 'in motion'. They therefore rejected the Epicurean goal of *ataraxia*, and asserted that 'one pleasure differeth not from another pleasure, nor is one pleasure sweeter than another pleasure'.[21] Pleasure for the Cyrenaics, moreover, existed only in the immediate present. It was neither to be had from 'the remembrance of past goods, nor expectation of future complete pleasure, as Epicurus thought, for by time and expectation the motion of the soul is dissolved.'[22] Aristippus' life, says Stanley, was lived in accordance with his teaching, having been 'employed in luxury, sweet unguents, rich garments, wine and women'.[23]

The sharp contrast between the undiscriminating abandon of Cyrenaic hedonism, and the temperate reasonableness of the Epicurean position is clearly seen in Epicurus' own defence of his doctrine of pleasure, as rendered in *Epicurus' Morals*:

When we say that pleasure in the general is the end of a happy life, or the chiefest good, we are very far from understanding those pleasures which are so much admired, courted and pursued by men wallowing in luxury or any other pleasures that are placed in the mere motion or action of fruition, whereby the sense is pleasantly tickled; as some, either out of ignorance of the right, or dissent of opinion, or prejudice and evil will against us, have wrongfully expounded our words; but only this . . . : not to be pained in body, nor perturbed in mind.

For it is not perpetual feastings and drinkings; it is not the love of, and familiarity with, beautiful boys and women; it is not the delicacies of rare fishes, sweet meats, rich wines, nor any other dainties of the table that can make a happy life; but it is reason with sobriety, and consequently a serene mind; investigating the causes why this object is to be elected and that to be rejected; and chasing away those vain, superstitious and deluding opinions which would occasion very great disquiet in the mind.[24]

The wise man, in Epicurus' conception, is prudent but not avaricious. He should 'proportion his expenses as still to be laying up somewhat for the future, yet without avarice, and the sordid desire of heaping up wealth. For it is not the part of a wise man to neglect his household affairs.'[25] A wise, temperate housekeeping will assist in the creation of the desired tranquillity of mind. Drunkenness and debauchery are to be avoided, because they impair the true pleasures of eating; for

> those who are daily used to more sumptuous entertainments have their palates so furred and imbued and their stomachs so oppressed and weakened by the continual use and ingurgitation of them, that they neither relish nor swallow their meats and drinks with pleasure comparable to that which a sober man receives, whose gusto is sincere and appetite strong.[26]

Epicurus consequently finds the greatest joy in simple, home-produced fare:

> For mine own part, seriously, when I feed upon simple bread and water, and sometimes (when I would entertain myself somewhat more splendidly) mend my cheer with a little cheese, I apprehend abundant satisfaction therein, and bid defiance to those pleasures which the ignorant and sensual vulgar so much like and cry up in the magnificence of great entertainments; and hereupon, if I have no more than brown bread, decocted barley, and clean water, I think my table so well furnished as that I dare dispute felicity even with Jove himself.[27]

Several passages in Cowley's *Essays* show clearly that the poet had attended to the recent defence of Epicurus,[28] and that, while he showed little interest in the more technical aspects of Epicurus' teachings, he felt personally drawn to the philosopher's ideals of retirement, abstemiousness and spiritual tranquillity. Though he uses the term 'Epicure' in the popular, pejorative, sense on a number of occasions,[29] he shows himself, in the substantial 'Pindaric' ode which forms the second half of 'The Garden',[30] to be well aware of the current debates about 'true' and 'false' Epicureanism:

> When Epicurus to the world had taught,
>   That pleasure was the chiefest good,
> (And was perhaps i'th' right, if righly understood)
>   His life he to his doctrine brought,
> And in a garden's shade that sovereign pleasure sought;
> Whoever a true Epicure would be,
> May there find cheap and virtuous luxury.[31]

And in the essay 'Of Liberty', Cowley defends Epicurus and his followers specifically against those who had charged them with the indulging in unbridled gluttony:

> Metrodorus [one of Epicurus' leading disciples] said that he had learnt . . . to give his belly just thanks for all his pleasures. This by the calumniators of Epicurus'

philosophy was objected as one of the most scandalous of their sayings; which, according to my charitable understanding, may admit a very virtuous sense, which is that he thanked his own belly for that moderation in the customary appetites of it which can only give a man liberty and happiness in this world.[32]

The true Epicurean, who 'rationally guides' his pleasures, 'and is not hindered by outward impediments in the conduct and enjoyment of them' is thus, in Cowley's view, to be clearly distinguished from 'he who blindly follows all his pleasures' and is thus 'but a servant' to his own luxuriousness.[33]

For Cowley, as for Gassendi and his English popularizers, the main tenets of Epicurus' ethical teaching are compatible with the teachings of Christianity. The Epicurean command to live in the present, for example, can be reconciled without much difficulty with Jesus' exhortation (Matt. 6:34) to 'take . . . no thought for the morrow; for the morrow shall take thought for the things of itself':

We are all *ephēmeroi*, as Pindar calls us, creatures of a day, and therefore our Saviour bounds our desires to that little space; as if it were very probable that every day should be our last, we are taught to demand even bread for no longer a time.[34]

The speech in which Horace's town mouse attempts to persuade his country host to visit the city reveals that Cowley had seen connections between the contrasting conduct and sentiments of Horace's two mice and the contrast (as much a matter of debate in first-century BC Rome as in seventeenth-century England) between 'true' and 'false' Epicureanism. But these connections are not as simple as they might seem at first sight. For Horace, a close inspection of the Latin original suggests, is not merely using the pretext of his animal fable to propound a straightforward moral distinction between the admirable 'Epicurean' country mouse and his deplorable 'Cyrenaic' visitor.

Commentators have noted the closeness in phrasing and sentiment of some of the town mouse's words to passages elsewhere in Horace's *œuvre* where the poet is writing *in propria persona*.[35] Several of Horace's *Odes*, they remind us, are cast in the form of an urgent exhortation to surrender to the pleasures of wine and relaxation, since time is passing rapidly by, and the grave will soon claim us all. *Odes* 1.11, for example, ends with the famous exhortation to the poem's addressee, Leuconoe: *carpe diem, quam minimum credula postero* ('seize the present day, putting as little trust as may be in the morrow'). *Odes* 2.3 exhorts the politician Dellius to surrender to the enjoyment of wines, perfumes and rose-blossom, in full recognition of the frail brevity of life. Another such injunction occupies the central stanzas of *Odes* 2.11. Youth and beauty, Horace there asserts, are speeding fast away. Old age will soon put an end to the sports of love, just as spring flowers and moonlight soon pass away. We should therefore drink wine, while we are still able, and recline in careless ease under a lofty plane or pine tree, our locks garlanded with fragrant roses and perfumed with Syrian ointments. And in *Odes* 4.12, Horace invites Virgil to join him in a drinking party, and, mindful of death's dark fires, to cast serious thoughts aside, *dum licet* ('while [he] can'). The similarity of all these sentiments (and of some of their phrasing) to those voiced by the town mouse in *Sermones* 2.6 is clear enough:

> 'terrestria quando
> mortalis animas vivunt sortita neque ulla est
> aut magno aut parvo leti fuga – quo, bone, circa,
> dum licet, in rebus iucundis vive beatus,
> vive memor quam sis aevi brevis.' (93–7)

'Since as all creatures that live on earth have mortal souls, and neither great nor small can escape from death, therefore, my friend, while you may, live rich and happy amid delights; live ever mindful of how brief your life is!'

Some commentators, noting the discrepancy between the note of urgent melancholy which informs the hedonistic exhortations in the *Odes* and the true Epicurean *ataraxia* of life on Horace's Sabine farm in *Sermones* 2.6, have implied that Horace gave such sentiments to the town mouse merely to guy them and to expose their banality.[36] Such critics might, indeed, point to the mixture of 'high style' phrasing in this passage (the genitive *aevi* after *brevis*, the pompous epicizing tmesis, whereby the phrase *quo circa* is interrupted by the vocative *bone*) with the colloquialism of the town mouse's words a few lines earlier – *vis tu homines urbemque feris proponere silvis?* ('wouldn't you put people and the city above these wild woods?') – to support their suggestion that the creature is here being ridiculed. And the phrase *aut magno aut parvo*, they might also point out, is a punning joke, either meaning (metaphorically) 'great or small' or (literally) 'big or little (like a mouse)'.

But there are problems with an argument which suggests that Horace is *merely* ridiculing the sentiments of the town mouse's speech. First, it implies that Horace was striving for a philosophical consistency in his poetry which many would claim was no part of his purpose.[37] Secondly, it assumes that, when he came to write the passages in the *Odes* cited above, either his heart was not in them, or he had forgotten his own earlier exposure of their inadequacy. Commentators on *Sermones* 2.6, moreover, have pointed out that Horace is less single- and simple-minded in his treatment of the theme of rural retirement than such an interpretation would imply. Horace's *Sermo*, they note, with its constant play of implicitly and explicitly self-mocking irony, is as much, or almost as much, concerned to reveal the potential difficulties and absurdities involved in embracing a philosophy of serene Epicurean contentment in the country as it is to celebrate its attainment.

When Horace's town dweller articulates his 'city' philosophy, the poet, to be sure, never lets us forget the comedy latent in having such sentiments come from the lips of a mouse. The *terrestria* of the mouse's philosophy denote, for the mouse himself, merely all 'creatures who live on earth'. But for Horace and his readers, the word also has a more specific meaning in context: 'mice who scuttle along the ground'.[38] The little creature's speech, however, has been felt by many readers to be invested with a genuinely persuasive appeal; it immediately convinces his country host, and its force and attractiveness are also, it has been plausibly suggested, intended to be felt by the reader.[39] On such a reading, the town mouse's pre-echoes of Horace's *Odes* should be seen not as a simple matter of self-parody-in-advance, but rather as Horace using the comic framework of his mouse fable to subject both the hedonistic yearnings expressed later in the *Odes* and the gentler Epicureanism advocated earlier in this very poem to a process of comic testing, which does not involve the simple dismissal or disparagement of either. Horace, on this reading, is embodying in the figures of *both* mice sentiments and philosophical positions to which he is himself strongly drawn. The fable form allows him to present both positions with a sympathetic warmth, while simultaneously exposing the inherent potential for absurdity in each of them. It allows him, that is, a more poised, teasing and inclusive perspective on his own concerns than could easily be achieved by more straightforward means.

Cowley's rendering supports such a reading. For in his version of this section, the English poet, while slyly alerting us to the fact that the town mouse is by no means merely prompted by high philosophical motives, invests the city dweller's address to his country host with a genuine warmth and affection. And though there is certainly an element of flattery and patronage in his words, the town mouse's appreciation of the country mouse's virtue and greatness of soul (34–5), and of the 'bounty' and 'civility' which we have seen with our own eyes is expressed in the tone of genuine feeling, and he is made to seem sincerely concerned that his friend's talents should not remain unrecognized (like those of Thomas Gray's 'village Hampden') in rural oblivion. The town mouse, moreover, does not want his friend to remain a social exile in his 'obscure retreat' (where 'obscure', we observe, denotes the darkness of the mouse-hole as much as its remote provinciality) and stresses that the 'luxury' of the Court is potentially 'generous' – that its wealth affords opportunities which are simply not possible in the depths of the country.

Cowley strengthens the town mouse's commendation of the city by deliberately making him recall the ancient hero whose distinctive quality was precisely his questing thirst for knowledge of the diversity of human society. For when the town mouse tells his country host that he 'should see towns, and manners know, and men', he recalls the opening of Homer's *Odyssey* (which had been commended and translated by Horace himself in *Epistles* 1.2). The appeal of the city, as Cowley's town mouse presents it, is thus not merely the appeal of unbridled 'Cyrenaic' debauchery. It is, we note, the claims of 'bright Honour' as much as 'soft Pleasure' (49) which tempt the country mouse to make his journey, and we thus do not feel, when he leaves his hole, that he does so for reasons that are simply despicable or ignoble. The tone, moreover, in which Cowley's town mouse reminds his friend of human mortality does not so much resemble the haunted melancholy of the foolish Court libertines[40] who, in Dryden's words, 'Disturb their mirth with melancholy fits',[41] as the sprightly, tripping gusto of Cowley's *Anacreontics* – those delightful 'familiar and festive' poems of 'voluptuous morality'[42] which Cowley clearly found so congenial to translate, yet which are so different in spirit from the ascetic austerity recommended in the *Essays*.

The point can be confirmed by comparing the nonchalant shoulder-shrug of Cowley's town mouse (42–5) with the distinctly more anxious note of Thomas Creech's version (which nevertheless draws on Cowley's rhymes):

> Since all must die, and must resign their breath,
> Nor great, nor little is secure from Death;
> Then spend thy days in pleasure, mirth and sport,
> And live like one that minds his life is short.

– or with the melancholy cadence of Fawkes':

> Since all must die that draw this vital breath,
> Nor great not small can shun the shafts of Death;
> 'Tis ours to sport in pleasures while we may;
> For ever mindful of life's little day.[43]

Though in life Cowley may, from his very earliest years, have always felt the attractions of a life of retirement and contemplative solitude more powerfully than he ever felt the lure of the Court,[44] he was able, in the comic context of 'The Country Mouse', to invest 'the generous luxury of the Court' with a genuine appeal, and to present its social, sexual and culinary lure in all its multiple, insidious attractiveness. Cowley's wit, like Horace's, brings together and fuses into an effortlessly delightful unity the appeal of the city for both mice and men. For the 'cakes and pies of London' which are on the city mouse's mind are both the luxury human fare of the Restoration capital[45] and a natural lure for domestic rodents. And the 'thousand beauteous shes' who, the town mouse promises, will 'move' 'about' the country mouse and 'by high fare' be 'pliant made to love' are, at one and the same time the finely-dressed belles who crowd the ballroom floor in contemporary paintings of the Restoration Court, and little creatures scuttling around and nudging into one another in search of crumbs and scraps which have been dropped by the rooms' human occupants.

The success and delightfulness of Cowley's wit, however, depends crucially on such thoughts being left subtly implicit. When Christopher

Cowley's Horatian mice

Smart's town mouse addresses his country host as 'your mouseship', and rests his invitation to the town on the claim that

> mortal lives must have an end,
> And death all earthly things attend,
> Nor is there an escape at all
> For man or mouse, for great or small,

the translator ruins the effect by making the distinction (and thus the analogy) between man and mouse crudely explicit. William Dunkin fares slightly better when he has his town mouse declare:

> Since animals but draw their breath,
> And have no being after death;
> Since nor the little, nor the great,
> Can shun the rigour of their fate;
> At least be merry while you may,
> The life of mice is but a day.

But here, despite the attractive last line, it is the contrast between 'little' and 'great' that is drawn too overtly to our attention. The distinctive play of Horace's and Cowley's humour depends (as in Virgil's treatment of the bees in *Georgics* 4) on the poets' ability to select terms which are equally, and tellingly, apt in worlds of both human beings and tiny creatures. The reminder of the shortness (in human terms) of a mouse's life (for both are 'mortal') serves simultaneously to remind us of our own frailty.

If the 'Epicurean mind' of Cowley's town mouse combines a reasoned relish of urban delights with the voluptuous abandon of the Cowleian Anacreon, the life and sentiments of his country mouse accord closely with the ideals of Epicurus himself, as expounded in English by the popularizers of Gassendi. Like the wise man of *Epicurus' Morals*, Cowley's country mouse is sober, serious-minded and frugal. He is justly proud to display the carefully variegated delights of his 'noble' banquet, and to share them with his guest. The joyous spontaneity with which he invites the city mouse to the feast, and his willingness to 'sacrifice the day' to his tutelary 'Genius', denote that he his capable of relishing life's present pleasures in a way which is utterly untrammelled by false delicacy, luxuriousness, envy or ambition. His Epicureanism is manifested not as a consciously held creed or doctrine (as becomes apparent later, he is entirely unaware of the blessedness of his existence), but implicitly, in his very gesture and tone of voice:

> 'Freely', said he, 'fall on, and never spare!
> The bounteous gods will for tomorrow care!'

The country mouse's second line recalls several passages in Horace's *Odes* (e.g. 1.9.9), and Cowley has here penetrated to the very heart of what, for a number of English readers at least, seemed to represent the truly Epicurean freedom of mind. Horace had, at the beginning of his fable, noted the admirable capacity of his normally austere, even stingy, country mouse to *solvere* ('loosen') an *animum* ('soul') that was normally *artum* ('tight-reined, narrow') in acts of bounteous hospitality. This phrase of Horace's seems to have epitomized, for some English readers, the 'feast of reason and the flow of soul'[46] which was both cause and effect of a truly Epicurean contentment. For when, in 1684, John Dryden came to translate the twenty-ninth *Ode* of Horace's third book, a poem which he regarded as the quintessence of Horatian Epicureanism, and in which, significantly, Horace is inviting Maecenas to share a simple meal with him at his Sabine farm, he remembered, and incorporated, the phrase *solvere animum* from *Sermones* 2.6 where there was no direct justification in the text of the *Ode* itself:

> Leave for a while thy costly country seat,
>   And, to be great indeed, forget
> The nauseous pleasures of the great;
>   Make haste and come;
> Come and forsake thy cloying store;
>   Thy turret that surveys from high
> The smoke, and wealth, and noise of Rome
>   And all the busy pageantry
> That wise men scorn, and fools adore;
> Come, *give thy soul a loose*, and taste the pleasures of the poor.
>
> (my italics)

Dryden's appropriation of the phrase seems, in turn, to have been remembered by later translators of *Sermones* 2.6, who re-appropriated it for their version of the poem from which it had been derived in the first instance. Here, for example, is William Dunkin's rendering of Horace's description of the country mouse's frugality:

> Thrifty he was, and full of cares
> To make the most of his affairs,
> Yet in the midst of his frugality
> Would *give a loose* to hospitality.

And Christoper Smart translated the same passage thus:

> This mouse was blunt and giv'n to thrift,
> But now and then could make a shift
> (However rigid or recluse)
> With open heart to *give a loose*.

Though Cowley does not directly translate the Horatian phrase which so impressed Dryden, his country mouse manifests abundantly the freedom and

Cowley's Horatian mice

'loose of soul' which it evokes. Not for this mouse are the artificially cultivated Frenchified delicacies of the Restoration gourmet's table. His bacon and cheese are offered as an *hautgoust* – the anglicized pronunciation of the culinary term (which commonly rhymed in seventeenth-century English with 'August') matching the strong, pungent, 'peasant' flavour of the dish itself. It is the very simplicity of the meal which, the narrator observes, makes it truly worthy of the gods. The cheese and bacon are accompanied by the feast's crowning glory, which we are presumably intended to see as towering above the diners:

> a large chestnut, the delicious meat
> Which Jove himself (were he a mouse) would eat,

– the perfect murine equivalent of Epicurus' favourite meal, as described in *Epicurus' Morals*:

> . . . if I have no more than brown bread, decocted barley, and clean water, I think my table so well furnished as that I dare dispute felicity even with Jove himself.

Cowley's firm identification of the truly Epicurean nature of the country mouse's life enables him, uniquely among the English translators, to invest the country mouse's banquet with a genuine grandeur and attractiveness, while simultaneously extracting the maximum comedy from discovering such philosophically impeccable conduct and such hearty relish among the humblest of creatures.

The effect of the country mouse's exhortation would be much less, of course, without the carefully imagined details with which Cowley, like Horace, has coloured his fable from the very beginning. Cowley expands Horace's local touches considerably, but always keeps his additions within carefully judged bounds. In this respect, his version differs markedly from the rendering of Wye Saltonstall, whose *The Country Mouse, and the City Mouse, or A Merry Moral Fable, enlarged out of Horace, Serm., Lib. 2, Sat. 6*[47] expands Horace's thirty-nine lines to make a shapeless poem of nearly fifteen times the length of the original and reminds us that significant economy of means is as crucial a weapon in the Horatian armoury as narrative deftness and accomplished versification. But as well as being economically managed, Cowley's additions allow a greater variety of tones, attitudes and perspectives to coexist simultaneously than the renderings of any of his rivals. For the other translators of *Sermones* 2.6 can all be seen to have achieved their effect by one or other kind of selection and simplification (and thus coarsening) of Horace's wit. Cowley is unique in the number of elements in the Horatian original which he has been able to assimilate, mobilize and combine as integral parts of an English poem.

Commentators on Horace's original have noted how, from the beginning of the fable, the poet's manner both serves as a credible representation of the garrulous over-deliberateness of the tale's ostensible narrator, the rural neighbour Cervius, and simultaneously allows a larger and more diverse play of mind over the situation.[48] The secret of Horace's wit in the opening section of the fable, as in the speeches examined earlier, lies in the poet's selection of terms which bring out both the human and mousely dimensions of the situation without ever allowing the reader's mind to dwell too long on one at the expense of the other. In receiving his visitor, Horace's country mouse becomes a *paterfamilias* and *hospes*, who is made, wittily, to dispense with magnanimity the bounteous hospitality which is expected of the head of a Roman household. The feast which he provides for his guest is not merely an ordinary *cena* ('meal') but a *daps* – Horace uses the epic word for a religious banquet.[49] The fare is, moreover, amusingly similar in significant respects to the meals which, as we have been shown earlier in the *Sermo*, Horace himself enjoys with his friends at his country retreat.[50]

At the same time, we are reminded that the country mouse brings in the food for the meal in his mouth (85). The bacon which he serves his guest has already been nibbled and discarded by one of the local peasants (85–6). The *lolium* which he eats, is, in fact, the wild cereal darnel.[51] The *acinus* which he carries in his mouth might be (as it appears in many translations) a 'raisin', but the term might just as easily denote a humble 'berry', or even a 'pip'. In stressing (84) that the oats which the country mouse provides are long-grained (in contrast to the round, pea-like, vetches which they accompany) Horace, momentarily, provides us with a recognizably mouse's-eye view of the fare.[52] And when we are told that the town mouse is scarcely prepared to touch the country mouse's food *dente superbo* ('with squeamish tooth'), the joke depends on our seeing him curling his lip in a manner which to a mouse in natural habit, but which to a human observer inevitably denotes fastidious disdain.[53]

In his version, Cowley pursues a similar train of anthropomorphic wit, but completely rethinks and recasts Horace's Italian details in English terms, and finds his own, quite different, means of conveying Horace's mock-naïve/mock-heroic narrative manner. In the very first line we are alerted to the diminutive size of the story's hero by having our attention immediately drawn to the position of his hole – 'at the *large foot* of a fair hollow tree'. But the residence occupied by this mouse is, from his own point of view at least, an equivalent of Jonson's Penshurst or Carew's Saxham, a 'commodious' (comfortable and convenient) ancestral 'Hall' which, like the manorial 'seat' of a seventeenth-century English aristocrat or gentleman-farmer, leads straight out on to arable land – in this case, the ploughed fields where the mouse forages for scraps when harvest is over. The country mouse is

Cowley's Horatian mice

'substantial': burly and thick-set (and perhaps a little plump), and also moderately wealthy – a respected figure in the neighbourhood, the murine equivalent, perhaps, of a local Justice of the Peace.

The earlier translators, Drant, Beaumont and Fanshawe, treat Horace's opening with a dry literalness that misses the humour of the poet's imaginings almost entirely. John Ogilby, whose verse-paraphrase of the 'Aesopic' version of the fable is, like several of the other versified *Aesops*, fleshed out from Horace,[54] produces a banquet which, however accurately it may or may not reflect a mouse's diet, destroys Horace's anthropomorphic poise, since it seems, from the human side of the equation, distinctly unappetizing:

> Yet had she fruit, and store of pulse and grain,
>   Ants eggs, the bee's sweet bag, a star's fall'n jelly,
> Snails dressed i'th'shells, with cuckoo foam and rain,
>   Frog legs, a lizard's foot, a newt's pied belly,
> The cob and hard roe of a pickled herring   (head)
>   Got for a dog,
> As they did prog,   (poke about in search of food)
> And a rush candle purchased by pickering.   (foraging, plundering)

The eighteenth-century renderings of the episode tend to adopt a jauntiness and/or archness which just as effectively destroys the delicate balance of Horace's anthropomorphism. So anxious, it seems, are these translators not to be thought naïve, that they signal their sophisticated superiority in an all-too-obtrusive fashion, thus achieving their humour, as it were, at the mice's expense. In Dunkin's rendering, for example, the country mouse's presentation of his meal seems desperately haphazard, as if the poor creature has, from the start, effectively abandoned hope of being able to please his guest. His fears turn out to be amply justified. In this version, the country mouse

>   goes and freely fetches
> Whole ears of hoarded oats and vetches
> Dry grapes and raisins crossed his chaps,
> And dainty bacon, but in scraps,
> If delicacies could invite
> My squeamish courtier's appetite,
> Who turned his nose at every dish,
> And, saucy, piddled, with a 'Pish!'

Pope's rendering of the same passage similarly dilutes Horace's wit, this time by adding contemporary allusions – to Swift, of whose version of the first half of Horace's *Sermo* Pope's is a continuation and imitation, and to the low-grade Suffolk skimmed-milk cheese colloquially known as 'bang and thump'.[55] Pope's references to his own world are, to be sure, deftly incorporated, but seem more designed to draw attention to the poet's own ingenuity in discovering modern analogies than to convey the Horatian grandeur-in-absurdity of the mousely banquet:

> He brought him bacon (nothing lean);
> Pudding, that might have pleased a Dean;
> Cheese, such as men in Suffolk make,
> But wished it Stilton for his sake;
> Yet to his guest though no way sparing,
> He ate himself the rind and paring.

The question of Horatian poise is equally important when considering the touches of mock-heroic style, which colour Horace's fable. Mock-heroic, as usually defined, consists of the deployment of epic sentiment and diction in distinctly non-epic situations. By being forced to register the discrepancy between lofty manner and banal matter, it is said, the reader is brought to a heightened sense of the triviality of the events and the ludicrousness of the personages being depicted. In Horace's description of the mice's journey to the city, we are certainly intended to register an epic dimension to the narrator's style. The poet employs formulae and phrases (*haec ubi dicta . . . propositum peragunt iter; iamque tenebat . . .*) which momentarily assimilate the two creatures' journey to the nocturnal ventures of epic warriors, such as those of Diomedes and Odysseus in *Iliad* 10. We are, at the same time, never allowed to forget that their *vestigia* ('steps') are also mouse foot-marks, and that the country mouse is *levis* ('light') as he *exsilit* ('leaps out of') his hole.[56]

While most of the English translators make little or no consistent attempt to imitate Horace's mock-heroic style, Cowley displays an ingenious resourcefulness in replacing Horace's touches of epic tone with periphrases reminiscent of the Jacobean and Caroline mythological narratives which were popular in his youth. The Ovidian fancy of the sun going to bed in the arms of the sea-nymph Thetis (52–5) is close, for example, to a passage like the following from Francis Beaumont's *Salmacis and Hermaphroditus* (1602):

> Now was the Sun environed with the sea,
> Cooling his wat'ry tresses as he lay,
> And in dread Neptune's kingdom while he sleeps,
> Fair Thetis clips him in the wat'ry deeps.[57] (embraces)

But it is also difficult not to see an amused self-reference in Cowley's reference to 'witty poets'. The extravagantly fanciful comedy of Thetis drawing 'the modest curtains of the night', as in a four-poster bed, is, after all, characteristically Cowleian.

Cowley's resourcefulness is also seen in his discovery of English analogues for the precise touches of Roman detail which mark Horace's description of the city mansion. Instead of, like Horace, noting the play of light on the scarlet draperies which cover the ivory couches in the room, he has his mice dwarfed by the huge and grandly 'noble' Mortlake tapestries on the walls, and notes that, when the room eventually becomes empty, that is because the human beings have gone off to another room, in the customary Restoration manner so often recorded in Pepys' *Diary*,[58] for an after-dinner dance.

In his version, Pope, too, finds English substitutes for Horace's Roman details, this time inserting references to the *à-la-mode* architectural fashions of the 1730s:

> Away they come, through thick and thin,
> To a tall house near Lincoln's Inn;
> ('Twas on the night of a debate,
> When all their Lordships had sat late.)
> Behold the place, where, if a poet
> Shined in description, he might show it,
> Tell how the moonbeam trembling falls
> And tips with silver all the walls;
> Palladian walls, Venetian doors,
> Grotesco roofs, and stucco floors;
> But let it (in a word) be said,
> The moon was up, and men a-bed,
> The napkins white, the carpet red;
> The guests withdrawn had left the treat,
> And down the mice sat, *tête à tête*.

Here Pope also slyly incorporates references to two modern works of literature – to Romeo's description of the moon 'that tips with silver all these fruit tree tops' (*Romeo and Juliet*, II.ii.108), and to the famous evocation of moonlight on the plains of Troy in his own version of the *Iliad* (8.691–4):

> Around her [i.e. the Moon's] throne the vivid planets roll,
> And stars unnumbered gild the glowing pole,
> O'er the dark trees a yellower verdure shed
> And tip with silver ev'ry mountain's head.

The moment is carried off with considerable verve and spirit. But, as before, there is an element of self-conscious virtuosity in Pope's treatment which, if his poem is being considered specifically as a rendering of Horace, seems alien to the original. For the mock-heroic style and circumstantial details in Horace's fable appear, in context, to be neither designed merely to expose the ludicrousness of the mice nor to show the poet's own skill at clever literary allusions. So firmly has Horace, by this stage, established a sense of the mice's humanity-in-mouseliness, and so effortlessly are our minds now passing from human concerns to those of mice and back again, that the mock-heroic treatment seems to work more subtly than the simple mockery of the textbook definition. By showing the mice participating in an enterprise which has grand, formidable, mysterious and beautiful dimensions that are far beyond anything dreamt of in their philosophy, Horace simultaneously alerts us to the precariousness, fragility and self-delusion of our own enterprises as human beings. The mice are, as it were, simultaneously aggrandized and diminished by being seen as heroic warriors, just as human figures in epic are both ennobled and diminished by being involved with immortal gods whose power far exceeds their own, but who, nevertheless, care about, and participate in, the activities of human beings. The mock-heroic joke, in Horace's hands, works, as it were, simultaneously in both directions. The trivial is made grand and the grand made trivial.

Just as Pope has simplified the mock-heroic dimension of Horace's fable, so has he diminished Horace's description of the urban banquet:

> Our courtier walks from dish to dish,
> Tastes for his friend of fowl and fish;
> Tells all their names, lays down the law,
> 'Que ça est bon! ah goutez ça!
> That jelly's rich, this malmsey healing,
> Pray dip your whiskers and your tail in.'
> Was ever such a happy swain?
> He stuffs and swills, and stuffs again.
> 'I'm quite ashamed – 'tis mighty rude
> To eat so much – but all's so good.
> I have a thousand thanks to give –
> My Lord alone knows how to live.'

Pope's comedy, though, once again, managed with virtuosic gusto, once again fails to convey the specific function of this scene in Horace's original. For here Horace had momentarily assigned to his city mouse the role of *praegustator*, the slave who, according to the very latest Roman fashion, was employed to taste each item of food being presented to his master to make sure that it was of acceptable quality.[59] Horace's town mouse *veluti succinctus cursitat hospes* ('bustles about, acting the host in waiter-style'), offering carefully selected tit-bits to his guest (who eats reclining, in the Roman manner), and returning with courteous relish the hospitality which he had received in the country. Pope's town mouse, by contrast, is made into a connoisseur of gourmet conversation, who tastes the various dishes so that he can patronize his country companion with his knowledge of courtly couisine. The country mouse, for his part, is made a glutton, gauchely blurting out his surprise at his new-found good luck, while simultaneously expressing servile gratitude to his 'lordly' host. Our mirth is certainly provoked, but it is *at* the mice rather than *with* them that we laugh. Horace's delicate balance of sympathy and amusement has been abandoned in the interests of a more farcically mocking humour.

Cowley's Horatian mice

In sharp contrast, Cowley's version stresses the 'bounties' entertained by the town mouse, and the warm camaraderie and shared pleasure of both the little creatures, and we are allowed to participate in their delights, both by being shown the 'delicious bits' with which the floor is strewn, momentarily, from their point of view, and as we observe (80) that, even in his transformed circumstances, the country mouse's old frugal habits die hard. This amusedly affectionate play of sympathy encouraged here is also apparent in the narrator's mock-portentous intervention a few lines later (84ff), when the mice's new-found bliss is interrupted by the servants and dogs.

Here, as before, the shortness and insignificance of a mouse's 'mortal' life is assimilated, by Horace's and Cowley's anthropomorphic wit, to the shortness and insignificance of human ideals and ambitions. Horace, Cowley's rendering suggests, has ended his sixth *Sermo* with a fable which was both intended to reinforce and, simultaneously, to subject to humorous exposure earnest Epicurean vows of the kind enunciated in the first half of the poem. Sabine farmers, Roman poets, epic heroes and mice, the fable's comic logic seems to suggest, are, for all their apparent differences, faced with life-problems which are essentially the same. Life is uncertain and short for all of them. All have to decide how they will spend the short space of time which is allotted to them. All have an exaggerated sense of their own importance in the larger scheme of things, and for that reason make themselves unhappy by neglecting the true goods of life – even, perhaps at those very moments when they are pursuing the quest for happiness with the greatest passion and resolve, and expressing their ideals with the greatest elegance and eloquence. But since this state of affairs is inevitable, the tale implies, it is saner to laugh than to cry.

In his portrayal of the two mice, Horace, I have suggested, involved some of his own most deeply cherished ideals and aspirations. When the country mouse begs, at the very end of the poem, to be allowed to return to his hole in the country, the two key words, *tutus* ('safe') and *tenuis* ('simple', 'homely') which he employs are terms which Horace regularly used in his own evocations of country happiness.[60] (The latter term is also used by Horace of the *style* of his writing in praise of simplicity and moderation.) The blend of sympathy and affectionate mockery which characterizes this moment, like the rest of the fable is, therefore, at one and the same time, an act of dramatic imagination and an act of self-knowledge and self-criticism on the poet's part. In embodying his own passionate convictions in the conduct and pronouncements of a pair of mice, Horace is, without cynicism or loss of integrity, hinting at the potential absurdity of his own attempts, of any human being's attempts, to defeat or deny the inevitable conditions of life.

Cowley, too, I have suggested, found himself personally implicated in the conduct and sentiments of his two mice. Whereas elsewhere in the *Essays* he had treated the subject of rural retirement with a uniform commitment and earnestness that can make a reading of the volume as a whole a slightly monotonous experience, he had discovered while composing his imitation of Horace's tale, a means of subjecting his ideals of retirement (as well as the hedonistic zest of his earlier *Anacreontics*) to a delightful extension by means of the comic scrutiny allowed by the mouse-fable form. For Cowley, as much as for Horace, the fable was a voyage of self-discovery and gentle self-mockery, in which his own cherished notions could, by being miniaturized, be put in a larger, more inclusive, perspective. As in Horace's original, the country mouse's final longing for 'peace' – a term, we might note, resonant with significance for a poet who had just lived through a civil war – prefaced by a vow of apocalyptic earnestness to be hidden in the deepest obscurity,[61] is his mousely version of the longing for 'liberty' which receives such extensive elaboration in the *Essays*. The poem's warmly attractive geniality of tone and humorous perspective, and the self-knowledge achieved by the poet in its composition, are thus twin sides of the same coin. But Cowley's geniality, like Horace's, is no mere compromise or fence-sitting. Cowley's conclusion is as firm in its 'moral' as any of the 'Aesopic' versions of the story, though more tellingly and convincingly so, because the situation has been imagined so comprehensively, and in such attentive detail. Without 'peace', the country mouse comes to realize, none of the other goods of life, whatever attractions they might genuinely hold, have any validity or worth whatsoever. The country mouse's fully Epicurean conclusion is the more impressive because it has been tested by experience and seen in the round. It is in this way that, for all his version's apparent infidelity to its original, Cowley was able to offer a more convincing and inclusive creative response to the end of Horace's *Sermones* 2.6 than many a more 'accurate' version. For in his free rendering of Horace's fable of the two mice, Cowley was indeed, in T. S. Eliot's phrase, 'giving the original through himself and finding himself through the original'.[62]

6

FIGURES OF HORACE IN DRYDEN'S LITERARY CRITICISM[1]

Paul Hammond

> atque ursum et pugiles media inter carmina poscunt.[2]
>
> est ubi recte putat, est ubi peccat.[3]
>
> ast opere in tanto fas est obrepere somnum.[4]

None of these lines occurs in Renaissance texts of Horace, yet each is quoted by Dryden in one of his critical essays as if it were Horace's own *dictum*. Dryden often quoted from memory (which is itself a tribute to the inwardness of his assimilation of Horace), and seems to have thought that if the words he attributed to Horace made Horace's point, then that was good enough: pedantry would be inappropriate in a man of letters writing the kind of urbane essay in which Dryden excelled. Horace could even be cited in support of this attitude:

> non ego paucis
> offendar maculis: quas aut incuria fudit,
> aut humana parum cavit natura.   (*Ars* 351–3)
>
> I shall not take offence at a few blots which a careless hand has let drop, or human frailty has failed to avert.

As it happens, this is actually one of Dryden's favourite quotations from Horace.[5]

To dismiss these misquotations as the product of idleness or ignorance, as some modern scholars have done, would be an over-hasty and anachronistic judgement. Sometimes Dryden's quotations from Horace substitute a word from the editorial glosses for a word in the text, and sometimes the Renaissance and seventeenth-century editions which Dryden was using have readings which are no longer found in twentieth-century texts. Indeed, discussion of how Horace was read in seventeenth-century England needs to recognize that 'Horace' was not simply the received Latin text of his poetry: no text is 'received' as if from the hand of God, or a godlike poet, however familiar the term 'received text' may have become. Texts are made, not born, and Renaissance texts of Horace were made by generations of editors. While the text of Horace is not as perplexed by variants and cruces as that of some other classical poets, there are nevertheless many points at which the words of the Horatian poems which Dryden was reading were different from those which we read today. Furthermore, the text of the poetry was surrounded by an elaborate framework of commentary: while this varied from edition to edition, it would normally include glosses, literary and historical annotation, and perhaps a continuous prose paraphrase. These different elements in the commentary were usually presented as typographically distinct columns on the page, so that readers were provided with several different kinds of material out of which they would construct 'Horace'. In these circumstances it becomes inappropriate to insist upon the familiar distinction between text and margin: the marginal glosses become part of the text which the reader makes when interpreting the poetry, while parts of the commentary may slip into or displace portions of the poem in the reader's memory. So when Dryden read what Horace has to say about the ideal length for a play:

> neve minor neu sit quinto productior actu (Ars 189)

let no play be either shorter or longer than five acts.

he evidently noted the editorial gloss *brevior* for *minor* in Lubinus, for it was this combination of text and commentary which lodged in his mind and generated this ostensible quotation from Horace in the *Essay of Dramatic Poesy*:

> neu brevior quinto, neu sit productior actu (1.34)

This may not be what Horace actually wrote, or even what any Renaissance editor actually printed, but it is one reader's rewriting (and one writer's rereading) of Horace. (The new line, with its different vocabulary and word-order, even scans, as one would expect Dryden to have ensured.)

This remaking of Horace at the detailed, local level, is a miniature version of the assimilation and rewriting of his critical precepts which had been a feature of literary theory since the Renaissance. The Horace which Dryden read was more than the collection of lines and glosses which he found when he opened his copy of Lubinus' edition: he was reading Horace via the Renaissance theorists who had codified and extended what they thought of as classical principles. He was also associating Horace with other ancient critics, particularly with Aristotle, and the two are frequently named together in Dryden's essays, forming a double-headed authority. Later on, when Dryden discovers Longinus, the treatise *On the Sublime* is added to the *Poetics* and the *Ars Poetica* as the texts which appear to generate and authenticate his critical theory, each text subtly modifying the way in which its companions

> 814   Q. HORATII FLACCI
> OMNE *tulit punctum, qui miscuit utile dulci,*
> *Lectorem delectando, pariterque monendo.*
> 345 *Hic meret æra liber Sosiis: hic & mare transit,*
> *Et longum noto scriptori prorogat ævum.*
> *Sunt delicta tamen, quibus ignovisse velimus:*
> *Nam neque chorda sonum reddit, quem vult manus*
> *& mens,*
> *Poscentique gravem persæpe remittit acutum;*
> 350 *Nec semper feriet, quodcumque minabitur, arcus.*
>   *Verum*

sublimes equis insidentes. *Nannius.* Turneb. lib. 19. cap. 9. & lib. 28. cap. 26. & lib. 29. cap. 35. *(Celsi prætereunt.*] Juvenes excelso animo contemnunt poëmata nulla voluptate condita. *Rhamnes, &c.*] Equites Romani à Romulo sic appellati.

343. *Omne tulit punctum.*] Omne suffragium abstulit seu meruit. Veteres suffragia ac sententias per tabulas ferebant. unde *lex Tabularia* dicta ea, qua illius, cui quisque astipularetur candidatorum aut competitorum, nomini punctum (vulgo *voces* vocamus) adscribebat. Horat.

Suffragiorum puncta non tulit decem.
Nannius. *Omne tulit punctum.*] Omnibus & senum & juvenum suffragiis ,præstantissimus Poëta judicatur, qui dulcis est in poëmate & utilis.

345. *Hic meret æra liber.*] Talis liber ditat bibliopolas, & in multas terras diffunditur. *Hic meret æra liber.*] Istiusmodi poëma pretium meretur & multos reperit emptores. *Sosiis.*] Sosii librarii insignes fuerunt, qui maximum quæstum vendendis libris faciebant : quorum etiam mentio Epist. 1. ad librum suum :

Scilicet ut prostes Sosiorum pumice mundus.
Nannius. *Sosiis*, Bibliopolis seu scriptoribus librariis. *Transit.*] Ad exteras nationes.

346. *Et longum noto scriptori.*] Talis, inquit, liber fama auctorem nobilitat,

& in multa sæcula durat. Horat. de seipso:
Exegi monumentum ære perennius.
Nannius. *Prorogat ævum.*] Nam præstantes Poëtæ etiam mortui vivunt.

347. *Sunt delicta tamen.*] Monet ignoscendum esse delictis, quæ occurrunt pauca in opere longo. Hoc confirmat duobus similibus; uno à citharœdis sumpto; altero à sagittariis. Causas autem ejusmodi delictorum exponit duas, injuriam & ingenii imbecillitatem. Dein per antithesin monet, non esse ignoscendum, si injuria nimis magna sit, ac proinde si delicta nimis multa, & contra virtutes nimis paucæ. Hanc sententiam confirmat item à similibus duobus; quorum prius à librario, posterius à citharœdo rursus sumptum est. *Piscator. Sunt delicta tamen quibus.*] Sunt quædam Poëtarum errata. *Velimus.*] Ignovisse oportet.

348. *Nam neque chorda sonum reddit.*] Probat superiora, exemplo soni ac toni. Non enim semper destinata mentis assequi possumus, neque perpetuo quem optamus cithara sonum reddet. Et hoc venia dignum, si rarum; si perpetuum, intolerabile. Nannius. *Chorda sonum reddit.*] Ut Musici aliquando errant, sic etiam Poëtæ. *Quem vult manus.*] Sonum, quem manus & voluntas expetit.

349. *Poscentique gravem.*] Citharœdo. *Remitti acutum.*] Reddit sonum acutum. 350. *Nec semper feriet.*] Probat altera

A page from *Q. Horatius Flaccus cum commentariis selectissimis variorum . . . Accurante Corn. Schrevelio* (Leiden, 1663), from the copy in the Brotherton Collection, Leeds University Library. The small capitals mark out line 343 as one of Horace's important *dicta*, while the notes provide glosses and paraphrases culled from various editors, together with the citation of parallel passages in Horace and other writers.

are read, and the three together encouraging a continually changing relationship between Dryden's respect for tradition and his delight in novelty, his equally strong attraction to restraint and to audacity. Furthermore, Dryden's reading of Horace was influenced by the combination of deference and difference which characterized his relation to his great predecessors in what seemed to him to be the English Golden Age: the sublime Shakespeare and the judicious Jonson. Jonson, as the deliberately classical dramatist, the self-assured critic, the man who had defined English classicism for his generation and for his 'sons', and, additionally, as the translator of Horace's *Ars Poetica*, was a dominating father-figure whom Dryden had to face, and he undid the massive, mythological status of Jonson partly by using some of the arguments about the value of change and modernity which he found in Horace.

Dryden and his contemporaries in the early 1660s were self-consciously engaged in the project of recreating English literary (and particularly theatrical) culture. The poems which greeted the return of Charles Stuart from exile in 1660, including Dryden's own *Astraea Redux*, made the appropriate Virgilian gestures which cast him in the role of the second Augustus, about to preside over a new Golden Age of peace and poetry.[6] In addition to being politically useful, the rhetoric of Augustanism provided an idiom for the development of a new literary criticism, a set of principles and formulae which helped to fashion a debate about the best kinds of dramatic form and language, about the ethics and strategies of satire, and about the comparative value of ancient and modern writing. All this was done partly as an act of self-definition, an assertion of difference and a claim for worth made by writers who were conscious both of their pre-war masters and of their contemporaries in France. Dryden was one of a group of writers who used Horace to work out a code and a vocabulary of literary criticism which would sustain, advertise and analyse the new creative achievement of Restoration England.[7] This criticism often relates somewhat awkwardly to the literary works themselves: sometimes the claims made in the manifestos are exaggerated; very often the poems and plays work in more complex ways than one might suppose from the comparatively limited terminology and scope of the critical essays. Moreover, this critical activity was never disinterested: it was always influenced by rivalries and friendships, both personal and professional, and was frequently skewed by flattery; for flattery was the inevitable idiom spoken by financially dependent writers in a feudal literary world dominated by vain and volatile lords. Horace is therefore used as a rhetorical flourish to authenticate a flagging argument, or to humour a conceited earl, as well as to work out a principled case. It is the purpose of this essay to explore the deployment of Horace by Dryden and his opponents in their rhetoric of criticism and compliment.

Figures of Horace in Dryden's literary criticism

In Dryden's first sustained work of criticism, the *Essay of Dramatic Poesy* (1668), Horace is frequently invoked as an authority in the debate between the four friends – Crites, Lisideius, Eugenius and Neander – over the theory and practice of drama. But how can Horace be used as an authority on this topic? The minute, often inadvertent, rewriting which takes place in some of Dryden's Horatian quotations reminds us that Dryden is as much the author of these *dicta* as Horace. Frequently Horace is deployed in the *Essay* because he is the pre-eminent classical critic who can be used to license and authenticate a form of modernism. The founding of Restoration modernism proceeds through the rhetoric of classicism: the assertion of independence licenses itself through the quotation of authority. The very practice of quoting Horace in fragments subordinates him to the needs of the modern writer, transposing his voice into the voice of Dryden. In the case of the *Essay*, however, Dryden himself speaks through several voices; his four characters articulate a range of views, and each uses Horace for his own purposes.

The *Essay* is particularly concerned with how contemporary playwrights should be judged in comparison with their precursors, both from the ancient world and from pre-war England. Crites (a figure based upon Dryden's brother-in-law Sir Robert Howard, a dramatist and translator) asserts that little contemporary writing is of any worth:

There are so few who write well in this age ... they neither rise to the dignity of the last age, nor to any of the ancients. (I.23)

But Eugenius (modelled on the Earl of Dorset) defends his contemporaries, and in order to establish his modernism effectively he cites one of the ancients:

there is no man more ready to adore those great Greeks and Romans than I am: but on the other side, I cannot think so contemptibly of the age I live in, or so dishonourably of my own country, as not to judge we equal the Ancients in most kinds of poesy, and in some surpass them; neither know I any reason why I may not be as zealous for the reputation of our age, as we find the Ancients themselves in reference to those who lived before them. For you hear Horace saying,
>indignor quicquam reprehendi, non quia crasse
>compositum, illepideve putetur, sed quia nuper. [*Ep*.2.1.76–7]

[I am impatient that any work is censured, not because it is thought to be coarse or inelegant in style, but because it is modern.]

And after:
>si meliora dies, ut vina, poemata reddit,
>scire velim, pretium chartis⁸ quotus arroget annus?
>[*Ep*.2.1.34–5]

> [If poems are like wine which time improves, I should like to know what is the year which gives fresh value to writings.] (1.23)

Here Eugenius is citing the quintessential classical authority in support of a modernist position. True classicism lies not in servile reverence for past masters but in learning from them, in emulating them, and – in so far as one's own abilities and the resources of the age permit – surpassing them. Eugenius' position is itself thoroughly classical, for it is in tune both with Horace and with Ben Jonson, who wrote in his *Discoveries* (himself translating Vives):

> I know nothing can conduce more to letters, than to examine the writings of the ancients, and not to rest in their sole authority, or take all upon trust from them... For to all the observations of the ancients, we have our own experience, which, if we will use, and apply, we have better means to pronounce. It is true they opened the gates, and made the way, that went before us, but as guides, not commanders.[9]

Crites himself is forced later in the discussion to concede that if Homer and Virgil had lived in the Restoration, they would inevitably have written differently:

> I will grant thus much to Eugenius, that perhaps one of their poets, had he lived in our age,
>
> > si foret hoc nostrum fato delapsus in aevum [S 1.10.68]
>
> [if he had fallen by fate on this age of ours]
>
> (as Horace says of Lucilius) he had altered many things; not that they were not as natural before, but that he might accommodate himself to the age he lived in. (1.43)

Dryden makes Crites articulate his own understanding of how one approaches the classical heritage: cultures change, and each age has its own distinctive resources:

> It has been observed of arts and sciences, that in one and the same century they have arrived to a great perfection; and no wonder, since every age has a kind of universal genius which inclines those that live in it to some particular studies. (1.26)

Hence one might expect Crites to argue that one should accommodate oneself to historical change by being faithful to the spirit rather than the letter of the classical tradition, but instead he exhibits an absolute regard for ancient literary achievement which is combined with a dogmatic disparagement of modern writers and modern society.

Whether or not this inconsistency in Crites' argument is a piece of mischief on Dryden's part, teasing his brother-in-law, it is an example of the inescapable tensions which are apparent in several of the attempts in the *Essay* to use Horace as an authority. At the beginning of their discussion the four characters discover that they need to define a play, 'because neither Aristotle, nor Horace, nor any other who writ of that subject, had ever done it' (1.25), and the definition which is offered by Lisideius (who represents the

Figures of Horace in Dryden's literary criticism

Francophile poet and dramatist Sir Charles Sedley) combines what sounds like the authentically Horatian aim of 'the delight and instruction of mankind' with a Jonsonian interest in the 'humours' (1.25). The *Essay* assumes that there is no problem here, no disjunction between the two sources of the vocabulary which informs this definition. The stress of appropriation becomes more apparent when Neander (the 'new man', standing for Dryden himself) defends the use of rhyme in drama against Crites; he argues that since tragedy

> is wont to image to us the minds and fortunes of noble persons, and to portray these exactly; heroic rhyme is nearest nature, as being the noblest kind of modern verse.
>
> > indignatur enim privatis et prope socco
> > dignis carminibus narrari caena Thyestae,   [*Ars* 90-1]
>
> [for the feast of Thyestes scorns to be told in the idiom of daily life which befits the comic sock.]
>
> says Horace). And in another place,
>
> > effutire leves indigna tragoedia versus.   [*Ars* 231]
> > [tragedy scorns to babble trivial verses.]   (1.87)

Moreover, says Neander, to deny a poet the use of rhyme is to deny him that liberty of daring anything, *quidlibet audendi* (*Ars* 10), which Horace claimed for him. Though this may seem to be an opportunistic, even a specious use of Horace, the argument for the nobility and naturalness of rhyme is an instance of Dryden's concern to work out a distinctively contemporary interpretation of classical principles.

When Lisideius praises the achievement of modern French drama, he is careful to use Horatian quotations to underline the value of those practices which differ most from the English. French dramatists, unlike the English, he says, ground their plays 'upon some known history; according to that of Horace, *ex noto fictum carmen sequar*' [*Ars* 240] [I shall aim at poetry moulded from what is known.] (1.46) He quotes Horace's praise of Homer:

> > atque ita mentitur, sic veris falsa remiscet,
> > primo ne medium, medio ne discrepet imum.   [*Ars* 151-2]
>
> [and so skilfully does he invent, so closely does he blend facts and fiction, that the middle is not discordant with the beginning, nor the end with the middle.] (1.46)

and explains that the French dramatist goes even further, for

> he so interweaves truth with probable fiction, that he puts a pleasing fallacy upon us; mends the intrigues of fate, and dispenses with the severity of history, to reward that virtue which has been rendered to us there unfortunate.   (1.47)

This clearly extends Horace's point so far as to make it a completely different one, for Horace is not complimenting Homer on his reshaping of history in the interests of providing a clear moral lesson: Horace is not Le Bossu, though Lisideius is enlisting him here in support of exactly that understanding of the need for dramatic or epic action to disclose an edifying principle which Le Bossu was to propose a few years later in his influential *Traité du Poème Epique* (1675). Similarly, when Lisideius discusses the French preference for avoiding certain kinds of action on stage, he quotes Horace's account of what it is fit to show and what to relate (*Ars* 179–88); he then offers a gloss on Horace's text and follows this with an extension of the argument into wholly new territory:

That is, those actions which by reason of their cruelty will cause aversion in us or, by reason of their impossibility, unbelief, ought either wholly to be avoided by a poet, or only delivered by narration. To which we may have leave to add such as to avoid tumult (as was before hinted), or to reduce the plot into a more reasonable compass of time, or for defect of beauty in them, are rather to be related than presented to the eye.
(1.53)

The first sentence quoted here is in the manner of (and probably follows) the gloss in Schrevelius' edition;[10] then, in that courteous assumption of Horace's permission to add to his text ('we may have leave to add') we see the Restoration's characteristic combination of reverence and nonchalance in its appropriation of Horace. The phrase 'we may have leave to add' may translate Schrevelius' *addendae*, but what it heralds is not an interpretative gloss on Horace but new political and aesthetic imperatives for the Restoration world. These gestures form a supplement, in the Derridean sense,[11] supplanting through appearing merely to add, and effacing Horace while ostensibly preserving his text and his name in order to give the new opinion a point of origin which confers on it Horatian authority, if not authenticity.

Underlying much of the debate in the *Essay of Dramatic Poesy* is the question whether the classical writers (with what is often seen as their privileged access to 'nature'), belong in some trans-historical realm where they exemplify eternally valid artistic principles, or whether they are to be read within history, thought of as being subject to the contingencies of their times, and particularly to the limitations of the language which was available to them. Eugenius calls attention to the difficulty of judging the wit in the comedies of Plautus, since they are written in a language which is now dead, and he cites Horace's observation that preceding generations praised Plautus' verse and wit, which to his own generation seemed crude. With changing times, judgement changes, and language changes. Eugenius quotes the lines in the *Ars Poetica* which observe that language alters along with everything else in nature; words wither and fall away like leaves on forest trees:

Figures of Horace in Dryden's literary criticism

> multa renascentur quae jam cecidere, cadentque
> quae nunc sunt in honore vocabula, si volet usus:
> quem penes arbitrium est et jus et norma loquendi. (*Ars* 70-2)

> Many terms that have fallen out of use shall be born again, and those shall fall that are now in repute, if usage so will it, in whose hands lies the judgement, the right and the rule of speech.

The recognition here that *usus*, usage, is the arbiter of language is important for Dryden. He does not advocate attempts to stabilize the language, or to dictate what is acceptable and what is not from some authoritative standpoint; rather, he understands that social usage shapes the language which writers employ, and therefore all writers are subject to criticism by their successors when the language has changed. Nevertheless, the fluidity of English when compared with Latin or Greek did trouble Dryden. In the Epistle Dedicatory to *Troilus and Cressida* (1679) he writes that he often has to test the accuracy of his own English by translating it into Latin, 'thereby trying what sense the words will bear in a more stable language' (1.239), while in the Preface to the same play he remarks that the Greek language at the time of Aeschylus 'was arrived to its full perfection; they had then amongst them an exact standard of writing and of speaking. The English language is not capable of such a certainty; and we are at present so far from it that we are wanting in the very foundation of it, a perfect grammar' (1.239). Accordingly, Dryden welcomed Lewis Maidwell's Latin grammar with a commendatory poem which saw the work as helping to provide a basis for good English.[12] Dryden has absorbed what Horace says about the instability of language, but applies this primarily to his own English tongue, regarding classical Latin as a stable resource by which contemporary vernacular usage may be judged. Social usage, then, is not the final arbiter: classical Latin is the ultimate touchstone.

The question of poetic language is one of the topics on which Dryden most frequently turns to Horace for support. Dryden's emphasis changes according to the particular case at issue, and according to the opponent whom he is answering, but he seems particularly concerned with the issue of poetic licence. In the *Defence of An Essay of Dramatic Poesy* (1668) he replies to Howard's denigration of the effort to establish rules for dramatic criticism. Howard had argued that dramatic poets are allowed considerable latitude in what they write, but Dryden contends that

> they cannot be good poets who are not accustomed to argue well. False reasonings and colours of speech are the certain marks of one who does not understand the stage; for moral truth is the mistress of the poet as much as of the philosopher: poesy must resemble natural truth, but it must *be* ethical. Indeed the poet dresses truth, and adorns nature, but does not alter them:

> ficta voluptatis causa sint proxima veris. [Ars 338]
>
> [fictions meant to please should be close to the real.] (1.120–1)

So the poet is always to follow nature, as Dryden had insisted in his defence of rhyme as a natural mode for writing tragedy. On the other hand, particularly after his discovery of Longinus, Dryden is also concerned to stress the poet's liberty of imagination, and to defend the use of audacious imagery. In this he is constructing a defence of his own use of strong metaphor, both in his early poems, where late metaphysical conceits are mixed with adaptations of Virgil's bold figures and Ovid's witty turns, and also in his heroic plays, whose extravagances were mocked in the *Censure of the Rota* pamphlets in 1673. In *The Author's Apology for Heroic Poetry and Poetic Licence* (1677) – which is appropriately prefixed to *The State of Innocence*, the operatic play in which Dryden's imagination tested the limits of theatrical representation in adapting *Paradise Lost* for the stage – he commends Horace for his own bold use of metaphor, saying that Horace and Virgil, 'the severest writers of the severest age, have made frequent use of the hardest metaphors, and of the strongest hyperboles' (1.200). He defends poetic licence, which is 'the liberty, which poets have assumed to themselves in all ages, of speaking things in verse which are beyond the severity of prose' (1.205), a licence which is properly used in the development of tropes and figures. Dryden pursues his ideas about poetic licence by reference to Horace:

> How far these liberties are to be extended, I will not presume to determine here, since Horace does not. But it is certain that they are to be varied, according to the language and age in which an author writes. That which would be allowed to a Grecian poet, Martial tells you, would not be suffered in a Roman. And 'tis evident that the English does more nearly follow the strictness of the latter than the freedoms of the former. Connection of epithets, or the conjunction of two words in one, are frequent and elegant in the Greek, which yet Sir Philip Sidney, and the translator of Du Bartas, have unluckily attempted in the English; though this, I confess, is not so proper an instance of poetic licence, as it is of variety of idiom in languages. (1.206)

In this passage Dryden still adheres to the rhetoric of authority and permission: poets need licence (in both senses: 'freedom' and 'authorisation'), but the licence needs limits. Since Horace has not spelt out the limits of the permissible, Dryden does not feel permitted to do so for himself. But this rhetoric is ultimately a way of asserting freedom and modernity, and of embracing historical change and difference: since languages have different capacities, the attempts by Sidney and Sylvester to make close imitations of classical diction ineptly constrain rather than liberate the poetic imagination. A more radical freedom, which is at once a more radical faithfulness, is required.

Figures of Horace in Dryden's literary criticism

In his 'Account of the Ensuing Poem' prefixed to *Annus Mirabilis* (1667) Dryden discusses two kinds of linguistic innovation which a poet can make: the coining of new words, and the development of metaphors through the reapplication of familiar terms in unfamiliar senses. Dryden praises Virgil for presenting nature in a particularly intense form, making us see things in a new way:

We see the objects he presents us with in their native figures, in their proper motions; but we so see them, as our own eyes could never have beheld them so beautiful in themselves . . . while we read him, we sit, as in a play, beholding the scenes of what he represents. To perform this, he made frequent use of tropes, which you know change the nature of a known word by applying it to some other signification; and this is it which Horace means in his *Epistle to the Pisos*:

> dixeris egregie, notum si callida verbum
> reddiderit junctura novum. [*Ars* 47–8]

[you will express yourself most happily if a skilful joining makes a familiar word new.] (1.99–100)

Dryden's analysis of language keeps returning to the idea of the 'natural'. Virgil's language heightens our perception so that in our imaginations we see objects 'in their native figures' but more beautiful; and this is achieved by 'changing the nature of a known word'. The difficulty of the topic is apparent in the paradoxical twists to which Dryden's language is subjected: it is through deviation from the 'natural' signification of words that the poet allows us to see nature more clearly, yet the 'natural' signification of a word can only be that meaning which it receives from usage, not from nature. Far from being a licence for bombast or far-fetched conceits, this position actually provides both a rationale for poetic invention and a check upon it: inventive metaphor is necessary to make us see nature clearly; at the same time, metaphor which does not achieve that end because it merely calls attention to its own ingenuity, has failed.

At the heart of Dryden's theory is the assumption that great writers are in closer touch with nature than the ordinary reader: Shakespeare, for instance, 'needed not the spectacles of books to read nature; he looked inwards, and found her there' (1.67). Readers can be helped to regain that closeness and clarity of perception through the apparent novelty (which is actually a radical faithfulness to nature) of poetic language. Hence imitation of such masters can lead the modern poet back to nature, provided that this imitation is not a servile copying but an imaginative recreation in the modern idiom which takes account of historical change. Dryden's own linguistic practice in *Annus Mirabilis* has, he says, been founded upon Virgil's, and he cites Horace once again in order to provide an authoritative justification for his practice of introducing new words or turns of phrase into English verse:

I have followed him everywhere, I know not with what success, but I am sure with diligence enough; my images are many of them copied from him, and the rest are imitations of him. My expressions also are as near as the idioms of the two languages would admit of in translation ... some words ... I have innovated (if it be too bold for me to say *refined*) upon his Latin; which, as I offer not to introduce into English prose, so I hope they are neither improper, nor altogether unelegant in verse; and in this Horace will again defend me:

> et nova, fictaque nuper, habebunt verba fidem, si
> Graeco fonte cadant, parce detorta. [*Ars* 52–3]

[words, though new and of recent make, will win acceptance if they spring from a Greek fount, and are drawn from there sparingly.]

The inference is exceeding plain; for if a Roman poet might have liberty to coin a word, supposing only that it was derived from the Greek, was put into a Latin termination,[13] and that he used this liberty but seldom, and with modesty: how much more justly may I challenge that privilege to do it with the same prerequisites, from the best and most judicious of Latin writers? (1.100–1)

This last sentence is an approximate translation of the lines which follow on from those which he has just quoted:

> quid autem
> Caecilio Plautoque dabit Romanus, ademptum
> Virgilio Varioque? ego, cur acquirere pauca
> si possum, invideor? cum lingua Catonis et Enni
> sermonem patrium ditaverit, et nova rerum
> nomina protulerit? (*Ars* 53–8)

Why indeed should Romans grant this licence to Caecilius and Plautus, and refuse it to Virgil and Varius? And why should I be grudged the right of adding, if I can, my little fund, when the tongue of Cato and of Ennius has enriched our mother-speech and brought to light new terms for things?

The 'liberty' which Dryden claims here is the freedom to imitate, so that independence and the ability to make an individual contribution to the language of poetry are figured as the imitation of the classical model. Appropriately, this assertion of independence is itself a translation: Dryden is revoicing Horace, in defence of his practice of revoicing Virgil.

The understanding of his own linguistic practice as being historically contingent goes along with a reappraisal of the language of his dramatic predecessors. In the *Essay of Dramatic Poesy* Dryden had said that Shakespeare's languge was 'many times flat, insipid; his comic wit degenerating into clenches, his serious swelling into bombast' (1.67), but it is Jonson who is subjected to the sharper scrutiny. In the Epilogue to *The Conquest of*

Figures of Horace in Dryden's literary criticism

Granada, Part II (1672) Dryden remarked that Jonson's comedy suffered from having been written in an unsophisticated age 'when men were dull, and conversation low'.[14] Subsequently the language both of writing and of ordinary social converse has become more refined. Elaborating this charge with detailed analysis of quotations from Jonson in his *Defence of the Epilogue* (1672), Dryden argues that the English language is now more exact and copious than in Jonson's day. But new words have to be used with caution:

> They, who have lately written with most care have, I believe, taken the rule of Horace for their guide; that is, not to be too hasty in receiving of words, but rather to stay till custom has made them familiar to us:
>
> quem penes arbitrium est, et jus, et norma loquendi. [*Ars* 72]
>
> [in whose power lies the judgement, the right and the rule of speech.] (1.176)

Once again, social custom is the arbiter of language.

Besides the addition of new words, the language is refined by the poetic development of metaphor. This, says Dryden, is what Horace meant in a contested passage:

> There is yet another way of improving language, which poets especially have practised in all ages: that is, by applying received words to a new signification. And this, I believe, is meant by Horace, in that precept which is so variously construed by expositors:
>
> dixeris egregie, notum si callida verbum
> reddiderit junctura novum. [*Ars* 47–8]
>
> [you will express yourself most happily if a skilful joining makes a familiar word new.]
>
> And, in this way, he himself had a particular happiness: using all the tropes, and particularly metaphors, with that grace which is observable in his Odes, where the beauty of expression is often greater than that of thought. (1.177)

Here Dryden is selecting from the commentators that interpretation of Horace which most suits his purpose: setting aside the majority opinion amongst Renaissance editors – that Horace is referring to how one links newly coined or borrowed words with familiar ones in order to make their significance clear – he seeks out instead the opinion recorded (though rejected) by Cruquius, that Horace is alluding to the creation of metaphors by the transferring of words from one signification to another.[15]

Horace did not innovate much, but he refined the language by his 'choice of words, and heightening of their natural signification' (1.177). Dryden describes this process as grafting new meanings on to old words, so that the poet becomes a horticulturalist, applying his art to nature in order to repair the loss of those words which have fallen away like leaves from the trees. Those poets who do this are themselves continually falling away and being replaced:

> By this graffing, as I may call it, on old words, has our tongue been beautified by the three forementioned poets, Shakespeare, Fletcher, and Jonson . . . And in this they have been followed especially by Sir John Suckling and Mr Waller, who refined upon them. Neither have they who succeeded them been wanting in their endeavours to adorn our mother tongue. (I.177)

Leaves, words and poets are all part of a natural historical process of decay and renewal. Hence Dryden's interest in the metaphor of poetic succession, of writers being like fathers and sons. Frequently Dryden's literary criticism maps out family resemblances, as between Ovid and Chaucer, or Spenser and Milton (II.270–1), and he more than once claims to be the heir of Horace himself (I.228, II.232).

The question of what it meant to be truly the heir to the classical heritage was at the heart of the debate between Dryden and the dramatist Thomas Shadwell, conducted in their prologues, epilogues and prefaces from the late 1660s to *Mac Flecknoe* in 1676, and beyond.[16] The stance adopted by Shadwell is self-consciously classical, and specifically Jonsonian and Horatian, at least in its trappings, if not in its spirit or substance. Shadwell's comedies *The Sullen Lovers* (1668) and *The Royal Shepherdess* (1669) both carry quotations from the *Ars Poetica* on their title pages; the former proclaims:

> num satis est dixisse, ego mira poemata pango,
> occupet extremum scabies, mihi turpe relinqui est,
> et quod non didici sane nescire fateri. (*Ars* 416–8)

> For it is enough to say, I fashion wondrous poems: the devil take the hindmost! It is unseemly for me to be left behind, and to confess that I really do not know what I have never learned.

and the latter:

> non quivis videt immodulata poemata judex. (*Ars* 263)

> not every critic discerns unmusical verses.

Taken from their context, and read in the light of the charges of ignorance and ineptitude which Dryden would make against Shadwell in *Mac Flecknoe*, these quotations seem ironically apt.

Figures of Horace in Dryden's literary criticism

In the Preface to *The Sullen Lovers*, Shadwell proclaims his admiration for Jonson and his adherence to the neo-classical unities, but is forced to a comically desperate application of a line from Horace to defend the repetitiousness of the play, and his lack of invention:

> Another objection that has been made by some, is that there is the same thing over and over: which I do not apprehend, unless they blame the unity of the action, yet Horace *De Arte Poetica* says,
>
> > sit quod vis, simplex duntaxat, et unum.[17] [*Ars* 23]
>
> [Let the work be what you will, let it at least be simple and uniform.]

In the Preface to *The Royal Shepherdess* Shadwell insists that the function of the comic poet is to instruct as well as to please,[18] and he predictably quotes Horace:

> > simul et iucunda et idonea dicere vitae. (*Ars* 334)
>
> to say things which are at once pleasing and helpful to life.

This is one of the chief issues over which Shadwell and Dryden disagree, with Shadwell maintaining that Jonsonian comedy of humours which instructs the audience by exhibiting human follies and vices, is the true model for a dramatist to follow, while Dryden defends the comedy of wit and repartee. Shadwell returns to the question in the Preface to *The Humorists* (1671), with a little anthology of quotations from Horace, asserting that 'a poet ought to do all that he can, decently to please, that so he may instruct', and claiming that in this he has taken the faultless Jonson as his model.[19] In all Shadwell's quotations from Horace the Latin appears as a simple proof-text, usually without Horace being named, as if the quotations were too familiar to need attribution, and so self-evidently authoritative that they need no discussion. This rhetoric of quotation never recognizes the different historical contexts of Horace and Shadwell, nor does it see any need to explore the nature of critical authority and the process of applying ancient precepts to modern drama.

Dryden's response to Shadwell's claim to stand for true classical principles takes several forms. At the beginning of his *Defence of the Epilogue* he firmly cites Horace in support of his contention that the critique of one's predecessors is an essential part of the function of a poet:

> I would so maintain my opinion of the present age as not to be wanting in my veneration for the past: I would ascribe to dead authors their just praises in those things wherein they have excelled us; and in those wherein we contend with them for the pre-eminence, I would acknowledge our advantages to the age, and claim no victory from our wit. This being what I have proposed to myself, I hope I shall not be thought arrogant when I inquire into their errors. For we live in an age so sceptical,

that as it determines little, so it takes nothing from antiquity on trust. And I profess to have no other ambition in this essay than that poetry may not go backward, when all other arts and sciences are advancing. Whoever censures me for this inquiry, let him hear his character from Horace:

> ingeniis non ille favet, plauditque sepultis,
> nostra sed impugnat; nos nostraque lividus odit. [*Ep.* 2.2.88–91]

> He favours not dead wits, but hates the living.

It was upbraided to that excellent poet that he was an enemy to the writings of his predecessor Lucilius, because he had said *Lucilium lutulentum fluere*, that he ran muddy [*S* 1.10.51]; and that he ought to have retrenched from his satires many unnecessary verses. But Horace makes Lucilius himself to justify him from the imputation of envy, by telling you that he would have done the same had he lived in an age which was more refined:

> si foret hoc nostrum fato delapsus in aevum,
> detereret sibi multa, recideret omne quod ultra
> perfectum traheretur, etc.   [*S* 1.10.68–70]

[had he fallen by fate upon this our age, he would smooth away much of his work, would prune all that trailed beyond the proper limit.]

And, both in the whole course of that satire, and in his most admirable Epistle to Augustus, he makes it his business to prove that antiquity alone is no plea for the excellency of a poem; but that, one age learning from another, the last (if we can suppose an equality of wit in the writers) has the advantage of knowing more and better than the former. (1.169–70)

Dryden insists that his careful critical appraisal and judicious praise of Jonson is a properly Horatian practice, unlike the indiscriminate adulation that Shadwell accords him, and the facile assumption that he is to be imitated as the only model for comedy.

On the specific question of whether comedy should both instruct and please, Dryden attempts to counter Shadwell's argument by reinterpreting the Horatian *dictum* which Shadwell had quoted against him:

in comedy... the chief end... is divertisement and delight: and that so much, that it is disputed, I think, by Heinsius, before Horace his *Art of Poetry*, whether instruction be any part of its employment.   (1.152)

Though Dryden does not pursue this point, it is nevertheless significant that he feels the need to undo Shadwell's apparently definitive quotation of Horace by embroiling the Horatian text with a doubting commentary from an authoritative Horatian scholar.[20]

Shadwell invokes as his supporters some anonymous 'men of wit and

1 Botticelli's *Primavera*: the iconography partly derives from a number of Horace's *Odes* (1.4 and 30; 4.7 and 12).

FOUR IMAGES OF HORACE

2a Classical Horace from Philippe Daniel Lippert's collection of 'antique gems'.

2b Medieval Horace from Holkham MS 318 fol. 35v.

3a Horace the scholar from an early printed book (1498), the first illustrated Horace.

3b Renaissance Horace from Raphael's *Parnassus*: the central figure is traditionally identified with Horace, with Petrarch to his right.

4 *Agriculturae Beatitudo* (*Epode* 2 provides the prime text), Otto Vaenius (1607).

5a *In Medio Consistit Virtus*, Otto Vaenius.

5b *Modum serva*, George Wither (1635).

EIGHTEENTH-CENTURY HORACE

6a Pope's grotto, sketch by William Kent: it carried

6b Apotheosis of Horace: title page to André Dacier's

7 *Horace's Exclamation against his Tree* (also known as *A Landstorm*), Philip James de Loutherbourg RA (1740-1812)

TOWN AND COUNTRY MOUSE

8a   Thomas Bewick

ONE place suits one person, another place suits another person. For my part I prefer to live in the country, like Timmy Willie.

8b   Beatrix Potter

honour, and the best judges',[21] and dismisses the rest with a lofty *odi profanum vulgus, et arceo* [I hate the rude crowd, and keep away. (*Odes* 3.1.1)]. He also dedicates several of his plays to the Duke of Newcastle (once Jonson's patron), calling him 'the only Maecenas of our age'.[22] But these gestures through which Shadwell associates himself socially as well as artistically with Horace and Jonson are outdone by Dryden in his Dedication of *The Assignation* (1673) to Sir Charles Sedley. Dryden uses the Dedication to make a public claim for both Sedley's patronage and his friendship, and he links his commemoration of Sedley with the practice of Horace and other Roman poets of recording their friendships in their poetry:

This was the course which has formerly been practised by the poets of that nation who were masters of the universe. Horace and Ovid, who had little reason to distrust their immortality, yet took occasion to speak with honour of Virgil, Varius, Tibullus, and Propertius their contemporaries... For my own part, I, who am the least amongst the poets, have yet the fortune to be honoured with the best patron, and the best friend... I can make my boast to have found a better Maecenas in the person of my Lord Treasurer Clifford, and a more elegant Tibullus in that of Sir Charles Sedley.(1.185)

And Dryden applies to Sedley the lines which Horace had written about Tibullus, in praise of his beauty, intelligence and generosity (*Ep.* 1.4.6–11). Moreover, Dryden claims that the conviviality of the Roman poets is reproduced amongst the circle of wits to which he and Sedley belong:

Certainly the poets of that age enjoyed much happiness in the conversation and friendship of one another... We have, like them, our genial nights, where our discourse is neither too serious, nor too light, but always pleasant, and for the most part instructive. (1.186)

(That Horatian formula associating the pleasant with the instructive seems inescapable, even when describing parties.)

Finally, Dryden claims an even more explicit association of himself with Horace when he returns to Shadwell's charge that he had denigrated Jonson, and returns also to his earlier defence, the comparison with Horace's strictures on Lucilius:

I am made a detractor from my predecessors, whom I confess to have been my masters in the art. But this latter was the accusation of the best judge, and almost the best poet, in the Latin tongue. You find Horace complaining that, for taxing some verses in Lucilius, he himself was blamed by others, though his design was no other than mine now, to improve the knowledge of poetry: and it was no defence to him, amongst his enemies, any more than it is for me, that he praised Lucilius where he deserved it: *pagina*[23] *laudatur eadem* [is praised in the same page. S 1.10.4]. (1.187–8)

Here Dryden and his enemies are seen to replicate precisely Horace and his enemies, so that nothing which Dryden can say will carry any weight with the enemies of poetry – except this uniquely powerful explanation as to why nothing will carry any weight.

When Dryden pilloried Shadwell in *Mac Flecknoe* (circulated in manuscript in 1676) as one who was truly the heir not of Horace and Jonson but of Richard Flecknoe, a writer who ineptly pretended to a Jonsonian role, the underlying argument was Horatian, even though the mode of personalized criticism may not have been. (Shadwell was to say that Horace should lash Dryden for not knowing the difference between libel and satire.)[24] The poem rejects the absolutism inherent in Shadwell's claim to dictate on literary matters: Flecknoe is said to have reigned 'through all the realms of nonsense, absolute' (line 6). Flecknoe himself blithely rejects a fundamental Horatian principle, for Horace had said:

> natura fieret laudabile carmen, an arte,
> quaesitum est: ego nec studium sine divite vena,
> nec rude quid prosit video ingenium. alterius sic
> altera poscit opem res, et coniurat amice. (*Ars* 408–11)

[Often it is asked whether a praiseworthy poem be due to Nature or to art. For my part, I do not see of what avail is either study, when not enriched by Nature's vein, or native wit, if untrained; so truly does each claim the other's aid, and make with it a friendly league.]

But Flecknoe advises his son: 'Trust nature, do not labour to be dull' (line 166), only to contradict himself a moment later: 'What share have we in nature, or in art?' (line 176).

That characterization of Shadwell is more than an adaptation of Horace: it is also an allusion to *An Allusion to Horace* (circulated in manuscript 1675–6), the poem in which Rochester turned *S* 1.10 into a survey of contemporary writers. Rochester compliments 'hasty Shadwell' as a practitioner of true comedy, whose 'unfinished works do yet impart / Great proofs of force of nature, none of art' (lines 43–5).[25] Dryden, meanwhile, is only gesturally credited with 'excellencies more than faults' (line 78), while the couplet which accords to Dryden the reverence which Horace gives to Lucilius –

> Nor dare I from his sacred temples tear
> That laurel which he best deserves to wear. (lines 79–80)

– reads ironically, satirically even, in a poem which mostly castigates Dryden for producing crude plays which pander to the worst forms of Restoration taste. Though some of Rochester's criticisms are not without foundation, they are far from being a balanced appraisal, and are often couched in personally abusive language. Besides lacking any clear principles of literary judgement, Rochester's poem also fails to match that persuasive literary persona, at once modest and assured, which Horace tries so hard to construct.

Dryden responded in his Preface to *All for Love* (1678). Dryden never names Rochester, thus maintaining a form of courtesy and decorum, and his use of plurals makes the essay an attack not on one opponent but on a whole self-important subculture which makes claims to cultural authority:

> those who are allowed for witty men, either by the advantage of their quality, or by common fame ... Men of pleasant conversation (at least esteemed so), and endued with a trifling kind of fancy, perhaps helped out with some smattering of Latin.
>
> (1.225–6)

The charge is brought home to Rochester himself through several allusions and half-concealed quotations from his poetry.[26] Not content with being a wealthy peer, Rochester must also be accounted a poet. Dryden remarks that 'Horace was certainly in the right where he said that no man is satisfied with his own condition' (1.226), and proceeds to demolish any claim that Rochester may have to being an Horatian figure. The appropriate classical precedent for him is not Horace but Dionysius or Nero, tyrants who demanded on pain of death that they be recognized as great poets. As for Rochester's role as a patron, he is no Maecenas, for Maecenas, recognizing that his own talent for poetry was meagre, determined to support Virgil and Horace,

> that at least he might be a poet at the second hand; and we see how happily it has succeeded with him; for his own bad poetry is forgotten, and their panegyrics of him still remain. But they who should be our patrons are for no such expensive ways to fame; they have much of the poetry of Maecenas, but little of his liberality.
>
> (1.226)

Dryden then claims that he is a true heir of Horace, while Rochester and his ilk usurp his name and authority to the detriment of genuine poets:

> They are for persecuting Horace and Virgil, in the persons of their successors (for such is every man who has any part of their soul and fire, though in a less degree). Some of their little zanies yet go further; for they are persecutors even of Horace himself, as far as they are able, by their ignorant and vile imitations of him; by making an unjust use of his authority, and turning his artillery against his friends. But how would he disdain to be copied by such hands! I dare answer for him, he would be more uneasy in their company than he was with Crispinus, their forefather, in the Holy Way; and would no more have allowed them a place amongst the critics than he would Demetrius the mimic, and Tigellius the buffoon:
>
> > Demetri, teque, Tigelli,
> > discipulorum[27] inter jubeo plorare cathedras. [S 1.10.90–1]

[Demetrius, and you, Tigellius, I bid you go whine amongst the chairs of your pupils.]

With what scorn would he look down on such miserable translators who make doggerel of his Latin, mistake his meaning, misapply his censures, and often contradict their own? (1.228)

The *Allusion* is represented as an anti-Horatian appropriation of Horace, which takes his name and applies a few of his observations to modern writers, but fails to recreate an Horatian text for the Restoration. Dryden is thus constructing an Horatian role for himself, which also entails the creation of a particular version of 'Horace' in a form which can support both his own *œuvre* and his understanding of contemporary culture.

After these struggles to enlist Horace in arguments over drama in the 1660s and 1670s, the development of a modern classicism which Dryden had been arguing for in the theatre happened in the 1680s in non-dramatic poetry: in Roscommon's verse essays, Oldham's satires and imitations, Creech's Lucretius, and the extensive programme of translation fostered by Dryden and Tonson. Dryden's poem *To the Earl of Roscommon, on his excellent Essay on Translated Verse* (1684) praises Roscommon for providing guidance of a properly Horatian kind, and when Dryden maps out his own theory of translation in the Preface to *Ovid's Epistles* (1680), he turns to Horace to support his rejection of the close, literal translation exemplified by Jonson's rendering of the *Ars Poetica*; the principle should be

> nec verbum verbo curabis reddere, fidus
> interpres.   (*Ars* 133–4)

Nor word for word too faithfully translate.   (1.268)[28]

Close adherence to the model is not only pedantry, says Dryden, but 'a faith like that which proceeds from superstition, blind and zealous' (like Shadwell's, we infer). The different characteristics of Latin and English make close translation a futile aim: *brevis esse laboro, / obscurus fio* [labouring to be brief, I become obscure (*Ars* 24–5)], as Dryden aptly quotes (1.269). Instead, faithfulness in translation demands a revoicing of the original, finding appropriate words in modern English for the thoughts of the author. This is, however, quite different from the revoicing which was known as 'imitation', where the modern poet seeks 'not to translate his words, or to be confined to his sense, but only to set him as a pattern, and to write, as he supposes that author would have done, had he lived in our age, and in our country' (1.270). Perhaps Rochester's work had made Dryden wary of such a

Figures of Horace in Dryden's literary criticism

method, though it was to be used with skill by Oldham, particularly in his version of *S* 1.9, and by Dryden himself in some passages of his translations. In his initial definition of translation, however, Dryden is seeking an Horatian stance: faithfulness to the writer's sense, combined with an awareness of linguistic difference, and not the effacing of historical difference by supposing that Horace could simply be translated to the streets of London. The licence which he issues is for a disciplined creativity.

Dryden's own translations in the 1680s turned particularly to existential questions, and the Horace who attracted him here was not the critic but the philosophical poet of *Odes* 1.9, 3.29 and *Epod.* 2. This was only part of Dryden's larger quest, and Horace could offer him only limited examples. But Horace remained an exemplary man of letters for Dryden, a model for use on important occasions when his own self-image was at stake: he offers his translation of *Odes* 1.3 to Roscommon, repeating the gesture by which Horace offered the original to Virgil, while his statement of faith, *Religio Laici* (1682), explicitly aims to imitate Horace's epistolary mode ('The Preface' lines 343–6), and echoes Horace's *sermoni propiora* [nearer to prose. (*S* 1.4.42)] in describing its verse as 'unpolished, rugged . . . fittest for discourse, and nearest prose' (lines 453–4). And it is particularly to Horace that Dryden turns when he wishes to defend that diffident, undogmatic exploration of different viewpoints which is his own most characteristic mode of writing: like Horace, he will 'not run into [the] fault of imposing my opinions on other men' (1.207), and will be content to 'write in a loose, epistolary way, somewhat tending to . . . the example of Horace' (11.232).

Shadwell called Dryden 'a servile imitator and a thief', adding a footnote identifying this little sample of his moderate muse as a translation of Horace's *O imitatores, servum pecus* (*Ep.* 1.19.19).[29] It was, however, precisely Dryden's refusal to be a servile imitator which made his citations of Horace a persuasive rhetoric: Horace is used as an authority, but that authority frequently advocates freedom, and the quotations form part of a discursive, epistolary mode of criticism which adapts Horace's own manner. Dryden's essays, erudite but easy, modest and self-assured, give both profit and pleasure: *omne tulit punctum qui miscuit utile dulci*, [he who has mixed profit and pleasure has won every vote. (*Ars* 343)]. Or, as Richard Flecknoe proclaimed on one of his title pages, in an unlucky attempt to display his Horatian credentials: *omne tulit punctam quae miscuit utile dulci*;[30] which only goes to show that some misquotations are merely misquotations.

7

HORACE'S *ODE* 3.29: DRYDEN'S 'MASTERPIECE IN ENGLISH'

Stuart Gillespie

IT IS MUCH more difficult to discover English poets of the later seventeenth century who were not imitators of Horace than to name ones that were. Between 1660 and 1700, new translations and adaptations of poems from the *Odes* alone were written by at least fifty different hands.[1] If the frequency with which gentleman-authors turned out their versions of Horatian odes did not quite match the rate achieved a generation or two later, in Pope's heyday, the uniformity of their productions and, one may thus infer, of their response to the *Odes* was perhaps even greater. Dryden himself is conventional enough in classifying the *Odes* into 'panegyrical', 'moral' and 'jovial' types, and in his apparent preference for the latter.[2] And the 'jovial' Horace – the bon viveur, the voluptuary, the lover – is a figure so frequently encountered in later seventeenth-century translators' work that we must suspect the period's usual sense of the poet to be extremely selective, if not positively eccentric. At least, most Restoration efforts to present this favourite Horace in English translation very clearly reflect the translators' own tastes and conspicuously lack qualities found in the *Odes* by readers of other periods. Horace tends to be made a spokesman for the Restoration gentleman's 'libertine' attitudinizing; in the process his poise becomes unbalanced, his moments of moral seriousness disappear and his wit is blunted and coarsened. Dryden's own work on Horace might on the face of it seem to fit this pattern only too well. Like many of his contemporaries he produced translations of a handful of the *Odes* which took his fancy, and the one he confesses to having spent most pains on, *Ode 3.29*, is a poem standing firmly in the *carpe diem* tradition.[3] Yet this translation has been recognized in each century after Dryden's death as a conspicuous success – as one of the most attractive renderings from the classics in his wide and varied work on them.[4] Other essays in the present volume deal with translators who have made more extensive inroads into the Horatian corpus than Dryden attempted, and with other periods in which different parts of that corpus have seemed assimilable; yet we would be hard pressed indeed to find any one Horatian translation by an English poet which achieves so powerful a stamp of conviction. Viewed as an independent

English work, Dryden's ode is – or should be, since it is still not well enough known – in itself a poem which compels our fullest attention, and any account of it must seek to do justice to its intrinsic appeal. But I hope to suggest in what follows that Dryden's translation is more than a highly successful exercise in manipulation of his original: it also constitutes an extremely challenging reading of Horace's *Ode*, with the potential to transform our sense of the Latin work.

This is not the place to rehearse the conflicting prescriptions translators have been offered by theoreticians over the centuries, or to attempt to establish principles governing the processes which might release the energies of such a poem as *Ode* 3.29 in the words afforded by the English language, and in the rhythms available to English verse. Others have tried to do so, in impeccably reasoned but empirically unreliable formulations;[5] Dryden's work seems to fit no one's model of translatorial procedure, and its success cannot be demonstrated by measurements of its relative proximity to the individual features of his original (in fact there are several points at which Dryden does not appear to be translating Horace's words, or even trying to emulate his local poetic effects, at all).[6] This translation seems to arise out of one of those rare and mysterious contacts between poets across the centuries which have given us, from time to time, a sudden, unlooked-for insight into a foreign text, and the explanations for which are reducible to no system or methodology; all we can do is to show how the translator's work seems to reshape our understanding of the original, filling with meaning a poem we had found speaking to us in whispers but not 'wi' the haill voice',[7] speaking in parts but not as a whole – and possibly never speaking fully home.

In a way, we perhaps expect too much of classical scholars. Though it may seem to us that the critical faculties have generally been valued at a discount in the twentieth-century study of Latin literature, our professors cannot be blamed for not being poets – for not affording us the insight which, as Dryden held, only poets can. All academic literary specialists need to remind themselves periodically that (as Michael Edwards has recently put it)

poets speak to poets, through the ties of friendship, or hostility, and across the ages, and that *here* is where poems are written, problems are raised and maybe solved, and new ways of thinking about poetry, and of thinking poetry, are discovered . . . poets are the professors of poetry.[8]

Those who have tested out the scholarly discussion available on Horace's *Ode* 3.29 have found their need for such thinking particularly acute. At worst it may seem, as it has to one recent writer, that 'although all [commentators] praise it, nobody has given a convincing reason for the praise'; that the available accounts tend to be so external that discussions of 'arithmetical correspondences of line lengths, of consonant and vowel interplay are offered as constituting what makes this the most impressive of the odes', and that there is 'the maximum possible amount of difference of opinion' about how the poem can be said to cohere.⁹ Undeniably, I think, interpreters of the *Ode*, both scholars and translators, have generally tended to make it seem either too slight to satisfy, or more weighty than its apparently slender frame can sustain. Perhaps the following bald summary from an introductory edition is enough to suggest how both possibilities arise:

A warm welcome awaits you, Maecenas, at my house: come then at once. Cease merely to gaze longingly on the country, and leave Rome for a while and all its magnificence and cares. Rich men sometimes find the change to a humble household a relief. The dog-days moreover are coming on, and yet you linger in town and worry about political contingencies. What is the good? Providence has sealed the future and mocks our efforts to read it. Calmly to deal with the present is wisdom; for life is like a river and moves along uncontrolled by us sometimes peacefully, sometimes like a raging torrent. He lives best who enjoys today; tomorrow Jupiter may send trouble but he cannot undo the past. Fortune is ever fickle: I accept her favour and put up with her frowns. In stormy weather I am not like a merchant fearful lest his rich cargo be lost: it is enough for me if I weather the tempest myself.

On the one hand there have been those over the centuries who have seen the *Ode* as very largely the invitation to the pleasures of friendship and wine which its starting-point and general structure seem to imply it is, and Horace's wider reflections as a mere extension of this (however elaborate a transformation of the traditional format might thus be produced). On this interpretation, Horace's references to change and loss are there to enhance the attractions good company offers much as snow outside is supposed to enhance the attractions of a log fire. Yet the *Ode* seems to bear readings of an altogether more rarefied kind too. Eduard Fraenkel went so far as to speak of the 'almost religious fervour that breathes in this ode', while the nineteenth-century scholar William Sellar spoke of the 'ethical grandeur' to which he felt it to rise.¹⁰ How does a poem proposing the pleasures of a country weekend come to bear this freight of 'philosophy'? Again, it requires little experience of Latin and Greek literature to see that nine-tenths of the 'precepts' Horace offers in the second half of his *Ode* must be thought of as conventional if not hackneyed: should any reading take these parts of the poem seriously – or is Horace, after all, committed only to the enjoyment of hedonistic pleasure?

There is no space here to work through Dryden's and Horace's poems in full detail; but if we plunge in at the centre, to the consequences the poet draws from the realization that the future is unknowable, the weightier and more difficult side of the *Ode* will come immediately to the fore. But where is the weight placed? Although Fraenkel was convinced that the *Ode* had extensive hidden depths of thought and feeling, he seems to have felt that it touches only lightly on the world outside. For him, that world is presented in

Horace's *Ode* 3.29

self-contained *tableaux* of which Horace's description of the Tiber is one – the 'finest ornament' of a poem which shows Horace's supreme 'eye for the picturesque' and 'ear for the suggestive sound'.

> quod adest memento
> componere aequus; cetera fluminis
>   ritu feruntur, nunc medio alveo
>   cum pace delabentis Etruscum
>   in mare, nunc lapides adesos
>
> stirpisque raptas et pecus et domos
>   volventis una non sine montium
>   clamore vicinaeque silvae,
>   cum fera diluvies quietos
> irritat amnis. (32–41)

Remember to make the best of the present moment with equanimity: the rest is carried along like a river, at one time peacefully flowing down in mid-channel to the Etruscan sea, at another whirling rocks it has eaten away and trees it has uprooted and cattle and houses all together, with a roaring echo from the mountains and nearby wood whenever a fierce flood excites the quiet river.[11]

What has Dryden made of this river? For him it is no 'ornament'; its importance does not seem to have lain for him merely in Horace's eloquence, but in the weight of experience the description imposes, as it were, on the utterly conventional sentiment which introduces it. Dryden translates:

> Enjoy the present smiling hour;
> And put it out of Fortune's power:
> The tide of business, like the running stream,
> Is sometimes high, and sometimes low,
> A quiet ebb, or a tempestuous stream,
> And always in extreme.
> Now with a noiseless gentle course
> It keeps within the middle bed;
> Anon it lifts aloft the head,
> And bears all down before it, with impetuous force:
> And trunks of trees come rolling down,
> Sheep and their folds together drown:
> Both house and homestead into seas are borne,
> And rocks are from their old foundations torn,
> And woods made thin with winds, their scattered honours
> mourn. (50–64)

Dryden begins by turning the river explicitly into an image of the implacable power of Fortune. This suggestion is only latent in Horace through the connection between Fortune and the watery grave the merchant's goods suffer at the close, yet once it is made it becomes inevitable that the river's destruction stands as an evocation of man's powerlessness in the face of the unpredictability of things. Dryden makes *cetera* refer to the whole of life outside the present hour; inspired by one of Cowley's Horatian poems, it seems, he calls this the sphere of 'business'. Here the power of Fortune dominates.[12] And the damage Fortune wreaks is not merely physical, but also – Dryden's language of transience and desolation implies – spiritual. It is possible to see in Dryden's lines a reflection of the arbitrary, chaotic changes, the abrupt discontinuities of his own life and times (a point to which I shall return); but whatever lies behind Dryden's words, the result of his recasting of the Latin at this point is to suggest unmistakably the feeling which some have discerned at various points in the original: an 'awareness of what is essentially a tragic view of man's condition'.[13] And yet there is something more. To some commentators, Horace's burden in this poem is that once the *fugiens hora* has been arrested, happiness is attainable because Man has overcome Nature's restrictions on him.[14] Dryden's rendering suggests a quite different possibility, and it is one which seems to account more fully for what all have praised as the astonishing vigour of Horace's description in this central stanza. The tragic note is only one element in Dryden's translation here. For all the destruction the flood unleashes, Dryden seems with one part of himself almost to relish its awesome force, and to communicate in the confident surge of his own verse a positive pleasure in contemplating the irresistible operation of Nature's process. The hero, so to speak, of Dryden's ode is not one who successfully resists the laws of Nature (to adopt a phrase Dryden used in translating Lucretius), but who gladly accepts them. I shall suggest later on further reasons for thinking this a convincing construction of Horace's mood rather than a wilful distortion of it.

'Mood' is a much better word here than 'thought'. It is crucial in responding to Horace's *Ode* not to imagine, as some have done, that its profundity is of the kind we might find in an exposition of philosophical principles.[15] This is particularly important with the stanza immediately following, a passage which has been taken to sum up 'Horace's philosophy of life', or to contain 'precepts' which constitute a recipe for happiness.[16] In commenting on his reasons for translating Horace, Dryden will have little to do with any of this, and concentrates instead on the special importance of his *manner*. He singles out Horace's 'elevated flights' and 'sudden changes of his subject with almost imperceptible connections' – 'Pindaric' features in Dryden's view, much in evidence in his own version of the stanzas on the river

Horace's *Ode* 3.29

– and explains that the characteristics of his style are inseparable from the animating spirit of his poetry:

That which will distinguish his style from all other poets', is the elegance of his words, and the numerousness of his verse; there is nothing so delicately turned in all the Roman language. There appears in every part of his diction, or (to speak English) in all his expressions, a kind of noble and bold purity. His words are chosen with as much exactness as Virgil's; but there seems to be a greater spirit in them. There is a secret happiness attends his choice, which in Petronius is called *curiosa felicitas*, and which I suppose he had from the *feliciter audere* of Horace himself. But the most distinguishing part of all his character seems to me to be his briskness, his jollity, and his good humour: and those I have chiefly endeavoured to copy.[17]

There can be no passage in which all this is more obvious than in these stanzas of *Ode* 3.29:

> ille potens sui
> laetusque deget, cui licet in diem
> dixisse 'vixi. cras vel atra
> nube polum pater occupato
>
> vel sole puro: non tamen irritum
> quodcumque retro est efficiet, neque
> diffinget infectumque reddet
> quod fugiens semel hora vexit'. (41–8)[18]

That man shall live as his own master and in happiness who can say each day "I have LIVED": tomorrow let the Father fill the sky with a black cloud or clear sunshine, yet he shall not make null whatever belongs to the past nor shall he alter and render undone what once the fleeting hour has carried away.

Horace's *Ode* does not *reason* that life should be lived for the present: in the coiled finalities of the Latin at this point, it dramatizes the spirit of one who is living according to that principle. And there is no translator who has so clearly brought over this spirit as Dryden. In the buoyancy of the rhythms and the vibrant simplicity of the language, and with a 'secret happiness' attending his choice of words of just the sort he had identified in Horace's, Dryden discovers in his own English the joyful energy which he felt was inseparable from Horace's wisdom – and hence discovers a much more deeply and convincingly 'jovial' Horace than the one his contemporaries so readily embraced. Here he very obviously rises to the level of his original, and in the quite independent conviction of the English verse we can see something of what Dryden was able to bring to Horace from his own resources:

> Happy the man, and happy he alone,
> He, who can call today his own:

> He, who secure within, can say
> Tomorrow do thy worst, for I have lived today.
> Be fair, or foul, or rain, or shine,
> The joys I have possessed, in spite of fate are mine.
> Not heaven itself upon the past has power;
> But what has been, has been, and I have had my hour. (65–72)

On the one hand, we must not imagine that Dryden was a passive vehicle through which Horace's sentiments flowed as through a conduit. No one could have written this stanza who had not reflected deeply on the few small English words on which it turns – today, yesterday, tomorrow. Yet we have no difficulty in recognizing Horace's lines (transformed into something familiar and domesticated) as Dryden's basis. Dryden's emphasis on the word 'lived', for example, is clearly inspired by the Latin, in which language the verb *vivere* is frequently used in the sense of enjoying or using life as opposed to merely existing (one need only recall Catullus' 'vivamus, mea Lesbia . . . '). Nor is the note we hear in this stanza the one Dryden himself usually sounded in summing up the ends of life – the one he felt appropriate for moments such as the close of his translation of Juvenal's Tenth *Satire*:

> Forgive the Gods the rest, and stand confined
> To health of body, and content of mind:
> A soul that can securely death defy,
> And count it Nature's privilege to die;
> Serene and manly, hardened to sustain
> The load of life, and exercised in pain
> Guiltless of hate, and proof against desire;
> That all things weighs, and nothing can admire. (548–55)[19]

In Dryden's Horace the note struck is not one of limitation, or of fortitude in the face of adversity, but of triumph. Commentators have disagreed over what note Horace's poem itself sounds at this point; Dryden's extraordinary lines force us to say whether we hear in it something like this:

to Maecenas he recommended a stoic indifference . . . Immunity to each day's vicissitudes and the security of the granted present – here is the best Horace can lay before Maecenas.[20]

or (from another twentieth-century exposition) something more like this:

Triumph is the atmosphere . . . so the country retreat is not . . . a place of refuge where the timid and the insignificant may hide themselves away. In stanza 12, [Horace gives] an impression quite opposite to defeatism; it serves to strengthen and prolong the tone of unshakeable confidence.[21]

Dryden's translation might not be able to provide 'evidence' about the way the Horatian *Ode* should be read. But his poetic resources can open our ears and our minds to possibilities which might otherwise be glimpsed only fleetingly – or never.

Two stanzas of the Dryden ode, three of Horace's, remain. Here we need to be alert to a paradox affecting the work of both men. The most obvious form of it has already been mentioned: although Horace's poem starts and ends with, and seems to depend for its effect on our sensation of involvement in, the most individual details of the poet's life, it also purports to speak for human experience at large. The close of the *Ode* has recently been described in this way by Peter Connor:

> From the predilections of Fortuna we note immediately that the giving and taking of honours and dignities picture a Horace who, as involved in public life as the stoutest Roman, can be exalted one moment and toppled the next. This is often interpreted as his willingness to renounce his Sabine farm if that became necessary. But the language contains a larger frame of reference or, at least, he is elevating his farm to equal significance with the most lofty gift of Fortuna granted to anyone.[22]

And the poem as a whole has been seen as working through this dual 'frame of reference':

> Though the poet draws us all in, he makes the words for *present* and *live* more serious, more intense, by his own personal concern, which is, we are made by his art to feel, both a concern shared with all men and the concern of a poet desirous of settling his principles of conduct.[23]

What is true of Horace in this respect seems to have been true of his translator. It is not necessary for us to relate Dryden's ode to the particular details of his situation in the 1680s; but it is evident that translating this poem enabled him to confront aspects of his own lived experience (and, again paradoxically, to do so in ways that his 'original' writing of the period did not). Paul Hammond has pointed out that at this date '[Dryden] had seen enough of public life to feel the power of Fortune, and to understand what it was like to live as Fortune's slave': tracing the play of Dryden's imagination over these subjects around this date, he shows how the concept of Fortune is for Dryden a symbol of a 'multifaceted problem which he is attempting to articulate and to solve', and finds a new departure in Dryden's treatment of it in his Horatian ode.[24] In this way, we may imagine, Dryden's writing involved him in the same kind of artistry several commentators have seen as lying behind Horace's, a process of 'test[ing] the inherited wisdom about life by bringing it to bear on his own experience',[25] at the same time confronting that experience through creative contact with his literary inheritance.

These are the penultimate passages of the two poems:

> fortuna saevo laeta negotio et
> ludum insolentem ludere pertinax

>   transmutat incertos honores,
>   nunc mihi, nunc alii benigna.
>
>   laudo manentem; si celeris quatit
>   pennas, resigno quae dedit et mea
>   virtute me involvo probamque
>   pauperiem sine dote quaero.   (49–56)

Fortune taking pleasure in her cruel job and stubborn at playing her high-handed game changes around her unstable honours, kind now to me, now to another: I praise her while she stays with me; if she shakes her swift wings, I give up what she has awarded me and I wrap my virtue close about me and go courting honest poverty that has no dowry.

>   Fortune, that with malicious joy,
>   Does Man her slave oppress,
>   Proud of her office to destroy,
>   Is seldom pleased to bless:
>   Still various and unconstant still;
>   But with an inclination to be ill;
>   Promotes, degrades, delights in strife,
>   And makes a lottery of life.
>   I can enjoy her while she's kind;
>   But when she dances in the wind,
>   And shakes her wings, and will not stay,
>   I puff the prostitute away:
> The little or the much she gave, is quietly resigned:
>   Content with poverty, my soul, I arm;
>   And virtue, though in rags, will keep me warm.   (73–87)

Once again we can say that what Dryden gives us is unmistakably his own. To 'puff the prostitute away' might be part of a line from a Restoration satire. Even the combination with Horace's prostitute of Virgil's Dido, *varium et mutabile semper / femina* (*Aeneid* 4.569), evinces a characteristically Drydenian cast of mind. And Dryden's expansiveness with respect to the Latin might suggest an almost irresponsible attitude to his duty as a translator. But in spite, or (I would argue) rather because of all these things, Dryden may in fact be said to find an English form in which Horace can live. Most translators water Horace down at this point, unwilling to make the passage turn on what seems a mere poeticism, the most hackneyed of tropes. For Dryden Fortune is not a mere allegorical figure, but a tangible female personality, a mistress, at once both alluring and dangerous. And there are further nuances behind the Horatian stanza to which Dryden seems to alert us. Poised though these lines are between seriousness and self-irony, some of the gravity which seems to underlie the Latin peeps through in Dryden's language. Horace's words here have often been felt to imply more than they say; and at this point commentators have been drawn to the thought that he was doing more than expressing a conventional faith in the *virtus* and *paupertas* to which he limits his expression of his resolution. Commager's reading is suggestive:

> May not *virtus* (55) have less to do with conventional morality than with something more private, something comparable to his proclaimed *fides* or *pietas*? His glad betrothal to *probam pauperiem* (55–56) recalls ... the blend of physical simplicity and the inner resources of the poet in the Hymn to Apollo ... Horace's exaggerations are deliberate, and suggest that he is trying to find a means of dramatizing the essentially undramatic quality of inner serenity.[26]

Dryden's language of religious consolation ('Content with poverty, my soul, I arm; / And virtue, though in rags, will keep me warm') has a corresponding resonance, for all the self-deflating humour both Horace and Dryden seem consciously to admit here.

But too exclusive an emphasis on the graver side of the poem would distort it. The final stanza leaves the reader not with solemnity but with a delighted enjoyment of the storm from whose dangers the poet is secure:

> If the mast split and threaten wreck,
> Then let the greedy merchant fear
> For his ill-gotten gain:
> And pray to gods that will not hear,
> While the debating winds and billows bear
> His wealth into the main.
> For me secure from Fortune's blows,
> (Secure of what I cannot lose),
> In my small pinnace I can sail,
> Condemning all the blustring roar;
> And running with a merry gale,
> With friendly stars my safety seek
> Within some little winding creek;
> And see the storm ashore. (91–104)

Dryden's transformations are significant. In Horace it was not the merchant but the sea that was 'greedy' (*avaro*, 61), and Horace said nothing about 'ill-gotten gain'. Dryden has not made the merchant unsympathetic on a whim, however, but through a deliberate emphasis: in the Latin there was already scorn in *ad miseras preces / decurrere et votis pacisci* ('dash off to offer up wretched prayers and strike bargains with the gods'). The effect is almost comic: tonally, we are at virtually the opposite extreme from Clarence's vision of the sea-bed:

> Methoughts I saw a thousand fearful wrecks;
> Ten thousand men that fishes gnawed upon;

>   Wedges of gold, great anchors, heaps of pearl,
>   Inestimable stones, unvalued jewels,
>   All scattered in the bottom of the sea.   (*Richard III* I.iv.24–8)[27]

Yet the Duke's vision of the horrors to which men lay themselves open through their lust for wealth is not totally alien to Horace's lines. The merchant is relevant to the poem not only because he depends for his happiness on Fortune; he is also one whose life is spent in hopes for the future (of his cargo), rather than contentment in the present – the condition the ode has defined as spiritually sterile. Dryden is content to end, however, with Horace's humour and fancifulness, in a final image which delights by its unexpectedness and generates a close which insists on nothing.

8

POPE AND HORACE
Robin Sowerby

POPE'S POETIC CAREER was consciously grounded in the Roman classicism[1] of which Horace was regarded in the Renaissance as one of the chief sources and embodiments. That this is so is apparent in the praise accorded to the Roman by the young English poet at the start of his career as he reviews the humanist heritage at the end of *An Essay on Criticism*, a work in which he sought to clarify for himself and for his readers the critic's role in relation to the art of the age. Surveying contemporary literary life, Pope gives us a vivid picture of chaos and confusion, then asks where in the modern world are to be found critics with the authority of the great ancients. In the appeal to antiquity that follows, Aristotle naturally comes first as the great legislative critic:

> Poets, a race long unconfined, and free,
> Still fond and proud of savage liberty,
> Received his laws . . .   (649–51)[2]

By contrast Horace is invoked next in what is the longest tribute in this roll call of six ancient names not as a legislator but first as an unmethodical critic who addresses us as a friend in a familiar style and 'talks us into sense':

> Horace still charms with graceful negligence,
> And without method talks us into sense,
> Will, like a friend, familiarly convey
> The truest notions in the easiest way.   (653–6)

Pope here characterizes the Horatian *sermo* which is the medium for most of Horace's criticism and which, though he has more apparent method than Horace, is ultimately the model for Pope's own *Essay on Criticism*. Then comes the tribute to Horace's critical judgement, coolly delivered where boldness might have been justified or expected:

> He, who supreme in judgement, as in wit,
> Might boldly censure, as he boldly writ,
> Yet judged with coolness, though he sung with fire;
> His precepts teach but what his works inspire.   (657–60)

Although he delivers precepts as Aristotle had delivered laws, a distinction is implied between the criticism of the philosopher and that of the poet. Given the intimate relation between wit and judgement established in the *Essay*, Pope's words seem to be referring to the poetic character of Horace as well as to his critical faculty, and the two are made inseparable in the final line where with exemplary decorum critical precepts teach what the poetic *œuvre* inspires. No one has ever defined so succinctly and expressed so justly the grounds for Horace's special critical authority.

As he is invoked in the *Essay* Horace is but a part of a tradition that extends before and beyond him, a tradition to which the *Essay* itself is but the latest addition. Yet Horace does have a special status in Pope's mind and if this is not already apparent from the terms of his tribute to him, it becomes so in the brief but brilliantly delivered sketch of cultural history that follows the invocation of the ancient critics.

> Thus long succeeding critics justly reigned,
> Licence repressed, and useful laws ordained.
> Learning and Rome alike in empire grew;
> And arts still followed where her eagles flew; (681–4)

But Rome falls to tyranny and superstition. With Erasmus the world is finally freed from monkish obscurantism and Rome is reborn. The Renaissance spreads north from Italy:

> Thence arts o'er all the northern world advance,
> But critic-learning flourished most in France;
> The rules, a nation born to serve, obeys;
> And Boileau still in right of Horace sways.
> But we, brave Britons, foreign laws despised,
> And kept unconquered, and uncivilised;
> Fierce for the liberties of wit, and bold,
> We still defied the Romans, as of old. (711–18)

The delicate surface raillery at the expense of the servile French and the bold but primitive early Britons (very much in the spirit of Horace's own representation of the different cultural aptitudes and achievements of the Romans and the Greeks in his *Ars Poetica* and elsewhere)[3] does not disguise other meanings. First, there is the historical fact that the revival of learning was a predominantly Latin phenomenon (and the civilization being revived was Roman rather than Greek) bringing with it the Roman predilection for laws, rules and methodizing. The history has been well told of the Romanization of Aristotle's *Poetics*,[4] many of the distinctive features of which, paradoxically, were only really comprehended after it had ceased to be the medium for classical influence.[5] Secondly, and equally a matter of literary history, is the more rigorous classicism of the French, here rather slightingly associated with 'critic-learning'. Thirdly, (and this is intimately connected with the whole purpose and tenor of the *Essay*) is the distinction made by Pope between Boileau, unflatteringly associated with critic-learning, and Horace, the greater representative of civilizing wit, hitherto resisted and only recently embraced by the British. The antithesis may be thought to be unduly sharp, especially since *L'Art Poétique* of Boileau (who also saw himself as a disciple of Horace) is a source of much of Pope's doctrine in the *Essay*. That doctrine, however, particularly with regard to the rules of art, is presented in a more flexible spirit by the English poet, and in this Pope doubtless believed not only that he was articulating a difference in tendency between the British and the French but also that he was doing this more in the spirit of the gracefully negligent Horace than of Boileau, 'the lawgiver of Parnassus', or of other British lawgivers following in the wake of the Frenchman.

Pope goes on to pay tribute to his immediate British predecessors who have 'here restored wit's fundamental laws', referring to Mulgrave's *Essay on Poetry* (1682) and to Roscommon who had translated Horace's *Ars Poetica* in 1680 and whose *Essay on Translated Verse* (1684), acknowledging Mulgrave, begins:

> Happy that author whose correct Essay
> Repairs so well our old Horatian way.[6]

'Wit's fundamental laws' are not specified but are to be generally understood as those principles underlying Horace and Pope and common to Mulgrave and Roscommon which have to do with 'the rules'.

That the poet needs genius and imitates nature is largely taken for granted. Horace has famous lines on the function of art in the *civitas* to which we shall return, but the fundamental principle that gives unity to the *Ars Poetica* is that the genius imitating nature must be subject to the moderating discipline of *ars*. In view of Pope's approval of Roscommon, the Horatian principles that follow are mediated by way of his version of the *Ars Poetica* which uses terminology akin to Pope's in the *Essay*. Knowledge of the classics and their example is essential:

> Consider well the Greek originals,
> Read them by day and think of them by night.
> (Roscommon, *The Art of Poetry*)[7]

So too is knowledge of the traditional kinds and of the styles associated with them:

> Why is he honoured with a poet's name
> Who neither knows, nor would observe a rule?
> (Roscommon, *The Art of Poetry*)[8]

Horace is seen here as the spokesman for his own and the general Roman practice of following the Greek tradition. At the same time in lines much quoted in the Renaissance, he recommends liberty in imitation:

> Nor word for word too faithfully translate,
> Nor (as some servile imitators do)
> Prescribe at first such strict uneasy rules,
> As they must ever slavishly observe,
> Or all the laws of decency renounce.
> (Roscommon, *The Art of Poetry*)[9]

We may recall here his own example in freely adapting Greek metres to the character of the Latin language to express Roman themes.[10] By his own example and in his precepts he is more liberal than the critic-learning enshrined in the notes encrusting the text of his *Ars Poetica* in Renaissance editions might suggest. He applauds Roman writers who have departed from the beaten track:

> Our writers have attempted every way,
> And they deserve our praise whose daring Muse,
> Disdained to be beholden to the Greeks,
> And found fit subjects for her verse at home:
> Nor should we be less famous for our wit,
> Than for the force of our victorious arms;
> But that the time and care that are required,
> To overlook, and file, and polish well,
> Fright poets from that necessary toil.
> (Roscommon, *The Art of Poetry*)[11]

It is the function of the *ars* to help remedy this deficiency by advocating attention to the technical aspects of poetry which can be learned and need to be perfected in the interests of a truly great national literature.

The restoration of wit's fundamental laws making possible the true civilization of British wit in Pope's account had already been accomplished. Mulgrave's *Essay*, however, bears a closer resemblance to Boileau than to Horace.[12] Roscommon's *Essay on Translated Verse* gave impetus to the growing interest in poetic translation and set it upon fruitful lines, but is necessarily restricted by its subject matter. More successfully than his English predecessors, and more successfully than through a formal translation of the Latin, Pope assumes the mantle of poet-critic in the Horatian manner and freely addresses the needs of his times. It is not, therefore, that he renews specific precepts that may be paralleled or found in the tradition that grew up around Horace but more a question of general attitudes common to both poets and advocated in a comparable spirit. As Horace urges respect for the Greek tradition as a necessary prerequisite while vindicating the Roman right to deviate from it, so Pope struck a comparable balance between on the one hand the just esteem to be felt for ancient rules and on the other liberty of wit, the traditional inheritance of brave Britons. Servile Frenchmen and brave Britons are thus counters wittily juxtaposed by Pope to present undesirable polarities; the force of tradition and native genius like wit and judgement in the *Essay* are held in a creative tension, the one acting upon the other as in Horace to result in a synthesis that represents a dynamic mean between the two.

The last of the critics to whom Pope pays tribute at the end of the *Essay* for daring to 'assert the juster ancient cause' is William Walsh who fulfilled for Pope the practical function of the candid critic in the spirit of Horace's recommendations when Pope submitted work to him for comment. Elsewhere Pope tells us that Walsh first put him on the road to 'correctness'[13] suggesting the drive of the period towards formal polish, metrical perfection and purity of diction, all that comes with the application of *limae labor* 'the labour of the file', and is the hallmark of Augustan art whether Roman or English. The labour of the file on its own, of course, can achieve nothing if the raw material is not shaped by genius; in the *Essay* Pope ridicules the 'correctly cold' (240). Roscommon had dubbed Mulgrave's *Essay* 'correct', but what cannot be doubted is that by virtue of greater poetic talent Pope is more correct than either of his predecessors and moreover 'correct with spirit', and so the better able to embody in his poetry the precepts he is advocating. This exemplary decorum of content and form gives the *Essay* the kind of status in its period that has been accorded to the *Ars Poetica* at Rome, and makes it the best example in English of the critical verse epistle whose only rival might be Pope's later imitation of Horace's 'Epistle to Augustus'.

In form and content and in attitude and style, the *Essay* is reconizably Horatian and since it was the ground of his subsequent career we can trace important Horatian elements in Pope's poetical formation at the beginning. But it was after composing poems in a variety of genres and after translating Homer that Pope 'moralized his song' (*An Epistle to Dr Arbuthnot*, 341) and turned consciously to a new kind of poetry with Horace as his guide, when, in 1729, he conceived the plan for a *magnum opus*, 'a system of ethics in the Horatian way',[14] of which *An Essay on Man* and the ethical epistles were to be a part. Here the hexameter poems of Horace were a model for Pope in the broad sense of being attractively didactic and touching on serious issues with wit and humour, *ridentem dicere verum* (S 1.1.19).

In famous passages in the *Ars Poetica* the Roman had declared that knowledge is the basis of good writing and that everyone applauds the poet who can mingle the useful with the pleasing:

> scribendi recte sapere est et principium et fons.
> rem tibi Socraticae poterunt ostendere chartae . . .   (309–10)

> omne tulit punctum qui miscuit utile dulci,
> lectorem delectando pariterque monendo. (343–4)

In John Oldham's version of these lines written in 1681 we can see how easily these Horatian notions could be accommodated in the late seventeenth century:

> Good sense must be the certain standard still
> To all that will pretend to writing well:
> If you'd arrive at that, you needs must be
> Well versed and grounded in philosophy: (494–7)
> ...
>
> But he, that has the knack of mingling well
> What is of use with what's agreeable,
> That knows at once how to instruct and please,
> Is quickly crowned by all men's suffrages. (555–8)[15]

Horace seemed his own best example in his hexameter poems. Though the *Satires* were composed at the beginning and the *Epistles* towards the end of his career, he seems to include both works under the title *sermones* 'conversations' (see *Ep.* 2.1.250); the *Epistles* are less satirical and often more elevated, and some of the *Satires* are in the form of dialogues, but many of the latter like the first addressed to Maecenas satirizing the human tendency to be dissatisfied with one's lot could be described not as diatribes but as moral epistles turning upon some general point of conduct treated in the manner of an essayist. (Horace has been a favourite of essayists from Montaigne to Cowley and Addison.) Overall Horace has no system to impart, but his *Sermones* have often been called Socratic in that Horatian irony prompts self-scrutiny in pursuit of the true goods of life. The *Sermones* have often been seen to embody, in an exemplary fashion, the quest for moral truth that for Horace is the prerequisite for poetic achievement and so to fulfil the highest function ascribed to poetry in the *Ars Poetica*. The exemplary fashion of 'the Horatian way' in poetry, is, in Oldham's words, the knack of doing this agreeably.

> est brevitate opus, ut currat sententia, neu se
> impediat verbis lassas onerantibus auris;
> et sermone opus est modo tristi, saepe iocoso,
> defendente vicem modo rhetoris atque poetae,
> interdum urbani parcentis viribus atque
> extenuantis eas consulto. (S 1.10.9–14)

Pope and Horace

> There must be brevity that the thought may flow and not be impeded by words that burden weary ears: and there is a need for a style, now grave, now gay, sustaining the part now of orator and poet and sometimes of the wit moderating his strength and controlling it with purpose.

Brevity is not to be achieved at the expense of clarity as he warns in the *Ars Poetica*: *brevis esse laboro, obscurus fio* (25), 'I strive to be brief, I become obscure'. Concision without obscurity is a fundamental Popean ideal given expression from the beginning in *An Essay on Criticism*:

> Words are like leaves; and where they most abound,
> Much fruit of sense beneath is rarely found.   (309–10)

> But true expression, like the unchanging sun,
> Clears and improves whate'er it shines upon;
> It gilds all objects, but it alters none.   (314–16)

In his couplet style Pope perfected a clear and fluent concision till it became second nature. Speaking of his decision to put the principles and maxims of *An Essay on Man* into verse he says: 'I could express them more shortly this way than in prose itself and nothing is more certain than that much of the force as well as of the grace of arguments or instructions depends upon their conciseness.'[16] At the end of the poem the invocation to his guide, philosopher and friend Bolingbroke recalls the Horatian ideal:

> Come, then, my friend! my genius! come along;
> Oh master of the poet and the song!
> And while the Muse now stoops, or now ascends,
> To man's low passions, or their glorious ends,
> Teach me, like thee, in various nature wise,
> To fall with dignity, with temper rise;
> Formed by thy converse happily to steer,
> From grave to gay, from lively to severe;
> Correct with spirit; eloquent with ease,
> Intent to reason, or polite to please.   (*Ep.* 4.73–82)

Pope has translated into his own terms the characteristics of the *sermo* style which is of a 'various nature' (not as is sometimes said invariably 'a plain style') falling and rising in pitch with artful transitions of tone and mood. The categories of *poeta*, *rhetor* and *urbanus* are not so clearly differentiated by Pope whose notion of poetry automatically subsumes the three: eloquence and urbanity are embodied in the polished control of the verse. There is wit, too, of a most subtle and sophisticated kind in these deceptively simple lines. For the passage gracefully alludes both to the tonal range and temper of the Horatian *sermo* and to the career and character of Pope's addressee Bolingbroke who fell from power in 1714 and whose fortunes rose again after his return from exile in the 1720s. Pope's friend who had guided him in his new philosophic undertaking in *An Essay on Man* is in fact transformed into the Horatian model becoming in the dignity and control of his bearing its very incarnation; it is his 'converse' (conversation and friendship) that is the poet's inspiration and guide. The conflation of Bolingbroke and Horace cleverly accounts for the genesis of the poem and its manner or kind; it also breaks down distinctions between literary style and conduct of life, as Pope generously acknowledges the value and stimulus of Bolingbroke's friendship for his art and also suggests a very human account of literary influence likening the ancient poet to an influential friend in the present. If it is allowed that the lines as a whole represent what Pope aimed for and in large measure achieved in writing 'in the Horatian way', then they also show how a poet using his own medium (and the Augustan heroic couplet has its own dynamic that sets it apart from the Latin hexameter) could appropriate the Horatian and make it his own, integrating past and present to create something new.

An Essay on Man, though written in the Horatian way, is a more systematically philosophical poem than anything in Horace, who cannot quite be imagined as writing to 'vindicate the ways of God to man' (*Ep.* 1.16). Pope's ethical epistles, however, while being equally in the Horatian manner are perhaps nearer to Horace in their treatment of such topics as inconsistency in human character and the abuse of riches. Even if Pope had not gone on to write the imitations, these epistles would have marked him as a disciple of Horatian rather than, say, Juvenalian satire. For, unlike Juvenal who so often treats monstrous crimes and perversions, Horace treats follies and vices to which all mankind are prone, and unlike Juvenal who, if he is to be taken seriously as a moralist,[17] has a more negative vision, Horace in his Socratic way makes an implicit appeal to reason which has made him a favourite with such writers of reforming satire as Erasmus and Ben Jonson. There is a further difference in method. Horace's injunctions concerning the *sermo* style are followed by the reflection (not used in Pope's epigraph)

> ridiculum acri
> fortius ac melius magnas plerumque secat res. (S 1.10.14–15)

Rochester in his *Allusion to Horace* (1675–6) translated the Latin in a way that suggests a difference often felt between Horace and Juvenal, and between English Augustan satire and the earlier satire of the Elizabethans and Jacobeans:

> A jest in scorn points out and hits the thing
> More home than the morosest satire's sting.   (28–9)[18]

Horatian 'jests in scorn' can often be sharp, but his fine raillery, jocular urbanity and subtle use of irony are in marked contrast to the more acerbic railing of the grandly declamatory Juvenal whose style moves dramatically from hyperbole to bathos. Horace differs from Juvenal in his restraint of language and familiar address, and differs, too, from the other Roman model for formal verse satire, the difficult and linguistically eccentric Persius, in the purity and ease of his style. The distinctive appeal of Horace for Pope as a satirical model, therefore, may be put down to a variety of reasons embracing the nature of his targets, the larger outlook on life (explicit and implicit) in the way that they are chosen and treated, and the method and style of his attack, both in respect of organization and language.

Much of this is to say that Horace represented the satirical model from the Augustan period at Rome when cultural life flourished and the greatest poets were accorded a recognized place in the body politic, existing in some kind of harmony with the ruling powers. Horace is not an alienated outsider like the later satirists living in darker times and more difficult circumstances. It is to be expected that the Augustan satirist will enjoy a special esteem in the period that has been called Augustan in English. Yet perceptions of the political situation and attitudes of Virgil and Horace varied in the period of Dryden and Pope, and modern scholars[19] disagree as to whether Pope, writing in very different circumstances, uses Horace and his situation as a positive touchstone to highlight contemporary cultural deficiencies, or whether, as an independent outsider, he is actually critical of Horace as Dryden had been in calling him 'a temporising poet, a well mannered court slave and a man who is often afraid of laughing in the right place; who is ever decent because he is naturally servile'.[20] There can be little argument, however, about Pope's affinity with the Augustan in Horace if this is considered aesthetically and primarily in a metrical meaning.

Horace's prescription for the style of the *sermo* occurs in one in which he criticizes the originator of the genre, the old Roman Lucilius; the lines, in fact, define qualities of good style that Horace finds lacking in Lucilius. He admires his predecessor but asks:

> quid vetat et nosmet Lucili scripta legentis
> quaerere, num illius, num rerum dura negarit
> versiculos natura magis factos, et euntes
> mollius?   (S 1.10.56–9)

> What is to stop me asking as I read the writings of Lucilius whether it was the harsh nature of the poet or of his subject matter that prevented his verses from being better made and more refined?

These lines appear as the epigraph to the two satires of Donne, one of which, 'The Impertinent', is loosely related to Horace's encounter with the 'pest' (S 1.9) which Pope published with the Horatian Imitations in the 1730s but which he tells us in the Advertisement to the poems he 'versified' some twenty years earlier. Donne is not simply a harsh and morose Elizabethan (and had Pope felt this way about him he would not have been attracted to the satires in the first place); nevertheless, in refining him the Augustan poet is asking the same question and answering it by subjecting the original material to a radical critical revision on Horatian lines, as will be apparent in the following comparison from 'The Impertinent':

> At home in wholesome solitariness
> My piteous soul began the wretchedness
> Of suitors at court to mourn, and a trance
> Like his, who dreamed he saw hell, did advance
> It self o're me: such men as he saw there
> I saw at court, and worse, and more. Low fear
> Becomes the guilty, not th' accuser: then
> Shall I, none's slave, of high born or raised men
> Fear frowns; and my mistress truth, betray thee
> For th' huffing braggart, puft nobility?
> No, no, thou which since yesterday hast been
> Almost about the whole world, hast thou seen,
> O sun, in all thy journey, Vanity,
> Such as swells this bladder of a court?
> . . .
> Bear me some God! oh quickly bear me hence
> To wholesome solitude, the nurse of sense:
> Where contemplation prunes her ruffled wings,
> And the free soul looks down to pity kings.
> There sober thought pursued the amusing theme
> Till fancy coloured it and formed a dream.
> A vision hermits can to hell transport,
> And force ev'n me to see the damned at court;
> Not Dante dreaming all the infernal state,
> Beheld such scenes of envy, sin and hate.
> Base fear becomes the guilty, not the free;
> Suits tyrants, plunderers, but suits not me.
> Shall I, the terror of this sinful town,
> Care, if a liveried lord or smile or frown?
> Who cannot flatter, and detest who can,
> Tremble before a noble serving-man?
> O my fair mistress truth! Shall I quit thee,
> For huffing braggart puft nobility?
> Thou who since yesterday has rolled o'er all
> The busy, idle blockheads of the ball,
> Hast thou, O sun! beheld an emptier sort
> Than such as swell this bladder of a court?
>
> (Satire IV. 155–68 and 184–205)

Pope and Horace

After hearing Pope, it is not difficult to realize why to the Augustan ear the lines of Donne seemed inharmonious, nerveless and prosaically flat. With the obvious metrical refinement come other changes in attitude and manner which bring the original more in line with the requirements of the Augustan *sermo*.

In his advertisement Pope argues that 'the poems of so eminent a divine as Dr Donne' prove 'with what indignation and contempt a Christian may treat vice or folly in ever so low or ever so high a station'.[21] Donne mourning in his piteous soul the wretchedness of courtiers and courtly vanity does indeed take the part of the solemn divine. Pope shares Donne's moral seriousness as he admires his wit but as the man of sense in detached contemplation, *vir urbanus*, he soberly pursues the *amusing* theme, uniting the grave and the gay with a more playful touch than Donne. There is humour and irony in Pope's reference to himself as a hermit, and a witty exploitation of incongruity in the transportation of the hermit to hell. Pope takes delight in witty paradox in the 'liveried lord' and the 'noble serving man', and in paradox with double meaning in the swelling of the 'emptier sort' and the 'busy idle blockheads of the ball'. The graver wit of the original is interpenetrated with a playful humour that has the paradoxical effect of intensifying rather than diluting the ridicule and of lightening it by making it more attractive. Pope differs from Donne too as *rhetor* in what might be called the oratorical pitch of his style. In his expansion of Donne and in the organization of his couplets, he has a more pronounced rhetorical structuring. The opening reaches a dignified climax in the full resounding line: 'And the free soul looks down to pity kings'. Notable is the management of emphasis in the three rhetorical questions 'Shall I . . . Care . . . Tremble . . . quit'; within this passage, the 'liveried lord' and 'noble serving man' form a prelude to 'puft nobility' which as the climax in a series of three gains emphasis accordingly. The movement of Donne's language by contrast is much more informal and mimics conversation. Since Horace elsewhere describes his satirical muse (though not without irony) as 'pedestrian' (*S* 2.6.17) and his *Sermones* as 'creeping along the ground' (*Ep*. 2.1.251) and even modestly disclaimed for himself the name of a poet in his hexameter verse (*S* 1.4.39–44), it may well be thought that Donne is nearer than Pope to what Dryden called 'the low style'[22] of Horace. Yet Dryden, who similarly found Donne's satire unrefined, also says of the 'Epistle to Augustus' that it is 'of so much dignity in the words and elegancy in the numbers that the author plainly shows that the *sermo pedestris* in his other satires was rather his choice than his necessity'.[23] Such dignity and elegance are habitual to Pope in his epistolary style which, it is generally true to say, is more often pitched at the upper register of Horace's varied scale, as it is in this instance in the revision of Donne.

The metrical refinement and fluency, the jocularity of the wit and the rhetorical panache sound the Augustan note in English, but Pope shares with Donne a proud independence of spirit and insistent assertiveness that are foreign to the Horatian manner. In his self-dramatization 'the terror of this sinful town' goes even further than Donne in projecting himself as incapable of flattery and utterly confident of his satirical talent. It has been well suggested[24] that Pope was drawn to this satire rather than to the Horatian poem to which it is loosely related precisely because, while Horace writes comically as an insider afflicted by a pestiferous social climber who envies his commerce with the great and the good, Donne foreshadowed Pope's stance in attacking a court which he believed to be corrupt and from which he wholly dissociates himself. The difference in stance and tone here between the English and the Roman is equally apparent in the Horatian imitations themselves, where opposition to the ruling powers gives Pope's satire consistently more bite than that of Horace.

Imitating Horace brought the English poet directly to the source of a major classical influence upon his poetical formation and practice that is recognizable even if Pope had never gone on to write the Horatian imitations. In translating Homer, Pope had sought to render ancient sense as faithfully as modern expression might allow (a formula that allows the translator considerable latitude) but in the freer form of the imitation ancient sense too may be subject not merely to modification but to a more radical revision, variation or even inversion. Indeed as imitator, Pope follows Horace's famous advice in the *Ars Poetica*:

> publica materies privati iuris erit, si
> non circa vilem patulumque moraberis orbem,
> nec verbo verbum curabis reddere fidus
> interpres, nec desilies imitator in artum,
> unde pedem proferre pudor vetet aut operis lex.   (131–5)

> Material in the public domain will become subject to your private rights if you do not linger along the broad and common track and are not concerned to render word for word as a faithful translator and do not in imitating plump for a narrow method where timidity or the rules of the genre impede your progress.

In all his poetry Pope's wit sought, in a variety of ways, to make a synthesis between ancient and modern, and in the imitations that synthesis took a new form as the text of Horace became for Pope *publica materies*, the traditional inheritance, that he seeks to appropriate and make new. The resulting transformation was successful for two related reasons. In the first place, because whatever differences Pope felt between his own outlook and circumstances and those of his predecessor, Horace as few other authors engaged his mind on topics about which he felt deeply and in a manner which, in a general sense, he had already made his own. Secondly Horace met a particular need in Pope's life in 1733:

The occasion of publishing these Imitations was the clamour raised on some of my epistles. An answer from Horace was both more full and of more dignity than any I could have made in my own person.[25]

Further light upon the occasion is thrown by Pope in an anecdote told to his friend Spence which recounts a visit to Pope by Bolingbroke who happened to take up a copy of Horace which lay on Pope's table and, 'turning over the leaves chanced upon the first satire of the second book. He observed how well that would hit my case, if I were to imitate it in English.'[26] Imitating Horace began and continued to be integrally a part of the poetic crusade against false taste and the abuse of riches that Pope had already begun in his moral essays. It sprang from the need for self-vindication and resulted in a self-defence that became more than merely personal as Pope used Horace to put the particular circumstances of his own case in a larger perspective.

Charged both with going beyond bounds in being too harsh in his satirical attack and with writing lines that are lifeless, Horace consults a lawyer Trebatius who advises him to give up, or if he must continue writing, to sing Caesar's achievements which will be more rewarding. The poet alleges lack of proper talent to do this. Each man has his own enthusiasm; Horace's delight is to follow in the footsteps of the old Roman writer of *sermones* Lucilius, who entrusted his secrets to his books so that his whole life was open to view. But he keeps his pen-power in check never taking the offensive unless provoked. Whatever his situation he will continue to write. Trebatius expresses fears that an important figure might cause his downfall. Horace points to the precedent of Lucilius who remained on good terms with Scipio and Laelius, who were not offended by his satirical verses against notables of their day:

>   scilicet uni aequus virtuti atque eius amicis.   (S 2.1.70)

>   To virtue only and her friends a friend.   (121)

Trebatius can find no fault with this but still urges caution, quoting the law against *mala carmina*, meaning both bad and libellous poems. But what if the poems are good and meet with Caesar's approval, if they attack those who deserve it while the poet himself is honest (*integer ipse*)? That being so, says Trebatius, there is no case to answer.

To make the answer from Horace convincing, Pope fits all the literary and political circumstances to his own case, and in so doing makes the circumstantial detail much more precise and particular than Horace. For Horace had given the charge against him in general terms and made mention only of Pantabolus and Nomentanus (thought by some scholars to have been names made notorious by Horace's model Lucilius) whereas Pope calls to witness many living individuals and uses identifiable nicknames for others. Where Horace had cordial relations with Augustus who honoured the poet's calling and fostered the arts through his friend Maecenas to whom the poet was indebted for his Sabine farm, Pope had no place at court where the king disliked poetry and the king's chief minister Sir Robert Walpole never succeeded in enlisting Pope on his payroll. In a later poem he prided himself on his independence gained from the proceeds of his Homer translation:

> But (thanks to Homer) since I live and thrive,
> Indebted to no prince or peer alive . . .
> *(The Second Epistle of the Second Book of Horace,* 68–9)

In the opening section of the imitation, therefore, Pope does not, like Horace, with seeming modesty suggest that he has not the talent necessary for epic or the public ode (he had already translated Homer and composed his St Cecilia Ode whereas Horace had not yet published any *Odes* before he penned the original) but with finely mocking irony exposes the hypocrisy and corruption of the system whereby hack writers are rewarded for their hollow celebration of an insignificant court indifferent to poetic merit:

> Or if you needs must write, write Caesar's praise:
> You'll gain at least a knighthood or the bays.
> P: What? like Sir Richard, rumbling, rough and fierce,
> With arms and George and Brunswick crowd the verse?
> Rend with tremendous sound your ears asunder,
> With gun, drum, trumpet, blunderbuss, and thunder? (21–6)

Where Horace warned by Trebatius that one of the great may cause his downfall invokes the example of Lucilius, Pope looks back to Boileau and Dryden pointedly contrasting his own position with theirs:

> Could pensioned Boileau lash in honest strain
> Flatterers and bigots even in Louis' reign?
> Could Laureate Dryden pimp and friar engage,
> Yet neither Charles nor James be in a rage?
> And I not strip the gilding off a knave,
> Unplaced, unpensioned, no man's heir or slave? (111–16)

Horace had made no such pointed contrast with Lucilius. Pope does not therefore scruple to change Horace to fit his own case.

At the same time there is a basic identity of values between the two poets, though the original is often rearranged to bring them out. In one instance Pope assumes the virtue of the golden mean, a favourite Horatian doctrine, for which there is no warrant in this particular poem:

Pope and Horace

> My head and heart thus flowing through my quill,
> Verse-man or prose-man, term me what you will;
> Papist or Protestant, or both between,
> Like good Erasmus in an honest mean,
> In moderation placing all my glory,
> While Tories call me Whig and Whigs a Tory. (63–8)

These neatly balanced lines with a verbal dexterity that sounds almost ticklish have the serious function of reminding readers that Pope's satire like his friendships ran across the main religious and political divisions of his time, and they serve his case well in their strategic position just before the central claim to satirical discretion:

> Satire's, my weapon but I'm too discreet
> To run amuck and tilt at all I meet;
> I only wear it in a land of hectors,
> Thieves, supercargoes, sharpers and directors. (69–72)

In another instance, Pope does not so much import an Horatian value as adapt and develop a hint from Horace when, in order to illustrate the honourable life of the satirist, the Roman represents Laelius and Scipio, the good and the great, retreating from the public arena to relax informally in the company of Lucilius

> nugari cum illo, et discincti ludere, donec
> decoqueretur olus, soliti. (73–4)

> they would turn to folly, and flinging off restraint would indulge with him in sport while their dish of herbs was on the boil.

The vivid phrase *discincti ludere* in its literal reference to wrestling and its figurative suggestion of bouts of verbal wit evokes the heroic simplicity of the old Romans. Pope turns all this to his own case adapting the imagery to the dignified but still informal pleasures he pursued in his elegant country house at Twickenham (then well outside the city of London):

> Know all the distant din that world can keep
> Rolls o'er my grotto and but soothes my sleep.
> There, my retreat the best companions grace
> Chiefs out of war and statesmen out of place.
> There St John mingles with my friendly bowl
> The feast of reason and the flow of soul:
> And he, whose lightning pierced th' Iberian lines,
> Now forms my quincunx, and now ranks my vine,
> Or tames the genius of the stubborn plain,
> Almost as quickly as he conquered Spain. (123–32)

Over his celebrated grotto, a pathway dug out under the main road that separated his house from his garden, he had inscribed a line from another Horatian poem: *secretum iter et fallentis semita vitae* (*Ep.* 1.18.103), 'the secret way and the path of a life unseen').

Pope is here wittily finding a literal application in his own life for what is in Horace a figurative expression recalling the Epicurean injunction *lathe biosas*, live a concealed life, that is a private life away from politics and the public world, for only such a life makes possible the attainment of *ataraxia*, tranquillity of soul and its Roman equivalent *otium*, the philosophic calm that is the goal of the Horatian life. In Pope as in Horace this is not to be found in solitary ascetic or even aesthetic contemplation but in friendship, enjoyment of the world and informal intellectual intercourse (a veritable humanist feast) which are delightfully concentrated in the celebrated couplet culminating in 'the flow of soul'. Horace's poetry celebrates rural joys, Pope takes delight in the ordering of nature in his garden at Twickenham. The impulse to cultivate one's own garden in withdrawal from the public world tempered by a desire seriously to engage that world in active critical debate is thoroughly Horatian, though it is something of a paradox that in the Latin poem, because the life of withdrawal is associated with the circle of Lucilius while Horace is asserting his desire to continue writing satire, the antithetical balance between these two impulses is less marked in Horace than it is in the English imitation.

The case for the satirist's defence rests on identical grounds but is presented with more direct emphasis in Pope. Horace makes indirect claim to autobiographical candour and integrity of motive in citing the precedent of Lucilius. Pope appropriates these claims directly to himself inviting comparison with the Latin text on the facing page. The determination to continue writing no matter what, the threat to use the powerful weapons at the satirist's disposal, the self-justification and the scorn for any opposition, all have their natural part in the case made by Horace but their emphatic expansion in Pope has the effect of making the case as he argues it more openly assertive and more sharply defined. Imitation of Horace, therefore, did not involve any dilution of his own poetic temper: on the contrary

> In this impartial glass my Muse intends
> Fair to expose myself, my foes, my friends;
> Publish the present age . . .   (57–9)

He sacrifices nothing of his satirical character; in fact he uses Horace to vindicate his own aggression and merrily rejoices in his capacity to make a poetic success of it:

> Its proper power to hurt each creature feels . . .   (85)

Pope and Horace

> Whoe're offends at some unlucky time,
> Slides into verse, and hitches in a rhyme,
> Sacred to ridicule! his whole life long,
> And the sad burden of some merry song.   (76–9)

Pope was the first to admit that the resulting expression of his own poetic self was rather different from Horace. In *The Epilogue to his Satires* (1738) he has the character of an impertinent censurer object:

> But Horace, Sir, was delicate, was nice;
> Bubo observes, he lashed no sort of vice . . .
> His sly, polite, insinuating style
> Could please at court and make Augustus smile:
> An artful manager that crept between
> His friend and shame, and was a kind of screen.
> (*Dialogue* 1.11–12, 19–22)[27]

Whether or not Pope is being critical of Horace for reasons similar to Dryden's or simply exposing the inadequacy of the objecting courtier's understanding of Horace, or even doing something of both, it is clear that for Pope this is a false Horace he wants nothing to do with. That his voice in the imitations so evidently continues to speak with accents modulated in the ethical epistles, and that the poetry of the imitations is equally successful, together invite the conclusion that far from adopting a false mask to function as a kind of smokescreen, Pope in taking up Horace found a new medium in which to channel his poetic energies and in the process extended his poetic self. In the *Ars Poetica*, Horace had declared *fungar vice cotis* (30), 'I shall function as a whetstone', sharpening awareness in others. So it proved with Pope. The imitations, in fact, may be regarded as dialogues with a sympathetic friend in the course of which the poet clarifies his stance upon a number of critical issues. In this instance it is the nature of the satirist's case (not just a case that Pope shares with Horace but one that embraces Lucilius, Boileau and Dryden with allusions to Juvenal and Persius too)[28] turning upon the distinction between satire and libel, and asserting the dignity and probity of this time-honoured genre. Nowhere else in Pope's work had there been so full an airing of the larger issues involved. Each imitation brought out something new in Pope. In the most famous of them his version of the 'Epistle to Augustus' (1736), Pope is inspired by Horace into writing a new style of literary criticism different from the negative critique of the *Dunciad* (1728) or the largely personal defence of *An Epistle to Dr Arbuthnot* (1735): 'a new battle of the ancients and moderns fought in favour of the moderns along Horatian lines'.[29] In *An Essay on Criticism* at the beginning of his poetic career, Pope had first assumed the mantle of poet-critic to mark out in the manner and spirit of Horace the general critical principles (derived largely from the ancients with many being specifically Horatian) to be adopted by the modern critic for the general health of contemporary culture; in the maturity of his genius he was prompted by Horace to assume the mantle of poet-critic again and this time to apply those principles in a more practical way in a judicious review of the English literary tradition.

Pope's summary of the argument of Horace suggests the easy affinity he felt with the original:

> Horace here pleads the cause of his contemporaries, first against the taste of the town, whose humour it was to magnify the authors of the preceding age; secondly against the court and nobility, who encouraged only the writers for the theatre; and lastly against the emperor himself, who had conceived them of little use to the government. He shows (by a view of the progress of learning and the change of taste among the Romans) that the introduction of the polite arts of Greece had given the writers of his time great advantages over their predecessors, that their morals were much improved, and the licence of those ancient poets restrained: that satire and comedy were becoming more just and useful; that whatever extravagances were left on the stage, were owing to the ill taste of the nobility; that poets, under due regulations, were in many respects useful to the state; and concludes, that it was upon them the emperor himself must depend for his fame with posterity.[30]

The circumstances of his own position perhaps disposed Pope to represent a greater distance between Horace and Augustus on one of the central questions at issue, the utility of poetry in the *civitas*, than is generally supposed to have been the case, but the contention that Horace is offering 'an apology for the poets in order to render Augustus more their patron' can be allowed. The imperial panegyric with which the epistle is framed, however genuinely conveyed, is essentially strategic.

The new literature for which Horace is critical advocate sought to achieve polish and refinement not only in the small-scale genres practised by the poets of the previous generation like Catullus but also in the large public genres of epic and drama that had formed the basis of the first Roman literature worthy of the name when poets like Ennius and Naevius began to adapt the Greek classics to Roman purposes after the Romans came into contact with centres of Greek civilization in the wake of the first Punic War. The conservative taste that he inveighs against continued to regard Ennius as a second Homer and resisted the new poetry of Virgil and Varius who wrote epic and in Varius' case tragedy as well. While he allows that the old Roman tragedy has spirit and vigour, he finds it shows ignorance and wants art. The criticism is of style and construction. The comedian Plautus, for example, is heavily censured for weakness in maintaining character and poor plotting. Despite the impediment of the poor taste of the crowd and of the upper classes seen in the popularity of spectacle in the threatre, Horace holds out the possibility of a

Pope and Horace

newly civilized literature of high standards inspired by and rivalling the classical example of the Greeks:

> The reflections of Horace and the judgements passed in his epistle to Augustus seemed so seasonable to the present times that I could not help applying them to the use of my own country.[31]

Pope's affinity is with the underlying critical principles which as poet-critic he endeavours to apply in his own judgements and embody in his own poetry, in the belief that they answer a general cultural need.

The repudiation of conservative prejudice in the opening section is based on good sense:

> If time improve our wit as well as wine,
> Say at what age a poet grows divine? (49–50)

Though made in playful rhetorical terms, it contains within it a serious plea enforced by Pope's own example for the exercise of true judgement:

> the people's voice is odd,
> It is and it is not, the voice of God.
> To Gammer Gurton if it give the bays
> And yet deny the Careless Husband praise,
> Or say our fathers never broke a rule;
> Why then I say, the public is a fool.
> But let them own that greater faults than we
> They had, and greater virtues, I'll agree . . .
> Milton's strong pinion now not heaven can bound,
> Now serpent-like, in prose he sweeps the ground,
> In quibbles, angel and archangel join,
> And God the father turns a school-divine.
> Not that I'd lop the beauties from his book,
> Like slashing Bentley with his desperate hook;
> Or damn all Shakespeare, like the affected fool
> At court, who hates whate'er he reads at school. (86–96, 99–106)

The judgement of Milton is not partisan nor is the dismissal of the classical scholar Richard Bentley who had recently published his eccentric and over-rationalistic edition of *Paradise Lost* (1730). The case of the courtier's response to Shakespeare is a reminder of the only too human origins of prejudice reinforced later when the rejection of the new is said to be frequently a matter of envy. The lines offer a critical challenge to the authority of learning and fashion:

> I lose my patience, and I own it too,
> When works are censured not as bad but new,
> While if our elders break all reason's laws

> These fools demand not pardon but applause.
> On Avon's bank, where flowers eternal blow,
> If I but ask, if any weed can grow? . . .
> How will our fathers rise up in a rage,
> And swear, all shame is lost in George's age! (115–20, 125–6)

Having produced his own edition of Shakespeare (1725) Pope had doubtless experienced this bardolatry at first hand, a continuing impediment in the pursuit of good judgement. The general example in Horace is made forcible by Pope's particularization.

The argument made for due critical regard to be given to the new concludes with the unanswerable question

> Had ancient times conspired to disallow
> What then was new, what had been ancient now? (135–6)

The mention of the new made by Horace in relation to the Greeks leads by elegant transition to humorous presentation of the desire for novelty on the part of the versatile Greeks which is then contrasted with the serious and businesslike life of the early Romans. Now the Romans have themselves become light-headed and been infected one and all by the itch for versifying. Nevertheless this is a harmless pastime and in fact poets can be useful in the community. We have now arrived at one of the main points in the argument.

We may recall here the famous lines in *Ars Poetica*:

> omne tulit punctum qui miscuit utile dulci
> lectorem delectando pariterque monendo. (343–4)

> But he that joins instructions with delight,
> Profit with pleasure, carries all the votes.
> (Roscommon, *The Art of Poetry*)[32]

The author of the *Odes* cannot have had a narrow conception of utility. Just before he advocates it, he makes the same telling contrast between Greek and Romans:

> Greece had a genius, Greece had eloquence,
> For her ambition and her end was fame;
> Our Roman youth is bred another way,
> And taught no arts but those of usury.
> (Roscommon, *the Art of Poetry*)[33]

As an advocate for poetry addressing a Roman audience, it is hardly surprising that Horace departs from the Aristotelian account that allows for an artistic autonomy which is more congenial to the modern world. The Greek philosopher, of course, was more directly an heir to the Periclean ideal which put a supreme value upon the love of beauty and the pursuit of truth for

Pope and Horace

their own sake. This had its counterpart at Rome but in the scale of values art is often secondary:

> tu regere imperio populos, Romane, memento,
> (hae tibi erunt artes), pacique imponere morem,
> parcere subiectis et debellare superbos.
> (Aeneid 6.851–3)[34]

Remember, Roman, to rule the nations with your power; these will be your arts, to impose the habit of peace, to spare the conquered and to quell the proud.

What could be a more persuasive argument for the value of poetry to the hard-headed Romans than that it is useful to the state, *utilis urbi* (124), and contributes to the progress of civilization?

Pope changes the cultural history wittily adapting the caricature of Greek instability to a humorous but serious critique of the pleasure-loving levity of the Restoration:

> No wonder then, when all was love and sport,
> The willing Muses were debauched at court; (151–2)

He had earlier referred to 'The mob of gentlemen who wrote with ease' (108). It is a major concern of Pope to vindicate the new seriousness ushered in by the new order following the revolution of 1688 (coincidentally the year of his birth).

The argument that poetry is useful to the state begins in Pope as in Horace with humour and irony:

> Of little use the man you may suppose,
> Who says in verse what others say in prose;
> Yet let me show, a poet's of some weight,
> And (though no soldier) useful to the state. (201–4)

Pope evidently knew the king's opinion of him: 'Who is this Pope that I hear so much about? I cannot discover what is his merit. Why will not my subjects write in prose?' The argument then becomes more serious:

> I scarce can think him such a worthless thing,
> Unless he praise some monster of a king,
> Or virtue or religion turn to sport,
> To please a lewd, or unbelieving court.
> Unhappy Dryden! – In all Charles's days,
> Roscommon only boasts unspotted bays. (209–14)

The king and court might at first seem to be Hanoverian, then become Stuart; cleverly they can be both. The independent spirit in which the judgement is applied is more marked in Pope than in Horace, who argues that the poet is a force for good in a variety of ways without specific example. In a line highlighted in Pope's Latin text he is *asperitatis et invidiae corrector et irae* (129) 'the corrector of asperity envy and anger'.

The general point is given particular force by Pope in the tribute he pays to the reforming zeal of Swift in lines which almost caused him to be prosecuted by the government:

> Let Ireland tell, how wit upheld her cause,
> Her trade supported, and supplied her laws;
> And leave on Swift this grateful verse engraved,
> The rights a court attacked, a poet saved. (221–4)

Lest it be thought that Pope's judgement is merely partisan signalling Tory opposition to Whig policy, and a predominantly political motive in the adaptation of Horace, it is worth noting that in previous lines he praises Addison who was not of his circle nor of his political persuasion. Moreover, given the previous censure of Addison in the portrait of 'Atticus' in *An Epistle to Dr Arbuthnot* (1735) the lines testify to the genuineness of Pope's effort to judge cases strictly on merit, and so enforce his argument by example.

Having asserted that the poet is actively a civilizing force, Horace then offers a complementary argument that the growth of civilization with the force of law has made the poet more responsible to his fellows. The example he gives concerns satire. The licence allowed in the old Fescennine satirical verses in rural festivals having been abused is now restrained. The account of the progress from the rustic to the urbane does not perhaps have quite the factual basis in English literary history that it may well have had in the Roman but there is a compelling symbolic truth and the culminating definition of refined and responsible satire reflects the balanced ideal to which Pope aspired in his moral essays and Horatian imitations:

> Hence satire rose, that just the medium hit,
> And heals with morals what it hurts with wit. (261–2)

The argument proceeds to the major impact upon Roman civilization provided by the Greeks.

> Graecia capta ferum victorem cepit et artes
> intulit agresti Latio. (156–7)

Captured Greece took her savage conquerors captive and brought the arts into rustic Latium.

Pope found a parallel in the recent French classical influence upon English:

> We conquered France, but felt our captive's charms;
> Her arts victorious triumphed o'er our arms:

Pope and Horace

>   Britain to soft refinements less a foe,
>   Wit grew polite and numbers learned to flow.
>   Waller was smooth; but Dryden taught to join
>   The varying verse, the full resounding line,
>   The long majestic march, and energy divine.
>   Though still some traces of our rustic vein
>   And splay-foot verse, remained, and will remain.
>   Late very late, correctness grew our care,
>   When the tired nation breathed from civil war.
>   Exact Racine, and Corneille's noble fire
>   Showed us that France had something to admire.
>   Not but the tragic spirit was our own,
>   And full in Shakespeare, fair in Otway shone:
>   But Otway failed to polish or refine
>   And fluent Shakespeare scarce effaced a line.
>   Even copious Dryden, wanted, or forgot,
>   The last and greatest art, the art to blot.   (263–81)

The final line in Horace to the effect that the early Roman tragic writers deeming it disgraceful were afraid to use the *litura* by which lines could be blotted out (and so revised) prompted in Pope the memory of Ben Jonson's remark in *Discoveries* 'I remember the players have often mentioned it as an honour to Shakespeare that in his writing (whatsoever he penned) he never blotted out a line. My answer hath been, would he had blotted a thousand'.[35] The application of the criticism to, Dryden whose versification Pope earlier praises so justly, pinpoints a difference between him and Pope that is now a commonplace. In his application of Horatian critical principles to the native tradition, like the Roman poet-critic before him he is himself the embodiment of the standards he applies and the attitudes he advocates. It may be said that he here defines the Augustan moment and that his judgement is vindicated in the refinement, urbanity and poise of the verse.

After a review of comedy and an energetic condemnation of contemporary theatrical taste, Horace concludes the *Epistle* with an address to Augustus: the prince who is jealous of his fame knows well enough that only good poets can bestow the laurel crown on Caesar. In adapting Horace to his own times in which Colley Cibber, later to be the hero of the revised *Dunciad*, had been made poet laureate (in 1730), Pope exhorts George Augustus not without irony to have a care for his fame or at least to appoint a Maecenas to act on his behalf:

>   Yet think, great Sir! (so many virtues shown)
>   Ah think, what poet best may make them known?
>   Or choose at least some minister of grace,
>   Fit to bestow the laureate's weighty case.   (376–9)

For the rest, there follows ironic praise and a spirited, dignified and humorous dismissal of the dismal efforts of servile flatterers.

Horace ended the poem by expressing the wish that no one should ever praise him in poor verse *ne rubeam pingui donatus munere* (267) 'in case I have to blush at the stupid gift', words used by Pope as an epigraph to his imitation. Horace addressing Augustus Caesar and Pope addressing George Augustus in widely differing circumstances are both concerned to uphold the dignity of the poet's calling and on this both are uncompromisingly immoderate:

> mediocribus esse poetis
> non homines, non di, non concessere columnae.   (*Ars* 372–3)

> But no authority of gods nor men,
> Allow of any mean in poesie.
> (Roscommon, *The Art of Poetry*)[36]

Poetry is not a gentleman's pastime or a trivial pursuit but an art that requires a lifetime's dedication and the most rigorous judgement in the weighing of words:

> at qui legitimum cupiet fecisse poema,
> cum tabulis animum censoris sumet honesti;
> (*Ep.* 2.2.109–10, 'To Florus')

> But the man whose aim is to have wrought a poem true to Art's rules, when he takes his tablets will take also the spirit of an honest censor.

The flexible good sense of Horace as literary guide and mentor to those who would see the import of his meaning is nowhere better illustrated than in his doctrine of poetic diction as delivered here in the 'Epistle to Florus' or more famously in *Ars Poetica*. In the perpetual cultural flux, there can be no hard and fast rules; the poet must be allowed licence to adopt new words as to revive old ones; in sifting, purifying and enlarging the dialect of the tribe the poet's judgement must be guided above all by usage:

> Men ever had, and ever will have leave,
> To coin new words well suited to the age:
> Words are like leaves, some wither every year
> And every year a younger race succeed . . .
> Use may revive the obsoletest words,
> And banish those that now are most in vogue;
> Use is the judge, the law, and rule of speech.
> (Roscommon, *The Art of Poetry*)[37]

Pope and Horace

In context Horace is defending the contemporary Augustan practice of Virgil and Varius against conservative Roman opinion that deplored innovation. For post-renaissance readers the doctrine served as a timely reminder that the purity of diction for which Horace is famous was achieved not by attempting to preserve traditional 'classical' expression but by the individual poet's mixing of ancient with modern (and native with foreign) in response to the speech of the time. Expounding and expanding the doctrine in his imitation of the 'Epistle to Florus', Pope eloquently defines the practice of his own lifetime's effort, and demonstrates in the easy vigour of his lines how that practice grew out of the traditional Roman *ars* as mediated by Horace; what seems like nature is the effect of art:

> But how severely with themselves proceed
> The men who write such verse as we can read?
> Their own strict judges, not a word they spare
> That wants or force, or light, or weight, or care,
> Howe'er unwillingly it quits its place,
> Nay tho' at court (perhaps) it may find grace:
> Such they'll degrade; and sometimes, in its stead,
> In downright charity revive the dead;
> Mark where a bold expressive phrase appears,
> Bright through the rubbish of some hundred years;
> Command old words that long have slept, to wake,
> Words, that wise Bacon, or brave Raleigh spake;
> Or bid the new be English, ages hence,
> (For use will father what's begot by sense)
> Pour the full tide of eloquence along
> Serenely pure, and yet divinely strong,
> Rich with the treasures of each foreign tongue;
> Prune the luxuriant, the uncouth refine,
> But show no mercy to an empty line;
> Then polish all, with so much life and ease,
> You think 'tis nature, and a knack to please:
> 'But ease in writing flows from art, not chance
> As those move easiest who have learned to dance.' (157–79)

The last couplet is Pope's equivalent of the Latin words that he appended as an epigraph to the imitation: *ludentis speciem dabit et torquebitur* (124) 'he will wear the expression of one at play and yet be on the rack'. The couplet is also almost a self-quotation from *An Essay in Criticism* indicative of the poet's self-dedication to his craft in the spirit of Horace that marks the whole of Pope's career. Ancient and modern are united by a kindred spirit, shared principles and a common dedication; following Horace, Pope's lines have a natural eloquence, a witty urbanity and an imaginative force harnessed together in the service of art that is refined and civilizing.

9

GOOD HUMOUR AND THE AGELASTS: HORACE, POPE AND GRAY

Felicity Rosslyn

HOW CAN ONE praise Horace without employing terms that could as easily be used to bury him? It is a peculiar fatality of his qualities that they so easily convert to defects, and his urbanity can strike the reader as mere worldliness, his humour as frivolity and his restraint as a basic lack of feeling. The ups and downs of his reputation would imply much the same – that the key to unlocking the wisdom that lies in his qualities and, more subtly, in their respective proportions, is easily lost, and once it is gone we are left with something degraded: the 'clubbable' Horace, or the courtier, or the satirist who does not bite, like Dryden's:

I must confess that the delight which Horace gives me is but languishing . . . I speak of my own taste only: he may ravish other men; but I am too stupid and insensible to be tickled. Where he barely grins himself, and, as Scaliger says, only shews his white teeth, he cannot provoke me to any laughter. His urbanity, that is, his good manners, are to be commended, but his wit is faint; and his salt, if I may dare to say so, almost insipid. Juvenal is of a more vigorous and masculine wit; he gives me as much pleasure as I can bear . . .[1]

The fact that Dryden, author of some of the most sympathetic and successful translations of Horace, had moods in which he could not say that he really enjoyed his author, may well give us pause. What is it in Horace's art that so rapidly spoils?

I want to dwell on the possibility that it is Horace's good humour itself that leads to faintly dismissive accounts of him; and that there is a problem in the way good humour touches off an ambivalent response in the reader. If one part of us delights in the free play of irony, another part demands to know 'where the author stands'; and if in one mood we find the smiling Horatian wisdom enough to live by, in another we may feel with Dryden that the salt lacks savour, and the wisdom is only valid for fair weather. We may wonder with Matthew Arnold what sustains the 'ideal, cheerful, sensuous, pagan life' when it is 'sick or sorry' – but, as he rapidly corrects himself, it never was;

Horace, Pope and Gray

'never at least shows itself to us sick or sorry . . .'² Is it not proper to be serious, sometimes, about serious things?

The Horace we meet in the *Sermones* would answer, I imagine, no. But the 'no' would be deeply considered, not the pagan 'light-heartedness' Arnold thought inadequate to the test. The difficulty is that Horace's convictions would prevent him from saying more, as would the 'good manners' Dryden commends; we cannot expect a defence of good humour from a truly good-humoured poet. But I would like to guess at what that defence would be, by way of substantiating the praise Horace won from the most intelligent of his French editors, as a kind of Socrates in verse. If Alcibiades compares the philosopher to an ugly Silenus with images of the gods tucked inside, so André Dacier sees the inner and outer meaning of Horace:

In the shape that Horace presents himself to us in his satires, we see nothing at the first view which deserves our attention. It seems that he is rather an amusement for children than for the serious consideration of men. But when we take away his crust, and that which hides him from our sight, when we discover him to the bottom, then we find all the divinities in a full assembly: that is to say, all the virtues which ought to be the continual exercise of those who seriously endeavour to correct their vices.³

But just as Socrates depended for his method on claiming to 'know' nothing, so Horace's teaching is indistinguishable from his willingness to amuse. It would have been disastrous, certainly, for him to announce his programme as Dacier describes it: 'To instruct us how to combat our vices, to regulate our passions, to follow nature, to give bounds to our desires, to distinguish betwixt truth and falsehood, and betwixt our conceptions of things, and things themselves . . .'⁴ This may well be the effect of reading him, but it could never be achieved by 'instruction': in such matters, the example is everything.

We may suppose, then, that Horace's playfulness knows what it is about, and the *Sermones* have an undeclared antagonist in view, in the shape of the reader who wishes to be serious about serious things – the agelast, to borrow a term from Rabelais, for whom laughter and seriousness do not go together.⁵ This can be a passing mood, as we know, a whole philosophy, or the tendency of an entire civilization; and Horace might have agreed with Rabelais, that nothing could be more central to the construction of human happiness at every level than recognizing the place of laughter in the moral scheme of things. More than this, says Rabelais, it has an immediate relation to our access to truth – and in *Gargantua*, Diogenes chases the agelasts away from his wine barrel, the 'gay truth' of undogmatic experience.⁶

Bakhtin has some remarks on Rabelaisian gaiety which throw an interesting light on humorous morality:

True ambivalent and universal laughter does not deny seriousness but purifies and completes it. Laughter purifies from dogmatism, from the intolerant and the petrified;

it liberates from fanaticism and pedantry, from fear and intimidation, from didacticism, naïveté and illusion, from the single meaning, the single level, from sentimentality. Laughter does not permit seriousness to atrophy and to be torn away from the one being, forever incomplete. It restores this ambivalent wholeness.[7]

On this showing, the freedom to laugh would be a test of true seriousness, and the seriousness that needs the protection of solemnity would be sham. Bakhtin quotes an apposite perception of Herzen on the variety of 'systems' by which the 'ambivalent wholeness' of humanity is compressed into false forms: 'In church, in the palace, on parade, facing the department head, the police officer, the German administrator, nobody laughs. The serfs are deprived of the right to smile in the presence of the landowners. *Only equals may laugh.*'[8] And it is no coincidence that the term 'agelast' was most recently revived by Milan Kundera for the *apparatchiks* of Socialist Czechoslovakia who, if they smiled at an interrogation, did so with a terrible earnestness.[9]

These disparate testimonies suggest the importance of what might otherwise seem to have no moral bearing: laughter is a declaration of freedom, a liberation of the human being from all partial definitions, whether from without (class, state, religion) or within (dogmatism, repression, conceit). In this context is is easier to understand Dacier's perception that what passes as 'amusement for children' in Horace deserves 'the serious consideration of men', for Horace's good humour would be the *sine qua non* of morality: without it, moral teaching undoes itself, and induces the very stress that makes for dogmatism.

We can see how well Horace knows this for himself from the suppleness of his strategies in the *Sermones*, from the way he anticipates the response of his invisible antagonist. If we take as an example *Sermo* 2.6, a satire which has been endlessly enjoyed and may therefore compress a great deal of hidden meaning. We may be struck by the very audacity of the subject: Horace's happiness, and what it is made of. The agelast objects, with Arnold, that Horace does not show himself 'sick or sorry'; Horace implicitly answers that happiness is more important. The agelast doubts that guilt and grief can be avoided; Horace implicitly says that these are largely within our power, and happiness, like other things, can be cultivated. He then goes on to show us how (but this is already to press too hard on an opening of fascinating tact: none of these things can be openly expressed).

It is made, for instance, out of gratitude, and a sense of the rarity of happiness ('my prayers are answered'); it is made out of wanting little things rather than great ('a smallish farm with a wood and a spring near the house') and not hungering then for little extras. (But before we can find Horace unbearably virtuous, he lends his imagination to that insatiability for us: 'Just that tiny corner, which spoils the shape of my small farm as it stands . . . '). Above all it is made out of being the friend of Maecenas, the patron who made the Sabine farm possible (and to whom Horace is also demonstrating his happiness as a thank-offering, as Fraenkel says).[10] But while being the intimate of Maecenas is a source of delicious pride ('honey-sweet, I admit'), it makes for difficulties too: it is precisely because of his important connections that Horace is intruded upon, pushed into false positions and swamped by others' partial definitions of him. In Rome his most urgent business is other people's, and while it is exhilarating to be courted, and to bustle through the day, bustle prevents one from engaging with anything that truly counts: in Dr Johnson's trenchant definition, it is 'getting on horseback in a ship'.

By stressing the inner frustrations of his public role, Horace evades the reader's potential envy, and also makes the essential point that happiness is not circumstantial: to be the friend of a great man is not a fixed state of bliss. Indeed, it makes the problem of distinguishing between real and illusory good more difficult – and more urgent – than ever. In the midst of all the distractions of Rome, he then brings us to a vision of what true happiness consists in; and it is typical of his good-humoured awareness of the awkwardness of his topic, that, for all the substantiality of the picture, he allows us to know that it is seen from afar – indeed, perhaps could only be seen with such clarity from the distance of Rome. The ingredients of real happiness are rural leisure, good books and sharing talk and home cooking with unpretending friends.

These are the delights Horace proposes to make famous by his prosaic Muse (*musa pedestris*), and in a passage of great *brio* he raises his claim for this *sermo* to the high level of *carmen*, lyric (20–4). The description of a country feast, enjoyed without ceremony among neighbours and house-slaves, at which men can finally ask the questions worth asking, is the point to which this *musa pedestris* has been tending. And to judge by the admiration this simple meal has drawn on itself, it is a classic instance of the observation that Horace's meaning must be searched for behind the 'crust' of appearances. What is it that justifies H. A. Mason (among many others) saying,

In this *sermo*, it seems to me, the context in which the question, what is happiness? is put may be fairly described as the most highly charged in European literature. All the realities are there in symbolic form.[11]

It is helpful to glance at a digest of Horace's meaning in prose:

Wasting the day amidst so much trivia I begin to dream of my country retreat. Oh, to be there with time to lie around, meditate and read good books! And with something comfortable on the table, like beans and greens. Those are the nights I remember, when I salute the gods of my hearth, and enjoy a meal with my neighbours, while the house-slaves amuse themselves as much as we do. Everybody drinks at his own pace, no silly rules: one man knocks it back and another mellows slowly, the way he likes it. The kind of talk that gets going then! No metropolitan gossip about who owns what, and who attended whose first night; we talk about what really matters, the things you have to make up your mind about: whether money makes people happy or principles, what makes for friendship, shared values or need, and what we mean by the good life. What form does it take at best? And someone will underline his point with an old wives' tale . . .

Thereafter follows the story of the town and country mouse, of which H. A. Mason says, 'there was no better way open to Horace to express his predicament, and there was no better way to prolong the dream of a happiness never to be fulfilled on earth'.[12]

What is meant by saying, 'all the realities are there in symbolic form'? We may guess that the most important of these is the meal; an obvious source of happiness that nonetheless grows more suggestive the longer one contemplates it. If Horace has an undisclosed antagonist in the shape of the reader who does not feel that laughter and seriousness go together, the same reader is likely to feel that philosophy and food belong to different planes of reality. (Drinking wine, perhaps – eating beans, no.) But Horace's aim for his *musa pedestris* is to celebrate quotidian pleasures, those things which make us human (and help keep us so); and therefore he makes no difficulty with the idea that the body is where we start from. The everyday business of feeding that body, healthily and moderately, is a test of true philosophy, and it is not a trivial matter to Horace any more than to his great follower, Montaigne. Indeed, it is a test of the greatest, that they are also willing to 'submit to the ordinary usage of life', as Montaigne puts it:

> When I see both Caesar and Alexander in the thickest of their greatest business, so fully enjoy human and corporal pleasures, pleasures so natural, and consequently so necessary and just, I do not hold that they slackened their souls, but wound them up higher, by vigour of courage, subjecting those violent employments and laborious thoughts to the ordinary usage of life: wise, had they believed the last was their ordinary, the first their extraordinary, vocation.[13]

Horace is still in touch, at however urbane a remove, with the classic assumption Homer makes – that when Achilles refuses any morsel of food in mourning for Patroclus, he reveals his lack of *aidōs* as unmistakably as when he drags Hector's body behind his chariot. And nothing better expresses his return to the human community than his simple invitation to Priam to eat with him, when they have both wept to exhaustion. Pope's translation underlines the Horatian significance of the moment:

> But now the peaceful hours of sacred night
> Demand refection, and to rest invite:
> Nor thou, O father! thus consumed with woe,
> The common cares that nourish life forego.   *Iliad* 24.753–6

There is greater humanity in stooping to those common cares than in denying them; though any noble nature is likely to have known the temptation.

Horace, Pope and Gray

It is an associated idea that what is served at the table is common food, food without status. Beans and greens in bacon fat are tasty and satisfying in themselves, but only to the man whose imagination does not dominate his palate. Anyone looking for acorn-fed boar from Umbria, or the best Falernian, will be disappointed: such things derive half their flavour from their exclusiveness, and they create a class system round the table as they are served. By the same token, there can be no drinking rules or competitions at this country feast. To be compelled to drink is an intimate form of bullying, and real hospitality allows each guest to 'mellow' at his own pace. And in the midst of all this bodily and spiritual freedom, vast social distinctions dissolve away, and partial forms of humanity are made whole again: the house-slaves confidently take liberties with an appreciative master (temporarily their equal), he shares their country rituals before the household gods, and he asks the central question of his neighbours as he would ask it of himself: 'What does "good" really mean?'

It is the most unexpected of all Horace's precautions against over-seriousness that, having brought us to a point where the agelast might hope for a moral, he veers off into a fable about two mice told by a neighbour. But in the light of Bakhtin's perception that laughter liberates 'from the single meaning, the single level, from sentimentality', this is the moment when Horace needs laughter most – when any definition of the 'good' would strike the ear as too thin, too simple. To present us with tiny rodents, however, who are as confused as any human being could be about whether 'the good life' is lived in the town or country, relaxes our strained attention, and allows us to experience an ambivalence we might otherwise have denied. It is not the 'truth' we get, but the liveliest sense of the difficulty of the choice; 'there was no better way open to Horace to express his predicament', says H. A. Mason, and it is humorously exposed for us to share.

Is it so obviously a good thing to live in the country, up against the grudgingness of nature? The country mouse is grateful for bacon rind (second-hand) and a withered berry: there is no value in isolation and hardship in themselves, and the town mouse, proposing to *carpe viam*, sounds as wise as Ulysses: 'Aren't men and cities more important than this?' Indeed, his injunction to his friend to live life in full awareness of its brevity is phrased like pure Horace: '*vive memor, quam sis aevi brevis.*' To be conscious of life's fragility adds a dignity to pleasure, whether of mice or men; even if the immediate form it takes is going to Rome to eat scraps. This expedition is treated by Horace with epic grandeur, by way of echoing the philosophic status of the mice's undertaking (*iamque tenebat / nox medium caeli spatium...*), and the rapture of the country mouse as he lolls among the remains of a banquet is feelingly conveyed. It is a wonderful thing to be exempt from labour and anxiety, to feel the presence of bounty and know nothing of where it came from. But it is only a dream: within half a line the door bursts open and realities reassert themselves in their ordinary relations. With a Molossian hound at one's tail, a hole in the woods is the only choice possible: *'et valeas'* – 'Goodbye!'

All sorts of ironic implications for the first part of the poem gleam out of this fable. Is Horace in Rome a mouse, browsing on the tit-bits of the great? Is there a *nemesis* pending as rough as that dealt by the hounds? Could anyone with a sense of the epic scale resist the lure of the city – and would anything but fear, or lack of imagination, keep anyone in the country? (It is also suggestive that the mouse does not know what country life is worth till he has had experience of the opposite.) All these deductions are possible, but we are not called on to make them; the profound charm of the story is that it deals with mice, not men, and the ambivalence and confusion it explores belong to a pair of rodents. What we do with their drastic discovery ('it is better to live in a hole than be eaten alive') is up to us. And how wise this approach is to human understanding shows in the way this has become one of the most famous and admired of Roman poems, adapted and translated by innumerable other poets for their own purposes, as David Hopkins illustrates (above pp.116–26). It belongs to whoever can make use of it, just as if it were the old wives' tale that Horace terms it himself.

The point of dwelling so long on this *Sermo* and its strategies was to give more substance to the idea that Horace's seriousness, like that of Socrates, does not lie in his statements so much as his method. Just as Socrates is at his most radical when he claims to 'know nothing' (what, therefore, is it, to 'know'?) – so Horace puts the defining of happiness aside to show us men and mice in pursuit of it, and most certain of what it is when they do not have it. But more than this, it is the very experience of reading the poem, the pleasure it gives and the way it gives it, that leaves us wiser – indeed, happier – than we were. What is so animating about the Horatian method is the way it spirits us out of the realm of effort and self-consciousness where most discussion of morality takes place.

If we nonetheless find at the bottom of his satire 'all the virtues which ought to be the continual exercise of those who seriously endeavour to correct their vices', as Dacier says, it is not because Horace ever uses the language of 'serious endeavour', vice and virtue. He renders goodness lovable, simply, and shows how good living can be made of the homeliest ingredients (hospitality, food, comedy, perspective). The 'virtue' the poem promotes is not present as a moral but as a demonstration – in the good humour it encourages in the reader, by its own good-humoured approach to a serious subject. The *Sermo* invites the reader freely to scrutinize the evidence, to view it from the back and sides, so to speak, and meditate at leisure (the sort of leisure provided by Sabine farms). The poem tolerates its own ambivalence,

Horace, Pope and Gray

and encourages the reader to do the same; and in its willingness to admit both the charm of its ideal, and humanity's likely distance from it, it leaves us in that state of 'ambivalent wholeness' that Bakhtin thought so characteristic of humorous morality.

This train of thought returns us to the earlier proposition that Horace's good humour is not surface charm but the *sine qua non* of moral education, for it alone takes account of the reader's resistance to being improved. It is the literary equivalent of genuine politeness in social relations – or, as Alexander Pope phrases it in a very Horatian passage of the *Essay on Criticism*, 'good breeding':

> Men must be taught as if you taught them not,
> And things unknown proposed as things forgot:
> Without good breeding, truth is disapproved,
> That only makes superior sense belov'd. (574–7)

The agelast might object to what sounds like a Jesuitical approach to the reader, flattering him into quiescence; but Pope would have replied that for truth to be 'beloved' rather than grudgingly admitted, the reader must feel he discovered it for himself. Nothing permits him to do this but the most careful display of authorial good manners: for good manners are a recognition of the reality of another person, whose errors (if that is what they are) are nonetheless dear to him. By granting the reader genuine freedom, the moralist shows how genuinely serious is his desire to share his wisdom. While the author may therefore seem 'at ease', his art is anything but easy, as Shaftesbury remarks of Horace and his contemporaries:

They are willing it should be known how serious their play was, and how elaborate their freedom and facility; that they might say as the agreeable and polite poet, glancing on himself,
> Ludentis speciem dabit et torquebitur

[wear the look of being at play, and yet be on the rack].[14]

To liberate the reader, and your own poetry, from the stress of any moral intention, is an art difficult enough to satisfy the most strenuous agelast.

It is not coincidental that the authors who entered most readily into Horace's stratagems and their unstated meaning were writing in the early eighteenth century, like Pope and Shaftesbury, or the late seventeenth, like Dacier (and Cowley, as David Hopkins shows). One of the effects of that profound investment in Roman culture that we call Augustanism was that, at least for some poets, Horace solved a problem besetting their civilization as much as his: how to cherish values without dogmatism, and share them without damage either to them or the recipient. Dacier's praise of his Socratic depth implies, indeed, that this difficulty was the key to a larger mystery, the way that humane culture can make for virtue; and this idea suffuses the Horatian satires and epistles of Pope, where the relation of seriousness to good humour, and good humour to goodness itself, is always to be glimpsed behind the ostensible subject.[15]

It is interesting to consider the course of eighteenth-century poetry in the light of these ideas, since Horace ceases to be so powerful an influence after Pope, and the idea that laughter could have moral prestige was slipping out of view, even in his lifetime. If the Horatian 'method' is as important as Pope and Dacier supposed, we should expect the poetry written without it to bear the marks of moral strain, and to show that over-serious seriousness Horace evades; and certainly the poetry of the 1740s and 1750s, with its graveyards, night thoughts and pursuit of the 'sublime', marks a new alliance between public morality and solemnity. One way of defining the gulf between Augustanism and emerging Romanticism in fact might be this preference the 'pre-Romantics' showed for 'the single meaning, the single level', with its risk of bombast on one side, and sentimentality on the other; and at least one contemporary author, Goldsmith, thought a disastrous confusion between solemnity and value had got abroad by 1760:

I should not have employed so much time in opposing this erroneous innovation [blank verse], if it were not apt to introduce another in its train, – I mean, a disgusting solemnity of manner into our poetry; and, as the prose writer has been ever found to follow the poet, it must consequently banish in both, all that agreeable trifling, which, if I may so express it, often deceives us into instruction . . . The finest sentiment, and the most weighty truth, may put on a pleasing face, and it is even virtuous to jest when serious advice might be disgusting. But instead of this, the most trifling performance among us now, assumes all the didactic stiffness of wisdom . . . The solemnity worn by many of our modern writers is, I fear, often the mask of dulness; for certain it is, it seems to fit every author who pleases to put it on.[16]

'One size fits all': solemnity can be as much of a fashion as anything else, and it guarantees nothing about the value of what the poet has to say.

In the second half of this essay I should like to dwell on what might justify Goldsmith's alarm, by way of substantiating the idea that when Horace's 'secret' goes missing, some of the best powers of poetry go missing too. Horace's ability to switch perspectives, mingle tones and make his teaching lovable, is not characteristic of pre-Romantic poetry; and perhaps more importantly, his willingness to fix his meaning in everyday reality is lost. As a result, the definition of what constitutes a poetic subject is narrowed as well as elevated, and English poetry develops what we might call an agelastic tendency that lingers (to my taste) to the present day. But these speculations convey little without illustration, and the best way of showing what was stirring Goldsmith's alarm might be to compare what Pope achieves in his mood of 'serious trifling' with his immediate successor, Gray.

Horace, Pope and Gray

A good example of Pope at his most Horatian would be Clarissa's speech from the *Rape of the Lock*, inserted in the poem in response to criticism that it lacked a serious moral. This is a parody of Sarpedon's famous speech in the *Iliad* on the relative value of life and glory, a passage Pope had translated with the utmost solemnity a few years before; so the shift into mock-epic perspective is quite as liberating to the author as a tale of two mice. What discipline is as hard in this world of belles, vanity and gossip as standing in the front line of battle? Only the maintenance of good humour:

> Say, why are beauties praised and honoured most,
> The wise man's passion, and the vain man's toast?
> Why decked with all that land and sea afford,
> Why angels called, and angel-like adored?
> Why round our coaches crowd the white-gloved beaus,
> Why bows the side-box from its inmost rows?
> How vain are all these glories, all our pains,
> Unless good sense preserve what beauty gains;
> That men may say, when we the front-box grace,
> Behold the first in virtue, as in face!
> Oh! if to dance all night, and dress all day,
> Charmed the smallpox, or chased old age away,
> Who would not scorn what housewife's cares produce,
> Or who would learn one earthly thing of use?
> To patch, nay ogle, might become a saint,
> Nor could it sure be such a sin to paint.
> But since, alas! frail beauty must decay,
> Curled or uncurled, since locks will turn to grey,
> Since painted, or not painted, all shall fade,
> And she who scorns a man must die a maid;
> What then remains but well our power to use,
> And keep good humour still whate'er we lose?
> And trust me, dear! good humour can prevail,
> When airs, and flights, and screams, and scolding fail.
> Beauties in vain their pretty eyes may roll;
> Charms strike the sight, but merit wins the soul. (5.9–34)

The absurdity of the mock-epic context (Belinda is about to revenge the loss of her favourite lock with a bodkin) enables Pope to approach his subject, and the reader, with radical freedom. He lingers with loving interest, even sympathy, on the outrageous worldliness and false values of the belle. Just as Horace can feel the rapture of his mice in Rome, so Pope can lend his imagination to the pleasures of dancing, dressing and coquetting; the details of this existence are intimately conveyed, and Clarissa's elegiac 'Oh!' is more than an obvious irony.

Pope's rendition of this world of glittering trivia is given additional lustre by his mock-epic diction, to the point where some readers have been unsure whether he was satirizing it at all. But the ambivalence is the essential point: this world is as lovely as it is insubstantial, and underlying it is the real pain of the predicament of women in Pope's day, which emerges with renewed force in the comic context. The salon is a Homeric arena of a kind, where fateful choices are made, almost as difficult as Sarpedon's. If the belle is petted, it is only for a few years, and on condition that she offers herself on the marriage market ('And she who scorns a man . . .'). The beauty that makes marriage possible is vulnerable to diseases with no cure ('Charmed the smallpox . . .') and nothing is more menacing, or certain, than haggard old age ('painted or not painted, all shall fade'). Sarpedon had only to choose a quick death, and eternal glory in song, to validate his existence; but the women of Clarissa's world confront the prospect of a slow erosion of what little selfhood they lay claim to through bad marriages, or disappointed hopes, and the spoiling of their temper by whispers in the market-place, and the sympathy of 'friends'. Small wonder that 'airs and flights and screams and scolding' are their usual weapons, or that Pope conceives of the salon as an area of battle – a point well taken by Samuel Johnson, who would not accept that this mock-epic lacked a genuine moral foundation. On the contrary, it had a better one than Boileau's mock-epic on the French clergy, he said:

The freaks, and humours, and spleen, and vanity of women, as they embroil families in discord and fill houses with disquiet, do more to obstruct the happiness of life in a year than the ambition of the clergy in many centuries. It has been well observed that the misery of man proceeds not from any single crush of overwhelming evil, but from small vexations continually repeated.[17]

The poem is firmly fixed in the realm of the quotidian, the world of 'small vexations continually repeated' where human misery is made. But by the same token, a small adjustment of perspective could make a large difference: just a shift of attitude could make happiness possible, though to take the first step might be as heroic as confronting an army at Troy. It is a matter of developing good humour; and clearly the term here has more than the mild implication of smiling through difficulties. It is Horace's own capacity to see himself in perspective and represent his lot as the common one, with no admixture of iron or irony, but only a pleasure that the fact is so. This good humour recognizes the intransigent facts of life – deformity from smallpox, the locks that turn to grey and the possibility of dying a maid; but because it knows about bleakness, its gaieties can be truly gay. It dissolves egotism, obsession and rage, in a relaxed perception of the place of the self in the scheme of things – and, since 'painted or not painted, all shall fade,' it can accommodate even death. It is the practical face of goodness, making happiness possible for oneself and others.

Horace, Pope and Gray

Just as good humour is Pope's subject, it is also (as with Horace) his method. This ideal of self-conduct in society is one of his most cherished convictions, as we know from how often he returns to it in his works;[18] but he puts it in the form of a Homeric parody, and into the mouth of the character who lent the Baron the scissors to cut the lock in the first place. He freely grants that no one paid Clarissa's excellent advice any attention: ' – no applause ensued;/Belinda frowned, Thalestris called her prude.'(5.35–6). But, disowned and inverted, the ideal glows with all the more radiance. We note that it runs against the grain of human egotism, but we also observe the cost of egotism in the hysterical 'battle' that follows. We feel, too, the politeness of the author in disappearing from his text and leaving us free to draw our own conclusions. It takes his genuine gaiety, on easy visiting terms with seriousness, to relax the reader's attention to the point where the moral can naturally take root.

Pope does not always write like this: in the same year that he published Clarissa's speech he also published 'Eloisa to Abelard' and 'Elegy to the Memory of an Unfortunate Lady', and the *Iliad* translation he was working on at the same time often censors Homer's openings for playfulness. But when most tempted by 'the single meaning, the single level,' and their potential 'sentimentality', a Horatian instinct seems to have prompted him to turn his serious subject upside down and treat it with a freedom he cannot entirely control, by way of compensation. The very earnestness of his intention then converts to a gaiety in proportion; and his career shows a series of earnest undertakings punctuated by parodic ones, much as a man on a high wire waves his balancing rod in both directions.[19]

Pope's friends in the Scriblerus Club were all, similarly, exploiters of 'mock' forms: mock-pastoral, epic, biography, opera, pamphlets. They seem to have shared an awareness of two cardinal points: that comedy gives a necessary home to ambivalence and contradiction, and that it requires just as much effort as serious writing. (Indeed, it may well outlast it, as the *Beggar's Opera* and *Gulliver's Travels* have.) But their confidence that 'serious trifling' was not at all to be confused with 'trifling' did not survive the growing taste for moral sentiment in blank verse, epitomized by Young's *Night Thoughts* (1742–5); and Goldsmith's reference to 'that agreeable trifling, which, if I may so express it, often deceives us into instruction' implies an audience that has not heard this proposition for a long time, and is not attuned to hear it.

We can perhaps see the consequences of this loss of confidence in the poetry of Gray: a poet who shares much of Pope's genius and many of his subjects, but in whom, by common agreement, great gifts came to surprisingly little. One way of describing what he did not share with Pope would be his difficulty in finding a role for his sense of humour. If Pope's works are startlingly varied in tone, moving swiftly between 'the single meaning' and the double variety,

Gray's poetry is actively divided against itself. It is difficult to find any connecting impulse between the intelligent savagery of his satire ('On Lord Holland's Seat') and the gory bombast of his worst odes ('The Fatal Sisters'), or the incomparable poise of the *Elegy* and the cluttered pedantry of 'The Bard'. Perhaps there is a kind of inverted similarity, however, between the light pieces and the more elaborate ones: in the latter, as Johnson says, Gray 'has a kind of strutting dignity, and is tall by walking on tiptoe',[20] while in the former he goes on all fours, like a grown-up indulging a child. The counterpart of his solemnity is a humour bordering on levity: not the good humour that brings us to the heart of the dilemma, but the temporary relaxation of a strained spirit.

Perhaps these remarks apply even to the delightful 'Ode on the Death of a Favourite Cat', where Gray comes very close to the mock-epic perspective of Horace and Pope. The context is vertiginously little and large – the cat has drowned in pursuit of fish, human beings perish in pursuit of false values – and it gives Gray a fine opening for humorous morality. But that is not quite what he gives us:

> 'Twas on a lofty vase's side,
> Where China's gayest art had dyed
>   The azure flowers, that blow;
> Demurest of the tabby kind,
> The pensive Selima reclined,
>   Gazed on the lake below.
>
> Her conscious tail her joy declared;
> The fair round face, the snowy beard,
>   The velvet of her paws,
> Her coat that with the tortoise vies,
> Her ears of jet and emerald eyes,
>   She saw; and purred applause.
>
> Still had she gaz'd; but 'midst the tide
> Two angel forms were seen to glide,
>   The genii of the stream:
> Their scaly armour's Tyrian hue
> Thro' richest purple to the view
>   Betrayed a golden gleam.
>
> The hapless nymph with wonder saw:
> A whisker first and then a claw,
>   With many an ardent wish,
> She stretched in vain to reach the prize.
> What female heart can gold despise?
>   What cat's averse to fish?

Horace, Pope and Gray

> Presumptuous maid! with looks intent
> Again she stretched, again she bent,
>   Nor knew the gulf between.
> (Malignant Fate sat by and smiled)
> The slipp'ry verge her feet beguiled,
>   She tumbled headlong in.
>
> Eight times emerging from the flood
> She mewed to every wat'ry God,
>   Some speedy aid to send.
> No dolphin came, no Nereid strirr'd:
> Nor cruel Tom nor Susan heard.
>   A fav'rite has no friend!
>
> From hence, ye beauties, undeceived,
> Know, one false step is ne'er retrieved,
>   And be with caution bold.
> Not all that tempts your wand'ring eyes
> And heedless hearts is lawful prize;
>   Nor all that glisters gold.

Nothing could be more deft than the substitution of that 'eight times' for the epic 'three', the mythic-elegiac note ('No dolphin came . . . ') and mock-sententiousness of the whole ('A fav'rite has no friend!'). But for all its real charm, the poem remains a trifle – an engagement with moralism rather than morality. It is an airy thing that, unlike the *Rape of the Lock*, does not tell either the cat or the girl what they might genuinely need to know. Nor is there more than a joking equivalence between the two; to yoke them in a moral is to underline the difference. (That girls should be less greedy than cats is no revelation, and as Johnson remarks of the conclusion, with titanic common sense, 'if what glistered had been "gold," the cat would not have gone into the water; and, if she had, would not less have been drowned'.)[21]

Johnson's sonorous impatience – 'the poem . . . was doubtless by its author considered as a trifle, but it is not a happy trifle' – is not unprovoked, if we consider that the 'serious trifling' of the humanist tradition has seemed worth the utmost pains of practitioners of the past.[22] When Gray does not attempt to mend the logic of the poem, or to deepen the joke by attaching it to a moral that could implicate him too, he is effectively saying that gaiety is 'only' gaiety to him; a mental reservation that colours the rest of his poetry, for it leads him down the primrose path of poetic solemnity, where what bars admittance to humour draws its claim to poetic status from that very fact.

Goldsmith pleads, 'let us, instead of writing finely, try to write naturally. Not hunt after lofty expressions to deliver mean ideas; nor be for ever gaping, when we only mean to deliver a whisper.'[23] In the context of *The Progress of*

Poesy and 'The Bard', published two years earlier, we can see what was making him uneasy: the most uncomfortable aspect of these odes, on which Gray lavished his art and learning, is their want of proportion and any saving self-awareness. In their determination to be sublime, they create a gulf between everyday reality and the realm of poetry that no humour could bridge. As we plunge into the Huncamunca world of 'The Bard',

> 'Ruin seize thee, ruthless king!
> Confusion on thy banners wait,'

we know that not only is smiling forbidden here, but even moving restlessly in one's seat: this is a realm where the truth that 'the body is where one starts from' is wholly suppressed. Poetic postures take over from a Horatian concern with the art of living, 'the single meaning' takes over from comic ambivalence, and for conclusive emphasis, the ode leaves every bard in Wales 'smeared with gore', and 'ghastly pale' in death. The bard of the title is the last survivor of the invasion of Wales by Edward the First, and he defies the English invader from a rock over the Conway on a note of Virgilian-cum-Celtic ecstasy:

> 'Be thine despair and sceptered care,
> To triumph, and to die are mine.'
> He spoke, and headlong from the mountain's height
> Deep in the roaring tide he plunged to endless night.   (141–4)

'Suicide is always to be had, without expense of thought', remarks Johnson of this; and we may note that a poem that would rather be 'fine' than 'natural' is condemned to be very fine indeed. The route back from the sublime to this world is a rocky one, and suicide exempts Gray's bard from finding it.

In this context, Bakhtin's remark about what is lost with the elasticity of good humour seems surprisingly germane. Laughter is not, he insists, the antagonist of seriousness – it is what is needed to keep it safe from 'atrophy': 'true ambivalent and universal laughter does not deny seriousness but purifies and completes it'. It liberates the human spirit from just those tendencies that afflict Gray's odes, 'pedantry ... didacticism, naïveté and illusion'; and above all, from the tendency to mean only one thing at a time: 'the single meaning, the single level, from sentimentality'. Laughter takes account of our human condition, which makes us ambivalent, and in which the wise poet will always leave room for his poetry to say more than he himself intends.

Is it stretching a point too far to go on to say that what afflicts Gray's poetry afflicts Romanticism in general, and one way of describing what is lost with Augustanism is the ability to be serious with good humour – a fact that gives our poetic tradition an agelastic turn from which it has never quite recovered?

10

HORACE AND THE NINETEENTH CENTURY

Norman Vance

HORACE WAS THE best-remembered classical author in nineteenth-century England.[1] He was the common possession of well-educated men, benignly presiding over cultivated masculine interchange in life and letters. Women were less impressed, even when their education had included the Classics. George Eliot knew her Horace, particularly the *Ars Poetica*, but made almost no use of him in her novels. Branwell Brontë attempted a translation of Horace's *Odes* which was commended by Hartley Coleridge, but his more famous sisters seem to have had no interest in poet or translation. The young Elizabeth Barrett had read Horace with her brother but always preferred Virgil and Homer. Horace was, supremely, the gentleman-poet for nineteenth-century gentlemen, the literary equivalent of the comfortable London clubs from which women were excluded.

It was hardly surprising that he was much quoted in that last retreat of male privilege, the House of Commons, 'the best club in London' according to Dickens's Mr Twemlow. When the *nouveau riche* newsagent and politician W. H. Smith acquired a magnificent house in Grosvenor Place it seemed natural, if unkind, for Lord Randolph Churchill to invoke Horace's poetically conventional disdain for vulgar display:

> Non ebur neque aureum
>   mea renidet in domo lacunar

No ivory or gold gleams on panelled ceilings in my house,   (*Odes* 2.18.1–2)[2]

In an age where men of taste seemed on the whole to prefer the poets of Greece Horace retained much of the popularity he had enjoyed in the previous century. This was partly because he offered comparatively easy access to the world of Greek letters and Greek civility by writing versions of Greek poetry in Latin. His work exemplified his own maxim that, culturally speaking, captive Greece captured her Roman conqueror (*Ep.* 2.1.156).

Horace, with Virgil and Homer, was at the heart of what every classically educated schoolboy needed to know: in the earlier nineteenth century at least prose authors were often comparatively neglected at school but it was expected that substantial quantities of Horatian and Virgilian verse would be committed to memory.³ Thackeray, much given to quoting Horace in private letters as well as in print, was not entirely joking when he made his waggish but erudite James Binnie report that Colonel Newcome's son Clive had acquired enough classical literature 'to enable him to quote Horace respectably through life, and what more do you want from a young man of his expectations?'⁴ The French, who continued to set the standard for European civility, had no doubt in the matter: Horace was described as the only classical author one could quote in polite society without incurring the charge of pedantry. For Victor Hugo Shakespeare's Bottom was aesthetically vindicated since Horace had found a vigorous speaking part for Priapus (S 1.8).⁵

Romantic taste was sometimes uneasy with Horace, but that hardly mattered. Influential critics such as Goethe felt that he was more of a technician than a true poet. Matthew Arnold gravely opined that he lacked 'seriousness': 'the best men in the best ages have never been thoroughly satisfied with Horace'. But both Goethe and Arnold knew ther Horace thoroughly. Like most nineteenth-century poets Arnold echoed Horatian phrases and in 1847 he attempted an Horatian poem, 'Horatian Echo', not published until 1887. Wordsworth may have translated Horace as a schoolboy exercise (early verse-translations have survived) but he also adapted and alluded to the celebrations of rural retirement and moral fortitude in the *Odes* in his poetic maturity and regarded Horace as his favourite Latin poet. His famous 'Ode to Duty' draws in part on Gray's 'Ode to Adversity', but Gray, and Wordsworth, had Horace's so-called 'Ode to Fortune' (*Odes* 1.35) very much in mind.⁶ Byron had hated Horace at Harrow (his own fault rather than Horace's, as he later admitted), but he attempted an updated, satiric *Ars Poetica*, entitled 'Hints from Horace' (1811), which 'imitated' Horace in the eighteenth-century fashion exemplified by Byron's beloved Pope.

To know Horace was to participate in the English as well as the Roman cultural tradition. Horace was not just a poet's poet: he had addressed public as well as private themes, Cleopatra as well as Lydia, and had mattered to men in public life, to Augustus and Maecenas, Milton and Marvell, the Earl of Chesterfield and the Earl of Chatham. He mattered to Mr Gladstone, who eventually published his translations of Horace's *Odes* into English verse in 1894. Sir Robert Peel quoted Horace rather too often in the Commons, which probably provoked the Duke of Wellington's advice to a young member 'Say what you've got to say, don't quote Latin, and sit down.'⁷

Robert Louis Stevenson, a less exalted student of the Classics, travelled

Horace and the nineteenth century

further both physically and imaginatively than Gladstone or Peel. But he too turned to Horace, in rather dramatic circumstances. Desperately ill in Davos, he startled an English clergyman by demanding: 'For God's sake, have you got a Horace?' It is tempting to conjecture that Stevenson felt in need of the consolations of pagan philosophy, the old Roman Stoicism of some of the *Odes*, but it turned out that his need was practical rather than moral, which may have relieved the startled cleric: he was preparing a collection of essays for the press and wanted to check the Horatian source of his title, *Virginibus Puerisque* ('to maids and boys', *Odes* 3.1.1). This was also the title of the first essay, a genially detached meditation on marriage and married people in life and literature.[8] Prosaic though the explanation is, it still highlights Stevenson's, and his publisher's, confidence that as late as 1881 an Horatian tag would be both recognizable and acceptable as the title of a (first) book of essays by a still-aspiring author, a way of establishing contact with an educated, but not necessarily a scholarly, reading public.

There are other, less dignified, testimonials to the ascendancy of Horace at this time, at least among male *cognoscenti*: he is the most frequently travestied classical author of the period. The iconoclastic Samuel Butler's sense of detachment from Victorian high seriousness was summed up in inspired misquotation: *dulce et decorum est disipere in loco* ('it is sweet and seemly to forget one's wisdom in the right place', conflating *Odes* 3.2.13 and 4.12.28).[9] From James and Horace Smith with their Regency drolleries (*Horace in London*, 1813), by way of G. O. Trevelyan (Macaulay's nephew) and his popular Cambridge burlesque *Horace at the University of Athens* (1861) to Charles Graves (uncle of Robert Graves) with his witty *Hawarden Horace* (1894), poking fun at Mr Gladstone and the politics of the day, parodies of Horace somehow managed to provide a word in season, and implied a readership capable of relishing the interplay of original text and contemporary occasion. George Eliot rather ponderously pilloried the intellectually dishonest Evangelical preacher Dr Cumming in the *Westminster Review* by sneering *Christianitatem, quocunque modo, Christianitatem* (compare *Ep.* 1.1.66).[10]

The various modes of appropriating Horace, in this and other periods, correspond to Horace's own ways of dealing with Greek poetry: they could be summed up as translation, parody, allusion or quotation and 'imitation' or recreation of Horatian effects in a different context. The categories constantly converge. It was agreed that a completely satisfactory translation of Horace was impossible, but it was not unduly difficult to produce acceptable English approximations because so many English poets had echoed Horace or imitated what they took to be his manner. The Oxford Professor of Latin J. C. Conington was justly admired as one of the best verse-translators of Horace: his *Satires and Epistles* (1870) were particularly effective because they were pastiche Cowper, a poet whose *Tirocinium* (1785) was seen as a sub-Horatian satire.

C. S. Calverley's adroit verse-translations of Horace include a version of *Odes* 1.24, the elegy for Quintilius, which represents Horace's complex stanza (the 'Fourth Asclepiad') in the distinctively rhymed quatrains of Tennyson's *In Memoriam*. This is appropriate enough since there are numerous Horatian allusions in Tennyson's poem, itself an extended elegy for a valued friend which wistfully commemorates shared landscapes and experiences. Translation could also work the other way: *In Memoriam* 107 offers hospitality despite harsh winter weather and partly derives from *Odes* 1.9 (*vides ut alta*). It begins 'The time admits not flowers or leaves / To deck the banquet' which becomes, very precisely, *non hora myrto, non violis sinit / nitere mensas*, neatly rendered into (back into?) Horatian Alcaics, the metre of 1.9. Not surprisingly, Calverley had a good 'feel' for the parodic possibilities of quasi-Horatian English verse. One of the best examples is the 'Ode to Tobacco', written in a kind of accentual rhymed approximation to Horatian Sapphics, praising the weed for banishing 'Black Care', alluding to the *atra Cura* of *Odes* 3.1.40.[11]

G. O. Trevelyan's *Horace at the University of Athens* includes jocular allusion to familiar Horatian tags, comically incorporated into English rhyming verse, convivial songs loosely translating *Odes* such as 1.27 (*Natis in usum*: 'Fighting with cups designed for pleasure is a Thracian habit'), itself a more formal drinking-song, and parodies of autobiographical passages in the *Odes* and *Epistles*. At times these amount to 'imitation' in the eighteenth-century sense as Cambridge stands in for the Athens where Horace studied, and the mid-Victorian volunteer movement and the American Civil War answer to the military encounter between Brutus and Mark Antony at Philippi in which Horace took part, only to throw away his shield. Or so he says (*Odes* 2.7.9–10), but the claim is itself an allusion to, an imitation or parody of Greek poems by Archilochus, Anacreon and Alcaeus in which the same thing seems to happen.[12]

These different appropriations select or construct a version of Horace serviceable for nineteenth-century purposes. This was the Horace of the *Odes* and sometimes the *Epistles*: the *Epodes* and *Ars Poetica* and the less formal *Sermones* were often largely ignored. He was perceived as a worldly, technically accomplished poet who reflected on civilized life. This life can be considered under four headings: transient love and gratification, male friendship and hospitality, national politics and war, and the sense of place.

In a romantic and religious age this Horace seemed to have obvious limitations. By comparison with other classical poets, notably Catullus, the emotional temperature seemed to be rather low, lacking the 'all-absorbing devotion of the heart'.[13] Despite light-hearted attempts, such as François

Horace and the nineteenth century

Ponsard's comedy *Horace et Lydie* (1850), to make Horace into a romantic lover, little of substance was detected beneath the conventional amorousness of the *Odes*. By comparison with Virgil there were few obvious indications of a modern religious sense or intuitions of an afterlife, so religious poets such as John Keble dismissed him as a genial worldling rather than a 'genuine poet', a view surprisingly similar to that of the reluctantly post-religious poet Matthew Arnold.[14] Arnold's friend Clough, however, invoked Horace in his poem of doubt, *Amours de Voyage*: the Dome of Agrippa, now Christianized as the Church of Sta Maria Rotunda, still seemed to Clough's protagonist Claude to belong with the pagan deities such as Vulcan, Juno and Apollo, so Claude aggressively translates Horace's celebration of them (*Odes* 3.4.58–64) in defiance of the newer Christian pieties.[15] Others again might complain of an excess of urbanity and sophistication in Horace, at the expense of 'sincerity' and 'originality'.

But these 'shortcomings' could appear as advantages in certain circumstances. As religious certainties waned after mid-century, leaving more space for unabashed hedonism and neo-pagan stoicism, and as a new post-Romantic aesthetic gradually emerged encouraging not passion but perfection of form and art for art's sake, Horace was more highly regarded than ever. This occasionally produced absurdities: the Dutch scholar Petrus Hofman-Peerlkamp and his successors applied such rigorous standards of what they took to be Horatian taste, formal perfection and logical coherence to individual poems that passages, and even whole poems, were rejected as spurious on aesthetic grounds alone and desperately ingenious but unwarranted emendations were forced upon the texts.[16] With more sanity the Irish scholar-critic R. Y. Tyrrell blamed Horace himself, pointing out in articles and published lectures what he regarded as errors of sense and literary tact. Noting poetic inconsequentiality or incoherence resulting from the technical difficulties of the metres to which everything else, perhaps, was sacrificed, he went so far as to compare Horace with the metrically ingenious but sometimes facile and vapid Irish Melodist Thomas Moore, author of 'The harp that once through Tara's halls'. The defensive tone of the latest version of Tyrrell's remarks (1895), accommodating strenuous opposition to his earlier comments, suggests that the legend of Horatian perfection died hard.[17] The late Victorians needed to believe that the poet of present pleasures was worth reading.

1 Transience

The satisfying humanistic *fin-de-siècle* Horace is admirably summed up in Andrew Lang's *Letters to Dead Authors* (1886): his Horace enjoys the good things of this life and does not 'look for more delight in the life beyond'; he sings of wine and women but not too much 'for passion frightens you, and 'tis pleasure more than love that you commend to the young'. He keeps faith not so much with the state religion as with a quasi-Wordsworthian 'pure and pious worship of rustic tradition, the faith handed down by the homely elders'.[18]

It is notable that this is very much the temperately Epicurean Horace, rather than the Stoic of some of the Roman *Odes*. There was a long tradition of Stoic–Christian dialogue, beginning allegedly with Seneca and St Paul, continuing with Jerome, Augustine and Calvin, but this seems to have had little influence on late Victorian views of Horace: Horace as stern Stoic moralist would be altogether too like the Archbishop of Canterbury or Arnold of Rugby to have much popular appeal. Matthew Arnold, uneasy with his Arnoldian legacy, imaginatively entertained but grew tired of a purely Epicurean Horace, whom he associated with the 'French Horace' Jean-Pierre Béranger (1780–1857). He soon dismissed both, rather unfairly, as *fade* or insipid. When he looked for Stoic models he did not reopen his Horace.[19]

Thackeray liked both Béranger and Horace rather more than Arnold, and found ways of adapting both poets in his man-about-town light verse. For Thackeray in this mood politics and moral philosophy are not to be taken too seriously: praise of Napoleon in Béranger and deference to Augustus in Horace give place to the poems about love and good humour and good food. Transient young love, described in *Odes* 1.5, 'To Pyrrha', is treated more breezily in Thackeray's version, 'The Age of Wisdom', and Pyrrha herself is refined out of existence:

> Ho, pretty page, with the dimpled chin
>   That never has known the Barber's shear,
> All your wish is woman to win,
> This is the way that boys begin, –
>   Wait till you come to Forty Year.

The high seriousness with which Horace presents Black Care (*atra Cura*, *Odes* 3.1.40) as the concomitant of oppressive wealth is transformed into the cheerful wisdom of Thackeray's Wamba the jester, measuring his distance from miserably proud chivalry:

> I will not have black Care prevail
> Upon my long-eared charger's tail,
> For lo, I am a witless fool,
> And laugh at Grief and ride a mule.

Thackeray's version of Horace's *Odes* 1.38 (*Persicos odi*), in which food is not mentioned, humorously transforms Horace's preference for Roman

Horace and the nineteenth century

simplicity instead of exotic Persian elaboration into a celebration of plain English fare:

> Dear Lucy, you know what my wish is, –
>   I hate all your Frenchified fuss:
> Your silly entrees and made dishes
>   Were never intended for us.
> No footman in lace and in ruffles
>   Need dangle behind my arm-chair;
> And never mind seeking for truffles,
>   Although they be ever so rare.
> But a plain leg of mutton, my Lucy,
>   I prithee get ready at three;
> Have it smoking, and tender and juicy,
>   And what better meat can there be?
> And when it has feasted the master,
>   'Twill amply suffice for the maid;
> Meanwhile I will smoke my canaster,
>   And tipple my ale in the shade.[20]

The moralizing author of *Vanity Fair* retained a certain imaginative complicity with the raffish world of the Regency, so it is appropriate that his bon viveur culinary version of Horace was anticipated in a complicated parody of the same *Ode* by the Regency poet Thomas Moore, the Irish Melodist, which begins:

> Boy, tell the Cook that I hate all nick-nackeries,
> Fricassees, vol-au-vents, puffs and gim-crackeries.[21]

Later in the century Horace as the poet of transient (if substantial) pleasures assists the process of transforming romantic despair into accomplished, conspicuously formal verse in the work of 'decadent' poets such as Ernest Dowson. Dowson's poetic persona looks back from a degraded and hopeless present to evanescent passion and fulfilment represented by the conventionalized Horatian delights of wine and roses and young love. In '*Non sum qualis eram bonae sub regno Cynarae*' ('I am not such as I was in the reign of good Cynara') and '*Vitae summa brevis spem nos vetat incohare longam*' ('The brief span of life forbids us to encourage prolonged hope') (1896) the extravagantly Horatian titles (from *Odes* 4.1.3–4 and 1.4.15) introduce stylized meditations which in a sense depend on the Horatian injunction *carpe diem* ('sieze hold of today') (*Odes* 1.11.8), seen not as a present imperative but as insufficiently regarded advice from the irretrievable past. The best that can now be said is that 'I have been faithful to thee, Cynara! in my fashion.' All that is left of love's possibility is stubborn memory and rueful reflection in the shadow of mortality.

> They are not long, the weeping and the laughter,
>   Love and desire and hate;
>   I think they have no portion in us after
>   We pass the gate.[22]

2 Male Friendship

Austin Dobson, who viewed the waning century with more equanimity, was nostalgic not so much for lost love as for an idealized eighteenth century, compounded of the aristocratic elegance of Watteau's paintings and the learned wit of Addison and Steele. Horace, much quoted in Addison's *Spectator*, much admired in France, was a natural point of contact with this lost world. Extensive classical attainments were no longer necessary to make the connections, for Sir Theodore Martin (biographer of the Prince Consort) had contributed to that useful series *Ancient Classics for English Readers* a gossipy biographical study of Horace (1870), subsequently reprinted as the preface to his rather facile *Works of Horace Translated into English Verse*. There were other pleasant introductions such as R. M. Hovenden's *Horace's Life and Character* (1877), which is actually a blank-verse translation of most of the *Satires* and *Epistles*. Like Martin in his translations, Hovenden is embarrassed by notorious passages such as *Sermones* 1.2 and 1.8, in which Roman coarseness and sexuality are altogether too frankly represented, and tactfully omits them.

This smoothly bowdlerized, popularized Horace is easily assimilated to the well-educated, sociable nineteenth-century man-about-town which middle-class readers without much Latin might wish to be. Martin describes Horace's social encounters very much in terms of the life of London or Paris. The dinner-conversation of Maecenas is compared with that of Talleyrand. The poem of invitation to 'the fair Tyndaris' (*Odes* 1.17) is compared to Milton's Sonnet 13 to his friend the musician Henry Lawes. This sets up a complex pattern of male solidarities, though the original was a poem of invitation to a woman. Horace is insinuated into a world of English male friendship which includes cultivated people such as Milton and Lawes and – by extension – those modern readers who know about them. A rather similar effect is achieved in Matthew Arnold's 'Horatian Echo', addressed 'To an ambitious friend', which echoes Milton's Sonnet 18 to Cyriac Skinner, itself derived in part from Horace (*Odes* 2.11.1–4). Martin speculatively relocates the sportsman Gargilius (*Ep.* 1.6.58) along the northern salmon-rivers that 'we' gentlemen fish in season: 'Have we never encountered a piscatory

Horace and the nineteenth century

Gargilius near the Spey or the Tweed?' Scenes in the life of Horace are casually linked with scenes from 'the pencil of Couture or Gérôme', or Shakespeare, or the eighteenth-century stage. 'We' accompany Horace to the theatre and encounter 'the Kynaston of the day' drunkenly playing Ilione (S 2.3.61), a knowing reference to a once-famous actor of the Restoration period who specialized in female roles. Horace's world becomes the world of the worldly who know about and are not unduly shocked by the Restoration theatre. This theatrical, artistic, companionable ambience is so much the world of Thackeray's bohemians and clubmen that it is not surprising that Martin proposes Thackeray as the nearest English approximation to his rather over-humanized Horace: both have 'the same keen eye for human folly, the same tolerance for the human weaknesses of which they were so conscious in themselves, the same genuine kindness of heart'.[23]

Dobson explicitly acknowledges Martin's picture of Horace in his poem 'To Q. H. F. [Quintus Horatius Flaccus], suggested by a chapter in Sir Theodore Martin's "Horace"'. Horace becomes a model and touchstone for the nineteenth century despite innovations such as the Albert Hall and Darwinian evolution which Horace had not envisaged:

> Walk in the Park – you'll seldom fail
> To find a Sybaris on the rail
>   By Lydia's ponies,
> Or hap on Barrus, wigged and stayed,
> Ogling some unsuspecting maid.[24]

Dobson's Horace is the poet of civilized friendship who also enrols the reader in literary friendship with other writers in a cosmopolitan world of letters. He was a companionable poet for a bookman, the 'friend of my friends' as Andrew Lang put it.[25] In some ways Dobson, a Civil Servant, rather resembles Horace, once a *scriba quaestorius* or 'Treasury clerk' in nineteenth-century parlance. Some of Dobson's poems are addressed to well-read Civil Service colleagues and friends such as Edmund Gosse, the famous critic, and it is implied that his anonymous readers are similarly cultivated. Horace had demonstrated to the *cognoscenti* his literary sophistication and technical credentials as a poet by imitating the Greek lyric metres of an older culture. In a consciously parallel demonstration Dobson wrote triolets, rondeaus, rondels, ballades and villanelles in the manner of the old French poets such as Villon and Charles d'Orléans. More modern Frenchmen, such as Théophile Gautier and Alfred de Musset, had admired and resurrected these intricate and demanding verse-forms. Since Horace had been admired by generations of English and French writers it was entirely appropriate that many of Dobson's virtuoso pieces should be translations of Horace.

The much-travestied *Ode, Persicos odi* (1.38) translates very neatly and fairly literally into a triolet: 'Davus, I detest / Orient display'. To assist the metre the unnamed 'boy' (*puer*) addressed in the original becomes 'Davus', the slave Horace mentions by name in the *Sermones* (2.7.2, for example), an artful substitution, but of course we all know who Davus was. The much-praised Bandusian fountain (*Odes* 3.13) plays once again for an appreciative audience, this time in the form of a rondeau. The form requires a refrain, for which there is no precedent in the Latin original, but a repeated 'O babbling Spring!' lamely but gamely keeps the fountain in mind. The most exacting of all the forms Dobson imitates is the villanelle, a series of alternately rhyming tercets concluding with a quatrain, calling for strategic repetitions of the first and third lines. Undeterred, Dobson uses it for a translation of *Odes* 1.11 'To Leuconoe' (*Tu ne quasieris*). Not surprisingly, the results are thin and disappointing. The sportive urgency of *carpe diem* becomes the languidly wistful

> Seek not, O Maid, to know
> (Alas! unblest the trying!)
> When thou and I must go.[26]

Horace presides more robustly over the sense of literary and intellectual fellowship in earlier nineteenth-century poetry. The Lake Poets Wordsworth and Coleridge and their circle shared a knowledge of Horace as well as theories of the imagination. Charles Lloyd, whose son was a pupil of Coleridge's and a friend of Charles Lamb, was on the edge of the circle; he sent Southey a copy of his verse-translation of *The Epistles of Horace* in 1813, even though Southey hated Horace.[27]

The proximities of student life at Oxford and Cambridge colleges could foster even closer intellectual and emotional friendships. In Trevelyan's Cambridge extravaganza *Horace at the University of Athens* Horace appears as a dandified freshman surrounded by a close circle of genially teasing male companions. The Trinity undergraduates for whom the burlesque was originally written could recognize him as 'one of us'.

Tennyson was at Trinity too, a little earlier than Trevelyan, and his closest friend there was Arthur Hallam, whose early death occasioned *In Memoriam*. While it would be absurd to give Horace all the credit for *In Memoriam*, the supreme Victorian poem of friendship and loss as well as of faith and doubt, it is clear that Horace's poems of nature and hospitality provided Tennyson with a literary model for the experiences he had once shared with Hallam.[28] Some of the allusions are fairly incidental: when Tennyson recalls (*In Memoriam* 89) how they would 'break the livelong summer day / With banquet in the distant woods' both the breaking up of the day and the distant woods may have Horatian parallels (*Odes* 2.7.6f and 2.3.6). In the same section, Hallam's as well as Tennyson's repudiation of 'The dust and din and steam of town', as both would have recognized, paraphrases Horace's similar sentiment in *Odes* 3.29.12.

More importantly, the address to the 'Fair ship' which carried Hallam's remains home from Italy (*In Memoriam* 9) ironically recalls Horace's prayer for a safe crossing for the ship carrying his poet friend Virgil (*Odes* 1.3). Hallam, also a poet, is made to play Virgil to Tennyson's Horace, but the worst Horace could have feared for his friend has already happened and there is only a corpse to bring home.

Horace's friendship with his patron Maecenas provides another model for Tennyson's friendship with Hallam (*In Memoriam* 84.37–44; 85.63f), but where Horace can only contemplate the melancholy prospect of Maecenas' death, the loss of half his own life, and propose to die on the same day to avoid separation (*Odes* 2.17.5–9, 21), Tennyson's friend is dead already and their friendship already participates in the Eternal, a concept derived from Christian teaching which alleviates the tragedies of Time in ways Horace could not imagine, or so Tennyson's use of the parallel implies.

The famous Tennysonian melancholy, and the residually Christian straining after a faintly apprehended larger hope beyond the finality of death's separations, are more Victorian than classical, perhaps, but Horace lies behind the well-spaced episodes of conviviality, such as *In Memoriam* 107 (recalling *Odes* 1.9, *Vides ut alta*), which frame the poet's grief. It took another Cambridge man, C. S. Calverley of Christ's, to emphasize the point by translating Horace into the stanzas of *In Memoriam* and rendering *In Memoriam* in Horatian Alcaics, as we have seen. That exacting scholar, critic and poet A. E. Housman pointed out that Calverley's Horace is 'too Tennysonian to be very Horatian',[29] but the antithesis is problematic at best.

Hallam and Tennyson had been members of the elite – or at least elitist – society, the Apostles, at Cambridge, and so had F. D. Maurice, later a celebrated if largely incomprehensible theologian with controversially liberal views about eternal punishment. In 1853 these forced his resignation from a professorship at King's College, London, a stuffily Anglican foundation. Tennyson expressed his sense of solidarity with Maurice, godfather of his eldest son, by writing (but apparently not actually sending) a very Horatian invitation to dinner, not at the Sabine farm but at his home on the Isle of Wight which was even further from the 'noise and smoke' (*fumum et opes strepitumque Romae*, *Odes* 3.29.12) of the metropolis. Maurice is represented as a choice spirit and a dear friend. To make the point Milton's Horatian celebration of civilized friendship interposes once again: Maurice is invited for the spring in terms which recall Milton's invitation to Edward Lawrence in Sonnet 17 as well as Horace in *Odes* 1.4.1 (*Solvitur acris hiems*):

> Come, Maurice, come: the lawn as yet
> Is hoar with rime, or spongy wet;
>   But when the wreath of March has blossomed,
> Crocus, anemone, violet,
>
> Or later, pay one visit here,
> For those are few we hold as dear;
>   Nor pay but one, but come for many,
> Many and many a happy year.

3 Politics and War

Tennyson promises Maurice 'Honest talk and wholesome wine'. The characteristically male conversation envisaged might turn on war, which overshadowed Augustan Rome, and mid-Victorian Britain during the Crimean campaigns, but it might also extend to 'Valour and charity' and the needs of the poor which were of particular concern to Maurice, a pioneer Christian Socialist. The substitution of theological controversy and Christian social concern for the business of the court of Augustus and civilized interchange at Horace's villa makes this the most revealing of all Victorian imitations of Horace. For many of the great issues of the day involved religious and moral issues, as that churchman and statesman and translator of Horace, Mr Gladstone, knew only too well.

Horace appealed to many involved with affairs of state or public administration not only because he had been part of their education but because he was close to Augustus and had taken part in a war. Tennyson, poet laureate and friend of Gladstone, and Matthew Arnold, pioneering Inspector of Schools, also knew something of public men and affairs. For all his coolness towards Horace, Arnold had served an Horatian apprenticeship which brought him to the fringes of public life. Trained in godliness as well as good learning at Rugby and Oxford, as Horace had studied with Orbilius in Rome before proceeding to Athens, he had then served as private secretary to Lord Lansdowne, Lord President of the Council, where Horace had served as a Roman Treasury official.

Arnold was working for Lansdowne when he wrote 'Horatian Echo'. This was addressed to an ambitious friend, possibly the journalist and parliamentary candidate John Blackett, to suggest that public life had its drawbacks, represented by 'the invading populace' and the 'imbeciles in present power'. There are other things in life than politics: one should cultivate love and personal fulfilment in the less tumultuous private sphere, while there is yet

Horace and the nineteenth century

time. The Horatian theme of *carpe diem* naturally mingles with conventionalized amorous dalliance with Lydia or Tyndaris, or 'Eugenia', who is Arnold's equivalent here.[30] Though the poem is deliberately formal and artificial, the impulse to retreat from the great world is characteristically Arnoldian as well as something Horace purports to have experienced on the Sabine farm. But by repudiating as 'no concern of ours' issues of foreign policy, popular politics and statecraft Arnold performs the Horatian trick of simultaneously dismissing and showing his privileged intimacy with affairs of state.

Other Victorians were to do the same. Gladstone retreated to his estate at Hawarden from time to time, to fell trees and translate Horace, but he kept in close touch with Westminster. Towards the end of Gladstone's career the Irish humorist Charles Graves (author of 'The Blarney Ballads') and some of his colleagues on the *Spectator* produced a series of Horatian parodies dealing with current affairs, later collected and expanded into *The Hawarden Horace* (1894) and *More Hawarden Horace* (1896). The civil and imperial wars that Horace had known provided uncomfortable parallels to political violence in Ireland and serious unrest in South Africa, problems which have not disappeared a century later. In 1886 Gladstone's colleague John Morley (later his biographer) had been sent to Ireland as Chief Secretary, 'a post of honour and danger'[31] which called for old-fashioned Roman fortitude in the wake of the Phoenix Park murders (1882) and the continuing terrorist activities of the 'Invincibles'. Horace's much-quoted *Ode, Integer vitae* (1.22) provides a word in season, its Moorish javelins and inhospitable Caucasus providing appropriate metaphors for Morley's possible reception. Gladstone is made to say:

> If clear be your conscience, my Morley,
>   No bullet-proof coat you'll require,
> Though often dispirited sorely
>   By Erin's Invincible ire:
> Nay further, discarding coercion,
>   You may with impunity fare
> On a midsummer moonlight excursion
>   Unarmed through the County of Clare.

Horace's poem ends musically with the sweet speech and laughter of Lalage; the parody ends with the diversions of actual music which the true-hearted man can relish, come what may:

> Were I doomed to despair on Sahara,
>   Or sentenced to dine with the Shah,
> Still I'd chant, to the tune of Ta-ra-ra,
>   The praises of Erin-go-Bragh.[32]

Gladstone's last administration had been harassed by the aggressive imperialism of Joseph Chamberlain, and its literary counterpart in the jingoistic verse of Alfred Austin, together with the problems of the South African gold fields and the ambitions of Cecil Rhodes who wanted to build a (British) railway from Capetown to Cairo. Horace's address to the Ship of State (*Odes* 1.14) becomes Gladstone's, complaining of the cares of office:

> Of old to me thou wast a weary weight,
> A source of anguish and regret of late;
>   O trust not Austin's odes,
> But shun the fatal gold reefs in the neighbourhood of Rhodes

(a comically laboured pun involving Cecil Rhodes and the island of Rhodes, the neighbourhood of which could be said to be the Cyclades which the ship of state is urged to avoid in the original (*Odes* 1.14.20)).[33]

The old Roman moderation and frugality commended by Horace and characteristic of Gladstone in private life might have a lesson for imperial Britain as well as imperial Rome. The wealthy Rhodes, a benefactor of Oxford University, is sardonically substituted for the unassuming Maecenas, patron of the arts, in an unusually serious travesty of *Odes* 3.16, 'Ad Maecenam', now redirected 'Ad Caecilium Africanum'. Gladstone's retirement to a small estate in Wales answers to Horace's retreat to the Sabine farm, and contrasts significantly with the overweening greed Graves associates with imperial adventure, corresponding to the dangerous, destructive wealth Horace condemns. Unlike Rhodes, Gladstone has no wish to control the De Beers Diamond Syndicate or become lord of Africa (*fulgentem imperio fertilis Africae*, *Odes* 3.16.31):

> Take it from me – no philosophic tyro –
>   Happier the man who limits his desires
> Than he who prances from Cape Town to Cairo,
>   Or spans the wastes of Africa with wires.
> Excessive wants on earth are never sated,
>   Nor mines nor millions avarice can assuage:
> Blest he, from Income-tax emancipated,
>   Who is content to earn a living wage.[34]

The serious business of war and politics attracted other and graver appropriations of Horace, who could be quoted on the imperialist as well as on the anti-imperialist side of the argument. It was not difficult to link the White Man's Burden with Roman ideas of self-sacrificing Duty, and Kipling was to make good fictional use of the 'Regulus' Ode (3.5) in a story of youth and empire published in 1908 and included in *A Diversity of Creatures* (1917). Long before, Turner's painting 'Regulus' (1828, reworked 1837), though not directly derived from Horace, had vividly commended Roman fortitude in the service of the state by showing the port of Carthage absorbed in painfully brilliant light.[35] This is how Carthage would have appeared to Regulus after his eyelids had been cut off, a punishment he knew he would suffer when he was brought back after refusing to negotiate a treaty in Rome. General Gordon, the hero of Khartoum, was a man of the same stamp, dying at his post rather than surrendering the city to the Mahdi though there was no hope of relief. Andrew Lang, normally restrained about such matters, could not forbear to make the connection: 'None but a patriot could have sung that ode on Regulus, who died, as our own hero died on an evil day, for the honour of Rome, as Gordon for the honour of England.'[36]

It was inevitable that patriots and politicians and the designers of war-memorials would recall that Horace had observed that it was sweet and seemly to die for one's country (*dulce et decorum est pro patria mori*, Odes 3.2.13). In the long peace between Waterloo and the Crimean War Britons had few opportunities to do so, but that did not deter them from recommending it to people of other nations. Liberal nationalist movements throughout Europe enjoyed widespread support in Britain, particularly from writers and intellectuals. Byron set the tone by dying for Greece at Missolonghi. Poland made repeated attempts to shake off Rusian domination, each rising more disastrous than the last, but aristocratic Polish exiles attracted energetic associates such as the poet Thomas Campbell, who organized the Literary Association of the Friends of Poland in 1832. W. E. Aytoun, later Professor of English at Edinburgh and a mainstay of *Blackwood's Magazine*, had been immensely impressed by the exiled Polish leader Prince Adam Czartoryski when he visited Edinburgh and dedicated *Poland, Homer and other Poems* to him in 1832. The volume opens with a grandiloquent invocation:

> Spirit of Freedom, shadow of the God
> Whom nations worship when he walks abroad . . .

The epigraph, predictably, is *dulce et decorum est pro patria mori*.[37]

Arthur Hugh Clough, a more reflective poet and political observer, was very much aware of the cause of Italian freedom in 1848, the year of European Revolutions: the Italian patriot Giuseppe Mazzini had lived in England and had many English friends. For a short time it looked as if a brave new Roman Republic might be established, which would have been particularly pleasing to classically educated Englishmen who knew all about the virtues of the old Roman Republic. But the following year Clough happened to be in Rome itself. The French were almost at the gates; Freedom was in mortal danger. But the issues were less clear-cut at close quarters. In Clough's travel poem *Amours de Voyage*, based on this experience, Italian politics, with love and religion, serve as examples of the problems of commitment and allegiance experienced by Clough himself. But the problems – and Horace – are treated ironically, an effect emphasized by fitting colloquial speech to accentual hexameters which mock the solemnities of classical verse. Clough's protagonist Claude writes home to his friend Eustace, remote enough from Rome to be an ardent patriot:

> *Dulce* it is, and decorous, no doubt, for the country to fall, – to
> Offer one's blood an oblation to Freedom, and die for the Cause; yet
> Still, individual culture is also something, and no man
> Finds quite distinct the assurance that he of all others is called on
> . . .
> Sweet it may be and decorous, perhaps, for the country to die; but,
> On the whole, we conclude the Romans won't do it, and I shan't.[38]

4 The Sense of Place

Amours de Voyage is among other things an Italian travelogue in verse, following in the tradition of the fourth canto of Byron's *Childe Harold's Pilgrimage*. Both Byron and Clough allude to country places that had Horatian associations, as do the Victorian guidebooks such as 'Murray' and 'Baedeker', even though wartime conditions in Italy prevented Clough from actually visiting any of them. Horace (and Byron) are liberally quoted in Murray's *Central Italy*, a bulky and bookish volume, and a few topographical tags of Horace survive in the much slimmer and less literary Baedeker.[39] Possible locations for the Sabine farm and the Bandusian fountain had fascinated generations of tourists, particularly English tourists – so much so that the country people in the valley of Licenza where Horace's villa may have been thought that Horace was an English poet.[40] Byron's friend John Cam Hobhouse wrote *Historical Illustrations of the Fourth Canto of 'Childe Harold'* (1818), an authorized companion-volume which amidst much else advises the scholarly tourist who pursues Horace from Rome to Tivoli and 'through the windings of the Sabine valley, till he detects him pouring forth his flowers over the glassy margin of his Bandusian fount'. Hobhouse airily accepts the contention of an eighteenth-century French savant that the Bandusian fountain was not in the Sabine valley but at Venusia on the Lucano-Apulian border where Horace was born.[41] Certainly there was a fountain there known as *Bandusinus fons* and asociated with Horace since the twelfth century or earlier, though the 'Fontagna della Oratini' near the probable site of the Sabine farm continued to be shown to visitors.

Even Italian landscapes which had little or nothing to do with Horace could somehow bring Horace to mind. In 'The Daisy' (1855) Tennyson employed a distinctive, approximately Horatian–Alcaic four-line stanza (similar to that used in the Horatian 'To the Rev. F. D. Maurice') to describe the shared pleasures of an Italian tour he had taken with his wife in 1851. There are no obvious Horatian allusions in the poem itself, though Virgil gets an honourable mention.

Painters as well as touring poets and scholars had followed in the footsteps of Byron and Horace. Turner had visited Italy in 1819, and in 1823 he exhibited 'The Bay of Baiae, with Apollo and the Sibyl'. The landscape is idealized and literary, emphasized by an accompanying quotation from Horace, *Odes* 3.4, which (rather incidentally) alludes to the delights of *liquidae . . . Baiae* (3.4.24). One of Turner's colleagues capped the quotation with *splendide mendax* ('splendidly false', *Odes* 2.11.35), for such light and landscape were never seen on sea or land.[42]

More generalized use of Horace's sense of place was widespread. He had ranged imaginatively among the remoter reaches of the Roman Empire and the known world, which led to some improbable adaptations. India in particular seemed to lend itself to Horatian treatment. Reginald Heber (1783–1826) had missed his wife very badly when he had been sent out on his own to be Bishop of Calcutta, so he wrote a long, bad poem to her: 'If thou wert by my side, my love.' Somehow or other Gladstone stumbled across it and decided it could appropriately be turned into Latin verse, into the Sapphic stanzas which Horace had so triumphantly made his own. The poem gains considerably in translation.[43] G. O. Trevelyan, like his uncle Macaulay and his father before him, served as an administrator in India in the 1860s and amused himself by parodying Horace. Gyges, the beloved of Asterie, had been detained in Bithynia (*Odes* 3.7), which was close enough to Rangoon to make no difference: he would soon return considerably enriched by trade (*merce beatum*):

> My dear Miss White, forbear to weep
> Because the North-West breezes keep
>   At anchor off Rangoon
> That youth who, richer by a lac,
> May safely be expected back
>   Before the next Monsoon.[44]

But closer to home, or closer to Rome, Horace sang of rural retirement. It was this aspect of Horace that had particularly appealed to earlier generations, but the nineteenth century was a little cooler about it. The anti-pastoral rural realism of Crabbe and Clare and Thomas Hardy, and popular French paintings such as Millet's *The Reapers* (1857) and *The Man with the Hoe* (1859–62), had offered different, less artificial perspectives on rural life. The famous second *Epode*, *Beatus ille* was still quoted, but it was drily pointed out that its conventional praise of country life was not necessarily Horace's own since it is spoken by the money-lender Alfius.⁴⁵

Horace the countryman was not ignored, however, as the parodies in *The Hawarden Horace* demonstrate. His manner lent itself to mannered humorous verse such as Tom Hood's 'Town and Country. An Ode' (1828), alluding to *Sermones* 2.6.60 (*o rus, quando ego te aspiciam*):

> O! well may poets make a fuss
> In summer time, and sigh '*O rus!*'
> Of London pleasures sick:
> My heart is all at pant to rest
> In greenwood shades – my eyes detest
> This endless meal of brick!⁴⁶

On the whole Horace, suitably selected, served the nineteenth century well as a kind of honorary Victorian, providing forms of words which said what people wanted to hear or feel, sometimes giving them opportunities to demonstrate their own superiority. He was never in any danger of being blackballed at the club. The sardonic Samuel Butler caught this establishment Horace neatly when he observed that 'Horace was often very priggish. Some say his "*Aurum irrepertum*", etc. [*Odes* 3.3.49], is worthy of Mr Tennyson himself. Well, I think it is.'⁴⁷ So much for Horace and Tennyson!

But occasionally Horace could challenge and subvert comfortably established attitudes. Dowson used him to articulate *fin-de-siècle* despair. Clough used him to assail the certainties of the Christian centuries. Hardy's poor country-boy Jude the Obscure, an autodidact excluded from the social and educational privileges of the well-born, increasingly ill at ease with conventional religion, finds the grave formal beauty of the *Carmen Saeculare* so unbearably moving on an evening when setting sun and full moon are both visible that he kneels to both and rapturously intones the whole poem, beginning with the invocation of sun-god and moon-goddess:

> '*Phoebe silvarumque potens Diana!*'⁴⁸

The lines speak to him across the ages, slipping below imposed barriers of culture, religion and class. That is what true poetry can do.

11

HORACE'S KIPLING
Stephen Medcalf

RUDYARD KIPLING COMMONLY wrote his most poignant and personal verse, when he had taken steps to be most removed from his own standpoint and circumstances. He laboured earnestly for what he calls 'the detachment of the true artist who knows that he is but the vessel of an emotion whence others, not he, must drink', to whom moreover life is the sweeter because he 'lives many lives in one'.[1] T. S. Eliot, admiring this unselfing, remarks on how well too Kipling knew 'the difference between the poem which forces its way into the consciousness of the poet and the poem which the writer himself forces'.[2]

Eliot instances Kipling's '"The Finest Story in the World"'[3], in which this difference is illustrated by two poems, one 'very good . . . in rather free verse', the other 'very bad . . . in regular verse'.[4] The story offers a double hypothesis about this: first, that 'the poem which the writer himself forces' was written with the utmost sincerity by a London clerk out of his own immediate feeling. (It had in fact been written in his adolescence by Kipling himself,[5] so that he had every right to tell us from what feelings it came.) Conversely, 'the poem which forces its way into the consciousness of the poet' was the clerk's vivid half-memory of an earlier incarnation.

Kipling probably entertained, but never fully believed, the doctrine of reincarnation. In another, and most powerful, story, '"Wireless"',[6] he presents a Brighton chemist's assistant who goes through the mental processes of Keats writing 'The Eve of St Agnes'. But the story suggests that this happens, not through reincarnation, but through possession by the mind and heart of Keats when various chances – wintry weather, and the fact that the young chemist is in love and ill with tuberculosis – have brought the dying man and the dead together.

'"Wireless"' is as much about reading poetry, conceived of as thinking the thoughts of a poet after him, as writing it. Both require, what these stories adumbrate, something to possess the poet or reader, which comes from outside the self of their ordinary experiences and responses. In writing poetry, Kipling called this his Daemon; in reading it, he used the poet's name. The

217

two acts came together when another poet provided him with a persona to protect the growth of a new poem out of his own heart and mind.

The poet who most possessed Kipling was Horace. Kipling tells in his autobiography *Something of Myself* how he first encountered Horace at school at Westward Ho! under William Crofts, the English and Classics master on whom he based Mr King in *Stalky & Co*:

I tried to give a pale rendering of his style when heated in a 'Stalky' tale, 'Regulus'[7] but I wish I could have presented him as he blazed forth once on the great Cleopatra Ode – the 27th of the Third Book.[8] I had detonated him by a very vile construe of the first few lines. Having slain me, he charged over my corpse and delivered an interpretation of the rest of the Ode unequalled for power and insight. He held even the Army Class breathless . . . C– taught me to loathe Horace for two years; to forget him for twenty, and to love him for the rest of my days and through many sleepless nights.[9]

What Kipling calles loathing of Horace did not prevent him from trying to translate the *Odes* into verse. Gilbert Murray, who met him in the Easter holidays of 1882, his last year at school, says:

I thought him extraordinarily clever and exciting, though there was something in him that repelled me. He threw his stick at a cat and he thought 'Do not be ashamed to marry the housemaid' was a correct Sapphic and a fine translation of *Ne sit ancillae tibi amor pudori*.[10]

Would Murray have objected to the version of *Odes* 3.9, the dialogue with Lydia, which Kipling printed in the school magazine[11] that year? It is deft and delightful, almost ominously clever for a sixteen-year-old, as if he would have no room for development. Male and female speak broad Devonshire, *dulcis docta modos et citharae sciens* becomes 'She can play the piano, she can', *tu levior cortice* 'An yeou shifts like cut net-floats, yeou du.' Kipling himself in later life may have thought that writing it was a sign of, if not loathing, at least inadequate love and understanding of Horace. He wrote it, he says, as an imposition, after he had suggested that he could do better with Horace if Latin verse 'rhymed as decent verse should'.[12] He never reprinted it, except among *Early Verse* in comprehensive editions of his work. And, although he wrote many poems based on Horace, he never again made an actual translation from him; he came to feel that translation 'of an idea that has been perfectly set forth' is impossible.[13]

Just as his translations from Horace in his last years at school modify, but do not destroy, his record that he then loathed him, so the occasional tags that appear in his work over the next twenty years modify, but do not destroy his statement that for that period he forgot him. They are commonly used facetiously, and at best are such 'totally unrelated Latin tags' as in 'Regulus' Hartopp the science master derides to King.[14]

Horace's Kipling

However, Kipling, as he said when he gave a talk on reading old books to his son John and others at Wellington College in May 1912, did 'attach a certain amount of importance to the spirit of a few old Latin tags and quotations. Some of them, not more than three lines long, give one the very essence of what a man ought to try to do. Others, equally short, let you understand once and for all, the things that a man should not do – under any circumstances'.[15] One such tag from Horace, *dis te minorem quod geris imperas* (*Odes* 3.6.5), rendered in 'Regulus', 'Thou rulest because thou bearest thyself as lower than the Gods', seems to be echoed in the poem prefixed to the original *Stalky & Co* of 1899 – 'Save he serve no man may rule.'[16] But 'Regulus' was not written yet, and the 'giddy' *Odes* of Horace only appear in that first collection as part of an examination paper to be sabotaged in proof – '"*Mutatosque deos flebit in antro*". "Mute gods weepin' in a cave", suggested Stalky.'[17]

In the 'Recessional' (July 1897) there are, as Carrington points out 'complicated metonymies in the Horatian mode'[18] like 'All valiant dust that builds on dust'. But the stylistic sources of these are probably not directly in Horace, but in the emblematic, or otherwise Horatian poets of the seventeenth century and later, in whom Kipling was revelling in Crofts' and the Headmaster's libraries, while Crofts pushed him through Horace. Nevertheless, he was being prepared in both ways for the time when Horace himself would affect him as poetry.

The closest he came in those twenty years to writing like Horace was in the imagery and complex lyric metre of *'L'Envoi'* to *Departmental Ditties* (1886), an apologia for writing verse while inspiration is absent, through the mouths of priests, who serve the altar of a Muse who has departed, because some wandering god may come and 'finding all in order meet / Stay while we worship at Her feet'.[19] The imagery may owe a debt to something which an old 'statesman who had been in charge of a great portion of the Empire' – Lord Dufferin – later pointed out to him in a conversation which Kipling reported at Wellington College. All Lord Dufferin 'took away from school and college was the fact that there were once peoples who didn't talk our tongue and who were very strong on sacrifice and ritual, particularly at meals, whose gods were different from ours and who had strict views on the disposal of the dead. Well, you know, all that is worth knowing if you ever have to govern India.'[20]

Both those highly intelligent men, Lord Dufferin and Kipling, will have taken seriously this reading of the Classics as a background for understanding other cultures, other faiths. Kipling had besides a deeper layer of experience to illumine the analogy between India and the ancient Mediterranean world. He was frequenting Hindu temples before he was seven: he learnt to perceive and to speak in India: and when he returned there, after nine years in England

and after having been pulled through Horace and Virgil, he found that the 'sights and smells . . . made me deliver in the vernacular sentences whose meaning I knew not'.[21] But it was only after he had published, in 1901, what is probably the most understanding evocation of India in English, *Kim*, that he wedded India in his writing with Horace and Virgil.

If we take 'twenty years' as seriously as is reasonable for Kipling's period of forgetfulness, we should look for his re-discovery of Horace within a couple of years of 1902. Two facts suggest 1904–5: first, that in *The Muse among the Motors*, a set of parodies by Kipling of his favourite authors on motoring, there was no Horatian poem in the original edition of 1904, and secondly that when in January 1918 he looked for old Horatian poems of his to collect in a 'Fifth Book' of Odes, he not only found a very deft motoring parody, the 'Carmen Circulare', which eventually went into the second edition of *The Muse among the Motors* in 1919,[22] but also 'The Pro-Consuls', an ode in honour of Lord Milner written between 24 March and 21 July 1905.[23]

'The Pro-Consuls' is a heavily moral poem, proclaiming that the builders of the world neither do, nor should, expect help or gratitude, in an image which develops that of '*L'Envoi*':

> For, so the Shrine abide, what shame – what pride –
> If we, the priests, were bound or crowned before it?

Its Horatianness may not originally have been deliberate, for in 1918 Kipling writes '. . . I perceive now that Horace wrote it. Rather a big effort for him and on a higher plane than usual – unless he'd been deliberately flattering some friend in the Government'.[24] But, much more than '*L'Envoi*', it reads as if Kipling wrote under the influene of Horace, at his most Stoic, moral and imperial, the Horace of the Roman *Odes*.

But why should he come more distinctly under the influence of Horace in the spring of 1905? Perhaps because he was preparing for a story about Roman Britain, a story brought to birth by his move to Burwash in the Weald of Sussex in 1902, his awareness of the presence of the past there in people, earth, water and trees increasing until he was set off by his cousin Ambrose Poynter, whose capacity to imagine and incapacity to write his imaginations was probably the model for the clerk in '"The Finest Story in the World"'.[25] 'Write a yarn about Roman times here', said Poynter, and suggested a narrator, a Roman centurion, and his name, Parnesius.[26]

On 25 September 1904, Kipling's wife Carrie noted him as at work on 'a fresh idea . . . the History of England told by Puck to children.'[27] It seems likely that he went to the Roman poets whom he had read at school, Virgil and Horace, to prepare for Parnesius. Carrie notes him as reaching his 'Roman Centurion story' in July 1905, so that he is likely to have been reading Horace in just the months when he wrote 'The Pro-Consuls'.

Horace's Kipling

To a large extent he imagined Roman Britain on the model of British India. *Kim* had been the crown of the first, the imperial and Victorian half of his writing. What followed with his final striking roots in England and Burwash T. S. Eliot calls 'the development of the imperial imagination into the historical imagination'.[28] It has at its beginning the Romano-Hindu *pietas* with which Parnesius, in 'A Centurion of the Thirtieth', describes how, before he left home to join his legion, 'we sacrificed to our ancestors – the usual little Home Sacrifice – but I never prayed so earnestly to all the Good Shades'[29] – or with which he addresses Puck as 'Faun', that is Faunus, the woodland and country god who would take his place easily among the Hindu gods – Muller in 'In the Rukh' (1893) describes Mowgli as Faunus.[30] These are religious acts which Horace could have shared.

Kipling's first collection of Puck stories, *Puck of Pook's Hill* (1906), is as much a Virgilian as a Horatian book in its sense of the land as expressing history, of the fall and rise of civilizations, and of life and death as a mixture of enjoyment, melancholy, ordinary duty and supererogatory heroism. It is Horace in an unusually Virgilian mood who seems to inspire the enchanting poem set before 'A Centurion of the Thirtieth':

> Cities and Thrones and Powers
>   Stand in Time's eye
> Almost as long as flowers
>   Which daily die:
> But, as new buds put forth
>   To glad new men,
> Out of the spent and unconsidered Earth
>   The Cities rise again . . .[31]

Horace, who probably learnt this pattern of the growth and decay of cities from the *Aeneid*, used the image of plants in their seasons to express it in *Odes* 4.4, when Hannibal says that after the fall of Troy, the Roman nation

> . . . as on Algidus the oak
>   Pruned by the biting axe anew,
> From wounds, from deaths, from every stroke
>   Resource and freshening vigour drew.
>
> (*Odes* 4.4.57–50)[32]

Such a tree often entered Kipling's awareness of Horace. There survive two sets of his illuminations for the *Odes*. In the fuller set, in Conington's edition printed and perhaps bought in 1908, there is a drawing at 4.4, with three other versions at other places, of a massive tree cut down to a stump, but alive. In the other set, in the Medici Press *Horace*, bought in May 1912, there are two versions, one of which is the frontispiece.[33] Has this tree become the flowers of 'Cities and Thrones and Powers'? It would make sense at least, considering

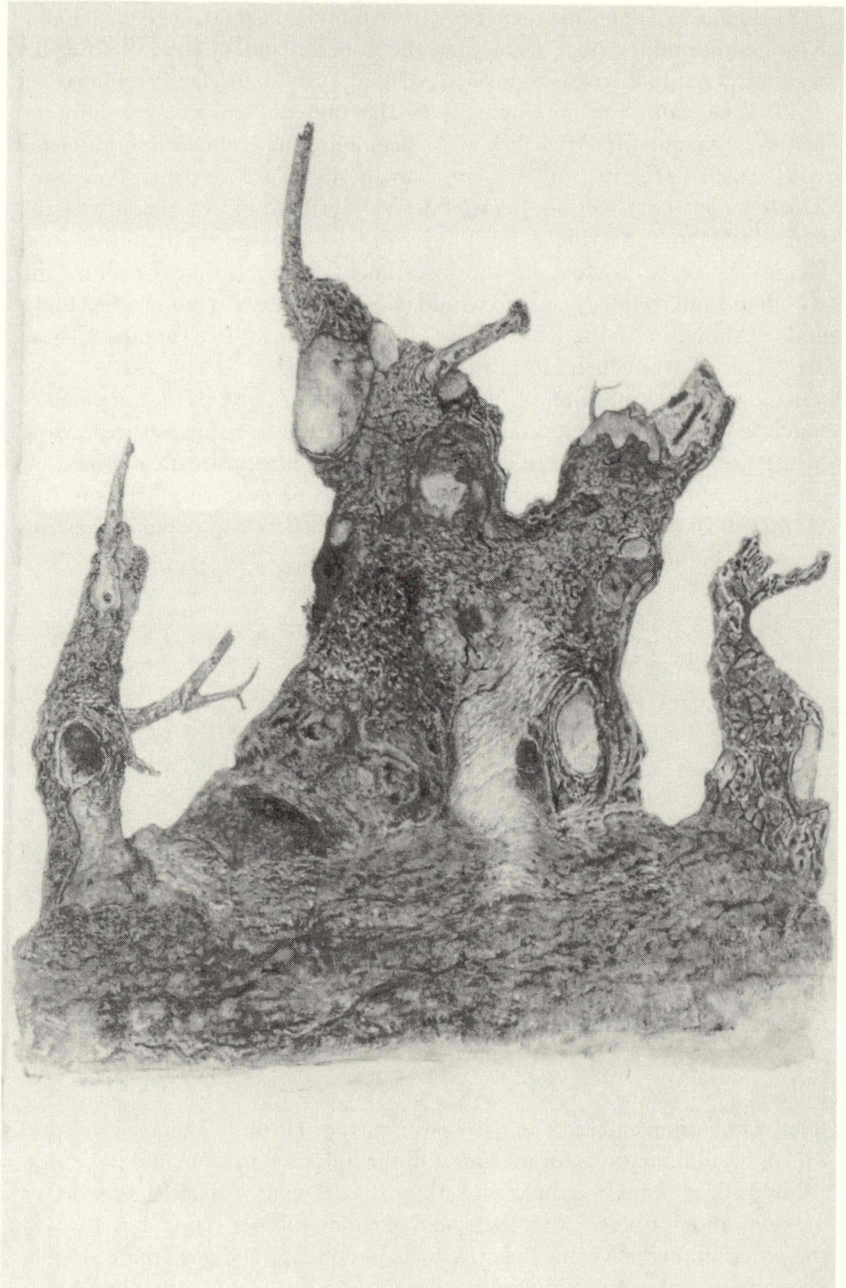

Horace's Kipling

the state of mind, about the history of England and the woods of the Weald, which Kipling brought to writing *Puck of Pook's Hill*, that it should be this image which first made him feel Horace as poetry. Perhaps it gave him too the pattern for English history in the whole book, which Puck sums up at the end of the last story, *The Treasure and the Law*, as 'as natural as an oak growing'.

If this oak gave the pathos and beauty of natural resurrection to describe the Cities at the beginning of 'A Centurion of the Thirtieth', perhaps it gave the hardihood that derives from blows to describe the City in the poem at its end, 'A British–Roman Song'. A Roman whose family have not seen Rome for generations invokes it as hive, heart and hearth of the Empire:

> Crowned by all Time, all Art, all Might,
> > The equal work of Gods and Man,
> City beneath whose oldest height –
> > The Race began![34]

He prays that it may, as hive, 'send forth again a brood / . . . that clings / To Rome's thrice hammered hardihood' – in this dense, Horatian style 'clings' suggests both hive and tree – as heart, send its blood through the Empire, and, as hearth, 'guard 'gainst home-born ills / The Imperial Fire!' The theme is Horace's sense of duty to Rome, but not exactly, for Horace's is a metropolitan's at the height of City and Empire, whereas Parnesius' (if he is the singer) is a colonial's, to which Kipling adds an unobtrusive bitterness by dating the song 'AD 406' the year of the barbarian invasion over the Rhine, which led four years later to the abandonment of Britain in the futile attempt to save Rome.

Both poems comment on what Parnesius' father says in the story between them, seeming to evoke *Odes* 3.6, ... *donec templa refeceris*: 'The great war with the Painted People broke out in the very year the temples of our Gods were destroyed. We beat the Painted People in the very year our temples were re-built . . . There is no hope for Rome . . . She has forsaken her Gods, but if the Gods forgive *us* here, we may save Britain.'[35]

In November 1906, Kipling began a new set of Puck stories which have for their 'underwood' the question 'What else could I have done?'[36] In 'The Tree of Justice', written in 1909, and made in 1910 the climactic story of the completed set, *Rewards and Fairies*, Horace appears again, after the fall of the Roman Gods, in the medieval and Christian world. Forty years after the battle of Hastings, Harold is found alive, 'witless, discrowned and alone', having done a lifetime of penance for making and breaking his oath to William to help him to the throne of England. He is protected by a certificate from Henry I's jester, Rahere, containing some Latin, which a clerk translates:

The charm, which I think is from Virgilius the Sorcerer, says 'When thou art once dead, and Minos (which is a heathen judge) has doomed thee, neither cunning, nor speechcraft, nor good works will restore thee!' A terrible thing! It denies any mercy to a man's soul![37]

The charm is the penultimate verse of *Odes* 4.7, *Diffugere nives*, and Horace is speaking of the inexorability of death: but everyone in 'The Tree of Justice' takes him to be speaking of the fate of the soul after death. Kipling makes Horace the type of the whole pre-Christian, pagan or Jewish world of the unmitigated Law. The climax of the story is Rahere's forcing from the administrators of law 'the King, his bishops – the knights,' the admission, just before Harold dies, that they dare not judge him. 'Well for your souls', says Rahere: so this is the answer to Horace. There is hope; but not in cunning, speech-craft nor good works: only in forgiveness in return for foregoing judgment. *Rewards and Fairies*, which begins its exploration of 'What else could I have done?' with a poem 'Cold Iron', making iron the type of both human service and the nails on the cross, ends it with the tree of justice, like the cross, becoming the tree of Mercy. Kipling, by setting him in this pattern, has begun to argue with the Stoic, moral figure whom he at first drew from Horace's *Odes*.

In his next Horatian exercise, he continues the argument, using *Odes* 3.6, from which he had taken both the tag about service in the poem prefixed to *Stalky & Co.*, and Parnesius' father's reflection on the gods, and adding 3.5, the Regulus *Ode*. It is that Stalky tale 'Regulus'[38] which we have heard him mentioning for its 'pale rendering' of Mr Crofts' style. He dates it 1908, but was still at work on it in May 1911.[39] In it, he has mellowed, is more willing to display the humanist aspects of education than in the original *Stalky & Co.* Those first stories were seen almost entirely from a boy's eye, the masters even where likeable were – apart from the Headmaster and the Chaplain – regarded as enemies, and even in the introductory poem with its Horatian ethic, which is the only point where a different dimension emerges and the masters are duly honoured, they are honoured exclusively for teaching good discipline. But in 'Regulus' we find King putting splendidly into practice the ideals of translation, of reading, of education, which Kipling presumably derived from Crofts, and which he expressed in his talk at Wellington in May 1912:

The reason why one has to parse and construe and grind at the dead tongues in which certain ideas are expressed, is *not* for the sake of what is called intellectual training ... but because only in that tongue is that idea expressed with absolute perfection. If it were not so the Odes of Horace would not have survived. (People aren't in a conspiracy to keep things alive.) I grant you that the kind of translations one serves up at school are as bad and as bald as they can be. They are bound to be so, because one cannot re-express an idea that has been perfectly set forth ... Yet, by a painful and laborious acquaintance with the mechanism of that particular tongue; by being made to take it to pieces and put it together again, and by that means only, we can arrive at a state of mind in which, though we cannot re-express the idea in any adequate words, we can realise and feel and absorb the idea.[40]

When King has brought them to take the Regulus *Ode* to pieces, and has himself put it together again, 'even the Army Class',[41] though incompetent to re-express Horace's ideas, do 'realise and feel and absorb' them. King as it were provides for them the experience of the Brighton chemist in '"Wireless"' with 'The Eve of St Agnes': an experience for which the model of decoding for understanding a poem, whether in one's own language or another, is inaccurate. The boys of the class only substitute English words as a temporary makeshift: Latin provides them with new words, for their own circumstances. King, for example, offers them a distinction in the behaviours of those surrounding Regulus as he returns, driven by honour, to face torture and death at Carthage. Horace contrasts *maerentes amicos*, 'the mourning friends', among whom are *obstantes propinquos* his kinsmen, with *populum ... morantem* the people. King explains *obstantes* and *morantem*: 'I take it that his kinsmen bodily withstood his departure, whereas the crowd – *populumque* – the democracy stood about futilely pitying him and getting in the way.'[42]

Presently Stalky is able to respond to the distinction, when Winton, a boy who is on his way to be caned by his studymate, is mocked by his fellows, and turns on them. King finds them at the close of the fight and suggests that they are the delaying *populus*. 'No, sir ... we're the *maerentes amicos*' says Stalky:[43] and King welcomes the implicit recognition that Winton is Regulus as proof that the boys have 'got what we poor devils of ushers are striving after – Balance, proportion, perspective – life.'[44]

The perspective gained is something beyond the capacity to model oneself on a hero. Behind and beyond King's aims, and not quite understood by him, are the Headmaster's. Winton, whose 'only fault' for the Headmaster 'is a certain costive and unaccommodating virtue',[45] has had his caning contrived for him – his first caning in seven years at the school – on the eve of his becoming immune from discipline as a member of the First Fifteen. The ultimate cause is a childish trick which he played on the art master, and which renders him 'penitent, perturbed and annoyed with himself'[46] – and, to the Headmaster, more human than he had been in all those seven years. Kipling, who glossed Horace's *integer vitae scelerisque purus* (*Odes* 1.22.1) 'The Pure and Perfect Bore', means his story not only as a vindication of Horace, but also as a dialectic which only begins with Horace's hierarchic Stoicism.

The habit of arguing with Horace brought Kipling closer to him. By itself, the discipline of taking a poet to pieces may provide either illuminations on experience, or a capacity to use the pieces facetiously. Stalky's remark trembles on the boundary between the two: and when Kipling published 'Regulus', in *A Diversity of Creatures* (1917), it was with three other Horatian writings which make the point well. Part of the point of '"My Son's Wife"' is the dense, comforting rurality of Edwardian Sussex, where drawing-room ballads are for ladies, Jorrocks for gentlemen and humorous perversions of Horace – '*injecto ter pulvere* – you've kicked half the ditch into my eye already'[47] – for a hunting lawyer. And the poem following 'The Village that Voted the Earth was Flat' turns the opening of *Odes* 4.3, one of Horace's serious aspirations to serve the Muse – *Quem tu, Melpomene, semel nascentem placido lumine videris* . . . into 'Who once hath lit . . . his pipe in the morning – calm / That follows the midnight stress . . . '[48] – a symptom of Kipling's own addiction to journalism.

'A Translation', however, which follows 'Regulus', is Kipling's closest representation of Horace's way of language and thought:

> There are whose study is of smells
>   And to attentive schools rehearse
> How something mixed with something else
>   Makes something worse.
>
> Some cultivate in broths impure
>   The clients of our body – these,
> Increasing without Venus, cure,
>   Or cause, disease.
>
> Others the heated wheel extol,
>   And all its offspring, whose concern
> Is how to make it farthest roll
>   And farthest turn.
>
> Me, much incurious if the hour
>   Present, or to be paid for, brings
> Me to Brundusium by the power
>   Of wheels or wings;
>
> Me in whose breast no flame hath burned
>   Life-long, save that by Pindar lit,
> Such lore leaves cold. I am not turned
>   Aside to it
>
> More than when, sunk in thought profound
>   Of what the unaltering Gods require,
> My steward (friend but slave) brings round
>   Logs for my fire.

The metre has something of the various stiffness, liquidity and bite of Horace's Sapphics: the syntax uses Latinate delays and metonymies, metaphors and allusions for terseness' sake: the shape of thought is that of the priamel, and is based on *Odes* 1.1 – only instead of the multitudinous throng of occupations in that poem, which Kipling in his Medici Press *Horace* glosses 'Sport, Politics, Finance / Trade, Liquor, Law, the Chase'[49] it is varieties of dependants on science who are dismissed to focus on Horace himself, who in both poems proclaims himself the disciple of the Greek lyrists. Thus, Kipling raises the ghost of Horace to approve King's feelings on the reading of the Classics, as against Hartopp's claims for science and technology. But this he does with an irony and ambiguity themselves Horatian.

The poem develops from King's use in 'Regulus' of Kipling's favourite tag, '(Thou rulest because thou bearest thyself as lower than the Gods) – making it a text for a discourse on manners, morals, and respect for authority as distinct from bottled gases.'[50] It seems that in Horace's world, the relation of Horace to his steward – 'friend but slave' – is, though complex, clear. The steward's business is to bring logs, Horace's is to command, because Horace bears himself as lower than the gods.

But the syntax of the last verse raises a doubt. Is it Horace himself or his steward who meditates on the will of the gods? The steward's mind takes up more of our attention than we might have expected: how does he bear himself in relation to the gods? The doubt spreads: while neither Horace nor Kipling seems to be in real doubt that Horace is right to rate the flame lit by Pindar above the logs, and the heated wheel, is Horace right to be 'much incurious' about all work, all technology? We recall that Kipling perhaps of all writers is the one who has paid most attention to men at work. And besides, Kipling himself was an enthusiastic motorist, and fascinated by medical research: yet it is Kipling who picks a metonymy from *Odes* 1.1 – *metaque fervidis / evitata rotis* – 'the heated wheel' and means by it in Horace's voice the chariot of an Olympic winner, in his own voice the motor car – which the poem spoken by both Horace and Kipling together condemns. The wit of the poem depends on our noticing that we are listening to two voices, from two worlds. And if we move outside Horace's world, then we know what we have already seen in 'The Tree of Justice', that his gods will alter. What then?

There is a parallel and a contrast between this poem and Ezra Pound's more or less contemporaneous rendering, in summer 1911, of the Anglo-Saxon 'Seafarer'.[51] Both poets are making play with personas of themselves in their translation or imitation of a poem from another culture, not coincidentally, but partly because they both enormously admired the similar experiments of Browning in *Sordello* and *Men and Women*. But in method they are near the opposite poles of translation. Pound in 'The Seafarer' – not entirely unlike Kipling in the verse attached to 'The Village that Voted the Earth was Flat', though not humorously – asks himself, 'What would this set of words be like if I had spoken them?' Kipling in 'A Translation' leaves that question to the overtone, to the secondary meanings of the poem as spoken in his own voice: of the poem as spoken in Horace's voice he asks 'What would I be like to have used these sets of words? – and in particular *Odes* 1.1?'

Kipling's Horace, then, in this poem at any rate, is not a mere persona of Kipling's but a clear and distinct personality who speaks with a voice derived from his own *Odes*. Kipling had conclusively begun what Jungians call an *Auseinandersetzung* – having it out with, coming to terms with Horace as both a familiar friend and a visitant within his own mind. And this sense of Horace as another person enabled him to make a discovery which is the special element in his affection for him as he described it at Wellington in May 1912. Of the Latin writers in general he says, as we heard earlier, that there are tags in them 'not more than three lines long', which tell us what we should or should not do.[52] Of Horace he says something more poignant: 'There are others – bits of Odes from Horace, they happen to be in my case – that make one realise in later life, as no other words in any other tongue can, the brotherhood of mankind in time of sorrow or affliction.'[53]

The emphatic phrase 'no other words in any other tongue' makes it possible to guess that one of the *Odes* in which he found this sympathy was the one he used in 'The Tree of Justice', *Diffugere nives*. For in the Medici Press *Horace*, which he acquired also in May 1912, there are not only the illuminations which we mentioned earlier, but also fifty-five annotations in verse. We cannot date them with any certainty: but there are half a dozen whose rusty ink, copperplate handwriting and distribution of capitals suggest that they form a group, and that this group was the first to be copied in, representing an initial ambition to comment on Horace as a Prior–Pope figure, in eighteenth-century verse: the other annotations are written more carelessly, in four or five different scripts. One of this group, probably copied close in time to the Wellington talk, and faintly echoed in it, is attached to *Diffugere nives*:

> If all that ever Man had sung
> In the audacious Latin Tongue
> Had been lost – and This remained
> All, through This might be regained.[54]

One can only guess in what time of affliction Kipling realized Horace's brotherhood with him. Just possibly there is an echo from *Diffugere nives* of the Graces dancing in the Spring in the poem about the Neolithic father Tegumai and his daughter Taffimai, in which Kipling, distanced as ever, expressed his bitter grief at the death of his own daughter Josephine in 1899 and set her on a walk taken near Guildford in June 1900 –

Horace's Kipling

> Comes Taffy dancing through the fern
> To lead the Surrey spring again[55]

But this is tenuous, and it is more likely that Kipling, having returned to Horace, as we have traced him, through ethics, found consolation in him later, perhaps when his parents died at the turn of the years 1910 and 1911. Kipling would not have wished us to know, and we do not.

We can be sure that he went to Horace for consolation in October 1915 after the disappearance of his son John in battle at Loos, and in the wretched period afterwards, before he was totally convinced of his death in 1917. The evidence for this is, again and characteristically, oblique and delayed.

In April 1917 he sent *A Diversity of Creatures* to C. R. L. Fletcher, an elderly Oxford don who was teaching at Eton as war service, asking for a Latin version of 'A Translation'.[56] He also enquired whether it was true that there was a rumour that a Fifth Book of Horace's *Odes* had once existed, as he wanted to write a story about it.[57] Fletcher denied that there had ever been such a rumour, and the story languished: but he liked 'A Translation', and asked if Kipling had any more such poems, to use in teaching his boys Latin.[58] In December Kipling sent him an imitation of Horace in his social satirical vein, 'Lollius', on the sale of honours under Lloyd George.[59] Fletcher responded by suggesting that they compose a Fifth Book between them.[60] Kipling dug out 'The Pro-consuls' and 'Carmen Circulare', answering on 2 January 1918 'It would be great fun if we could eventually make a little collection of 'em – something to keep one's mind at play sometimes.'[61] In February they agreed to have 'fresh hands in the game', and Kipling wrote to Charles Graves, to provide more poems like his earlier skit on Gladstone, *The Hawarden Horace*:[62] fortunately as it turned out.

On 11 March 1918 Kipling wrote the only poem which he expressly created for the Fifth Book, 'A Recantation'. It is a lament for his son. The opening verse is written in his Medici Press *Horace*, at the Hymn to Apollo, *Odes* 4.6, beside the last verse, where Horace tells the choir who are to sing at the Secular Games, *nupta iam dices: ego dis amicum / . . . / reddidi carmen . . .* – 'At your marriage you will say, "I sang the hymn that pleased the gods."' Kipling's verse is a heart-rending comment, both on 'the unaltering Gods' of 'A Translation' and on the loss of such a future for his son:

> What boots it on the Gods to call
> Since – answered or unheard –
> We perish with the Gods and all
> Things made except the Word.[63]

By itself, this verse, like most of Kipling's annotations, was part of a conversation with Horace. But 'A Recantation' as a whole is addressed 'To

Lyde of the Music Halls', who, in spite of the change of sex, probably represents Harry Lauder. The first verse was eventually printed in italic: the next nine verses, in which Kipling speaks in a Horatian voice but very much in his own person, are in ordinary type, emphasizing a change of tone. Formerly, he says, he judged Lyde's art 'O'erblown and over-bold'.

> But he – but he, of whom bereft
>   I suffer vacant days –
> He on his shield not meanly left –
>   He cherished all thy lays.

On New Year's Day 1917, Lauder had received the news 'Thy son had – followed mine', but, following an artist's duty as both and he and Kipling understood it, continued at the Shaftesbury Theatre with his successful revue *Three Cheers*.[64] Kipling pays tribute to him, and ends:

> Singer to children! Ours possessed
>   Sleep before noon – but thee,
> Wakeful each midnight for the rest,
>   No holocaust shall free!
>
> *Yet they who use the Word assigned*
>   *To hearten and make whole*
> *Not less than Gods have served mankind*
>   *Though vultures rend their soul.*[65]

Kipling joins Lauder with Horace – both addressing young men and girls – adds Shakespeare by echoing the Fool's last words in *King Lear*,[66] and ends the part of the poem in his own person with an implicit reproach to the gods in the word 'holocaust'. In the last verse, he returns to italic and to the voice of the first verse, which now seems to come from a perspective beyond either his own or Horace's. But the original desolate faith of this voice in the endurance of song is transformed into a comparison of those who console by song – Lauder, Horace, Shakespeare, Kipling – with, not the gods, but Prometheus.

Unfortunately, Fletcher disliked 'A Recantation', and said that A. B. Ramsay, whom he had brought in as a translator, objected that Horace had no son.[67] Kipling wrote to him on 24 March: 'What you say about the Recantation, of course, ends the game for me. It was a very delightful game while it lasted, but one can't play under a Censorship and just now I haven't any right to play at all as I've been shoved into a heavy job which will take all my time.'[68] 'A Recantation' was published in *The Years Between*[69] and Kipling provided no more poems for the Fifth Book, although he gave Charles Graves abundant and fruitful suggestions.[70] He was clearly wounded in a way that, for this project, fettered his Daemon.

His next published Horatian poem addressed the question of the reference of griefs expressed in poetry to actual occasions. It was generated by the best of Charles Graves' contributions to the Fifth Book, a poem for which Kipling himself supplied, says Graves, a 'very full scenario'.[71] Virgil, drinking with Horace and Maecenas, opens his heart till dawn: asked how he, serene, conceived 'hearts torn with passion' he answers 'Ah! but I knew them', and tells of two sisters at Mantua, and a Gallic prisoner of Caesar's, his models for Dido, Anna and Turnus.[72] There was a Latin version of this by July 1918.[73] In 1919 Kipling wrote an exactly parallel poem about Shakespeare, transposed to the Mermaid, and even signed, as it were, with a quotation in acknowledgement of Graves in the last line - 'Busied upon shows of no earthly importance? Yes, but he knew it!' Its Horatianness is evidenced in a terseness of diction governed by its Sapphic metre. Kipling uses an historical instance – the suicide of Katharine Hamlett in the Avon in Shakespeare's boyhood, which very probably did attach itself in Shakespeare's mind to the funeral in the churchyard nearby of his son Hamnet, and the legend of Hamlet, to create Ophelia[74] – to which he adds others, including, with a gesture to Horace's emphatic *ebria*, 'drunk', in the Cleopatra *Ode*, Shakespeare's own Cleopatra 'Drunk with enormous, salvation–contemning / Love for a tinker.'[75]

The poem develops the idea of Horace's gift of brotherhood in affliction. Its thesis, that poetry derives its occasions and its force from the poet's human sympathy, and from incidents observed which in feeling and essence are similar, in circumstance widely different, to what they become in poems, is true of Kipling's own work, and likely enough to be true of Horace's, as of Shakespeare's. But for Kipling, the virtue of a poem depends on transformation of the original occasion by the poet's other self, his Daemon. Thus he praises Horace's *Ode* 4.13, to Lyce, in language suggestive of that with which he describes the chemist's thoughts in '"Wireless"' – 'unclean as we count uncleanliness' – before they are transformed into 'The Eve of St Agnes':

> This thing was born of bitter spite
>   But that sure Daemon at his side
> Allowed the vengeful Bard to write
>   The first twelve lines – then turned the tide
> Of ancient and uncleanly wrath
>   To that eternal song of pain
> When Beauty, bilked of all she hath,
>   Solicits even Death in vain![76]

Kipling here exercised the faculty for which Eliot praised him – distinguishing a poem which has forced its way into Horace's consciousness from others which Horace himself has forced. Those others which, because Horace has forced them, have lost all sense of any original experience, are for the most part *Odes* in which he tries to express kinds of ecstasy. Curiously, three of these are the three nineteenth *Odes* – 1.19 lust, 2.19 inspiration and 3.19 drunkenness – as if Horace had consciously tried to set an ecstatic poem at that point in each book, and failed for very self-consciousnes. Of 2.19, *Bacchum in remotis*, in which Horace has tried to describe a vision of his Daemon, who to him is Bacchus, Kipling says it is a 'thrice-faked lay', made up of 'book-passions' and 'self-made wind',[77] and of its companion, 3.25, *Quo me Bacche*, in which Horace claims he is actually being carried away by Bacchus as he writes, Kipling says he is '(officially) screwed / But not too screwed to speak',[79] which is paralleled by his comment on 3.19, *Quantum distet ab Inacho*, 'This is the way that poets write / But never the way that men get tight'.[79]

The drunkenness of 3.19 has as a minor component Horace's desire for Glycera, which is the main theme of 1.19, *Mater saeva Cupidinum*. Kipling makes his feelings clearer on the latter poem by dividing it. In the first twelve lines, where Horace portrays his desire for Glycera as an irresistible assault of Venus, Kipling says that Venus can hear 'docile Horace whoop' in 'Words without one touch of passion'.[80] That is, 'the detachment of the true artist who knows that he is but the vessel of an emotion whence others, not he, must drink'[81] has spilt over – from Horace as artist, creating the passion – to Horace who is created to experience it. Kipling clearly excludes the alternative possibilities (that Horace is creating himself with ironic humour, or describing the peculiar coldness with which, like Lucretius and Ovid, he sometimes experiences lust) although he seems to interpret more light-hearted *Odes*, like 3.21 to the wine-jar, or 4.11 to Phyllis, in one or other of these ways.[82] (About half of his annotations, but rather little of his other dealings with him, are light-hearted and concern Horace as a writer of *vers de sociéte*.)

But in 1.19 'the Power shines / In those last four clear-cut lines!'[83] where Horace 'very strong on sacrifice and ritual,'[84] though not on religious or erotic ecstasy, sacrifices to Venus at a turf altar. For ritual lends itself, as here, to a point of technique of which Kipling, like his contemporaries the Imagists, approved, that is to transitory but clear-cut sensuous images which crystallize the particular quality of a particular person at a particular instant. Such images are a great part of Kipling's own narrative technique, and specially of the uncanny way in which his historical tales convince their readers, as the clerk's description of water brimming over the sides of a boat convinces the narrator of '"The Finest Story in the World"' that he is recalling his death in an earlier incarnation.[85] In 1925 Kipling recorded in a poem what comfort he found in the apparent eternity of such images in Horace.

Again the poem seems to arise quite incidentally. After A. D. Godley (who ultimately edited the Fifth Book) died, Fletcher, who was writing his memoir, found among his papers a Latin poem which puzzled him. Kipling wrote (21

Horace's Kipling

September 1925) explaining that it was an acknowledgement of a cheque for his share in the sales of the book, in which Horace, as an 'amplificatio of "Exegi monumentum"' expresses his 'gratification that, in the stress of the war, and the submarine campaign, and the general negation of the Decencies, men took comfort from his songs, some of which he specifies. Their survival, when Rome and the Caesars have perished, makes him wonder at Fate.'[86] The Latin poem was a joke: but presently Kipling quotes, as what it was trying to say, two draft verses from a poem which is not a joke, although it looks as if it were based on the Latin one. He originally called it 'Exegi monumentum',[87] but presently attached it to a story written in the spring of 1923, 'The Janeites', and changed its title to 'The Survival'.[88] In the story, Jane Austen's novels challenge the unspeakable experience of the Great War: in the poem the wars, which bards promised their Kings to commemorate, are forgotten, while images of other things survive. All the images listed are from Horace – *prima nocte . . . sub cantu querulae . . . tibiae* (3.7.29–30) – *alga litus inutili* (3.17.10) – *ara multo fumat odore* (3.19.708) – *coronae . . . simplici myrto* (1.38.2–5):

> Mere breath of flutes at eve
>   Mere seaweed on the shore
> A smoke of sacrifice;
>   A chosen myrtle-wreath;

These are only details in the *Odes*, but they are also phrases which typify a certain quality in Horace – what Helen Waddell in her novel *Peter Abelard* (1933) makes her twelfth-century Epicurean canon Gilles, quoting the first two of these lines as if directly from Horace, describe as '*bonnes bouches*: jelly of quinces and salted almonds',[89] and presently compare to the beauty of Heloise, perfection of texture combined with something rich. It may be Pyrrha, who herself *simplex munditiis* (1.5.5) embodies this quality, whom Kipling has in mind in his next line, although he is becoming freer now, and follows it with a line that might apply to a number of poems:

> An harlot's altered eyes;
>   A rage 'gainst love or death;

Then he seems to conflate Soracte, *nive candidum* (1.9.1) with the Thracian mountain, also *nive candidam* (3.25.10), seen by the wakeful Bacchanal in the *Ode* to Bacchus which otherwise he despised, and ends the list with another detail from Soracte, *veteres agitantur orni* (1.9.12):

> Glazed snow beneath the moon;
>   The surge of storm-bowed trees . . .

Kipling was of course well aware that the endurance of these images is not only not what Horace promised Augustus, but not even what he, as a rule, consciously intended. Kipling's gloss on the well of Bandusia (3.13) recognizes that that is just such an image, consciously intended by Horace, 'For the drip of the water pleased his ears':⁹⁰ but his glosses on some of the poems alluded to in 'The Survival' as wholes pay no attention to their images. 'Mere seaweed on the shore', for example, is scarcely even implicit in one version of the gloss on 3.17, 'A message that the glass was falling', and altogether absent from the other, 'a list / Of Christmas-in-the-country pleasures.'⁹¹ Consequently, 'The Survival' ends with a question, once again about the altering gods:

> The Caesars perished soon,
>   And Rome Herself. But these
>
> Endure while empires fall
>   And Gods for Gods make room . . .
> Which greater God than all
>   Imposed the amazing doom?

The full power of this poem is only felt when one realizes that its speaker is Horace. Though there is no faked ecstasy, he speaks as one astonished by the changes of time from the opening lines, 'Securely after days / Unnumbered, I behold . . . ', to the closing question. This is the only poem in which Kipling hears him speaking as having survived when his world has become the remote past. It is also the first poem in which, in place of a doubt being raised about the completenesss of his world, he asks the question himself.

Two of the other three Horatian poems in the same book, *Debits and Credits* (1926), also end in questions about the gods. 'The Portent', which does not, is the least impressive, a satire in which, as in 'Lollius', Horace attacks a twentieth-century folly (Prohibition in America) as if it were an issue in Augustan Rome. Of the others, 'To the Companions' is attached to a Stalky story, 'The United Idolators', in which Kipling recalls a period at Westward Ho! when, as he had written in 1895 to Joel Chandler Harris, under the influence of his book, *Uncle Remus* 'we used to go to battle (with books and bolsters and such like) . . . to the tune of *Hi! Yi! tingalee: I eat um pea I pick um pea*'.⁹² The poem is, in Kipling's voice, about the nostalgia of writing such a story: in Horace's it is about the variety of gods who rule a life – Venus, Liber, Power, Avarice – after the time when the God of Mirth

> . . . withdrew from sight and speech,
>   Nor left a shrine. How comes it now,
> While Charon's keel grates on the beach,
>   He calls so clear: 'Rememberest thou?'⁹³

In the Medici Press *Horace*, the first lines of 'The Last Ode' are attached to *Odes* 2.17, in which Horace assured Maecenas that he will not long outlive him. Kipling's poem is set in the brief period of his doing so. But it also relates

Horace's Kipling

to another *Ode* about friendship and death, 1.24, the consolation to Virgil for the death of Quintilius, and to Virgil's own Messianic Eclogue, the Fourth. It is a poem about beginnings. Horace recalls the Bantine woods which he associated with his childhood:

> As watchers couched beneath a Bantine oak,
> > Hearing the dawn-wind stir,
> Know that the present strength of night is broke

so Virgil at his death knew that change is coming on the gods, and a new Star rising, who is plainly Christ, and with it, 'the lost shades that were our loves restored / As lovers, and for ever'.

> Maecenas waits me on the Esquiline:
> Thither to-night go I . . .
> And shall this dawn restore us, Virgil mine,
> To dawn? Beneath what sky?[94]

The poem is set ambiguously between 'The Eye of Allah', a story which forecasts the end of medieval Christianity, and 'The Gardener', which concerns resurrection and the presence of Christ. Kipling imagines Horace pressing against the limits of the ancient world and wonders through him, if the fact that what lies beyond those limits is Christianity with its promises means that Christianity is the final truth. But the three poems which end in questions, together move towards a God who is concerned not with the perceptions of Kings but with those of persons, not with power but with mirth, a God in whom what will survive of us is love.

These questions are continued in 'The Church that was at Antioch',[95] written in May 1928. An old-fashioned Roman police-chief in Syria c. AD 50, Lucius Sergius, encounters the religions of the East, like his successors in British India, with some sympathy but without belief. His talk, like the country lawyer's in '"My Son's Wife"' is 'studded with . . . out of date Roman society verses'[96] which are Horace's or reminiscent of him – 'I'm not the uncle with the rough tongue'[97], *patruae verbera linguae* (3.12.3), or 'Prime companion – how does it go? – we drank the long, long eastern day out together',[98] *prime sodalium / cum quo morantem saepe diem mero / fregi . . . / Syrio . . .* (2.7.5–8). Moreover, there was a song in Antioch against Christians, which after the manner of slang, draws allusively on some of the apostles' having been fishermen, on St Peter's dream of a sheet full of the beasts of the earth, on the symbol of Christ as a fish, and on St John's word *opsarion*, pickled fish, for the fish of the feeding of the five thousand,[99] to prophesy derisively the triumph of Christ, when 'the Gods themselves decline' and 'the Pickled Fish of Galilee ascend the Esquiline'.[100] Lucius Sergius' comment, talking to St Peter and St Paul, is drawn from Horace.

'That'll be something of a flood – worse than live fishes in trees! Hey?',[101] *piscium et summa gens haesit ulmo* (1.2.9). But Peter and Paul know, as we do, that it will happen: once again a quotation from Horace presses towards the limits of his world and the downfall of his gods.

Lucius Sergius' nephew, who has adopted another of the Eastern religions, Mithraism, is assassinated just after he has ordered the evening trumpet call, '"Let night also have her well-earned hymn", as Uncle 'ud say',[102] *dicetur merita nox quoque nenia*' (3.28.16). He dies with what Peter and Paul recognize, though he does not, as Christ's dying words in his mouth, 'Don't be hard on them . . . They get worked up . . . They don't know what they are doing.'[103] The juxtaposition of Horace's coolness and a young man's warmth is probably a further memorial to John Kipling, who had himself baptized a month before the war in which he died.

The collection in which 'The Church that was at Antioch' appeared, *Limits and Renewals* (1932), was, as its title suggests, much concerned with limits of endurance and kinds of new life. It includes a poem put in the mouth of St Paul, based on a saying of his 'I am made all things to all men',[104] which fascinated Kipling because it seemed to apply to his own sense of himself as artist. At the end of his life, Paul prays 'Ah Christ . . . Restore me my self again!'[105] Kipling's dealings with Horace in the four years of life which remained to him, suggest some such wish to find himself, and, while remaining an artist, to be such an artist as speaks out of himself.

On 23 May 1932, he published 'The Storm Cone', which uses the image of the ship of state making way in a storm that goes back through *Odes* 1.14 to Alcaeus:

> This is the midnight – let no star
>   Delude us – dawn is very far
> This is the tempest long foretold –
>   Slow to make head but sure to hold.
>   . . .
>
> It is decreed that we abide
>   The weight of gale against the tide
> And those huge waves the outer main
>   Sends in to set us back again.
>
> They fall and whelm. We strain to hear
>   The pulses of her labouring gear,
> Till the deep throb beneath us proves
>   After each shudder and check, she moves![106]

Kipling here no more speaks in Horace's person than Horace did in Alcaeus'. And although the poem's message, that the war which began in 1914 is only halfway through, has often and rightly been acclaimed as prophetic, it is a

Horace's Kipling

prophecy which springs not from any inspiration forcing itself on his consciousness, from outside, but from the normal conviction of Kipling's distrust of Germany and his pessimistic realism.

On 29 May 1932, the other side of his heart, his love of companionship, was pleased by his installation as an honorary fellow of Magdalene College Cambridge, at the invitation of the Master, A. B. Ramsay, one of the translators of the Fifth Book.[107] His first response, on 31 May, was to send the college magazine thirteen of his glosses on Horace.[108] His second was involved with another gloss, that on 3.28, source of the tag about night's well-earned hymn which Lucius Sergius' nephew mocked. Like all Lucius Sergius' tags, and most, though not quite all, of the glosses sent to Magdalene College Magazine, this gloss suggests the Epicurean Horace rather than the Stoic and moral Horace with whom Kipling had begun:

> He drank the strenuous Caecuban
>   With Lyde at the close of day
> And I recall another man
>   Whose instincts also turned that way –
>   A Latitudinarian
>   (So Deb and Mercer had to pay)
> Yes! Through the age-old tale there creeps
> The note – the very note of –
>   Pepys![109]

The handwriting and the freshness of the ink show that this is one of Kipling's latest glosses. It must have been written in connection with the Horatian poem which he published in *The Times* on the tercentenary of Samuel Pepys' birth, 23 February 1933. Pepys too was a member of Magdalene College, and Kipling gave the poem the same title as he did to the one attached to 'The United Idolators', 'To the Companions'.[110]

We have no guidance whether the speaker of 'To the Companions' is Kipling in an opulently Horatian style, or Horace conceived as alive in Kipling's day looking back on Pepys; so that we had best hear them in this, Kipling's last Horatian poem, altogether united. It helps Kipling in imagining Pepys, a man from a culture only partly like our own, to have Horace with him, in four overlapping ways:

First, in speaking about aspects of humanity which are perhaps permanent, at any rate in civilized humanity. The poem begins with an oak like that on Algidus which was involved with Kipling's first love of Horace: but this oak illustrates the history not of a nation, but of a single person:

> Like as the Oak whose roots descend
>   Through earth and stillness seeking food

which, felled, furnishes 'dense indomitable wood' for the mole at Ostia, or the Liburnian galleys of the Cleopatra *Ode* – but which, as a tree, may wed a vine or harbour doves: so Pepys who – the poem glances at the dangers of 'The Storm Cone' – remade the Navy, also followed Venus and Liber after pleasures public and secret. Thus far the poem could be said to enlarge on a comparison Kipling had drawn in 1913 between Pepys and an ancient Egyptian 'Minister of Agriculture' – probably Menna, 'Scribe of the Fields' to Tuthmosis IV – whose tomb-paintings at Luxor manifest clear delight in his business, recreation, family, but a religion that remained to Kipling opaque.

Secondly, however, Pepys would have heard in his lifetime and approved the comparison of Restoration England with its peculiar sophistication, classicism and political ambitions to Augustan Rome.

And, thirdly, Kipling now moves to something which he thinks of himself as sharing with Horace and Pepys (but not with Menna), the artist's Daemon, whom Horace's gods enable him to speak of more casually and urbanely than in modern Engish, even in one breath with Pepys' and Horace's carnal pleasures, with Liber and Venus:

> . . . His life betrayed
> No gust unslaked, no pleasure missed.
> He called the obedient Nine to aid
> The varied chase. And Clio kissed;

Finally, there is, by Clio's gift, no barrier (such as Menna's remote time and his decorous self-presentation before the gods of the dead create), to the inner life of Pepys. 'To the Companions' ends by praising him as the kind of artist whom Kipling had scarcely considered before, one who lives no other life than his own, and writes only that, but so to the full that he achieves the same result as the artist who lives through other selves – 'that sinners undiscovered, like ourselves, might say – "'Tis I!'".[111]

'To the Companions', if we take it as by Horace and Kipling conjointly, does not suggest that either of them is the kind of artist that Pepys was. It does suggest that all three share in the three states of the oak, the flourishing delights of its leaves, the public use of its wood and the still, secret life of its roots. The last of these, something inward to do with self-consciousness, religion and guilt, Kipling could make nothing of in Menna, but, rightly or wrongly, implies that he shares with Pepys and Horace. He does not define it so closely as to make it identical in the three. But in the gloss of his 'Medici Press *Horace*', he models Horace's attitude to Lyde on Pepys' to Deb and Mercer, maidservants dismissed because their master chose to flirt with them. All three, Kipling, Horace, Pepys, and in the poem 'ourselves', acknowledge an indulgence for which someone else has to pay. Kipling's first poems in Horace's voice had represented him as the poet of unaltering law: in 'The Tree of Justice' he set Horace's sense of the world against the willingness to forego judgement, and in 'The Church that was at Antioch' the easygoing *homme moyen sensuel* aspect of his verses against passionate forgiveness. Now he deepens his earlier discovery in Horace of brotherhood in affliction by finding fellowship in responsibility, in something which guilt is too specifically Christian to describe. Perhaps one cannot go beyond 'shared inwardness'.

The recognition "'Tis I!' is balanced by the title 'To the Companions'. When Kipling came to make his final description of what Horace meant to him he did not use the image of possession or reincarnation, as he had done in parallel cases. In the autobiography which he was still writing when he died, he used again the language of companionship: to love him 'for the rest of my days and through many sleepless nights'.[112] *Something of Myself* remains, unlike Pepys' journal, a self-revelation which gives very little away. But a man like Kipling, who expects his privacy to be valued by others as by himself, may also want from them the sympathy that picks up small public signals. 'Through many sleepless nights' means a great deal from a man who, in addition to the ordinary human pains, had lost in bitter circumstances two out of three beloved children, and was within a few months of dying from a duodenal ulcer. It means a knowledge of the *Odes* gained by weighing each word, each syllable of the elaborately interwoven and weighed sentences which ask for that treatment, and respond to it; it means a love of them – knowing them 'by heart' as we carelessly say – exactly adapted to finding out Horace's peculiar but not at all careless uses of words. It means an appreciation of the various, and sometimes alien, aspects of Horace which Kipling had honoured like a critical and loving friend. It means an ability to see through Horace's eyes what Kipling could not have seen through his own, and to attain between both their visions a perspective from outside their separate worlds, on the worlds of their gods and God.

Kipling's final view of Horace is not one of any kind of identification, as the models of possession or reincarnation would have implied. Neither is it of any kind of detachment. In the fifty years since Kipling's death, it has become the automatic response of most literary theorists to shy away at any image which suggests that reading is a response of person to person. But, regardless of whether Kipling got any particular fact about Horace's literary or social persona right, regardless even of whether he or we could state with conviction what the relation between such personas in Augustan Rome is likely to have been, what he provides in his relation with Horace is a model, qualified by his own passionate assertion of those points by which literature is rightly distanced from personality and immediate experience, to show that the response of person to person can be simply what good reading is. The model is companionship.

12

SOME ASPECTS OF HORACE IN THE TWENTIETH CENTURY

Charles Tomlinson

IT WOULD BE impossible for any writer in the twentieth century – with scarcely a decade to go, this generalization has a fair chance of proving to be fact – to identify his poetic concerns so completely as Alexander Pope with those of his great Roman precursor, Horace. Pope's *Imitations of Horace* counted on a familiar acquaintance with that poet among its readership – after all, he was, from school days, in the possession of most literate males and evidently also of some educated women. For Mrs Aphra Behn, Lady Mary Wortley Montagu and Anna Seward, the Swan of Litchfield, all wrote imitations of one of Horace's most famous *Odes*, 'Ad Pyrrham'. As earlier chapters of this book have shown, the ground had been prepared for an English Horace ever since Ben Jonson put him into couplets and an Horatian tone entered his own original poetry. Previously both Surrey and Sidney had tried their hand at Englishing him, but it was not until the creative effort initiated by Jonson and continued by Fanshawe, Cowley, Oldham and Dryden that Horace became, so to speak, a fully fledged English poet. Dryden's version of *Odes* 3.29 ('Descended of an ancient Line / That long the Tuscan Scepter sway'd . . . ') is perhaps the greatest single translation of a Horace poem to date – the date of its publication and, one might add, the present time. Thus, when Jacob Tonson in 1715 brought out his edition of Horace, translated by numerous hands, he could assemble from chiefly contemporary writers a team of remarkable quality. The balance, but also the audacity of Horace, had entered into the bloodstream of many of these, so that the term Horatian can be applied to much original English poetry of the seventeenth and eighteenth centuries in a way that would not fit our contemporary verse. Most readers of poetry do not know Horace even in translation; the several Penguin versions of the *Odes, Epodes* and *Sermones* do little to convey the verbal corrugation of the original; in my own lifetime universities have ceased to require Latin for student entrance. So the generalization with which I began seems set to be confirmed, since poets of future generations are the products of educational requirements. Individuals, of course, will diagnose and seek to remedy their own cultural vitamin

Some aspects of Horace in the twentieth century

deficiencies. For example, in 1979 and in America, where the high schools had long since abandoned any pretence of a humanistic education, the young poet Robert Pinsky, in making his debut with the ambitious book-length poem *An Explanation of America*,[1] incorporated into this work a version of Horace's *Epistles* 1.16 where, says Pinsky, Horace

> Implies his answer about aspiration
> Within the prison of empire or republic.

He then goes on in a meditation on Horace's poem to discover common ground with this Roman freedman's son whose youthful enthusiasm had found him, 'Along with other enthusiastic students / (Cicero's son among them)', on the wrong side at Philippi:

> Horace came back to Rome a pardoned rebel
> In his late twenties, without cash or prospects,
> Having stretched out his wings too far beyond
> The frail nest of his freedman father's hopes,
> As he has written.

Pinsky's poem is in some ways an Horatian reply to the subjectivity implicit in those psycho-dramas of the self, the poetries of Lowell, Berryman, Sexton and Plath. Given the moment of its appearance, perhaps there is even something honourable in its running the risk of seeming at times verbally somewhat undernourished. It is Horatian in the democratic moderation of its imaginings of a possible future for Pinsky's country and his children, and also in the unapocalyptic tone in which it patiently 'explains' the present, avoiding the Manichean black and white of ready simplifications (Vietnam was one of the uneasy issues whose visionary yeast had activated much bad poetry). Pinsky's 'two lame cheers for democracy that I / Borrow and try to pass to you' and his suspicion of 'that tyrant / And sycophantic lout, the majority' are given force and context by his realization that

> Denial of limit has been the pride, or failing,
> Well-known to be shared by all this country's regions,
> Races and classes; which all seem to challenge
> The idea of sufficiency itself . . .

His 'idea of sufficiency itself' finds tempered scope in the expression of the Horatian *Epistle* that precedes this statement. In a poem addressed to his children (who, as he realizes, may never read it), it is right and proper that questions of family and of paternal regard should be primary:

> Horace's father, who had been a slave,
> Engaged in some small business near Venusia;
> And like a Jewish or Armenian merchant

> Who does well in America, he sent
> His son to Rome's best schools, and then to Athens
> (It's hard to keep from thinking, 'as to Harvard')
> To study, with the sons of gentlemen
> And politicians, the higher arts most useful
> To citizens of a Republic . . .

Pinsky opts for the 'middle style'. His unshowy, even relaxed way of writing, derives for the epistolatory Horace and not from the denser, more compacted style of the *Odes*. It was this latter style that appealed to a number of literary modernists born earlier in the century than Pinsky, namely Pound, Bunting and Auden (though Auden also has an Horatian epistle in 'The Sea and the Mirror', Alonso's 'Dear Son, when the warm multitudes cry . . . '). Pinsky's style harks back, with whatever differences, to the Horatianism of an American belonging to an older generation than all these, Robert Frost, and aims, like Frost, at an effect of almost casual conversation. Frost himself had been anticipated in this vein by Emerson and also in the use of a convention whereby the man who lives close to the soil – shades of Horace's Sabine farm – can chasten the rootless townee with his own more elementary satisfactions. There is even an Horatian touch, when in Emerson's 'Hamatreya', Death puts in an appearance among these rural solidities:

> "Tis good, when you have crossed the sea and back,
> To find the sitfast acres where you left them.'
> Ah! the hot owner sees not Death, who adds
> Him to his land, a lump of mould the more.

Emerson, however, cannot sustain this unity of tone and before long we have left the world of Horatian nature and are listening to the spirit of Earth purveying a rather different kind of wisdom. It was Frost himself who, as Reuben Brower[2] has remarked, Americanized the Horatian *sermo*, Pope's couplets suggesting the technical means, as in a poem like 'The Lesson for Today' where Frost considers the historic gap between quantitative verse such as that used by Horace and the reversion in medieval Latin poetry to stress and end rhyme:

> Yet singing but Dione in the wood
> And *ver aspergit terram floribus*
> They slowly led old Latin verse to rhyme
> And to forget the ancient lengths of time,
> And so began the modern world for us.

'The ancient lengths of time', of course, refers to the quantitative measures of Roman verse – the medieval 'ver aspergit terram floribus' with the addition of 'And' at the beginning of the phrase, makes a perfect modern accentual

Some aspects of Horace in the twentieth century

iambic pentameter. Two speakers are imagined as exchanging views in this poem, a common device in Horace's (and Pope's) satires. 'The dramatic mode of the debate', says Brower, 'is also Horatian', as Frost addresses an aristocratic poet of a previous epoch:

> Let's celebrate the event, my distant friend,
> In publicly disputing which is worse,
> The present age or your age.

However, 'And so began the modern age for us' ushers in elsewhere a somewhat bleaker prospect (Horace, of course, could be bleak, but not with the lonely and romantic nihilism of the post-Nietzschean generations). New Hampshire, whatever earthy wisdom it had to teach, was hardly the Sabine farm for Frost. Sheer endurance, the sense of being alone up there, are the marks of both Frost and his protagonists. The Horatian modes are social and often convivial, but in a poem like 'Directive' Frost has to face out the overmastering awareness of geological ages – those disappearing quantities, the cancellation of 'ancient lengths of time', are more than simply a metrical matter:

> There is a house that is no more a house
> Upon a farm that is no more a farm
> And in a town that is no more a town.
> The road there . . .
> May seem as if it should have been a quarry . . .
> Besides the wear of iron wagon wheels
> The ledges show lines ruled southeast-northwest,
> The chisel work of an enormous Glacier
> That braced his feet against the Arctic Pole.

This is a vaster and more troubling universe than that of Horace and in 'Directive' the sustaining fiction of dialogue has fallen away. The voice in the poem addresses 'you', meaning us, but we have no more means of replying than the aristocratic poet from years back. Although the protagonist in the poem, exploring this deserted spot, takes up a broken drinking goblet which he likens to the Grail, we know this Grail does not contain Christ's blood, and we know also that the 'you' at the poem's conclusion, while it gestures towards a community of listeners, falls on the lonely desertion of Panther Mountain:

> Here are your waters and your watering place,
> Drink and be whole again beyond confusion.

Yet the confusion was endemic to Frost and to his time and not to be got rid of by an invented ceremony among the ruins. He finds himself, before taking refuge behind the persona of the bluff, no-nonsense New Englander (his formative years until the age of twelve were spent in San Francisco), a houseless spirit threatened by the aftermath of a thinker whose perception of Horace is part of our story, that is Nietzsche himself.

Nietzsche, like the early Frost, was a divided man, a product of the Protestant north who yearned towards the Mediterranean. Having begun by endorsing the music of Richard Wagner and its re-embodiment of Teutonic mythology, he succeeded in persuading himself that the music which really appealed to him was that of Bizet with its evocation of the unsubjective south (of a Spain, in fact, on which Bizet had never set foot). Here was the opportunity to 'be whole again beyond confusion': 'How such a work [*Carmen*] brings one to perfection. One becomes a "masterpiece" oneself', as he wrote to the composer Peter Gast. The south, he tells us, in *Beyond Good and Evil*,[3] is 'a great school of recovery for the most spiritual and the most sensuous ills' and teaches us to be 'somewhat on guard against German music'. As far as literature goes, in his rejection of Wagnerian subjectivity (he sees Wagner as poet as well as musician), his attraction towards the south and 'the Mediterranean clearness of sky' leads, according to the testimony of his later years, to Roman in preference to Greek culture: 'We do not *learn* from the Greeks: their mode is too foreign, it is also too unstable to operate imperatively or "classically". Who would ever have learned to write from a Greek!' It is as a writer that Nietzsche is speaking, and when he says of the Greeks, 'they *cannot* be to us what the Romans are', the Roman he particularly thinks of is Horace. The section 'My Indebtedness to the Ancients' in *The Twilight of the Idols*[4] contains a passage on the effect of Horace's style very different from anything expressed or incorporated by a poet like Frost into his own mode of writing. The insights in Nietzsche's account of Horace, uncannily accurate in defining the way the original Latin works, point forward to what it was that drew Pound, Bunting and other moderns to the Horatian *Ode* rather than the *sermo*. D. M. Hooley in his book *The Classics in Paraphrase*[5] speaks of the *Odes* giving 'some crucial stimulus to the modern poet's technical artifice', and goes on: 'Horatian metrical virtuosity, its mosaic cohesiveness, its love of contrast and surprising turns – all find their analogues in *Briggflatts* and Bunting's two books of *Odes*.' The word 'mosaic' in this comes from Nietzsche's passage:

Up to the present I have not obtained from any poet the same artistic delight as was given me from the first by an Horatian ode. In certain languages that which is obtained here cannot even be hoped for. The mosaic of words in which every word, by sound, by position and by meaning, diffuses its force right, left, and over the whole, that *minimum* in the compass and number of signs, that *maximum* thus realised in their energy, – all that is Roman, and if you will believe me, it is *noble par excellence*. All other poetry becomes somewhat too popular in comparison with it – mere sentimental loquacity.

Some aspects of Horace in the twentieth century

Before going on to see how this conception of a 'mosaic of words' affords 'some crucial stimulus to the modern poet's technical artifice', in Hooley's phrase, first an example from Horace himself of what Nietzsche has in mind. Dr Frank Stack includes in his *Pope and Horace*[6] an account which can scarcely be bettered of the first eight lines of *Odes* 4.1, a poem made familiar to us by both Ben Jonson and Pope and which exists in an elegant contemporary version by James Michie. Dr Stack begins by quoting from the poem:

> *Intermissa Venus diu*
> *Rursus bella moves? parce precor, precor!*
> *Non sum qualis eram, bonae*
> *Sub regno Cynarae: desine, dulcium*
> *Mater saeva Cupidinum,*
> *Circa lustra decem flectere mollibus*
> *Jam durum imperiis: abi*
> *Quo blandae juvenum te revocant preces.* (1–8)

(Christopher Smart's trot runs: 'After a long cessation, O Venus, again are you stirring up tumults? Spare me, I beseech you, I beseech you. I am not the man I was under the dominion of good-natur'd Cynara. Forbear, thou cruel mother of soft desires, to bend one bordering upon fifty, now too harden'd for your soft commands: go whither the soothing prayers of youth invoke thee'.)[7]

Our scholar and critic comments:

This is what Nietzsche calls the mosaic of words. Adjectives are placed well before the nouns they modify, suspended to arouse interest in what it is they refer to and only 'completed' when their nouns are discovered: *intermissa . . . bella* ('Suspended . . . warfare'), *bonae . . . Cynarae* ('good . . . Cynara'), *dulcium . . . Cupidinum* ('sweet . . . desires'), *mollibus . . . imperiis* ('soft . . . commands'), *blandae . . . preces* ('wheedling . . . prayers'). Contrasting words are yoked together: *dulcium . . . saeva* ('sweet . . . fierce'), *mollibus . . . durum* ('soft . . . hardened'). The words *imperiis* ('commands') and *durum* ('hardened') are juxtaposed without syntactical connection in order to emphasize the paradox. But within this complex pattern how powerful is alliterative *parce precor, precor* ('Show mercy, I beg and beseech you'); and how simple and haunting is *Non sum qualis, eram bonae / Sub regno Cynarae* ('I am not the man I was under the rule of good Cynara'). Finally, how distinctive is the rhythm: the metre is the Second Asclepiadean, a graceful metre used, significantly, in many of Horace's earlier love poems:

$$- - - \cup \cup - \cup \underline{\cup}$$
$$- - - \cup \cup - \| - \cup \cup - \cup \underline{\cup}$$

The heavy syllables at the beginning of every line tend to give strength and calm, the light syllables movement and grace.

Ezra Pound, beginning with the curious proposition that Horace was 'the first Royal Academy', moves reluctantly away from his ambivalence about him, and at the end of his poetic career, writes three masterly versions of the *Odes* to which I shall return later. A sense of 'the mosaic of words' and an awareness of the role of metre, comparable with that in Stack's analysis, already appear in an article Pound published in *The Criterion*[8] for 1929–30, where we read: 'Apart from Catullus, he was the most skilful metrist among the Latins . . . [He gives pleasure] to the connoisseur by his verbal arrangements . . . This literary pleasure is not due to the passion of Horace, but to the order of words and their cadence in a line measured by the duration of syllables.' Basil Bunting, never having doubted the mastery of Horace, admonishes another Poundian, Louis Zukofsky, in a letter of 1948, 'Horace works wonders with a word order which was crabbed even to his contemporaries, as one may see by reading Lucretius and Ovid on either side of him. It is not right to banish such effects . . . ' Like Frost, both Pound and Bunting were exercised by the fact that verse had 'forgotten the ancient lengths of time'. Discussing Horace's genius in 'changing the whole mood of a poem in a single line', Bunting says, 'Quantity is no doubt one element in it – there are semibreves as well as crotchets etc., in music. To write pure quantitative poems in English, as Sidney, Spenser, Campion sometimes did is very difficult because the stress in English is so strong that people, at least in the south of England, don't notice anything else. Besides, the stress sometimes modifies the quantity. English phrases with stress on a short syllable are not common. But a poet ought to be always aware of the quantities and it is a very good exercise to imitate quantitative patterns.'[9] That people 'at least in the south of England' can hear nothing *but* accent and gloss over the differentiation of vowel lengths, points to the fact that perhaps only a northerner could have achieved the differentiations in the opening lines of Bunting's masterpiece *Briggflatts*:

> Brag, sweet tenor bull,
> descant on Rawthey's madrigal . . .

'I'd see what could be done in the way of adapting Greek quantitative patterns into English', he had already advised a young poet George Marion O'Donnell in 1934. In his own work, in translating Horace's *Odes* 1.13 he bases his accentual English cadences on the Second Asclepiadean metre, that is used also in *intermissa Venus diu / rursus bella moves*. Pound even half persuaded himself, 'I think the desire for vers libre is due to the sense of quantity reasserting itself after years of starvation.' His own response to this was the metre of *Homage to Sextus Propertius*. 'As to quantity', mulling over the same question in 1913, he had written: 'it is foolish to suppose that we are incapable of distinguishing a long vowel from a short one.' He wanted to

Some aspects of Horace in the twentieth century

know when he first read Marianne Moore's syllabic verse 'whether you are working in Greek quantitative measures . . . '. Eliot, as D. S. Carne-Ross has recently reminded us, said of Pound's poem 'The Return' that it was 'an important study in verse which is really quantitative.' Carne-Ross in this same *Arion*[10] article audaciously argues that in this poem where Pound sets out to resurrect the presences of classical poetry –

> See, they return; ah, see the tentative
> Movements, and the slow feet,
> The trouble in the pace and the uncertain
> Wavering!

– there is an attempt to reconstitute the effect of that very Sapphic stanza Horace adapted from the Greek:

The tentatively moving feet we are called on to see are those of the ancient gods, returning to us after their long absence. On the poem's secondary level we are invited to *hear* the feet of the ancient poems that celebrated their presence, the Greek poems composed in the quantitative measures now returning to assume new forms in English verse.

The mosaic of words, Horace's ability to '[change] the whole mood of a poem in a single line' (Bunting's phrase), the role of quantity in achieving this, all these elements in the ongoing drama of a Horace poem, derive their complete force from the fact that Horace is writing in an inflected language, whose positioning of adjective in relation to noun, for example, cannot easily be reproduced in our uninflected English. But what of the all-over form of an Horatian *Ode*, in terms, that is, of its track from start to finish? Can its movement be transposed into English poetry and how can that movement be defined? An attempt to answer these questions brings into our account another American poet, but one of a rather different constituency from that of Pound and his friends, J. V. Cunningham.

Cunningham, having published *The Helmsman* in 1942, went on to write a commentary on the poems this book contains, *The Quest of the Opal*[11] (1950). The title poem 'The Helmsman' is, very consciously, an Horatian *Ode* and Cunningham's reflections on the form contain some of the most enlightening insights about it I have come across. Like Frost and Pound, Cunningham has pondered the loss of 'the ancient lengths of time' and the poem is an attempt 'to achieve in English the effect of the Alcaic strophe' by combining dissyllabic and tri-syllabic feet, rhyme being 'admitted here and there as a figure of diction'. My own feeling is that the substance of the experiences alluded to in 'The Helmsman' is more successfully handled in the accentual metres of two other poems. 'August Hail' and 'Montana Pastoral'. The trouble with Cunningham's Alcaics is that (unlike, say, Tennyson's imitation of this stanza in his tribute to Milton, 'O mighty-mouthed inventor of harmonies') the lines lack metrical bite, and the occasional appearance of rhyme has the effect, in so controlled a poem, of seeming almost desultory. However, Cunningham's reflections on 'the track' of the Horatian *Ode* contain a most arresting passage. He located, he says, the unity of the *Ode* in 'the unformulable feeling that, as the poem unfolded, its length and the arrangement of parts were proper and inevitable: "that just now is said what just now ought to be said."' And then comes – he speaks of himself in the third person – the most brilliant insight and simile of the entire commentary: 'He found that the progression from detail to detail was by a kind of imagic shift or transformation image which, like a train through a tunnel, brings one to a new prospect on the other side of the divide.'

One has only to look, say, at *Odes* 1.37, the so-called Cleopatra *Ode* (the poem Marvell imitated in that portion of his own 'Horatian Ode' which deals with the execution of Charles I), to see the justice of Cunningham's image. *Nunc est bibendum*, we are told, and what we are drinking to is the defeat of Cleopatra's navy at Actium and of her 'contaminated gang' in Smart's prose version. Caesar has brought her back to reality, her mind swimming in Mareotic wine. His pursuit of her is compared to the hawk pursuing the tender doves or the nimble hunter the hare in the plains of snowy Thessaly. A certain sympathy is here reserved for the *molles columbas* and the *leporem*, but we are not allowed to forget that this is 'a destructive monster of a woman who . . . ' (and here the syntax takes an unforeseen turn, prompted perhaps by that note of sympathy and by the way Caesar has forced her mind back to reality). This is the kind of thing Bunting alludes to when he speaks of Horace 'changing the whole mood of a poem in a single line'. We are, in Cunningham's image, coming out of the tunnel to our new prospect: 'who' introduces 'seeking to die a more generous death / displayed no womanish fear . . . ' And the concluding portion of the poem, twelve lines of it, shows us a woman with as steady an eye as Marvell's Charles, gazing at her ruined palace and, with courage and fortitude, taking hold of the asps that will kill her, rather than letting herself be dragged off by the Liburnian sailors ('rough Liburnian tars,' says Smart). The triumph is entirely hers – she whose defeat the poem had begun by calling on us to celebrate.

A contemporary poet who seems to have taken careful note of Cunningham's image of the tunnel is Donald Davie, in a poem that follows the turns of the Horatian *Ode* in dealing with, of all improbable themes, the miners' strike under Arthur Scargill (Davie and Scargill are both Yorkshiremen). Unlike Cunningham, he does not try to imitate Horatian metre, but Horatian syntax. He writes in free verse of a neo-American variety, verse guided (as in Horace) to its unpredictable goal by the firmness of its syntactic connectives:

Some aspects of Horace in the twentieth century

WOMBWELL ON STRIKE

Horace of course is not
a temporizer, but
his sudden and smooth transitions
        (as, into a railway tunnel,
          then out, to a different landscape)

it must be admitted elide,
and necessarily, what
happens up there on the hill
        or hill-ridge that the tunnel
          of syntax so featly slides under.

I have been reminded of this
when, gratefully leaving my native
haunts, the push-and-pull diesel
        clatters into a tunnel
        under a wooded escarpment:

Wentworth Woodhouse, mounded
or else in high shaws drifted
over the miners' tramways.
        Horace's streaming style
        exhorts me never to pause;

'Press on,' he says, and indeed his
suavities never entirely
exclude the note of alarm:
        'Leave the unlikely meaning
        to eddy, or you are in trouble.'

Wombwell – 'womb well': it is
foolish and barbarous wordplay,
though happily I was
        born of this tormented
        womb, the taut West Riding.

Yours was solid advice,
Horace, and centuries have
endorsed it; but over this tunnel
        large policemen grapple
        the large men my sons have become.[12]

When, over thirty years ago, I first discovered Cunningham's image of the tunnel and the 'new prospect on the other side of the divide', a piece which immediately came to mind was Marianne Moore's 'Poetry'. Did this follow the formal path of an Horatian *Ode*? I soon realized that it didn't quite, but the abruptness of the transitions, whether intentionally or not on the part of the poet, recalled Horace, and the heavily Latinate diction together with the indented syllabic lines of the stanza form, eschewing traditional accentual verse, reinforced the association. The Moorish style suggests rather than exemplifies classical practices – hence Ezra Pound's puzzlement as to 'whether you are working in Greek quantitative measures'. She was not, and presumably one of the few ways of doing so in English would be to follow Swinburne's approach in his 'Sapphics', allowing stress and quantity to coincide and keeping to the same syllable count as Sappho's hendecasyllabics:

> All the night sleep came not upon my eyelids,
> Shed not dew, nor shook nor unclosed a feather,
> Yet with lips shut close and with eyes of iron
>   Stood and beheld me.

This is precisely what Bunting did in his version of Catullus' imitation of Sappho's most famous ode, No. 20. Bunting, who must be one of the very few major twentieth-century poets (Pound was another) to be an enthusiastic admirer of Swinburne as metrist, uses the same method in his translations of Horace's *Odes* 1.13 and 3.12. The first of these, as noted above, is in the Second Asclepiadean, and Bunting's accentual cadence is hewn close to the rhythm of Horace's Latin:

> Please stop gushing about his pink
>   neck smooth arms and so forth, Dulcie; it makes me sick . . .

Odes 3.12 is in the *ionic a minore* (∪ ∪ − − / ∪ ∪ − −) which Bunting once more effectively mimes, letting the metre show from time to time, rather than governing every turn of the poem:

> Yes, it's slow, docked of amours,
>   docked of the doubtless efficacious
>   bottled makeshift . . .

His version of *Odes* 2.14 is far darker in tone, as befits its subject, and an excellent example of the way Bunting follows out the winding inevitability of Horace's syntax. This was written in Bunting's seventy-second year:

> You can't grip years, Postume,
> that ripple away nor hold back
> wrinkles and, soon now, age,
> nor can you tame death
>
> not if you paid three hundred
> bulls every day that goes by
> to Pluto, who has no tears,
> who has dyked up

Some aspects of Horace in the twentieth century

> giants where we'll go aboard,
> we who feed on the soil,
> to cross, kings some, some
> penniless plowmen.
>
> For nothing we keep out of war
> or from screaming spindrift
> or wrap ourselves against autumn,
> for nothing, seeing
>
> we must stare at that dark, slow
> drift and watch the damned
> toil, while all they build
> tumbles back on them.
>
> We must let earth go and home,
> wives too, and your trim trees,
> yours for a moment, save one
> sprig of black cypress.
>
> Better men will empty
> bottles we locked away,
> wine puddle our table,
> fit wine for a pope.

In a recorded interview made for the New York Center for Visual History[13] in 1984, Bunting both reads and comments on this poem. We have heard much of Pound's stress on 'the ideogrammatic method', a technique whereby he juxtaposes many verbal fragments in his *Cantos* on the basis of his understanding of Chinese characters. Bunting is sceptical about Pound's reliability in this area and, asked to comment on the nature of the ideogrammatic method, he replied

> It ultimately has nothing whatever to do with the Chinese character. Though Pound saw an instance of it there, you could find it just as well in Horace... It is as if you set two things side by side... But it's not the case of one ideogram against another. It's the case of a whole page of ideograms one against another so to speak... In Horace you find this continually... He leaves you to fill in the connections.

The example he then reads is 'You Can't Grip Years, Postume'. Aren't we back once more ('set side by side, a whole page of ideograms one against another') with Nietzsche's idea of 'the mosaic of words'? – the difference between Bunting's and Pound's (also between Horace's and Pound's) construction of the mosaic being, that Bunting believes in syntax and that Pound, at any rate in the *Cantos*, believed in the paratactic confrontation of a poem's elements, with the role of syntax greatly diminished.

Bunting, of course, spent a very small portion of his life actually translating Horace, but the Horatian presence in his own work is very audibly there. The Horatian cast of thought and the attention to the inter-meshings of sound pattern, have caused one critic, David Gordon, in *Paideuma*[14], to call Bunting 'A Northumbrian Sabine'. As to sound and rhythm, Gordon writes of the Horatian cross-fertilization in *Briggflatts*:

In Bunting's own *vers libre* we find a rough and irregular metric pattern, unusual sequences of trochees, spondees and dactyls, as well as of long or heavily stressed syllables, e.g., 'tight / néck córds? Axe rusts. Spíne / pícked báre.' And we hear arresting echoes of bits of the logaoedic measures of Horace, which Bunting formed according to the rhythmic needs of his poem, e.g., 'Loáded with | maíl of | línked líes' (an aristophanic from the Second Sapphic); 'kíng líft tŏ fíght' (from the Alcaic); 'spíne / pícked | báre bў rávĕns' (from the Alcaic); 'ínért | bráin névĕr | wíse' (from the Fourth Asclepedean). 'Thére wĭll bĕ | nóthĭng ŏn | Stáinmóre | tŏ híde' (from the Second Pythiambic); 'stópped tĭll | lóng flíght' (from the Alcaic); 'éndĕd ĭn | bále ŏn the fellsíde' (from the Alcmanic).

The moral austerity and stoicism of the Northumbrian Sabine draw this comment from Gordon: '. . . certainly Bunting would have found this stern morality, self-reliance, self-mastery, this equanimity in facing life or death in Villon and in the Persian poets, but he undoubtedly found them first in Horace.'

In the twentieth century the influence of Horace and of classical poets generally has led to a far more widespread modification of English metrical form than it did in the seventeenth and eighteenth centuries, those great ages of classical influence and translation. The linguistic intrusion of another poetry is most radically felt in some of Pound's versions in his *Confucian Anthology* where he gives us something English and something irreducibly foreign and distant. A compromise, but also a meeting of cultures, comes in the reconciliation of accent and quantity. Hardy, our third Swinburnian, tried this – his scansion of 'Sapphics' is to be seen in his own copy of Swinburne's poems – and conceivably the influence filtered to W. H. Auden, though there was a further element needed for the full intrusion of foreignness in the 'Horatian' Auden. This came about through his adoption of the Moorish style in the syllabics of 'In Memory of Sigmund Freud'. Eventually he will combine Moore's syllabic lineation with an increasing regard for that imagined reader he speaks of who can recognise choriambs and bacchics. Line and sentence length are also to become important, line emphasizing the cruces of meaning and sentence lengthily deploying a complex syntax, while rhythm, playing across the two, dances through ingenious equivalents of Latin spondees, dactyls and anapaests. For my own

Some aspects of Horace in the twentieth century

money this use of the long sentence, miming aspects of Latin syntax, achieves its most striking display of artistry in 'In Transit', a poem which memorably recreates the homeless feeling of a stop-over in a strange airport in a landscape we shall never get to know:

> Let out where two fears intersect, a point selected
>   Jointly by general staffs and engineers,
> In a wet land, facing rough oceans, never invaded
>   By Caesars or a cartesian doubt, I stand,
> Pale, half asleep, inhaling its new fresh air that smells
>   So strongly of soil and grass, of toil and gender,
> But not for long: a professional friend is at hand
>   Who smiling leads us indoors; we follow in file . . .

And the sentence of this first stanza winds to completion four lines on into stanza two with an Horatian audacity. Appositely to the effect here, Richard Johnson in *Man's Place: an Essay on Auden*[15] comments:

The pattern of internal rhymes helps to create both the music and the spatial pattern of the poem. It almost serves as a system of inflections, drawing words together across the patterns of line and phrasing [and] our attention to connections and resemblances, which, because the pattern is neither schematic nor familiar, as in end-rhymed forms, come to the reader as sudden discoveries.

'In Praise of Limestone', 'Ischia' and 'Ode to Gaea' also contain elements of Horatian procedures and evidence of a growing taste for Horatian attitudes – a distrust of romantic extravagance, the selection of a modest Mediterranean hideaway (a house on Ischia, later to be exchanged for more northerly premises at Kirchstettin in Austria) and a preferene for 'moderation' (sometimes getting to sound a little too satisfied with itself as in 'Read *The New Yorker*, trust in God; / And take short views'). 'The Horatians' decides that 'Flaccus and [his] kin' are to be found not in Grand Opera or Opera Buffa, but are more likely to turn up as the amateur detective in a whodunit who solves the murder 'thanks to your knowledge of local topography' (by this point the poem is getting a little 'gabby', an adjective Frank Kermode once used to describe Auden's 'The Aliens'). Auden's Horatians are also to be found among 'Natural bachelors / and political idiots',

>   Zoological and Botanical Gardens,
> museum-basements displaying feudal armour
>   or old coins: there too we find
>   you among the custodians.
>
>   Some of you have written poems, usually
>   short ones, or kept diaries, seldom published

till after your deaths, but most
make no memorable impact

except on your friends and dogs . . .

Is not all this making Flaccus and his kin slightly twee and the 'Horatian' just a formula for resolutely minor achievements? One takes the point that the tastes of Horatians 'run to / small dinner-parties, small rooms, / and the tone of voice that suits them'. Though whether Auden himself ever quite attains that tone of voice consistently is another matter, for the compulsive talker tends just to chunter on. Horace is never a tour guide to the Sabine villa; Auden even takes us into his lavatory.

The aim of this essay has been to touch on certain saliences. These would be incomplete without mentioning two more, the versions of C. H. Sisson and also Ezra Pound's late tribute to a poet about whom he had once been ambivalent. Before rendering a number of Horace's *Odes*, Sisson had been concerned with seeing how much pressure might be brought to bear on the unadorned declarative sentence. His verse was then being honed towards precision in his versions of Catullus. The declarative sentence which can sometimes be telling for Catullus is less helpful in Englishing Horace, though Horace also, for all his polish, often chooses the unresonantly prosaic phrase to counter our over-emotive expectations. Sisson's choice of a still plain but now slightly more elaborate style dwells on this side of Horace, a stylistic trait that combines with a certain relish for Horace's no-nonsense attitudes ('a poet invaluable in our time not least because of his lack of sympathy with our most current prejudices').

The most surprising item among Sisson's odes is his attempt at the *Carmen Saeculare* which 'comes near to being a new start from the old original', in short an imitation rather than a direct translation, often with old instances which are updated or re-applied as in Johnson's use of Juvenal in 'The Vanity of Human Wishes'. An imitation of Horace's most Virgilian poem, celebrating the emperor as the lineal descendant of Anchises and Venus, the head of Church and State, permits some interesting parallels. One of the pleasures of classical imitation being the pleasure of recognition, there is a parallel here that gains both wit and point if the reader sees it. In 'The Secular Ode' Aeneas sails from Troy to Rome and finds it better than what he left behind him. Sisson's British parallel to this is a legend David Jones makes much of in *The Anathemata* – the legend of the Trojan Brutus who, according to tradition, came to settle in England. What Sisson's poem brings home is that it could only have been written by an Englishman, and by an Englishman for whom Christianity and the monarchy continue to matter. Sisson can still

Some aspects of Horace in the twentieth century

write out of a profound sense of national unity – of England not just as the sum of economic developments, oil finds and balanced budgets, but 'England as a poetic idea', as Donald Davie puts it. This phrase implies the idea of inherited unity that, as a nation of monarchists, we invest in the symbol of the crown. Sisson, once Under-Secretary at the Ministry of Labour, spells out much of this in his prose work, *The Spirit of British Administration* of 1959. His version of Horace's 'Secular Ode' unselfconsciously celebrates the idea of unity as he looks at London in the perspective of Rome, but without any plangent evocations of vanished imperial splendours, though the fact of empire enters this poem as part of England's story and part of the poem's story. England 'as poetic idea' must here also balance itself against the ironies of history and the sense of both human frailty and human fragility:

> The ways that have led here are multifarious,
> Even Brutus from Troy, our ancestors believed,
> But whatever they left they found better here.
>
> We have been through it all, victory on land and sea,
> These things were necessary for your assurance.
> The King of France. Once there was even India.
>
> Can you remember the expression 'Honour'?
> There was, at one time, even Modesty.
> Nothing is so dead it does not come back.
>
> There is God. There are no Muses without him.
> He it is who raises the drug-laden limbs
> Which were too heavy until he stood at Saint Martin's . . .
>
> He bends now over Trafalgar Square.
> If there should be a whisper he would hear it.
> Are not these drifting figures the chorus?

Besides his odes, I must mention in passing Sisson's translation of the *Ars Poetica*, written in long lines which seem to owe something to the hexameters of Arthur Hugh Clough in *Amours de Voyage*.

When in 1964 Pound's anthology *Confucius to Cummings*, compiled with the aid of Marcella Spann appeared, it contained three translations of Horace by Pound, *Odes* 1.31, 1.11 and 3.30, done respectively in 1963, 1964 and 1964. Here we have what Hopkins meant when he wrote of poetry's power to 'bid' us:

> By the flat cup and the splash of new vintage
> What, specifically, does the diviner ask of Apollo? Not

> Thick Sardinian corn-yield nor pleasant
> Ox-herds under the summer sun in Calabria, nor
> Ivory nor gold out of India, nor
> Land where Liris crumbles her bank in silence
> Though the water seems not to move . . .

Great translators have sometimes found support in their spiritual crises by expressing them through another mouth. Dryden did this via Lucretius and Ovid, Cowley via Anacreon. In the twentieth century perhaps the most moving example is Ezra Pound. Amid the wreckage of his late years, his *Cantos* a botch (or so he thought), we see him turning to Horace and away from trying to save the universe. In his version of *Odes* 1.11,

>   Winter is winter
> Gnawing the Tyrrhene cliffs with the sea's tooth.
>
> Take note of flavors, and clarity's in the wine's manifest.
> Cut loose long hope for a time.

In 1.31, contenting himself with 'olives . . . endives and mallow roots' ('Delight had I healthily in what lay handy provided') he asks

> Grant me now, Latoe:
>   Full wit in my cleanly age,
> Nor lyre lack me to tune the page.

The third version rephrases a famous Horatian boast: 'This monument will outlast metal and I made it' and qualifies with 'Bits of me, many bits, will dodge all funeral' – using Horace's own qualification to point to Pound's scattered triumphs and the nuggets in the sprawling *Cantos*. How few people know these three masterpieces of translation – a pity, for they alter our sense of Pound and reveal his capacity for humility.

These three poems tell us less about Horace's original text and its dense implications than Pope's more extended work, but like the Pope, they are activated by a personal electricity. At the same time, there is a putting aside of the merely personal. D. M. Hooley says well when he sums up this phase of Pound's activity. 'The three translations', he writes, 'form as effective a "crown" to Pound's career . . . as any he could devise. And it is significant, not just curious, that so fitting a closure comes through translation. It is not just that Pound thought best through the matrices of other languages, literatures, traditions. Rather, through resigning himself to their influences, he transfigured their impulses into startling new creation . . . in both the Propertius and the Horace there is some resignation of self, of dogmatism . . . Horace dictates a kind of reorientation of the poet to his verse and the verse to the world. Horace, the master of technique, pressures Pound just as he does Bunting . . .'[16]

Some aspects of Horace in the twentieth century

Pound's Horace does not exactly dispose of the generalization that stands at the head of this essay, but it leaves a salutory dent in it; so that perhaps the claim should be modified, with also Bunting's and Sisson's versions in mind, to say that, given our angle of approach – inevitably a more fragmented business than Pope's – we must rest content with 'bits . . . many bits [that] will dodge all funeral'.

13

DENIABLE EVIDENCE: TRANSLATING HORACE
C. H. Sisson

A POET WHO is also a translator may justly be suspected of a partiality for his own methods. In this essay I shall admit the charge from the first, not claiming, however, that the way I have found myself doing this is superior to that of other people. What I shall try to do is to offer evidence of a possible way of proceeding – one that I know is possible because it has presented itself to me as the best I could do. What follows, therefore, is not an argument but a piece of evidence.

My first attempt at translation – as distinct from mere construing – was undertaken at the request of a French master. Knowing that I had produced some English verses which were considered locally to be better than those of most fifteen-year-olds, he instructed me to do a version of some Romantic poet – I believe, Lamartine – 'to show that it can be done'. After considerable and worried efforts I reported, slightly to the master's annoyance, that it could *not* be done. I have never since seen any reason to depart from that youthful judgement, as regards Lamartine or any other poet whatsoever. A poem is what it is, and not something else: there is no such thing as an equivalent. That goes for every line of every poem, and those who assert the contrary are talking about something other than poetry.

Nearly another fifteen years passed before my next major attempt as a translator. This was as an NCO in the army in India, when I relieved my boredom by producing some versions of Heine which reflected not only the original but, implicitly and sometimes explicitly, my immediate surroundings. The third landmark was when I had already turned fifty. With two small volumes of verse behind me, I had begun to feel the need of some technical refurbishing. In the hope of effecting this I turned, almost for the first time since leaving school, to the Latin classics, and translated one or two, and after some hesitation all, of the poems of Catullus. This was followed a year or two later, by bits of Virgil and Horace, this time not because I saw in them direct models – which they could hardly be, for a poet in the 1960s, or at any rate certainly not for me – but because I had found that such attempts were the best way, for me, of re-vising these authors.

Translating Horace

You may say that my concern was with *literature*, rather than with Latin literature, but I knew that in literature there are no such things as generalities, only particulars – particular works which inevitably reflect particular persons and particular times and places – and, although far from anything which could be called scholarship, I helped myself as best I could with Ellis' *Commentary on Catullus* and other non-current monuments of learning. The task, however, was always to see what *I* could get out of my author, which meant in the end how close I could get to him in the verse I could write at the time. In the case of my *Reading of Virgil's Eclogues* this meant giving as it were only the shape and main lines of the original; the project started with a rhythm which in fact commanded the progress of the work. Those who think of the process of verse-translation from outside are apt to imagine a 'right' form in the vernacular. What is in question with the poet who produces anything like a poem from a foreign original is rather the confluence of two streams – one carrying the original poem and the other being the stream of the poet's own development. That may seem outrageous arrogance, but a moment's reflection will show that something like that operates with Dryden and Pope as with lesser fry. The ultimate concern of such a translator must be the vivacity of the vernacular text that he produces.

The possibilities of a text produced in this way are multifarious. None is right; none is absolutely wrong and the degrees of wrongness can be measured only against a standard of objectivity which is itself suspect. When I attempted Horace, *Odes* 1.11, what came into my mind was:

> You do not ask – unless to ask, Leuconoë –
> What ends the gods will give, to me, to you.

The Chaldeans have already disappeared, but not much else, by any ordinary metaphrastic reckoning. The shape of the vernacular rendering was already determined, and is in effect the control in what follows, as much, and ultimately more, than the minutiae of the Latin text itself. Any other proceeding would involve a degree of wilfulness which no poet would allow himself. If you are inclined to lay down laws extraneous to those which govern the poet himself, you can say that the 'translation' was wrong from the start but if the opening lines are accepted – which means perhaps no more than being read with some of the pleasure English verse can give – you can hardly say that it should go on differently so as to accommodate, for example, Jupiter and the Tuscan coast with its possibly porous rocks. The rest of my version reads:

> Consult no augurers. Suffer what comes,
> Whether some winters still, or this one only
> Which now wears out the sea under the cliffs.
> Think, take your wine. You are better off with sleep

> And no long hopes. For, while we speak, age falls.
> Collect your day, and have it. The next, you may not.

It seems to me quite creditable, and even Horatian, so far as the drift of the Latin poem can be conveyed to an English reader of the twentieth century.

A proceeding such as this does not necessarily involve the erasure of palpably classical references, or the 'modernization' of the matter. But what cannot be evaded is that translation of whatever kind *is* a form of modernization. It is the words of here and now which are to be used for those of far-off and then, and the writer of English verse which is to have any liveliness must be acutely aware of the shadow of associations which he cannot make acceptable in the context. There is no difficulty about the odd deity, where his function is obvious, as 2.10:

> Jupiter brings in the shapeless
> Winters but he also
>
> Takes them away. If things are bad now, and have been,
> They will not always be so. Sometimes Apollo
> Rouses the silent Muse with his lyre; he is not
> Always stretching his bow.

But the temptation is always there, for the poet who is as deeply concerned with his own art as with Horace's, to substitute local or contemporary references for those of the Latin. So, in 2.15:

> Where there were once forests a region of
> Concrete. Until quite recently
> There were meadows at Westminster.
> The salmon leapt where Raleigh was beheaded.

One may even be steered away from the original to express a malice of one's own:

> Once there was only nature for ornament.
> Then there was ornament and art flourished;
> Now there is only the South Bank
> And, of course, the Arts Council.

A perfect tact with both the English and the Latin would not be tempted to such excesses, but where is such virtue to be found? And if it is found, that does not invalidate this slightly freakish version, or its debt to Horace who, perhaps – if he can be imagined bothering himself with such trivialities – would not object to exercising this touch of influence on a barbarous tongue which certainly has need of his presence.

The *Carmen Saeculare*, with its deep undercurrent of good wishes for Rome and her future, and its evocation of an idealized past, may well be best

Translating Horace

understood by the contemporary reader who is so little persuaded by the prejudices of our own happy time as to be not without parallel feelings in relation to his own country. A translator so seized might, without metaphrastic inhibitions, discard the Phoebus and Diana of the opening line for

> O sun, and moonlight shining in the woods

– the luminaries which shine on us still. Thus released, is it absurd to go on

> Now, at this season when selected girls
> And the boys who are about to venture upon them,
> Though still in bud, sing what will please London,

and so to abandon the gods who loved the Seven Hills for the one formerly recognized in our own capital city? Such recklessness is not unprincipled, in the substitution of local products for the gifts of Ceres and of Jove, or even, I would say, in following the suggestions of *fetus* into our own usage rather than that of the text:

> Rich in apples, yes, and seething with cattle,
> The succulent earth is dressed in barley whiskers.
> And grow plump, embryo, from the natural gifts.

There is less temptation not to use the concepts of the original where Horace speaks of *Fides et Pax et Honor Pudorque*, but such virtues have to be spoken of in terms which are possible in the discourse of our own day, which does not readily invoke them:

> Can you remember the expression 'Honour'?
> There was, at one time, even modesty.
> Nothing is so dead it does not come back.

My version ends shamelessly with the God who 'bends over Trafalgar Square'. Take it or leave it, and faint as the echo of Horace may be, is it any fainter than in other twentieth-century versions one can think of, *verbo verbum* though they be?

The problems in relation to the *Ars Poetica*, which I attempted much later, are quite different and in several respects simpler. Although one can, in general, make too much of the distinction between translation and imitation, it might almost be said that there is an invincible case for the latter. At least the choice must be between a version which, with all the equipment of scholarship, attempts to reproduce Horace's account of Augustan poetics and one which requires a knowledgeable practitioner who is moved, as in past centuries a number have been, to go over the same ground with his eye on his own language and the contemporary scene. My own version aspires to be included in the latter class, and my zeal for what I consider to be good practice goes so far as to include some fifteen pages of notes designed to spread – I would not say that they have actually succeeded in spreading – enlightenment among young poets. There was never any question of attempting a successor to Jonson's literal version. Oldham would have been a more likely influence, though I cannot say that he was particularly in my mind at the time, and indeed no model is needed for the sort of adaptation to the contemporary English scene which was simply the only attempt I felt qualified to make. The result hardly belongs to Horatian studies, except so far as it demonstrates, by the closeness of the parallels on a variety of occasions, how little the absurdities of poetasters have changed from one age to another. I was even able to recall, with little departure from Horace's original, a contemporary expert on poetic suicide, Mr Alvarez.

Whatever our preferences, as between metaphrase and paraphrase, it is an invincible fact of literary history that the surivival of any verse translation depends not on its 'accuracy' but upon its having some claim to be a poem in its own right. And when we look at the versions of a particular original, done in more or less widely separated times, the overwhelming impression is of reading a poem of the translator's time. Each generation has to confront the past anew, for itself. For the sense of a spark across time which the reading of a foreign original, whether in a classical or a modern language, can give, there is no substitute for attempting to decipher the original itself. Translations cannot make the attempt unnecessary; at best they can assist our approach to it. Helps are of many kinds, linguistic, historical, sometimes philosophical, and that of the translator who produces a readable version can hardly be accounted among the chief of them. What he can do is to give some not unuseful indications of the drift of the original. To the reader for whom poems are living entities this may give valuable, if always incomplete, clues as to how the poem is to be read.

One can understand the scholar, properly proud of his own professionalism, being reluctant to admit the legitimacy of what must seem to him a wayward discipline, and indeed one should scrutinize with care any claim for special treatment by people who think that, as artists, their obligations are less than other people's. It is arguable that Milton's translation of *Odes* 1.5, should be a model for all: 'Rendered almost word for word without Rhyme according to the Latin measure, as near as the Language will permit'. This description at least contains the essential admission, that the language will not permit everything the scholar would wish, and carries the implication that Chaucer would not have used the language of Milton, and that we should not attempt to do so either. Milton's piece exhibits a rare degree of technical competence, as we should expect, but this youthful exercise should not be allowed to overrule the mature practice and principles of such as Dryden, nor should a great name scare us away from all enquiry. It is hardly for a non-scholar to comment on Milton's handling of 'the Latin measure', but I should be surprised to learn that he is to be regarded as more successful, in this matter, than Thomas Campion, whose *Observations on the Art of English Poetry* (1602) is the classic apology for the adoption of classical metres in English. Campion was himself a superb technician, unsurpassed except by Shakespeare in the rhymed and accented forms of the lyric, and Milton's version of the Fifth Ode is surely less full of life, to an English ear, than

>   Rose-cheeked Laura, come:
>   Sing thou smoothly with thy beauty's
>   Silent music, either other
>   Sweetly gracing.

Campion, however, was not there wrestling with the problems of translation. Milton's claim to have kept close to the original can hardly be faulted, unless one counts the slight aberration in the last line where, A. J. Macleane remarks in his commentary on Horace (1869 edn, p. 21) he 'translates "the stern god of sea," not observing that "potens" governs "maris"'. Yet one cannot say that even Milton has produced the irrefutable translation, even for his own time. Charles Tomlinson's *Oxford Book of Verse in English Translation* contains versions of the same poem by Fanshawe and by Cowley, the former born in the same year as Milton, the latter ten years later. Cowley takes thirty lines, as against Horace's sixteen, and trails along behind his text, pleasingly enough, without casting any new light on it. Fanshawe manages with sixteen. He imports some phrases and omits some, but might have claimed, as Dryden would have it, that he has 'the sense' of the original if the 'words are not so strictly followed'. As Tomlinson points out in his Preface: 'Once one has put things like this it is... difficult to limit the elements of adaptation.' Of course there is no legal limit, in this sort of driving, nor in general as to what one literature may suggest to another. Fanshawe's performance, however, is very creditable within the limits of 'translation', and if he is further from 'the words' than Milton, it could be claimed that on some points he gives a more vivid interpretation of the 'sense'. The opening

>   What stripling now Thee discomposes
>   In Woodbine Rooms, on Beds of Roses...

loses the point that the young man was stinking of scent – a point which Milton's 'bedew'd with liquid odours' can hardly be said to make very clearly; he loses the cave or recess apparently prepared for the occasion. In what follows

>   For whom thy Auburn Haire
>   Is spread, Unpainted Faire?

Milton has the advantage, overwhelmingly, with 'Plain in thy neatness' instead of the mere 'unpainted' for *simplex munditiis*, yet it suggests some Puritan girl rather than the Pyrrha Horace had in mind. Fanshawe (perhaps getting on too fast with the scene as it presents itself to him) gives us the hair loose rather than bound up. But when Milton says rather pedantically

> O how oft shall he
> Of Faith and changed Gods complain,

one may sympathize with Fanshawe in thinking that this literalness will mean less to the contemporary reader than

> How will he one day curse the oaths
> And heaven that witness'd your betroaths!

and if the 'cuckold' which he then introduces is a rather sledgehammerly treatment of the Latin, it is hardly more redolent of his own Cavalier milieu than Milton's curious 'stern god of sea' is of Milton's Puritan retirement. And perhaps, in the first line of all, 'discomposes' is a more exact word for Horace's *urget*, than Milton's too vague 'courts'. Fanshawe certainly knew more of the world than Milton did, when they wrote their respective versions, in which this difference shows up. And it is not only translators who show themselves up in this way. One may smile, surely, at the tone of Macleane's apparently indignant (and certainly superfluous) comment: 'That 1.5 expresses any but a poetical jealousy on the part of Horace I do not believe.'

The question remains, what can be learned about the peculiarities of Horace from the evidence later and almost always lesser poets have left on the way his poems have affected them. Too much weight should not be given to the evidence offered by any individual poet. The influences bearing down upon anyone at the time of writing are many and various, and are predominantly determined by the state of the language in which he writes, including the state of the art of poetry, in which a few times are fortunate and many unfortunate, even to the extent of utter incapacity for particular tasks. But can one not conclude, from the successive attempts which have been made to translate Horace, something about the characteristics which have made his work so central to the European tradition? If poets have so often been tempted away from what pass for literal versions to versions in which the substance of the poems is presented, to a more or less degree, in particulars which are of the translator's times rather than of Horace's, may it not be because Horace himself was so much of his own place and time? And may it not be the penetration of Horace's mind, as exercised on his particular circumstances, which through the centuries has made readers find him so close to their own times? Horace is, certainly, a social poet. If Virgil is a poet for whom tears are never far below the surface of things, Horace might be said to be one for whom laughter is never very far away, and laughter is a social phenomenon. It must be hard even for a fine scholar to be sure that he had identified all the ironies which an intelligent Roman contemporary might have detected in Horace's most impeccable sentiments.

When one of the editors first suggested that I might care to write for this volume a poem to or about Horace, I replied, truly enough, that I did not have the knack of such deliberate, *ad hoc* productions, but that if anything turned up, I would let him have it. There is however a further difficulty. More than twenty years ago I addressed some no doubt presumptuous stanzas to the master, and if I made a second attempt now it would be as one who is less sure than he was what sort of man he was addressing.

Instead, I offer a version of *Epode* 2 which is less a translation than a commentary. I would say that it is never without a certain tenuous connection, direct or indirect, with the words of the original but it is reckless in exploiting the point made by a number of commentators about the relationship between the body of Horace's poem and the last stanza. Macleane points out that Manicelli 'saw that a good deal of the language and sentiments of this ode was unsuited to Alphius', the usurer who is supposed to have spoken so beautifully about the pleasures of a country life, and he himself expresses the opinion that 'some parts of the language suit and some do not suit the character of Alphius.' E. C. Wickham adds: 'There does not seem to be any attempt to make the usurer speak in character through the poem; the pleasures named are those which any Roman poet would have named . . . It is the irony of the conclusion which turned an Idyll into an Epode. Its point is rather the strength of the "ruling passion" than, as has been suggested, the elaborate hypocrisy of a money-lender who makes his panegyric of a rustic life an excuse for pressing his debtors for repayment, while he means all the while to put the money out at interest again at the next settlement day'. All this betrays a certain uneasiness. I have light-heartedly made Alphius speak throughout as a city man who is far from being at home in the country, but I do not pretend to have begun to solve the problem which would be in making this clear while sticking close to Horace's words.

HORACE: EPODES, 2

Happy the man who, free from business
    As Adam was when innocent,
Pretends to farm paternal acres
    And never thinks of the investment.
Nobody sends him tiresome papers
    Which leave him utterly at sea;

He is not harried by his brokers
    Or people better off than he.
Oh no! He cultivates his vineyard
    And lets his vines get out of hand;
His cattle graze without regard
    To the condition of the land.
In pruning, he will always sever
    The fruiting branch, and leave the new;
At shearing, finds the sheep so clever
    He likes their wool best where it grew;
Finds honey sticky in the autumn
    And fruit a bit above his head;
He does not pick the pears, they all come
    Bouncing on top of him instead.
His wine is fit for a libation
    Upon the ground, but not to drink;
He much enjoys the preparation
    And he is proud if it is pink.
His private stream meanwhile runs purling,
    The birds sing as they're paid to do;
His fountains never tired of plashing
    And they are soporific too.
But when the proper sporting weather
    Arrives, he has to take a gun
And stir up something in the heather
    As gentlemen have always done,
Or even venture out on horse-back
    And hope a fox will come his way;
How awkward he should lose the pack
    So very early in the day!
With such delights he can forget
    That tiresome girl at the week-end:
He plans to have, but not just yet,
    A wife on whom he can depend.
– Children perhaps – some sunburnt lady,
    He'd feel a proper farmer then;
She'd bring in firewood, have tea ready,
    He'd come in tired, not curious when
She penned the geese or milked the cows,
    So long as she'd drawn cider and,
From home-grown chicken and potatoes,
    Prepared a meal with her own hands.
No Yarmouth oysters could be sweeter,
    Smoked salmon, turbot, what you please,
Not any delicacy caught here
    Or found, long dead, in the deep freeze.

Translating Horace

It's not too bad to dine off pheasant
      But home-grown olives do as well,
And what he finds extremely pleasant
      Is chewing meadow-sweet and sorrel:
Which one of course can supplement
      By hedgerow herbs that taste of tar,
Or better, when such boons are sent
      A lamb run over by a car.
'Amidst such treats as these, how fine
      To see beasts by your own front door,
The latest plough, the latest combine,
      And plan what you will use them for.'

So spoke the city man, and sold
      The lot, preferring stocks and shares.
Too bad that he had not been told
      The full extent of rural cares.

POSTSCRIPT

IMAGES OF HORACE IN TWENTIETH-CENTURY SCHOLARSHIP
Don Fowler

THE HISTORY OF scholarship is a form of history, and as such can lay no claim to the status of a privileged metadiscourse. There is no history without plot, but plot is not 'out there' waiting to be discovered: it has to be provided by the historian from her cultural stock. For the history of Horatian scholarship in the twentieth century, various general plots are to hand. There is the positivist plot of scientific advance: the scholarly world (singular) learning more and more each year about its subject strides confidently towards its goal of total mastery. On this plot, books and articles are milestones or signposts: Kiessling–Heinze, Pasquali, Fraenkel, Nisbet–Hubbard flash past our window on the road to Truth. Or there is the supposedly more sophisticated plot of Kuhnian Cultural Revolution: our milestones become paradigm shifters, and after each movement of the furniture the little men of 'normal science' come in to dust the books and tidy things up a bit. But classicists have some plots of their own. There are the monastic heroics of the Great Tradition: in a hostile barbarian world, a small band of scholars preserve the ancient truths from oblivion. Or there is the thrill of the barricades as texts that tell of love and life are snatched from the hands of dusty old dominies and held proudly aloft in the youthful breeze. More to *fin-de-siècle* taste perhaps are various darker tales: decadence and decline, the failure of hope as meaning slips away, the sun sinking slowly in The West.

It is not that these plots are simply distortions or falsifications: there is no other way to tell history, no MetaPlot against which they can be set. It is not absurd to prefer one to another; rational grounds for doing so can exist. But it is well to think also of the chaotic mass of 'facts' to which they attempt to give structure and meaning.[1] Hundreds of scholars in different countries writing books and articles over a period of ninety years: schoolchildren construing the *Odes*, lectures on the *Epistles*, doctoral theses on the *Sermones*. Already by calling all this (or some of it) 'scholarship' we are making connections that need justification: if an English man of letters between the wars and a young American professional classicist looking for tenure both write on Horace, it is

Postscript

far from obvious that they are doing the same thing. And that's before we start taking 'Horace' him / itself apart: Horace the man, Horace the text, or Horace *'all-the-forces-that-moulded-the-text-plus-its-reception'*?[2]

The most obvious plot goes like this. At the beginning of the century – or let us move down a few years to justify the term 'Edwardian' – Horace is firmly Horace the man, and the image of him in English scholarship is of an honorary Englishman. Here is R. S. Conway in an address first given in 1903 on 'Horace as Poet Laureate':[3]

A long line of statesmen and governors through more than a thousand years – King Alfred, Thomas à Becket, Thomas More, Philip Sidney, Clive, Pitt, Durham, Dufferin, Cromer, to mention no other names – have all learnt to understand the poetry of Horace in the years when a boy's training makes the deepest imprint in what Roger Ascham called 'the faire, cleane wax of his mind'. In no other country of Europe has the study of Latin struck deeper, if even so deep, into the fibres of national life; and in spite of the abuses which grow round every ancient custom, it has borne great fruit. The standards of public conduct in this country – and, we may add, in America – have been formed on Roman models. This whole chapter of practical ethics has been drawn not so much from the New Testament as from Cicero and Horace, Vergil and Livy. In the Gospels every Christian community finds the deepest springs of ethical life; but where in the New Testament is there any counsel how to govern a conquered dependency, how to administer a public office?

Let us test this briefly and simply. What do we think to be the typical British virtues in public life? This question admits of many answers; but among them every one would wish to count at least four: justice in administration; moderation in victory; a saving sense of humour, and, chief of all, steadfastness, – sticking grimly to the guns.

Now these virtues are the favourite themes of Horace; you cannot read a page of his writings in which some one of them is not enforced. Beneath the portrait of Warren Hastings in the Council Chamber at Calcutta is written the motto from Horace, *Aequa mens rebus in arduis*. And you may read in Lord Roberts' story of *Forty-one Years in India* how at the height of the India Mutiny, in the midst of the fateful struggles on Delhi Ridge, young Quentin Battye, as he fell mortally wounded, whispered to an old friend beside him, *Dulce et decorum est pro patria mori*.

American appropriation was no less striking: here is E. K. Rand addressing a Harvard audience in 1937:[4]

Horace is the prince of club men,[5] with old and young in his circle. He is a pleasant counsellor, a perfect Freshman adviser, always at home, always at leisure, ever ready to pour out for us a glass of one of the mellower brands and to expound the confortable doctrine of *nil admirari*, caught from Socratic irony and handed on to choice souls down the ages. The *sprezzatura* of the Renaissance, French wit in any period, Oxford reserve, and, rightly understood, Harvard indifference, these are the links in a golden chain.

As always, there is no history without cheating: both of these pieces are from 'popular' lectures, and mainstream scholarship was more restrained. Nevertheless, the change of tone fifty years on is striking. Here is R. G. M. Nisbet reviewing J. Perret's *Horace*[6] in 1960:

> There have been too many agreeable introductions to Horace, and the appearance of a new one may cause some foreboding. M. Perret writes with clarity and taste, he shows a humane appreciation of his author, most of what he says is true. Perhaps it is not enough.

'Taste' and 'humanity' have changed their sign. Reviewing the major commentary on *Odes* Book One that Nisbet produced with M. Hubbard ten years later, the Italian Marxist scholar A. La Penna[7] will compliment the authors for remaining 'relatively insensible to the spell that decorum and false sublimity have cast over so many interpreters, especially academics': twenty years later again Nisbet will argue that *dulce et decorum est* is not even what Horace wrote.[8]

That is: at the beginning of the century Horace was the common property of men of culture, 'one of us', while towards the end there is a growing critical distancing, a move from man to text, a stress on alterity. From a broad-based and facile humanist appropriation, we move to a narrow historicism: at the beginning of the century Horace is read warmly and badly by large numbers of gentlemen, towards its end his text is read coolly but well by a small group of players.[9] Such a plot can of course be used more widely to structure the history not only of classical literary studies, but also of literary criticism in general, and of many other aspects of Western culture. Many factors can be brought into play: the changing place of Classics within English education, the increasing professional organization of classical studies, developments in literary methodology (the shift from author to text, and then to reader), the growth of historical and ethnographic relativism, the experience of literary modernism, the rise of feminism, the loss of the British Empire. But anyone writing from Oxford will inevitably foreground the seminal contribution of Adolf Hitler.

Although ancient history in England[10] had begun to become more professional before the second world war, classical literary studies were still essentially amateurish before the great influx of Jewish refugees in the 1930s brought scholars like Jacoby, Maas, Pfeiffer and especially Eduard Fraenkel to Oxford. The agenda of the German scholarship that they brought with them had been set back at the time of the foundation of the Prussian state, when historicism as a methodology had found its canonic expression in Wilamowitz's quarrel with Nietzsche over the 'Philology of the Future': 'undiverted by any presuppositions about the end result, thinking truth alone to be noble, to stride forward from finding to finding, to grasp all historically produced phenomena in terms of the assumptions of the time in which they

Postscript

developed, and to see their justification in terms of their own historical necessity'.[11] The experience of Nazi Germany, which in other scholars produced a reaction against this historicist tradition, in the case of the classicist emigrés seems to have intensified it, perhaps in reaction to the humanist warmth of English appropriation. Here is Fraenkel already in 1946, reviewing L. P. Wilkinson's *Horace and His Lyric Poetry*:[12]

> This is a pleasant little book. It can be recommended to all who wish to brush up their school-day recollections of Horace and enjoy him again without being shocked by unfamiliar aspects, or being induced to tackle in earnest the difficulties of great poetry.

Fraenkel's main criticism of Wilkinson was that 'nowhere is a serious effort made to view the poetry of Horace in its historical setting': and it was a historicized view of Horace that Fraenkel attempted to provide with his own *Horace* published by Oxford in 1957. In the preface, he comments that 'what has induced me to write this book was my desire to remove from the poems of Horace some of the crusts with which the industry of many centuries has overlaid them and to enable a sympathetic reader to listen as often as possible to the voice of the poet and as seldom as possible to the voices of his learned patrons'. The anonymous reviewer in the *TLS*[13] saw this as one of the book's most important characteristics: noting the decline of the myth of the English Horace with the 'self-confident and cultured colonialism which supported it', he praises Fraenkel for setting Horace 'firmly in his historical and cultural context as an Italian poet, separated from our own tradition by profound differences of temperament as well as language and background'.

One of the most important aspects of this historicization was Fraenkel's treatment of Horace's politics. As several recent studies have shown,[14] there had always been an ambivalence in English attitudes to Augustus, with facile adoration of the Golden Age tempered by Tacitean suspicion. The experience of the dictators of the 1930s, which found its most celebrated scholarly reflection in Ronald Syme's *The Roman Revolution*,[15] had reinforced this distaste: here for instance is the poet Alfred Noyes, the great opponent of Joyce and modernism, in his *Portrait of Horace* written just after the war:[16]

> Our modern world boasts of its freedom from worship of place and power, and demands a new moral standard for kings and governments, as well as for private individuals; but the historians continue the old evil into the new age. With a strange, unconscious snobbery, they make obeisance before the blood-stained throne of Caesar and whisper with awe the grandiose name Augustus, forgetting that he bestowed it on himself after careful consideration of its semi-divine significance, a proceeding which they would view with contempt in anyone not endowed with worldly grandeur.

This clear-headedness does not lead however to a New Historicist exposure of Horace's engagement in the régime: throughout his (well-written and intelligent) book Noyes tries to excuse Horace, to negotiate a way around the politics. Similarly, Patrick Wilkinson in his previously mentioned *Horace and his Lyric Poetry* of 1945 had explicitly put the stress on the private poetry of Horace: in his survey of Horace's 'Character and Views' 'Religion, Life and Death, Morality, Love and Friendship, The Country, Humour' are given pride of place over 'The State'. This had aroused Fraenkel's ire:[17]

> As soon as Augustus comes into the picture, many people begin to see red. If a poet refuses to cold-shoulder the Princeps, they suspect him of sinister motives or at any rate regard him as lacking in spirit and strength of mind.

Accordingly, Fraenkel put the stress on the political poetry, with results well summarized by C. O. Brink:[18]

> He portrays an Horace whose political poems are at the very centre of his lyric production and who, in his lyric verse, rose from an unreal position of an individual addressing and exhorting the people to one that inspired him to speak on their behalf – in the *Carmen Saeculare*, 'the greatest triumph of Horace's achievement as a lyric poet' (p. 382) and finally reached the 'we' of 'his most mellow lyrics' in *Odes*, Book IV (p. 452).

At least, that is one way to put it. David Armstrong had been more forceful in 1964:[19]

> Fraenkel's *Horace* is a book which pretends that a great deal of Horace's poetry is not really coherent; that he was a mediocre satirist in the strict sense of the word; that he was an insignificant love-poet; and that he only found his true voice in the odes he wrote in honor of Augustus and the Roman State – and not all of them either.

The *fortuna* of Fraenkel's book is in fact a curious one: the only book on Latin that he published during his tenure of the Corpus Chair, it remains in print and sells steadily, but is largely ignored in scholarly discussion and is treated as an embarrassment alongside the monumental achievement of the commentary on Aeschylus' *Agamemnon*.[20]

In retrospect, of course, it is clear that Fraenkel's historicization of Horace was only superficial. Even his fellow German F. Klinger in a laudatory review had unconsciously put his finger on the element of self-presentation in Fraenkel's view of Horace:[21]

> The author says in his preface (p. vii) that Horace was an exacting author, unconcerned with the general reading public and preferring to write for a small circle of educated men, who were capable of giving their concentrated attention to those works of art; one might say the same of his own work.

With many of the refugee scholars – one thinks especially of the greatest of them all, Eduard Norden – their sufferings under National Socialism, and in some cases the bravery of their resistance, can easily blind interpreters to the

Postscript

way that their early works were produced in an atmosphere of authoritatian scholarly conservatism which was one of the breeding grounds of Fascism.[22] La Penna had no difficulty in showing that this was also true of Fraenkel, with his 1925 piece *Die Stelle des Römertums in der humanistischen Bildung*,[23] and Fraenkel's favourite Ode[24] remained 4.5, perhaps of all Horace's *Odes* the easiest to read as straightforwardly fascist. As La Penna observed, 'Just as the cult of Greece in Germany became in the end a Nietzschean obsession with irrationality, so the cult of Rome became in the end a superstitious reverence for the state and for racial purity.' For all his boast of approaching Horace with an 'unprejudiced mind', Fraenkel's view was as much the product of his time as Noyes' or Wilkinson's, though in many ways that time was the 1920s not the 1950s. The pretence of objectivity, the avoidance of the obvious analogies between Augustus and Hitler and Mussolini, had an honourable cause, the attempt to knit together the ends of the German tradition of philology which the Nazis had torn apart: but the effect was bizarre.

In one respect, however, Fraenkel's *Horace* was very much of its time. At Oxford, he played an important part in establishing the (still dominant) tradition of the individual work of literature as the focus of attention, in reaction to the dismembering of works to provide atoms of historical evidence which had been dominant: his principal teaching instrument was the seminar on a single play of Greek tragedy. So too his *Horace* is structured around the discussion of individual poems, and he is at pains to stress throughout the principle of 'poems, understanding of, not dependent on outside information' as a celebrated entry in the index has it:

Those kind readers who from time to time feel tempted to supplement a Horatian poem by reading into it what in their opinion the poet has failed to say himself are respectfully but firmly asked to shut this book and never to open it again: it could only disappoint and distress them. My interpretations are, without exception, based on the conviction that Horace, throughout his work, shows himself both determined and able to express everything that is relevant to the understanding and the appreciation of a poem, either by saying it in so many words or by implying it through unambiguous hints.[25]

Although Fraenkel's views here can be traced without difficulty to German romanticism, it would be hard to find a clearer expression of the principles of the New Criticism, at least in its English vulgar reception.[26] This attitude may seem a surprising partner for historicism, but both are ways of denying the influence of one's own time upon one's interpretation. The direct influence of Fraenkel as a respectable academic in encouraging the acceptance of 'New Critical' practice (not that he knew that was what it was) was not inconsiderable, but much more important was the indirect effect when the reaction set in that produced works like Gordon Williams' *Tradition and*

Originality in Roman Poetry and Nisbet and Hubbard on *Odes* Book One, works whose stress on the systems of meaning that need to be grasped before the individual poem can be tackled in retrospect looks like the first-beginnings of structuralism.

I have dwelt for some time on Fraenkel's *Horace* because it shows how *difficult* it is to write the history of Horatian scholarship. The clear outlines of the map with which we started – the simple plot of a move from facile involvement to cool historicism – become fractal as we move closer in: the English enthusiasm for Horace the public poet transforms itself into an ambiguous exaltation of the private voice, to be challenged by a German political refugee in the name of a historicism whose chief characteristic is a flight from history. It is difficult to keep out of our discourse that most Horatian of words 'ironic'. This complexity can be seen in many other areas of Horatian scholarship as well. One of the central oppositions in his works is that between Greek and Roman culture, expressed optimistically in his famous boast in *Odes* 3.30 to be 'the first to have led down Aeolian song to Italian measures'.[27] Reviewers rightly singled out the Italian elements in Fraenkel's Horace, and Fraenkel's own enthusiasm for Italy was a striking trait that he had inherited from Wilamowitz and which he passed on to many of his pupils. By contrast, the scholarship of the 1960s, 1970s and 1980s paid ever increasing attention to the Greek background to Horace's poetry: and on to that opposition of Roman and Greek came to be projected an opposition between reality and fantasy, life and literature.[28] But the scholar who had most brought the Greek elements into prominence was an Italian, Giorgio Pasquali, with his *Orazio Lirico* of 1920.[29] Pasquali had studied in Germany, and he was bitterly attacked by Italian reviewers for his lack of patriotism in devoting so much space to Greek, especially Hellenistic, elements: moreover his attention to 'sources' was anathema to Croceans who wished to stress the birth of poetry in the spirit of the individual artist.[30] Such disputes over *Romanità* were to become strident in the early years of Fascism, until the alliance with Germany caught out the less careful nationalists. Pasquali's own politics are almost as hard to grasp as Horace's: he had published *Socialisti Tedeschi* in the same year as *Orazio Lirico*, but was soon enmeshed in the cultural politics of Fascism by his friend Giovanni Gentile, and his precise relationship to Fascism remains a subject of warm dispute amongst Italian classicists.[31] Again, it all seems very ironic: an Italian Germanophile who defends the Greek elements in Horace against Fascist criticism before himself succumbing (or not) to the cult of the Roman.

Doubtless similar tales could be told of the history of classical scholarship in relation to other authors, but with Horace the great myths fail more easily: we never find the easy battle-lines that can be drawn up for Virgil and the elegists, the 'Whose side are you on?' of the wars over Augustanism. Horace seems *especially* slippery, *especially* prone to catch his interpreters out. This is itself a commonplace of the scholarly literature: 'the number of recent Horaces is large and their diversities are bewildering'.[32] In part, this is clearly a result of the variety of genres in which Horace wrote (iambus, lyric, satire, didactic): there is a similar multiplicity about Ovid. So, for instance, Patrick Wilkinson is happy to admit that 'for me Horace is the poet of the Odes and Epodes'[33] while there has been a tendency in recent criticism to foreground works like the *Sermones* or *Epodes* which merely embarrassed earlier scholarship.[34] But Horace's Hellenistic *poikilia* itself demands an explanation, a narrative into which it can be inserted. The story I like pushes this back to Horace himself. Central to all his work is an ideal of the connected life, where sex and politics and drinking and poetry somehow come together, where we know that there is no centre but we fashion one all the same. Already Horace himself pretends to complain people tear him apart[35] (*Ep.* 2.2.58–64):

> denique non omnes eadem mirantur amantque:
> carmine tu gaudes, hic delectatur iambis,
> ille Bioneis sermonibus et sale nigro.
> tres mihi convivae prope dissentire videntur,
> poscentes vario multum diversa palato.
> quid dem? quid non dem? renuis tu, quod iubet alter;
> quod petis, id sane est invisum acidumque duobus.

Then, not everyone admires and loves the same things: you like the lyrics, he gets pleasure from the iambic poetry, this one from the Bionic conversations and black salt. My three dinner-companions all seem to disagree, all wanting different things for their different palates: what am I supposed to give them, what hold back? You turn down what the other one asks for: what you want is hateful and bitter to the other two.

It is no surprise to learn that one of the concepts critics most frequently grasp for when trying to capture this multiformity is that of Romantic Irony: not only in instances like the 'Heinesque surprise at the close'[36] of *Epodes* 2 or *Odes* 3.3 but also more generally:

But this too is romantic. The game here conforms completely to the aesthetic theory of Friedrich Schlegel. It is 'Romatic Irony' which is already infiltrating this ode of Horace [1.22] – indisputable proof of his vitality when one considers that it will have to wait eighteen centuries to find its theoretical formulation. This romantic irony, the keyword of all lively poetry, instructs the poet to make it seem that his art is nothing but a game, a gratuitous act, an arabesque where freely blossoms exuberant emotional energy and the over-rich sap of a fertile genius. This pre-romantic Ode of Horace could easily be one of Heinrich Heine's, a Heine expressing himself in Latin.[37]

And my own next move will be equally unsurprising. This image of Horace as ironically fashioning a unity from extreme cultural diversity, this slippery Horace who always escapes the reader's grasp: where does it come from? At the end of my tendentious survey, the dreaded 'p' word cannot be avoided. For Horace the romantic, Horace the classic, Horace as Kipling or Horace as Pound, I offer you Horace 'the most modern',[38] Horace the postmodern, the poet who always (already?) will have beaten you to it. If you like.[39]

NOTES

1 INTRODUCTION

I am endebted to the following for help, advice, or inspiration: Catharine Edwards, Denis Feeney, Julia Hoffbrand, Michael Liversidge, Michelle Martindale, Stephen Medcalf, Joanna and Robert Parker, Niall Rudd, and especially Duncan Kennedy, *iudex et amicus candidus*. To all of them I apologize for my 'unHoratian' obstinacy. For an earlier, more 'humanist' discussion see my 'Ovid, Horace and Others', in *The Legacy of Rome: A New Appraisal*, ed. Richard Jenkyns (Oxford 1992) 177–213.

1 Cited (critically) by L. P. Wilkinson, *Horace and his Lyric Poetry* (Cambridge 1945, 2nd edn 1951) 2, note 2.
2 Ezra Pound, 'Horace', *Criterion* 9 (1929–30) 217–27, reprinted in *Arion* 9 (1970) (nos. 2 and 3, Horace issue) 178–87 (178–9).
3 John Heath-Stubbs, *Artorius* (London 1973) 24.
4 See J. K. Newman, *Augustus and the New Poets, Latomus* (Brussels 1967) 303–14. cf. T. S. Eliot's warning that Milton's style 'is not a *classic* style, in that it is not the elevation of a *common* style, by the final touch of genius to greatness. It is, from the foundation, and in every particular, a personal style' ('Milton II', in Frank Kermode, ed., *Selected Prose of T. S. Eliot* (London 1975) 267–8). Tennyson's revisions of his Horatian invitation poem 'To the Rev. F. D. Maurice' show the influence of the idea of Horace's purity of diction: he alters (rightly) the twee 'Here in the sweet little Isle of Wight' to '(Take it and come) to the Isle of Wight'; but the vigorous, jokey writing of the original eighth stanza is replaced by something altogether flatter, and a stanza of violent but effective satire on religion is deleted altogether. See Christopher Ricks, ed., *The Poems of Tennyson*, 2nd edn, 3 vols. (London 1987), II.497ff. I am grateful to Niall Rudd for directing my attention to this material.
5 For a fuller account see my essay 'Unlocking the Word-hoard: in Praise of Metaphrase', *Comparative Criticism* 6 (1984) 47–72 (60f).
6 The most interesting discussion is still Steele Commager's, in *The Odes of Horace: a Critical Study* (Bloomington and London 1962) 88ff, a classic of the 'New Criticism'. See also Gregson Davis, *Polyhymnia: the Rhetoric of Horatian Lyric Discourse* (Berkeley and Oxford 1991) 233–42. Davis is illuminating on the structural obliquities of the *Odes*; see, for example, his analysis of 1.6 (33–9), 4.1 (65–71) and 4.2 (133–43), poems discussed below.

7 For these poems see David Amstrong, *Horace*, Hermes Books (New Haven and London 1989) 62f; John Henderson, 'Suck It and See (Horace, *Epode* 8)', in Michael Whitby, Philip Hardie, Mary Whitby, eds., *Homo Viator: Classical Essays for John Bramble* (Bristol 1987) 105–18; Amy Richlin, *The Garden of Priapus: Sexuality and Aggression in Roman Humor* (New Haven and London 1983) 109ff. I am particularly indebted to Duncan Kennedy who provided me with material for my discussion of the *Epodes*.
8 Eduard Fraenkel, *Horace* (Oxford 1957) 57.
9 See Gordon Williams, *Horace*, Greece and Rome: New Surveys in the Classics No. 6 (Oxford 1972) 6.
10 See A. D. Nuttall, 'Fishes in the Trees', *Essays in Criticism* 24 (1974) 20–38 (reprinted in *The Stoic in Love: Selected Essays on Literature and Ideas* (New York and London 1989) 68–81).
11 Christopher Ricks, ed., *A. E. Housman: Collected Poems and Selected Prose* (London 1988) 307. Housman may, however, be wrong on the particular textual point: cf. Tibullus 1.4.18 *longa dies molli saxa peredit aqua*; *Odes* 1.11.5 (*hiems*) *oppositis debilitat pumicibus mare* (I owe these parallels to Niall Rudd).
12 This formulation combines elements from Derrida, Gadamer and Jauss. For J. Derrida e.g. *Dissemination*, trs. B. Johnson (London 1981); for H.-G. Gadamer, *Truth and Method*, trs. G. Barden and J. Cumming (London 1975); for H. J. Jauss, *Towards an Aesthetic of Reception*, trs. T. Bahti (Brighton 1982), chapters 1 and 2. I hope to defend this view in detail in my forthcoming book, *Redeeming the Text: Latin Poetry and the Hermeneutics of Reception* (Cambridge).
13 See Donald F. Bond, ed. *The Spectator*, 5 vols. (Oxford 1965) vol. 4, 139. The motto for the essay is inevitably *Odes* 2.10.5–8.
14 For information and iconography, I am grateful to my colleague Michael Liversidge. For Bentley's Horace see C. O. Brink, *English Classical Scholarship: Historical Reflections on Bentley, Porson, and Housman* (Cambridge and New York 1986), chapters 2–4.
15 Niall Rudd, *The Satires of Horace and Persius*, Penguin Classics (Harmondsworth 1973) 32, headnote to translation.
16 See Reuben A. Brower, *Alexander Pope: the Poetry of Allusion* (Oxford 1959) 293.
17 For this poem see Frank Stack's outstanding study *Pope and Horace: Studies in Imitation* (Cambridge 1985) 78ff, especially pp.87f; cf. John G. W. Henderson, 'Not "Women in Roman Satire" but "When Satire Writes Woman"', in Susan H. Braund, ed., *Satire and Society in Ancient Rome*, Exeter Studies in History 23 (Exeter 1989) 89–125; 'Satire writes "woman": Gendersong', *Proceedings of the Cambridge Philological Society* 215 NS 35 (1989) 50–80; Leo C. Curran, 'Nature, Convention and Obscenity in Horace, Satires 1.2', *Arion* 9 (1970) 220–45 (241–5).
18 Bond, *The Spectator*, vol. 5, 113.
19 The quotations are from Terry Eagleton, *The Function of Criticism: from The Spectator to Post-Structuralism* (London 1984), chapter 1: 11, 14, 18f, 21.

cf. 20: 'The critic as *flâneur* or *bricoleur*, rambling and idling among diverse social landscapes where he is everywhere at home, is still the critic as judge; but such judgement should not be mistaken for the censorious verdicts of an Olympian authority.'
20 C. S. Lewis, 'Addison', in Walter Hooper, ed., *C. S. Lewis: Selected Literary Essays* (Cambridge 1969) 154–68 (168).
21 See Caroline Goad, *Horace in the English Literature of the Eighteenth Century* (New York 1967, first published 1918) 562, with further instances; for melancholy cf. e.g. the Homeric image of men as leaves in *Ars* 60ff.
22 e.g. by Cowley, *Essays*, ed. J. Rawson Lumby, revised Arthur Tilley (Cambridge 1938) 44: 'There was never ... such an example as this in the world, that he should have so much moderation and courage as to refuse an offer of such greatness ... '
23 cf. Nicholas Mann, *Petrarch*, Past Masters (Oxford, New York 1984) chapter 6 ('The Life as Work of Art').
24 Fraenkel, *Horace*, 260 and index; cf. Ronald Syme, *History in Ovid* (Oxford 1978) 173f.
25 Fraenkel, *Horace*, 15–16.
26 Ronald Syme, *The Roman Revolution* (Oxford 1939) 452.
27 Fraenkel, *Horace*, 21; the subsequent quotation is from pp. 417f. Similarly Fraenkel will entertain no possibility of irony in Maecenas' request to Augustus in his will *Horati Flacci ut mei esto memor* ('The full worth of Maecenas appears in the clause ... which admits of no comment'); 17.
28 David Amstrong, '*Horatius Eques et Scriba*: Satires 1.6 and 2.7', *TAPA* 116 (1986) 255–88 (267, 275, 277, 279, 285).
29 I. M. leM. Du Quesnay, 'Horace and Maecenas: the Propaganda Value of *Sermones* 1', in Tony Woodman and David West, eds., *Poetry and Politics in the Age of Augustus* (Cambridge 1984) 19–58 (19).
30 See Stack, *Pope and Horace*, xv, 16f, 265–74 (168 for Seneca quotation).
31 See R. G. M. Nisbet and M. Hubbard, *A Commentary on Horace: Odes Book One* (Oxford 1970) 376ff (for Johnson p. 377).
32 Gordon Williams, *The Third Book of Horace's Odes* (Oxford 1969) 76.
33 My account of Derrida owes most to Bernard Harrison: 'Deconstructing Derrida', *Comparative Criticism* 7 (1985) 3–24, and chapters from his recent book which he kindly showed me in advance of publication: *Inconvenient Fictions: Literature and the Limits of Theory* (New Haven and London, 1991). For a sensible introduction see Christopher Norris, *Derrida*, Fontana Modern Masters (London 1987) with bibliography. Whether my reading of Derrida is regarded as 'convincing' or not does not affect the argument itself.
34 See Howard D. Weinbrot, 'Masked Men and Satire and Pope: Towards an Historical Basis for the Eighteenth-Century Persona', in *Eighteenth-Century Satire: Essays on Text and Context from Dryden to Peter Pindar* (Cambridge 1988) 34–49.
35 It may not be close. The case of Caelius is instructive. It is hard to reconcile Cicero's attractive, witty correspondent with what we know of his actions from other sources. Hence the paradox that Romans can seem from their

writings more like modern Europeans than what we know of their lifestyle and culture gives us the right to expect. See, on the question of personality, the useful remarks of P. E. Easterling, 'Constructing Character in Greek Tragedy', in Christopher Pelling, ed., *Characterization and Individuality in Greek Literature* (Oxford 1990) 83–99 (especially 88f).
36 cf. D. F. Kennedy, review of Averil Cameron, ed., *History as Text*, *Journal of Roman Studies*, 81 (1991) 176–7. Barthes' position is a shifting one; closer to that adopted here are *A Lover's Discourse* and *Roland Barthes by Roland Barthes*.
37 See Harrison, 'Deconstructing Derrida', 21.
38 Stack, *Pope and Horace*, 280.
39 Goad, *Horace in the English Literature of the Eighteenth Century*, 564.
40 See Howard D. Weinbrot, *Augustus Caesar in 'Augustan' England: the Decline of a Classical Norm* (Princeton, 1978) especially 120ff, with many further illustrations (for Wicksted, 126; for Dryden, 129).
41 See Stack, *Pope and Horace*, 225–7.
42 James Boswell, *Life of Johnson*, 3 vols. (London 1912) III, 199 (the conversation occurred in 1781).
43 Quoted by Daniel M. Hooley, *The Classics in Paraphrase: Ezra Pound and Modern Translators of Latin Poetry* (London and Toronto 1988) 16, from Ronald A. Knox, *Let Dons Delight* (London 1939) 264f. The speaker is an economics lecturer.
44 R. G. M. Nisbet, 'Horace's *Epodes* and History', in Woodman and West, *Poetry and Politics*, 9. For this whole section I owe much to the writings of Duncan Kennedy, especially his review of Woodman and West, *Liverpool Classical Monthly* 9, no. 10 (December 1984) 157–60; '"Augustan" and "Anti-Augustan": Reflections on Terms of Reference', in A. Powell, ed., *Roman Poetry and Propaganda in the Age of Augustus* (Bristol, 1992).
45 Syme, *Roman Revolution*, 299, 461.
46 They are gathered in *Colin Macleod: Collected Essays* (Oxford 1983) chapters 23–5.
47 For some meanings of *otium* see R. G. M. Nisbet and M. Hubbard, *A Commentary on Horace Odes Book 2* (Oxford 1978), introduction to *Otium divos* 252ff.
48 Eagleton, *The Function of Criticism*, 10–11, 15.
49 Cowley, *Essays*, 36.
50 Paul Zanker, *The Power of Images in the Age of Augustus*, trs. Alan Shapiro (Ann Arbor 1988) 31. Such certainty, however, is scarcely warranted, and Zanker too readily accepts the assumptions of Roman moral discourse.
51 Quoted in *Arion* 1970, 132.
52 Walter Benjamin, *Illuminations*, trs. H. Zohn, (London 1968) 258.
53 Quoted in *Arion* 1970, 128.
54 Quoted from J. V. Cunningham, *The Quest of the Opal*, in *Arion* 1970, 176.
55 Dryden, *Preface to Sylvae*, in George Watson, ed., *John Dryden: of Dramatic Poesy and other Critical Essays*, 2 vols. (London and New York 1962) II.31.

56 T. S. Eliot, 'Andrew Marvell', in Kermode, ed., *Selected Prose of T. S. Eliot* (quotations from 162f, 164f, 170).
57 Gordon Williams, *Tradition and Originality in Roman Poetry* (Oxford 1968) 57, 673f (for his discussion of the *Ode*, 148–52); see also William Fitzgerald, 'Horace, Pleasure and the Text', *Arethusa* 22 (1989) 81–103; Ralph Hexter, '*O Fons Bandusiae*: Blood and Water in Horace, *Odes* 3.13', in Whitby, ed., *Homo Viator*, 131–9.
58 A. Y. Campbell, *Horace: a New Interpretation* (London 1924) 2; David West, *Reading Horace* (Edinburgh 1967) 129–30.
59 Dryden's translation of Horace, *Odes* 3.29, 49–52.

2 HORACE AT HOME AND ABROAD: WYATT AND SIXTEENTH-CENTURY HORATIANISM

1 *Inferno* 4.89
2 Thomas Drant, *A Medicinable Morall* (London 1566) sig. a4^a.
3 Niall Rudd, *The Satires of Horace* (Cambridge 1966) 195.
4 See D. R. Shackleton Bailey, *Profile of Horace* (London 1982) 15.
5 Rudd, in *The Cambridge History of Classical Literature: Latin Literature*, eds. E. J. Kenney and W. V. Clausen (Cambridge 1982) 391 cites *S* 2.7.28–9 and *Ep.* 1.8.12 to show Horace's sense that people should not be monolithic. See also Rudd, *The Satires of Horace* 201.
6 Abraham Cowley, *The Essays and other Prose Writings* ed. A. B. Gough (Oxford 1915) 160. David Hopkins' essay in this volume brings out another side of Cowley's Horace.
7 Bailey's *cornicula*, crow, is a more probable inhabitant for a grain store, but I have retained the reading of sixteenth-century texts.
8 *The Satires: a Renaissance Autobiography* ed. Peter de Sa Wiggins (Athens, Ohio 1976) 247–65.
9 R. S. Kilpatrick, *The Poetry of Friendship: Horace Epistles I* (Edmonton 1986) 11–12 explores the legal overtones of the phrase and argues that it may not mean 'I give it all back', but 'I rebut any connection between myself and the fox.'
10 *Q Horatii Flacci . . . opera cum commentariis Acronis* (Basle 1527) [henceforth 'Acron'] 720, 'dicens malle sibi omnia recipi a Mecenate quam tam gravi servitio cogi'; 'saying he would rather give everything back to Maecenas than be compelled to such a harsh servitude'.
11 Acron 601; cf. *Q. Horatii Flacci opera cum commentariis . . . Mancinelli et . . . Ascensii* (Paris 1511) [henceforth 'Ascensius'] fol 1^b.
12 *Ep.* 1.10.6–7: 'tu nidum servas, ego laudo ruris amoeni / rivos et musco circumlita saxa nemusque'.
13 Drant, *A Medicinable Morall* sigs. C3^b–D3^a.
14 Wiggins, *The Satires* xv, notes that *Regrets* 150 imitates Ariosto's Satire 1.12.
15 *Reliquiae Wottonianae* (London 1651) 530–40. The Wottons were family

friends of the Wyatts, *ibid.*, fol. b6^b. Wotton's 'The Character of a Happy Life' was copied by Ben Jonson and Robert Herrick, see C. F. Main, 'Wotton's the Character of a Happy Life', *The Library* Series 5, 10 (1955) 270–4, and Norman K. Fowler, 'Poems from a Seventeenth Century MS with the Hand of Robert Herrick', *Texas Quarterly* 16 (1973), Supplement 51.

16 *Life and Letters of Sir Thomas Wyatt* ed. K. Muir (Liverpool 1963) 44, 117, 135. For the role of diplomacy in Wyatt, see my review 'An Augustan Wyatt', *English* 36 (1987) 148–58.

17 For Alamanni's admiration of Ariosto, see Satire III in *Opere toscane* (Florence 1532) 370, and Piero Floriani, 'Sulle *Satire* di Luigi Alamanni', *Giornale storico della letteratura italiana* 161 (1984) 30–59.

18 See H. Hauvette, *Un exilé florentin à la cour de France au XI siècle, Luigi Alamanni (1495–1556)* (Paris 1903).

19 *Opere toscane* 400.

20 *Ibid.* 402.

21 All quotations from Sir Thomas Wyatt, *The Complete Poems* ed. R. A. Rebholz (Harmondsworth 1978).

22 Acron 601; *Q. Horatii Flacci Odarum libri . . . sermonum libri duo. Epistolarum totidem . . . Joanne Britan, Brixi interprete* (Venice 1520) fol. 139^a.

23 See G. R. Elton, *The Tudor Constitution* 2nd end (Cambridge 1960, 1982) 59–87. On the influence of the Treason Act on Tudor literature see my review of Alistair Fox, *Poetry and Politics in the Reigns of Henry* VII *and Henry* VIII, *Essays in Criticism* 41 (1991) 51–61.

24 *Policy and Police: the Enforcement of the Reformation in the Age of Thomas Cromwell* (Cambridge 1972) 263–326.

25 *Opere toscane* 392. cf. Ariosto 3.70ff; 7.124ff.

26 cf. the list of diplomatic goals opposed to the static delights of home in Ariosto, Satire 3.55–7: 'Chi vuole andare a torno, a torno vade: / vegga Inghelterra, Ongheria, Francia e Spagna; / a me piace abitar la mia contrada.' (Whoever wants to range around, let him range: let him see England, Hungary, France and Spain; for me it's enough to dwell in my native land).

27 See Ascensius fol. 69^b; Acron 731.

28 *Letters and Papers Foreign and Domestic of the Reign of Henry* VIII eds. J. Gairdness and R. H. Brodie (London 1896), vol. IX, Item 182, 55–7; Item 405, 133; vol. XV, Item 629, p. 303. This may have been a member of the Gloucestershire branch of the family. On the several John Pointzes of the period, see J. Maclean, *Historical and Genealogical Memoir of the Family of Poyntz* (Exeter 1886) 33, 113.

29 H. A. Mason, *Sir Thomas Wyatt: a Literary Portrait* (Bristol, 1986) 297–308.

30 Muir, *Life and Letters* 198.

31 See, e.g., Mason, *Sir Thomas Wyatt* 308.

32 Ascensius fol.1^b.

33 See, e.g., 'laetus sorte tua vives sapienter, Aristi', *Ep.* 1.10.44; 'quod satis est cui contingit, nihil amplius optet' *Ep.* 1.2.46.

34 Acron claims that Horace is trying to persuade Bullatius, who refuses to leave

home since he likes the Tiber so much, to go abroad, Acron, 724–5, which prompted a vigorous response from Ascensius fol. 65a. This may have drawn Wyatt's eye to the epistle; but since the poem describes the psychological effects of shuttle diplomacy, it would have certainly meant something to him.
35 *The Satires of Horace* 240.
36 Most notably Roger Ascham, *English Works* ed. W. A. Wright (Cambridge 1904) 224–9. See also Du Bellay, *Les regrets* 31.
37 For the circumstances which produced the satire, see the excellent article by David Starkey, 'The Court: Castiglione's Ideal and Tudor Reality: Being a Discussion of Sir Thomas Wyatt's Satire Addressed to Sir Francis Brian' *Journal of the Warburg and Courtauld Institutes* 45 (1982) 232–9.
38 *Life and Letters* 86; *Letters and Papers Foreign and Domestic* XIII pt.1, Item 924, p.384; Garrett Mattingly, *Renaissance Diplomacy* (London 1955) 272–4.
39 Muir, *Life and Letters* 135.
40 Ibid. 139.
41 *Reliquiae Wottonianae* fol. c2^a.
42 *Letters and Papers Foreign and Domestic* XIII, pt.1, Item 117, p. 41.
43 Rebholz, *The Complete Poems* 450.
44 Sir John Harington, *Letters and Epigrams* ed. N. E. McClure (Philadelphia 1930) 121, 255.
45 *Arundel Harington MS of Tudor Poetry*, ed. R. Hughey, 2 vols. (Columbus, Ohio 1960) 173, l.27; cf. Egerton MS 'She fedeth on boyled bacon, meet and roost.'

3 THE BEST MASTER OF VIRTUE AND WISDOM: THE HORACE OF BEN JONSON AND HIS HEIRS

1 Horace seems to make the political situation deliberately vague, see Gordon Williams, ed., *The Third Book of Horace's Odes* (Oxford 1969) 42.
2 Line references to Jonson's plays and to *Discoveries* are to C. H. Herford, Percy and Evelyn Simpson, eds., *Ben Jonson* (corrected edn Oxford 1954–63) xi v.
3 There are translations and imitations by William Hammond, Archbishop Sancroft, William Cartwright, Robert Farley, George Daniel, William Habington, Mildmay Fane, Henry More, Milton, Waller, Cowley and Thomas Flatman. References may be found in my unpublished Oxford D. Phil. thesis 'The Response to Horace in the Seventeenth Century' (1977) 214–5, 398, which contains fuller documentation on many of the points raised in this essay. I should like to record here my gratitude to my supervisor, Miss M. E. Hubbard, for her many suggestions and corrections, when my thesis was being written.
4 Storm imagery carries the resonance of Boethius' and others' use of the metaphor of the storm of Fortune, see J. F. Danby, *Elizabethan and Jacobean Poets* (London 1965) 81f, and Emrys Jones, *The Origins of Shakespeare*

(Oxford 1977) 209–10. On the storm of Civil War, see Earl Miner, *The Cavalier Mode from Jonson to Cotton* (Princeton 1971) 178–9 and *passim*.

5 There are perhaps reminiscences of *Odes* 2.3.1–4 and 4.9.34–44 here as well. Croke died in 1641. The poem was not printed in Denham's lifetime; Denham's modern editor, Theodore Howard Banks, *The Poetical Works of Sir John Denham* (2nd edn, 1969), does not say much about manuscript circulation, but presumably Marvell could have seen the poem in manuscript as it was certainly written before his own.

6 Marvell's attitude to Cromwell in the 'Horatian Ode' has, of course, been hotly debated; that he supported Cromwell by the time of 'The First Anniversary' is not in dispute. For my own view that Marvell turned to Horace to present a complex view of Cromwell in the Ode by imitating both the impartiality of the Cleopatra Ode in discussing past events and the controlled enthusiasm of the later Odes to Augustus in discussing future glories, see Martindale, 'Response to Horace', 300–12. In a recent contribution to the debate David Norbrook, 'Marvell's "Horatian Ode" and the politics of genre', in Thomas Healy and Jonathan Sawday, eds., *Literature and the English Civil War* (Cambridge 1990) 147–69, argues that the poem is a pro-Republican answer to Horace.

7 J. M. Wallace, 'Marvell's "lusty Mate" and the Ship of the Commonwealth', *Modern Language Notes* 76 (1961) 106–10.

8 See further Barbara Everett, 'The Shooting of the Bears', in R. L. Brett, ed., *Andrew Marvell: Essays on the Tercentenary of his Death* (Oxford 1979) 65–6, and Howard Erskine-Hill, *The Augustan Idea in English Literature* (London 1983) 189–95. I share their view that 'Tom May's Death' is by Marvell; though this is questioned in G. deF. Lord's edition, *Complete Poetry* (New York 1968), xxxi-ii.

9 Thomas Creech, trans., *T. Lucretius Carus the Epicurean Philosopher* (1682) b3v: Thomas Otway, 'Epistle to R. D. [Richard Duke] from T. O.', lines 57–64. See further Martindale, 'Response to Horace' 357–61.

10 This is the approach of Katharine Eisaman Maus, *Ben Jonson and the Roman Frame of Mind* (Princeton 1984).

11 This aspect of Ben Jonson has been amply illustrated in Richard S. Peterson's *Imitation and Praise in the Poems of Ben Jonson* (New Haven 1981).

12 Martindale, 'Response to Horace', 121–2; Erskine-Hill, *Augustan Idea*, 169.

13 In 'The Purpose and Technique of Jonson's *Poetaster*', *Studies in Philology* 42 (1945) 225–52.

14 The phrase is Niall Rudd's, *The Satires of Horace* (Cambridge 1966) 128. See further his discussion, 124–31, on *Sermones* 2.1. and J. K. Newman, *Augustus and the New Poetry* (Brussels 1967) 282–98.

15 See *Discoveries* 2434–2443, which adapts *Art of Poetry* 440–1. See also 'To the Memory of Mr William Shakespeare' 58–62, and Peterson's discussion of Horatian motifs in the poem, *Imitation and Praise* 158–94.

16 See David Riggs, *Ben Jonson: a Life* (Cambridge, Mass., 1989) 80–4. His whole discussion of the poets' quarrel is useful, 72–84.

17 Line references for *Satiromastix* are to Fredson Bowers, ed., *The Dramatic Works of Thomas Dekker*, vol. 1 (Cambridge 1953).
18 Another Horatian source is *Odes* 3.29.57–64. Other classical sources for this passage are discussed by Peterson, *Imitation and Praise* 112–57. On the importance of the Stoic figure for Ben Jonson, see Thomas Greene, 'Ben Jonson and the Centered Self', *Studies in English Literature* 10 (1970) 325–48; Isabel Rivers, *The Poetry of Conservatism* (Cambridge 1973) 26–33.
19 But see Horace's old woman poems, *Odes* 1.25 and 4.13 for a more savage tone, which might have appealed to Jonson.
20 See Wesley Trimpi, *Ben Jonson's Poems: a Study of the Plain Style* (Stanford 1962) 153–7, 213.
21 B. Partenio, in the commentary owned by Ben Jonson, explains Horace's scheme as the preferability of genius to wealth and notes how he elaborates it with concrete details, *Bernardini Parthenii Spilimbergii in Q. Horatii Flacci Carmina atque Epodos Commentarii* (Venice 1584) 94, 95v. After Jonson, the rejection of rich furnishings was taken up by a number of poets, e.g. Herrick, 'A Panegyric to Sir Lewis Pemberton', Carew, 'To my Friend G. N. from Wrest', Mildmay Fane, 'My Happy Life, to a Friend', George Daniel, 'A Pastoral Ode'.
22 For associations between Augustus and the heroes, see *Odes* 1.12.25–33, 3.14.1–4; *Epistles* 2.1.5–17; *Aeneid* 6.791–805. On the *doctor ineptus* figure, see W. S. Anderson, 'The Roman Socrates: Horace and his Satires', in J. P. Sullivan, ed., *Critical Essays on Roman Literature: Satire* (London 1963) 29–37. For mockery of the *sapiens*, see *S* 1.3.120–42; *Ep.* 1.1.106–8. For pictures of personal poise, see e.g. *Odes* 2.16.37–40; *S* 1.6.110–31; *Ep.* 1.18.104–12. Rudd, *Satires of Horace* 199–201, thinks that Horace admired Stoic consistency but found his personal ideal in controlled variety; M. J. McGann, *Studies in Horace's First Book of Epistles* (Brussels 1969) 72–3, thinks that Horace admired adaptability; Steele Commager, *The Odes of Horace* (Bloomington 1967) 255–306, thinks that Horace particularly admired the ability to change.
23 *Poetry and Politics in the English Renaissance* (London 1984) 187. Norbrook seems to me to be distorting the meaning of the passage in *Discoveries* which he paraphrases here. The context (lines 2578–98) shows that the judgement being talked about is *literary*, not moral: Horace is a good literary critic because he is a practitioner. There could well be a source in Daniel Heinsius, from whom the surrounding context is translated. The phrase 'best master both of virtue and wisdom' comes from 'To the Reader' in Heinsius' 1612 edition of Horace. In answer to Norbrook, we may also note that in his imitation of *Epode* 2 in 'To Sir Robert Wroth', Jonson omits the trick conclusion.
24 I find a more attractive political reading of Jonson's poems that of Annabel Patterson, *Censorship and Interpretation* (Madison 1984) 120–44, where she argues that the *Underwood* sets out to the attentive reader the tensions between the poet and his environment, his private self and his public

relations, in 'a voice that whispered of careerism, of the limits of idealism, of necessity, of the impossibility of independence'; or Rivers, *Poetry of Conservatism* on tensions between private and public in Jonson 21–71.

25 *Augustan Idea* 118–19, and see also 169–70. Jonson often echoes *Odes* 4.8 and 9 on the immortalizing power of poetry, e.g. in 'Epistle to Elizabeth Countess of Rutland' (*Forest* 12), 41–63.

26 See further Martindale, 'Response to Horace' 151–4. Herford and Simpson, 1.254 thought that the underlinings in Partenio's edition were by Jonson; David MacPherson, 'Ben Jonson's Library and Marginalia: an Annotated Catalogue', *Studies in Philology* 71(5) (1974) 10–11, 53–4, is more sceptical, and notes that there are some marginalia probably not by Ben Jonson. In a lecture delivered to the Oxford Bibliographical Society entitled 'Ben Jonson's Library Revisited' H. R. Woudhuysen agreed with MacPherson. I am grateful to Dr Woudhuysen for directing me to the Magdalene Horace.

27 Partenio, *Commentarii* 138.

28 Partenio constantly stresses this feature of Horace in his commentary, see e.g. on *Odes* 2.18, where he says that Horace's method of detailing the forms of wealth is special to good poets, 94. See also Cowley on the difference between modern poetry and Pindar: 'The old fashion of writing was like disputing in enthymemes, where half is left out to be supplied by the hearer; ours is like syllogisms, where all that is meant it expressed', first note to his translation of Isaiah 34 in *Pindaric Odes*. On Marvell's imitation of this feature of Horace's style in the 'Horatian Ode', see Everett, 'Shooting of the Bears' 78–80.

29 '*Iapeti genus*', the son of Iapetus, i.e. Prometheus. The identification of Iapetus and Japhet seems to have been common in the Renaissance; there is a chapter on it in an appendix to Conti's *Mythologiae* (Lyons 1653), quoted by John Carey and Alastair Fowler, eds., *The Poems of John Milton* (London 1968) 655–6.

30 Alastair Fowler, *Conceitful Thought* (Edinburgh 1975) 134.

31 In a classic discussion, L. C. Knights in *Drama and Society in the Age of Jonson* (London 1937) 193–8 compared 'the quiet recognition of the inevitable' in this passage with Horace and contrasted the sentimentalities of Landor.

32 Thomas M. Greene, *The Light in Troy* (New Haven 1982) 273.

33 285, 278–84. On Jonson's classicism, see also George Parfitt, *Ben Jonson: Public Poet and Private Man* (London 1976) chapter 6; Robert B. Pierce, 'Ben Jonson's Horace and Horace's Ben Jonson', *Studies in Philology* 78 (1981) 20–31.

34 On the *neque iam* motif see Partenio's commentary, 12v.

35 J. B. Leishman, *The Art of Marvell's Poetry* (2nd edn London 1968) 273–7 describes this linguistic tradition. It often colours translations of Horace's *Odes*: Soracte for example gains a 'periwig' of snow in Sherburne's translation of *Odes* 1.9. See further Martindale, 'The Response to Horace' 49–51.

36 It seems worth emphasizing this point, as commentators seem to think that the imitation of 2.10 does not begin until line 29 (see e.g. Miner, *Cavalier*

Mode 121). If we do not see the relation of the first twenty-eight lines to stanza one of Horace's *Ode*, we may miss, as Miner does, the irony of lines 5–15.
37 R. G. M. Nisbet and Margaret Hubbard, *A Commentary on Horace: Odes Book 2* (Oxford 1978) 151–7.
38 For the rejection of politics in Horace's symposiac *Odes*, see e.g. *Odes* 2.11.1–4; 3.29.25–33.
39 For comments on this poem, see Miner, *Cavalier Mode* 299–300; James D. Simmonds, *Masques of God: Form and Theme in the Poetry of Henry Vaughan* (Pittsburgh 1972) 122–6; Jonathan Post, *Henry Vaughan: the Unfolding Vision* (Princeton 1982) 51–6. The two latter in emphasizing the bitterness of Vaughan's satire seem rather to forget the strong satire of Jonson.
40 *Augustan Idea* 169–74. See also Stuart Gillespie, *The Poets on the Classics: an Anthology* (London 1988) 116–18. Earlier, Earl Miner's *Cavalier Mode* gave full recognition to the importance of Horace for the Cavalier poets. Another factor which helps to obscure the frequency of imitation of Horace by poets of this period is that they are free in their approach to genre, imitating ode in epistle and *vice versa* and using a variety of metres.
41 For Dryden's Horatian old age, see e.g. the conclusion of Theseus' speech in Dryden's translation of Chaucer's 'The Knight's Tale', where Boethius is turned into Horace, or 'Epistle To my Honoured Kinsman, John Dryden of Chesterton'; Rachel Trickett, *The Honest Muse: a Study in Augustan Verse* (Oxford 1967) 76–9. On Cowley's Horatianism in the *Essays in Prose and Verse* and his later imitators, who include Charles Cotton, John Norris, Katherine Philips, Anne Finch and Lady Mary Chudleigh, see Martindale, 'Response to Horace' 313–40, 370–83 and David Hopkins in this volume.
42 Miner, *Cavalier Mode* 285–6 saw this poem as a Horatian ode.
43 On the *Anacreontea* and Cowley's translation of 'The Grasshopper', see Tom Mason, 'Abraham Cowley and the Wisdom of Anacreon', *Cambridge Quarterly* 19 (1990) 103–37.
44 *Mathiae Casimiri Sarbievii e soc Iesu Lyricorum Libri* IV (Antwerp 1632) 178.
45 Miner, *Cavalier Mode* 287–8.
46 Compare *Odes* 2.2.9–12, 3.16.25–8, 39–44; *Epistles* 1.10.32–3.
47 *Art of Marvell's Poetry* 188. For the mixture of prose and lyricism in the *Odes*, see J. K. Newman, *Augustus and the New Poetry* 314, 437–54.
48 J. B. Leishman, *Themes and Variations in Shakespeare's Sonnets* (2nd edn London 1963) 95–101 distinguishes between *carpe florem* and *carpe diem*. 'De Rosis Nascentibus', sometimes attributed to Ausonius, is a poem from the Virgilian appendix. For Lucretius, see *De Rerum Natura* 3.931–51; 2.1–61. On the parallels between *carpe diem* and Epicurus and the Sermon on the Mount, see R. G. M. Nisbet and Margaret Hubbard, *A Commentary on Horace: Odes Book 1* (Oxford 1970) 142. On Epicurus in the seventeenth century, see T. F. Mayo, *Epicurus in England (1650–1725)* (Dallas 1934); Martindale, 'Response to Horace' 254–7; David Hopkins in this volume.
49 From *The Odes and Satires of Horace that have been done into English by*

the Most Eminent Hands, published by Jacob Tonson (1715). The pseudo-Rochester translation of 1.4 will also be found in this volume.

50 e.g. Roger B. Rollin and J. Max Patrick, eds., *'Trust to Good Verses': Herrick Tercentenary Essays* (Pittsburgh 1978); Alastair Fowler, 'Robert Herrick', *Proceedings of the British Academy* 66 (1980) 243–64; Ann Baynes Coiro, *Robert Herrick's 'Hesperides' and the Epigram Book Tradition* (Baltimore 1988).

51 I assume the priority of Jonson's poem though the precise dating of either is not known: 'Sir Robert Wroth' was not published until 1616; 'A Country Life' is said by L. C. Martin to be datable to c.1610.

52 Here Herrick combines S 2.7 with *Odes* 2.3.1–2 'thy equal thoughts', as well as imagery from Cicero, Aristotle and Virgil: see Martindale 'Response to Horace' 193–4.

53 Not elegiacs, *pace* Miner, *Cavalier Mode*, 276; see J. C. Maxwell, *Notes and Queries*, NS 8 (1961) 309. The iambic distich is an iambic metre, consisting of an iambic trimeter followed by an iambic dimeter; elegiacs consist of a hexameter followed by a pentameter. The connotations of the metres are different. Jonson and Herrick are writing not love-elegy, but moral poems in the manner of *Epode* 2.

54 e.g. Miner, *Cavalier Mode* 278.

55 Lines 1–4 are from *Odes* 2.14.1–4; lines 7–8 are from *Odes* 1.28.19–20; lines 9–12 are from *Odes* 2.14.21–4; lines 13–14 are a variation of *Odes* 2.16.25–6; 'our holiday' of line 16 recalls the *dies festos* of *Odes* 2.3.6–7; lines 18–20 recall *Odes* 4.7.13; lines 25–7 are from *Odes* 4.7.14–15; line 30 combines *Odes* 1.4.16 and 4.7.16.

56 e.g. 'Upon Prudence Baldwin her Sickness', 'To his Maid Prue', 'Upon Prue his Maid', 'Upon his Spaniel Tracy'.

57 Vegetarian diet, e.g. *Odes* 1.31.15–16; *Epod.* 2.45–60; S 1.6.111–8, 2.6.63–76, 83–9; sleep *Odes* 2.16.15–16, 3.1.17–24; *Epod.* 2.23–8; *Ep.* 1.10.18; rack-renting *Odes* 2.18.23–8.

58 For examples of the pose of small man, see also 'Lar's Portion and the Poet's Part' and 'A Hymn to the Lares'. On Herrick's 'exquisite diminution', see Fowler, 'Robert Herrick' 245–6; *Kinds of Literature* (Oxford 1982) 197–8.

59 Geoffrey Walton in *From Donne to Marvell*, ed. Boris Ford, rev. edn (Harmondsworth 1982) 210.

60 See also the article by John L. Kimmey, 'Robert Herrick's Persona', *Studies in Philology* 67 (1970) 221–36. Coiro ignores the non-urban unsatiric Horatian country-house side of Martial, seen in e.g. *Epigrams* 3.58.

61 J. Max Patrick, ed., *The Complete Poetry of Robert Herrick* (New York 1968).

62 *The Classics and English Renaissance Poetry: Three Case Studies* (New Haven 1978).

4 MARVELL AND HORACE: COLOUR AND TRANSLUCENCY

All translations, unless otherwise specified, are my own.
1 All quotations from Marvell are taken from *The Poems and Letters of Andrew Marvell*, ed. H. M. Margoliouth, 3rd edn revised by Pierre Legouis with the collaboration of E. E. Duncan-Jones, 2 vols. (Oxford 1971).
2 'Andrew Marvell: *An Horatian Ode Upon Cromwell's Return from Ireland*: the Thread of the Poem and its Use of Classical Allusion', *Critical Quarterly*, 11 (1969) 325–41. Reprinted in Arthur Pollard, ed., *Marvell: Poems: a Casebook* (London 1980) 176–98.
3 'Ovid Immoralised: the Method of Wit in Marvell's "The Garden"', in my *The Stoic in Love* (Brighton 1989) 90–9, esp. p. 97.
4 *Q. Horatius Flaccus*, ed. Gaspar Orellius, 3rd edn, curavit Georgius Baiterus, 2 vols. (Zurich 1850–2) 1.579.
5 Both Wickham and Commager have defended the conflation of the two Scipios. See E. C. Wickham, ed., *Quinti Horati Flacci Opera Omnia*, 2 vols. (Oxford 1896) 1.314, and Steele Commager, *The Odes of Horace: a Critical Study* (New Haven and London 1962) 319.
6 Orellius, *Q. Horatius Flaccus*, 582.
7 *A Diversity of Creatures* (London 1917) 249.
8 In her 1977 Oxford D. Phil. thesis 'The Response to Horace in the Seventeenth Century (with Special Reference to the Period 1600–1660)'. This admirable work, most oddly, has not been published.
9 Exceptions are Blair Worden, 'Andrew Marvell, Oliver Cromwell and An Horatian Ode', in Kevin Sharpe and Steven N. Zwicker, eds. *Politics and Discourse: the Literature of Seventeenth-Century England* (Berkeley 1987), 147–80, and David Norbrook, 'Marvell's "Horatian Ode" and the Politics of Genre', in Thomas Healey and Jonathan Sawday, eds., *Literature and the English Civil War* (Cambridge 1990), 147–69.
10 'Marvell's "Horatian Ode"' 149–52, 154.
11 'Andrew Marvell', in *The Force of Poetry* (Oxford 1984) 40. This essay first appeared in C. A. Patrides, ed., *Approaches to Marvell: the York Centenary Lectures* (London 1978).
12 *Devotions upon Several Occasions*, ed. John Sparrow (Cambridge 1923) 11. My attention was drawn to this passage by Nigel Smith.
13 Cited by Kitty Scoular Datta (following Ruth Wallerstein and Christopher Hill) in her 'New Light on Marvell's "A Dialogue between the Soul and the Body"' *Renaissance Quarterly*, 22 (1969) 242–55, esp. 243.
14 'Marvell's Horatian Ode', *Review of English Studies*, NS 12 (1961) 150–72.
15 Taken from the Oxford Text, *Cornelii Taciti Annalium ab excessu divi Augusti Libri*, ed. C. D. Fisher (Oxford 1906).
16 The Oxford Text, *Cornelii Taciti Historiarum Libri*, ed. C. D. Fisher (Oxford 1911).
17 *The Odes of Horace. Translated by James Michie* (Harmondsworth 1964) 14.

18 *Ovid: Metamorphoses*, with an English translation by Frank Justus Miller, 3rd edn revised by G. P. Goold, 2 vols. (London 1977) 1.3.
19 Compare the analogous idiom with *volo*, 'I wish' in Plautine comedy, *Mostellaria*, 1074, and, in a passage of almost racy reported conversation in Horace, *Epistles*, 1.7.60–1, *dic / ad cenam veniat*, 'Tell him to come to dinner.'
20 13 (5) in *Anacreon*, ed. Bruno Gentili (Rome 1958) 12.
21 Appended to his short story, 'Regulus', in his *A Diversity of Creatures* (London 1917) 239–72.
22 I have followed the (heavily restored) text given as no. 137 in *The Oxford Book of Greek Verse*, ed. Gilbert Murray et al. (Oxford 1931) 170. The poem may be found in its unrestored form in Denys Page, *Sappho and Alcaeus: an Introduction to the Study of Ancient Lesbian Poetry* (Oxford 1955) 300.
23 In *Oxford Book of Greek Verse in Translation*, ed. T. F. Higham and C. M. Bowra (Oxford 1938) 203.
24 See Richard Perceval Graves, *A. E. Housman: the Scholar–Poet* (London and Henley 1979) 171–2.
25 e.g. in his 25th Elegy, 'His Picture'. On this, see John Carey, *John Donne: Life, Mind and Art* (London 1981) 65–6.
26 *W. B. Yeats: The Poems*. ed. Daniel Albright (London 1990) 261–3.
27 *The Poems of Alexander Pope*, ed. John Butt (London 1963) 601.

5 COWLEY'S HORATIAN MICE

1 For statements of such views which have been influential on several generations of students during the post-war period, see G. Walton, *Metaphysical to Augustan : Studies in Tone and Sensibility in the Seventeenth Century* (London 1955) and Patrick Cruttwell, *The Shakespearean Moment and its Place in the Poetry of the Seventeenth Century* (London 1954).
2 For earlier editions of Cowley, see M. R. Perkin, *Abraham Cowley : a Bibliography* (Folkestone 1977); on the history of Cowley's reputation, see A. H. Nethercot, 'The Reputation of Abraham Cowley (1660–1800)', *PMLA* 38 (1923) 588–641, and Jean Loiseau, *Abraham Cowley's Reputation in England* (Paris 1931).
3 The report derives from Milton's widow; see John Milton, *Paradise Lost*, ed. T. Newton, 2 vols. (London 1749) I.lvi.
4 John Dryden, *Of Dramatic Poesy and Other Critical Essays*, ed. G. Watson, 2 vols. (London 1962) I.203.
5 Joseph Spence, *Observations, Anecdotes and Characters of Books and Men*, ed. J. Osborn, 2 vols. (Oxford 1966) I.89; 'The First Epistle of the Second Book of Horace, Imitated' 78.
6 William Cowper, *The Task* 4.729–30.
7 Samuel Johnson, *Lives of the English Poets*, ed. G. B. Hill, 3 vols. (Oxford 1905) I.37.
8 M. L. Peacock, *The Critical Opinions of William Wordsworth* (Baltimore

1950) 311, 233. The new edition of *The Collected Works of Abraham Cowley*, to be published in 6 volumes by the University of Delaware Press (of which volume I appeared in 1989) should help to rekindle an interest in Cowley's work among a new generation of readers.

9 Abraham Cowley, *The Essays and Other Prose Writings*, ed. A. B. Gough (Oxford 1915) 108; a useful general introduction to Cowley's volume is provided by A. H. Nethercot in 'Abraham Cowley's Essays', *Journal of English and Germanic Philology* 29 (1930) 114–30.
10 Cowley, *Essays* 145, 154.
11 See Maren-Sophie Røstvig, *The Happy Man : Studies in the Matamorphosis of a Classical Ideal: vol.* I : *1600–1700*, 2nd edn (Oslo 1962) 41–3.
12 *The Works of Horace, in English Verse, by Mr Duncombe Sen., J. Duncombe, MA, and Other Hands, vol.* III, 2nd edn (London 1767) 197–8.
13 (made more simply celebratory in the English version, since Horace's ironical conclusion is omitted)
14 On Epicurus himself, see C. Bailey, *The Greek Atomists and Epicurus* (Oxford 1928); G. Panichas, *Epicurus* (New York 1967); J. M. Rist, *Epicurus : an Introduction* (Cambridge 1972); on Epicurus' *Nachleben*, see C. T. Harrison, 'The Ancient Atomists and English Literature in the Seventeenth Century', *Harvard Studies in Classical Philology* 45 (1934) 1–79; T. F. Mayo, *Epicurus in England (1650–1725)* (Dallas 1934); R. H. Kargon, *Atomism in England from Hariot to Newton* (Oxford 1966); L. S. Joy, *Gassendi the Atomist* (Cambridge 1987); Howard Jones, *The Epicurean Tradition* (London and New York, 1989); Fred S. and Emily Michael, 'A Note on Gassendi in England', *Notes and Queries* NS 37 (1990) 297–9.
15 See R. P. Jungkuntz, 'Christian Approval of Epicureanism', *Church History* 31 (1962) 279–93 and D. C. Allen, 'The Rehabilitation of Epicurus and his Theory of Pleasure in the Early Renaissance', *Studies in Philology* 41 (1944) 1–15 for partial exceptions to this generalization.
16 See Harrison, 'The Ancient Atomists' 1–19.
17 See L. Sharp, 'Walter Charleton's Early Life, 1620–59, and Relationship to Natural Philosophy in Mid-Seventeenth Century England', *Annals of Science* 30 (1973) 311–40 (317–18).
18 4 vols. 1655–62; the section on the Cyrenaic sect first appeared in vol. II (1656).
19 Thomas Stanley, *The History of Philosophy*, 3rd edn (London 1701) 134.
20 Stanley, *History* 135.
21 Stanley, *History* 134.
22 Stanley, *History* 135.
23 Stanley, *History* 133.
24 Walter Charleton, *Epicurus' Morals, Collected and Faithfully Englished*, ed. F. Manning (London 1926) 15.
25 Charleton, *Epicurus' Morals* 37.
26 Charleton, *Epicurus' Morals* 43.
27 Charelton, *Epicurus' Morals* 48–9.
28 Nethercot ('Abraham Cowley's Essays' 129) suggests that Cowley may have

read Gassendi's work in the original Latin; see also Richard Aldington, 'Cowley and the French Epicureans', *New Statesman*, 5 Nov. 1921 133–4.
29 See, for example, 'The Enjoyment' (in *The Mistress*) and *Essays* 114.
30 An essay significantly addressed to John Evelyn, one of the leading figures in the current English Epicurean revival.
31 Cowley, *Essays* 173.
32 Cowley, *Essays* 120.
33 Cowley, *Essays* 121.
34 Cowley, *Essays* 206.
35 See, for example, *Les œuvres d'Horace: Satires*, ed. P. Lejay (Paris 1911) 536; N. Rudd, *The Satires of Horace* (Cambridge 1966) 250; F. Stack, *Pope and Horace: Studies in Imitation* (Cambridge 1985) 233.
36 See F. Villeneuve, ed., *Horace: Satires* (Paris 1932) 196.
37 See, for example, W. S. Maguiness, 'The Eclecticism of Horace', *Hermathena* 27 (1938) 27–46.
38 See David West, 'Of Mice and Men' in T. Woodman and D. West, eds., *Quality and Pleasure in Latin Poetry* (Cambridge 1974) 67–80 (75).
39 See C. O. Brink, *On Reading a Horatian Satire : an Interpretation of Sermones* II.6 (Sydney 1965); W. S. Anderson, 'The Roman Socrates: Horace and his Satires' in *Critical Essays on Roman Literature : Satire*, ed. J. P. Sullivan (London 1963) 1–37 (36).
40 On the association of Epicureanism and Libertinism after the Restoration, see Mayo, *Epicurus in England* and Dale Underwood, *Etherege and the Comedy of Manners* (New Haven and London 1957) 10–40.
41 'Translation of the Latter Part of the Third Book of Lucretius: Against the Fear of Death' 98.
42 The phrases are Johnson's ('Life of Cowley'); on the *Anacreontea* and their appeal for Cowley, see Tom Mason, 'Cowley and the Wisdom of Anacreon', *Cambridge Quarterly* 19 (1990) 103–37.
43 Other translations of *Sermones* 2.6 cited in this essay are as follows: Thomas Drant, in *Horace, his Art of Poetry, Pistles and Satyrs Englished* (London 1567; facs. rpt. New York 1972) 261–8; Sir John Beaumont in *Bosworth-field* (London 1629) 37–43; Sir Richard Fanshawe in *Selected Parts of Horace* (London 1652) 79–82; Thomas Creech in *The Odes, Satyrs and Epistles of Horace*, 2nd edn (London 1688) 473–8; Alexander Pope and Jonathan Swift, 'An Imitation of the Sixth Satire of the Second Book of Horace' in *The Twickenham Edition of the Poems of Alexander Pope* vol. IV: *Imitations of Horace*, ed. J. Butt, 2nd edn (London 1953) 250–263; William Dunkin in Philip Francis, *The Satires of Horace*, 9th edn (London 1791; first pub. 1746) 236–51; Francis Fawkes (see note 13 above); Christopher Smart in *The Works of Horace*, 4 vols. (London 1767) 3.248–63.
44 In the essay 'Of Myself', Cowley quotes from the retirement poem 'A Vote', first included in *Sylva* (1636), a collection published when he was seventeen or eighteen, and which he says was composed when he 'was but thirteen years old'.

45 See *The Diary of Samuel Pepys* vol. x: *Companion*, ed. R. Latham (London 1983) 144, 147.
46 Pope, 'The First Satire of the Second Book of Horace, Imitated' 128.
47 This poem, nevertheless, seems to have been very popular. The second edition, the first to have survived, is dated 1637, and a 12th edition, dated 1683, is in the Pepys collection at Magdalene College, Cambridge. There appear to be no extant copies of the other ten editions. In *Small Books and Pleasant Histories: Popular Fiction and its Readership in Seventeenth-Century England* (London 1981) 57, Margaret Spufford comments interestingly on the possible appeal for country readers of its extended descriptions of city fare.
48 P. Lejay and David West, for example (see *Satires*, ed. Lejay 525; West, 'Of Mice and Men' 70) see the *chiasmus* and wordplay of Horace's lines 79–80 as an attempt to imitate Cervius' laboured manner of narration.
49 West, 'Of Mice and Men' 52.
50 Rudd, *Satires of Horace* 250.
51 West, 'Of Mice and Men' 54.
52 See *The Works of Horace*, ed. E. C. Wickham, 2 vols. (Oxford 1891) II.185.
53 West, 'Of Mice and Men' 56.
54 John Ogilby, *The Fables of Aesop, Paraphrased in Verse*, 2nd edn (London 1668) 18; for other 'Horatian' *Aesops*, see, for example, Edmund Arwaker, *Truth in Fiction: or Morality in Masquerade* (London 1708) 84–9; *Aesop's Fables, with Morals and Reflections . . . done into a Variety of English Verse*, 4th edn (London 1720) 21–5.
55 I am grateful to Miss Judith Williams for explaining this reference. In *The Farmer's Boy* (1800), Robert Bloomfield commented on the properties of Suffolk skimmed milk and its conversion to cheese :
> Its name derision and reproach pursue,
> And strangers tell of 'three times skimm'd sky-blue'.
> To cheese converted, what can be its boast?
> What but the common virtues of a post!
> If drought o'ertake it faster than the knife,
> Most fair it bids for stubborn length of life,
> And, like the oaken stuff whereon 'tis laid,
> Mocks the weak efforts of the bending blade;
> Or in the hog-trough rests in perfect spite,
> Too big to swallow and too hard to bite.
56 See West, 'Of Mice and Men' 76.
57 See N. Alexander, ed., *Elizabethan Narrative Verse* (London 1967) 182.
58 See Pepys' entries for 26 Oct. 1665, 31 Oct. 1665, 14 Mar. 1666, 28 Aug. 1666, 9 Nov. 1666, 26 Mar. 1668, 23 Feb. 1669.
59 See West, 'Of Mice and Men' 72; Rudd, *Satires of Horace* 246.
60 See West, 'Of Mice and Men' 78.
61 Compare Rev. 6:15–16.
62 Eliot's phrase (from his Introduction to *The Selected Poems of Ezra Pound* [1928]) is aptly applied to Cowley's poem by Charles Tomlinson (*Poetry and Metamorphosis* (Cambridge 1983) 84).

6 FIGURES OF HORACE IN DRYDEN'S LITERARY CRITICISM

1 The question of which edition or editions of Horace Dryden used has not been satisfactorily settled. J. McG. Bottkol in his pioneering article 'Dryden's Latin Scholarship', *Modern Philology* 40 (1943) 241–54, demonstrated that Dryden made careful use of the commentaries by a range of Renaissance editors in his translations from classical poetry, but could find no evidence as to which edition of Horace Dryden employed. The editors of Dryden's translations of Horace in the California edition of *The Works of John Dryden*, edited by H. T. Swedenberg et al., 20 vols. (Berkeley 1956–) III.293, guess that he may have used Heinsius' edition of 1629. But the evidence offered in the present essay, together with that which will be provided in the annotation to the Horatian translations in my forthcoming edition of Dryden's poetry in the Longman Annotated English Poets series, points to Dryden having made use of the following editions:

Cruquius: *Q. Horatius Flaccus . . . opera Iacobi Cruquii* (Antwerp 1578).
Lubinus: *Quinctus Horatius Flaccus* accuratissime emendatus, & explicatus paraphrasi nova scholastica Eilhardi Lubini (Frankfurt 1612).
Heinsius: *Q. Horati Flacci Opera.* Cum animadversionibus & notis Danielis Heinsi (Leiden 1612).
Lambinus: *Q. Horatius Flaccus . . . opera Dionys. Lambini* (Paris 1617).
Schrevelius: *Q. Horatius Flaccus* cum commentariis selectissimis variorum . . . accurante Corn. Schrevelio (Leiden 1653).
Dacier: *Remarques critiques sur les Œuvres d'Horace avec une nouvelle traduction*, 10 vols. (Paris 1681–9).

For reasons which will be apparent from this essay, it is not appropriate to follow the conventions of this volume in quoting from the Teubner text of Horace, so all quotations from Horace (apart from those made by Dryden himself) are taken from the edition of Lubinus, which Dryden undoubtedly used; spelling and capitalization in these quotations are modernized, but the punctuation is not. After Dryden's quotations from Horace I have interpolated a translation of the Latin (generally based on the Loeb version) inside square brackets.

2 John Dryden, *Of Dramatic Poesy and Other Critical Essays*, edited by George Watson, 2 vols. (London 1962) 1.46; subsequent quotations from Dryden's critical essays will be from this edition, with references by volume and page number. Dryden here is adapting Horace's *Ep.* 2.1.185–6, which Lubinus prints as *media inter carmina poscunt / aut ursum aut pugiles* ('call in the middle of a play for a bear or for boxers').

3 1.86, adapting *Ep.* 2.1.63, which Lubinus prints as *interdum vulgus rectum videt, est ubi peccat* ('at times the public see straight; sometimes they make mistakes'). Dryden may have been influenced by Schrevelius' gloss *recte judicat* ('it judges rightly') for *rectum videt*.

4 1.19, adapting *Ars* 360, which Lubinus prints as *verum opere in longo fas est obrepere somnum* ('when a work is long it is permitted to snatch some

sleep'). Dryden, referring here to the likelihood that there are errors in his play *The Conquest of Granada*, changes 'a long work' to 'such a work'.
5 See I.77, I.197, II.29, II.236.
6 See H. T. Swedenberg, 'England's Joy: *Astraea Redux* in its setting', *Studies in Philology* 50 (1953) 30–44; Howard Erskine-Hill, *The Augustan Idea in English Literature* (London 1983) 213–22.
7 The most significant use of Horace in critical works by Dryden's contemporaries include: the Earl of Rochester's version of *S* 1.10 as *An Allusion to Horace* (circulated in manuscript 1675–6), on which see Howard D. Weinbrot, *Eighteenth-Century Satire* (Cambridge 1988) 68–79; the Earl of Roscommon's translation of *Ars*, *Horace's Art of Poetry* (1680), and his *Essay on Translated Verse* (1684); and John Oldham's translation of *Ars* in his *Some New Pieces* (1681), collected in *The Poems of John Oldham*, edited by Harold F. Brooks and Raman Selden (Oxford 1987), on which see Paul Hammond, *John Oldham and the Renewal of Classical Culture* (Cambridge 1983) 86–111. Horace was to some extent read via Boileau's *Art poétique* (1674; translated by Soame and Dryden 1683): see A. F. B. Clarke, *Boileau and the French Classical Critics in England 1660–1830* (Paris 1925).
8 The reading *chartis pretium* in modern editions is also found in Cruquius, but Dryden would have read *pretium chartis* in Lambinus, Lubinus, Heinsius and Schrevelius.
9 *Ben Jonson*, edited by C. H. Herford, Percy and Evelyn Simpson, 11 vols. (Oxford 1925–52) VIII.567.
10 Schrevelius says: 'ut sunt res nefariae ac immanes, item impossibiles; quibus addendae turpes ac foedae ... Quia res est visu foeda, vel nimis atrox & incredibilis' (p. 803; 'such as things which are impious and monstrous, or impossible; to which may be added things shameful and loathsome ... Because something is loathsome to the sight, or too cruel and incredible').
11 Jacques Derrida, *Of Grammatology* (Baltimore 1976) 144–5.
12 See John Barnard and Paul Hammond, 'Dryden and a Poem for Lewis Maidwell', *Times Literary Supplement*, 25 May 1984 586.
13 Here Dryden is virtually translating from Schrevelius' note (p. 786) : 'si e Graeca lingua derivata, desinant & exeant in casum seu finem Latinum' ('if they are derived from the Greek language, they end in Latin cases or terminations').
14 Line 4. Dryden's poems are quoted from *The Poems of John Dryden*, edited by James Kinsley, 4 vols. (Oxford 1958).
15 The editors who interpret the passage as referring to the deployment of new words are Cruquius, Lambinus, Lubinus and Schrevelius. Lambinus (alone amongst those whom I have consulted) adds another interpretation: 'haec est huius loci sententia, quicquid alii somnient de verbis translatis: quam tamen testimonio, & auctoritate M. Tull. confirmabimus' ('this is the meaning of this passage, which others idly believe to concern the transferring of words: which, however, we may support from the testimony and authority of Cicero'). He then cites book 3 of *De Oratore*, where Cicero discusses the extension of vocabulary through the transferring of words.

16 The exchanges between Dryden and Shadwell are collected by Richard M. Oden in *Dryden and Shadwell* (Delmar 1977); for a discussion see Paul Hammond, 'Flecknoe and *Mac Flecknoe*', *Essays in Criticism* 35 (1985) 315–29, and *John Dryden: a Literary Life* (Basingstoke 1991) 74–81.
17 Thomas Shadwell, *The Sullen Lovers* (London 1668) sig. a^v.
18 Thomas Shadwell, *The Royal Shepherdess* (London 1669) sig. A3^r.
19 Thomas Shadwell, *The Humorists* (London 1671) second unsigned page, and sig. a^r–a4^v.
20 Watson says that 'Dryden's memory is at fault' (I.152), and the California edition concurs. But the question is not so simply dismissed. In the separately paginated section '*In Q. Horatium Flaccum Animadversiones et Notae*' included in his edition, Heinsius has a long discussion (pp. 78–99) of *Ars* 270–72, the lines which condemn Plautus for the crudity of his wit. Heinsius calls this a *durum . . . judicium* ('harsh judgement'; p. 78), and proceeds to give a defence of Plautus and a discussion of the various kinds of laughter which are provoked by different forms of Greek and Roman comedy, providing an account of the range of functions which comedy can serve. Heinsius stresses that comedy gives pleasure: in discussing Menander and Terence, for example, he says: 'qui ut sapientibus voluptatem potius afferrent, quam risum plebi violenter excuterent, duplici jucunditate utilitatem condierunt; imitatione vitae humanae, et inimitabili lepore . . . in usum venit nova. Cuius unicum propositum, humanos nosse atque imitari mores . . . Omnis autem imitatio, ut postea dicemus, natura delectat.' (p. 80: 'in order that they might bring pleasure to the wise, rather than violently stir up laughter in the common people, they brought usefulness together with a double pleasure, the imitation of human life, and an inimitable charm . . . the sole aim of new comedy was to know and imitate human manners . . . All imitation, as we shall argue later, delights by its very nature'). Heinsius is not denying that comedy may be edifying, but his vocabulary suggests that delight is the key to the way comedy functions. Dryden is no doubt simplifying Heinsius' discussion for his own polemical purposes, and is evidently working from memory, but his citation of Heinsius at this point is not without foundation.
21 *The Humorists* sig. a^r.
22 Thomas Shadwell, *Epsom-Wells* (London 1673) sig. A2^r.
23 Renaissance and modern editions read *charta*. I have not been able to find *pagina* in any edition, though other glosses are offered: *poemata* (Cruquius and Schrevelius) and *satyra* (Cruquius, Lambinus and Lubinus).
24 Thomas Shadwell, *The Medal of John Bayes* (London 1682) 2.
25 Rochester is quoted from *The Complete Poems of John Wilmot, Earl of Rochester*, edited by David M. Vieth (New Haven 1968).
26 See *The Works of John Dryden* XIII.402–3, and Paul Hammond, 'Two Echoes of Rochester's *A Satire against Reason and Mankind* in Dryden', *Notes and Queries* 233 (1988) 170–1.
27 Dryden changes the gender from *discipularum*: Rochester and his circle may be men, but they take the role of Horace's unthinking and indiscriminate

women. Lambinus and Schrevelius explain why *discipularum* is the correct reading, but there seems to be no tradition of printing *discipulorum* instead.
28 Dryden is following Denham's rejection of any aim to being *fidus interpres* in his Preface to *The Destruction of Troy* (*The Poetical Works of Sir John Denham*, edited by Theodore Howard Banks, 2nd edn (1969) 159).
29 *The Medal of John Bayes* 6.
30 Richard Flecknoe, *A Treatise of the Sports of Wit* (London 1675) title page.

7 HORACE'S *ODE* 3.29: DRYDEN'S 'MASTERPIECE IN ENGLISH'

1 See my article 'A Checklist of Restoration English Translations and Adaptations of Classical Greek and Latin Poetry, 1660–1700', *Translation and Literature* 1 (1992) 52–67. For further discussion of contemporary translation of the *Odes* see Valerie Edden, 'The Best of Lyrick Poets', in C. D. N. Costa, ed., *Horace* (London 1973) 135–60; Maren-Sofie Røstvig, *The Happy Man: Studies in the Metamorphosis of a Classical Ideal*, 2 vols. (Oslo 1954–8); and my own 'Dryden's *Sylvae*: a Study of Dryden's Translations from the Latin in the Second Tonson Miscellany, 1685', Ph.D. dissertation, Cambridge 1987, 145–60.
2 Preface to *Sylvae*, *The Works of John Dryden*, ed. E. N. Hooker *et al.*, 20 vols. (Berkeley 1956–) III.16. All quotations from Dryden are taken from this edition.
3 Preface to *Sylvae*, *Works of Dryden* III.16–17. Dryden writes: 'I have taken some pains to make it my masterpiece in English.' At least three translators other than the several who wrote complete versions of the *Odes* attempted *Ode* 3.29 in the period 1660–1700: see the checklist referred to in n. 1.
4 Modern commentators who have regarded Dryden's *Ode* 3.29 as an especially impressive performance include H. A. Mason, 'Living in the Present: Is Dryden's "Horat. Ode 29. Book 3" an Example of "creative translation"?', *Cambridge Quarterly* 10 (1981) 91–129; Paul Ramsay, *The Art of John Dryden* (Lexington 1969) 23–4; George Steiner, *After Babel: Aspects of Language and Translation* (London 1975) 426–9; and George Wasserman, *John Dryden* (New York 1964) 134–5. But Dryden's work was perhaps regarded even more highly by readers of previous centuries: see for example Samuel Rogers' comment to the effect that Dryden's Horatian translations surpass the originals (*Recollections of the Table-Talk of Samuel Rogers*, ed. Alexander Dyce (London 1887) 89–90).
5 See for one example the arguments of J. B. Leishman in the introduction to his *Translating Horace* (Oxford 1956), and the deeply unconvincing accompanying translations.
6 This point is discussed by Mason, 'Living in the Present' 112–20.
7 i.e., 'with the whole voice': Edwin Morgan's translation of Mayakovsky's title *Vo ves' golos*.

8 Michael Edwards, *Of Making Many Books: Essays on the Endlessness of Writing* (London 1990) 34.
9 Mason, 'Living in the Present' 102–3.
10 Eduard Fraenkel, *Horace* (Oxford 1957) 228; W. Y. Sellar, *The Roman Poets of the Augustan Age: Horace and the Elegiac Poets* (Oxford 1899) 166.
11 Horace is quoted from Shackleton Bailey; for the editions used by Dryden, see p. 294 n.1 in this volume. There is only one minor variant affecting passages discussed here (see n. 18 below). The English prose translation quoted here and below is that of Gordon Williams, ed. *The Third Book of Horace's 'Odes'* (Oxford 1969) 146–7.
12 Compare Cowley's couplet 'The st[r]eam of business does begin, / And a spring-tide of clients is come in' in 'Upon Liberty' (*The English Writings of Abraham Cowley* ed. A. R. Waller, 2 vols. (Cambridge 1905–6) II.389). Paul Hammond, 'Dryden's Philosophy of Fortune', *Modern Language Review* 80 (1985) 769–85, makes the point that 'it is Dryden who introduces Fortune' here (775), ascribing the change (implausibly I think) to the influence of Machiavelli. Dryden's 'tide of business' should be construed as a tide not only of 'official or professional duties' (*OED, business*, 12), appropriate to Maecenas, but in the light of more general senses such as *OED* 5, 'anxiety, solicitude, care; distress, uneasiness'.
13 R. A. Hornsby, 'Horace's Ode 3.29', *Classical Journal* 54 (1958) 129–36 (136). Hornsby's stress on this aspect of the *Ode* is, however, generally felt to be too exclusive.
14 See for example Steele Commager, *The Odes of Horace* (1962; rpt London 1967) 315.
15 Thus far one might wish to concur with Fraenkel's comparison of *Ode* 3.29 with several passages in the *Epistles*: the latter are 'not inferior to the ode in dignity ... but they demonstrate and teach, they do not sing' (*Horace* 228). For the importance of ethics in Horace's *Odes* see the various pieces by Colin Macleod gathered in his *Collected Essays* (Oxford 1983).
16 This section of the *Ode* was excerpted by several Restoration translators for separate treatment in this way: John Norris of Bemerton, for example, includes a version of lines 25–56 titled 'The Advice' in his *A Collection of Miscellanies*, 1687. Buckingham, similarly, calls his 'paraphrase' of part of the *Ode*, 'To Fortune': see Christine Phipps, ed. *Buckingham: Public and Private Man; The Prose, Poems, and Commonplace Book of George Villiers, Second Duke of Buckingham* (New York and London 1985) 152.
17 Preface to *Sylvae*, *Works of Dryden* III.16.
18 *pater* is taken to be vocative by Shackleton Bailey; the quotation here is adapted to accord with Dryden's and Heinsius' (n. 11) readings of it as nominative.
19 See also H. A. Mason's comparison with Dryden's version of Persius' *Satire* 5, ('Living in the Present' 126–7), a passage approaching slightly closer to the temperature of the Horatian *Ode*.
20 Commager, *Odes of Horace* 314–15.

21 Peter Connor, *Horace's Lyric Poetry: the Force of Humour* (Victoria 1987) 138.
22 Connor, *Horace's Lyric Poetry* 138.
23 Mason, 'Living in the Present' 104.
24 Hammond, 'Dryden's Philosophy of Fortune' 776.
25 Mason, 'Living in the Present' 121.
26 Commager, *Odes of Horace* 343.
27 Quoted from *Richard III*, ed. E. A. J. Honigman (London 1968).

8 POPE AND HORACE

There are three full-length studies of Pope and Horace devoted chiefly to the imitations of Horace:
   Thomas E. Maresca, *Pope's Horatian Poems* (Columbus 1966)
   John M. Aden, *Something Like Horace: Studies in the Art and Allusion of Pope's Horatian Satires* (Nashville 1969)
   Frank Stack, *Pope and Horace* (Cambridge 1985)
The latter is outstanding, and has a full bibliography of the subject.

1 For Horace as literary critic see C. O. Brink *Horace on Poetry*, I: *Prolegomena to the Literary Epistles* (Cambridge 1963); II *The Ars Poetica* (Cambridge 1971); III *Epistles Book II: the Letters to Augustus and Florus* (Cambridge 1982); also Niall Rudd *Horace Epistles Book II and Epistle to the Pisones* ('Ars Poetica'), Cambridge Greek and Latin Classics (Cambridge 1989).
2 See *The Twickenham Edition of the Works of Alexander Pope*, general ed. J. Butt, 10 vols. (London and New Haven 1938–68) I.313. All quotations from Pope are from this edition. Vol. IV contains all the imitations of Horace.
3 See *Ep.* 2.1.90–110 and *Ars* 323–32.
4 See *passim*, Bernard Weinberg *A History of Literary Criticism in the Italian Renaissance*, 2 vols. (Chicago 1961).
5 See Marvin T. Herrick, *The Poetics of Aristotle in England*, Cornell Studies in English 17 (New Haven and London 1930).
6 *Critical Essays of the Seventeenth Century*, ed. J. E. Spingarn, 3 vols. (Oxford 1908) II. 297.
7 Wentworth Dillon, *An Essay on Translated Verse 1685 and Horace's Art of Poetry Made English 1684* (Menston 1971) 18: translating *Ars Poetica* 268–9. In the absence of line numbers, references to Roscommon are to page numbers.
8 Roscommon, *The Art of Poetry* 7 translating *Ars* 86–7.
9 Roscommon, *The Art of Poetry* 10–11 translating *Ars* 133–5. The passage is cited later in this chapter on page 170.
10 See *Odes* 3.30 and *Ep.* 1.19.19–34.
11 Roscommon, *The Art of Poetry* 19–20 translating *Ars* 285–91.

12 See Spingarn II.354 commenting on Mulgrave's *Essay* which is included in this volume (286–90).
13 See *Joseph Spence, Observations, Anecdotes and Characters of Books and Men*, ed. J. M. Osborn, 2 vols. (Oxford 1966) I, no. 73 cited with commentary by Maynard Mack in *Alexander Pope: a Life* (New Haven and London 1985) 111–12.
14 Pope's own phrase in a letter to Swift 28 November 1729; see *The Correspondence of Alexander Pope*, ed. George Sherburn, 5 vols. (Oxford 1956) III.81.
15 *The Poems of John Oldham*, ed. H. F. Brooks and R. Selden (Oxford 1987) 104.
16 *The Twickenham Edition* III.i.7–8.
17 See H. A. Mason 'Is Juvenal a Classic?', in J. P. Sullivan, ed., *Critical Essays on Roman Literature: Satire* (London 1963) 93–176. Mason argues that Juvenal is to be valued as a wit rather than a moralist.
18 *The Poems of John Wilmot Earl of Rochester*, ed. Keith Walker (Oxford 1984) 100.
19 See Howard T. Weinbrot, *Augustus Caesar in 'Augustan' England: the Decline of a Classical Norm* (Princeton 1978) chapter 6; Howard Erskine-Hill, *The Augustan Idea in English Literature* (London 1983) 324–34 and Stack, *Pope and Horace* 152.
20 'A Discourse concerning the Original and Progress of Satire' in *The Works of Dryden*, ed. H. T. Swedenberg *et al.* (Berkeley and Los Angeles 1956–) IV.65.
21 *The Twickenham Edition* IV.3.
22 'Discourse' in *The Works of John Dryden* IV.64.
23 'Discourse' in *The Works of John Dryden* IV.64.
24 See Howard Erskine-Hill, 'Courtiers out of Horace' in A. J. Smith, ed., *John Donne: Essays in Celebration* (London 1972) 273–307 especially 295–end. On Donne and Horace, see Niall Rudd, 'Donne and Horace', *Times Literary Supplement*, 22 March 1963.
25 *The Twickenham Edition* IV.3.
26 *Spence*, ed. Osborne, I no. 321a cited by John Butt in *The Twickenham Edition* IV.xiii at the opening of his introduction – q.v. for an account of all the circumstances surrounding the composition of the imitations of Horace.
27 *The Twickenham Edition* IV.298–9. for further discussion see Stack, *Pope and Horace* 277–8.
28 See Maresca, *Pope's Horatian Poems* 50–1.
29 Stack, *Pope and Horace* 152.
30 *The Twickenham Edition* IV.191–2.
31 *The Twickenham Edition* IV.191.
32 Roscommon, *The Art of Poetry* 24.
33 Roscommon, *The Art of Poetry* 22.
34 *P. Vergili Maronis Opera*, ed. R. A. B. Mynors (Oxford 1969).
35 *Ben Jonson* ed. C. H. Herford and P. and E. Simpson, 11 vols. (Oxford 1925–47) VIII.583. Cited in *The Twickenham Edition* IV.218.

36 Roscommon, *The Art of Poetry* 25–6.
37 Roscommon, *The Art of Poetry* 5–6 translating *Ars* 58–63 and 70–2.

9 GOOD HUMOUR AND THE AGELASTS: HORACE, POPE AND GRAY

1 John Dryden, *Of Dramatic Poesy and Other Critical Essays*, ed. G. Watson, 2 vols. (London 1962) I.129–30.
2 Matthew Arnold, *Complete Prose Works*, ed. R. H. Super, 11 vols. (Ann Arbor 1960–77) III.222, 228.
3 André Dacier, quoted by Dryden in amends for his own moderation, *Of Dramatic Poesy*, I.140.
4 Dacier, quoted in *Of Dramatic Poesy*, I.140.
5 Gk. *a-gelastes*, a non-laugher.
6 Rabelais, *Gargantua* 3 Prol.
7 Mikhail Bakhtin, *Rabelais and His World* (Cambridge, Mass. 1968) 122–3.
8 Bakhtin, *Rabelais* 92 n.37.
9 For his debt to Rabelais see Milan Kundera, *The Art of the Novel* (London 1988) 159.
10 Eduard Fraenkel, *Horace* (Oxford 1957) 143.
11 H. A. Mason, *The Cambridge Quarterly* 8 (1978) 15.
12 Mason, *CQ* 8 17.
13 Montaigne, *Essays* trans. Cotton, 3 vols. (London 1930) III.371.
14 Shaftesbury, *Characteristics*, ed. John M. Robertson, 2 vols. (Gloucester, Mass. 1963) I.152.
15 See particularly his imitation of *Sermo* 2.2, and the *Epistle to a Lady*.
16 Oliver Goldsmith, *Collected Works* ed. Arthur Friedman, 3 vols. (Oxford 1966) I.319–22.
17 Samuel Johnson, *Lives of the English Poets*, ed. G. B. Hill, 3 vols. (Oxford 1905) III.234.
18 It is suggestive that Pope defined the whole aim of the *Essay on Man* as 'to put morality in good humour' (*Correspondence*, ed. George Sherburn, III.117).
19 The 1728 *Dunciad* follows his edition of Shakespeare, and his elaborate plans for a neo-Virgilian epic, *Brutus*, are counterpointed by the 1742 *Dunciad* revision.
20 Johnson, *Lives* III.440.
21 Johnson, *Lives* III.434.
22 The phrase belongs to Erasmus, and the great tradition of *The Praise of Folly*. Pope illustrates the pains involved by publishing the *Rape of the Lock* in three distinct versions (1712, 1714, 1717) with innumerable minor adjustments.
23 Goldsmith, *Collected Works* I.322.

10 HORACE AND THE NINETEENTH CENTURY

1 For example, over half the Latin quotations in Trollope's forty-seven novels are from Horace; of the 200 or so Latin quotations in Thackeray 140 are from Horace, 104 from the *Odes*. See Richard Mullen, *Anthony Trollope: a Victorian in his World* (London 1990) 73; Elizabeth Nitchie, 'Horace and Thackeray', *Classical Journal* 13 (1917–18) 294.
2 All translations mine unless otherwise specified. Quoted by T. E. Page, Introduction to C. L. Graves, *More Hawarden Horace* (London 1896) ix.
3 M. L. Clarke, *Classical Education in Britain 1500–1900* (Cambridge 1959) 57.
4 W. M. Thackeray, *The Newcomes* (London 1853–5) chapter 8.
5 Etienne de Wailly in his translation of the *Odes* (1817); Victor Hugo, 'Réalité (1859) in *Les Chansons des rues et des bois* (1865) I.ii.2, both quoted in Jean Marnier, *La Survie d'Horace à l'époque romantique* (Paris 1965) 22, 138.
6 F. W. Riemer, *Mittheilungen über Goethe*, 2 vols. (Berlin 1841) II.644; Matthew Arnold, 'On the Modern Element in Literature' (1857) in *On the Classical Tradition*, ed. R. H. Super (Ann Arbor 1960) 36. See William Wordsworth, *Poems*, vol. I, ed. J. O. Hayden (Harmondsworth 1977) 76, 141f, translating *Odes* 1.31 and 3.13; Wordsworth's allusions to Horace, notably in 'Liberty' (1829), are listed in M. R. Thayer, *The Influence of Horace on the Chief English Poets of the Nineteenth Century* (1916) (New York 1968) 53–64.
7 Quoted in Herbert Paul, 'The Decay of Classical Quotation', *Men and Letters* (London 1901) 50.
8 Recounted in T. R. Glover, *Horace, a Return to Allegiance* (Cambridge 1932) 9f; see also Jenni Calder, *RLS, A Life Study* (London 1980) 156f.
9 *Further Extracts from the Note-Books of Samuel Butler*, ed. A. T. Bartholomew (London 1934) 92. The entry was made some time between 1874 and 1883.
10 George Eliot, 'Evangelical Teaching: Dr Cumming' (1855) reprinted in *Essays*, ed. T. Pinney (London 1963) 175.
11 C. S. C[alverley], *Verses and Translations* (1862), 12th edn (London 1888) 150, 124, 55; *The Poems of Tennyson*, ed. C. Ricks (London 1969) 960 (all subsequent Tennyson quotations are from this edition).
12 Archilochus fr.5 (West), Anacreon fr.28 (Bergk), Alcaeus fr.32 (Bergk); the extent to which these provide precise parallels is debated.
13 Sir Theodore Martin (trs.), *The Works of Horace*, 2 vols., new edn (Edinburgh 1888) I.ci.
14 John Keble, *Oxford Lectures on Poetry 1832–1841*, trs. E. K. Francis, 2 vols. (Oxford 1912) II.468; compare Arnold's 'On the Modern Element in Literature', *On the Classical Tradition* 36.
15 A. H. Clough, *Amours de Voyage*, ed. Patrick Scott (St Lucia, Queensland 1974) I.viii, 156–71.

16 Peerlkamp's edition of the *Odes* was first published in Haarlem in 1834: see W. S. Teuffel and Ludwig Schwabe, *History of Roman Literature*, trs. G. C. W. Warr, 2 vols. (London 1900) I.466f and J. E. Sandys, ed., *A History of Classical Scholarship*, 3 vols. (Cambridge 1958) III.276–8.
17 R. Y. Tyrrell, *Latin Poetry* (London 1895) 165f, 194–205.
18 Andrew Lang, *Letters to Dead Authors* (London 1886) 223, 228, 233.
19 See W. D. Anderson, *Arnold and the Classical Tradition* (Ann Arbor, 1965) 135. For Béranger as the French Horace see Jean Touchard, *La Gloire de Béranger*, 2 vols. (Paris 1968), esp. I.465.
20 W. M. Thackeray, *Works*, vol. XI (including *Ballads*) (London 1894–9) 440, 499f, 471.
21 Thomas Moore, *Complete Poetical Works* (London 1869) 142.
22 See *Poetry of the Victorian Period*, ed. J. H. Buckley and G. B. Woods, 3rd edn (Glenview 1965) 841f.
23 Martin, *Works of Horace* I.lxxx, lxxxiv, cxvi, lxxxv, lxxxii.
24 Austin Dobson, 'To Q. H. F.', *Vignettes in Rhyme* (1873) in *Collected Poems* (1897), 5th edn (London 1902) 122. Sybaris is the sportsman unmanned by Lydia's love in *Odes* 1.8; Barrus is the man pathologically eager to be thought handsome in *Satires* 1.6.30.
25 Lang, *Letters to Dead Authors* 234.
26 Dobson, *Collected Poems* 463, 479, 485.
27 E. V. Lucas, ed., *Charles Lamb and the Lloyds* (London 1898) 233–5.
28 For Horace in college life see also the parodies in Owen Seaman, *Horace at Cambridge* (London 1895); for Tennyson's use of Horace see W. P. Mustard, *Classical Echoes in Tennyson* (New York 1904) chapter 9, 'Tennyson and Horace' 107–20.
29 Housman to John Drinkwater, 25 December 1922, in Henry Maas, ed., *The Letters of A.E. Housman* (London 1971) 209.
30 *The Poems of Matthew Arnold*, ed. Kenneth Allott (London 1965) 57f.
31 F. W. Hirst, 'Morley, John', *Dictionary of National Biography* (1922–1930 Supplement).
32 C. L. Graves, *The Hawarden Horace* (London 1894) 27, 31.
33 C. L. Graves, *More Hawarden Horace* (London 1896) 15.
34 Graves, *The Hawarden Horace* 83.
35 Exhibited at the British Institution in 1837, the painting is now in the Turner Collection at the Tate Gallery in London. It is reproduced in, e.g., *The Turner Collection in the Clore Gallery, an Illustrated Guide* (London 1987) 63.
36 Lang, *Letters to Dead Authors* 230f.
37 W. E. Aytoun, *Poland, Homer and other Poems* (London 1832) 5.
38 Clough, *Amours de Voyage* II.ii, 30–3, 46f.
39 [Octavian Blewitt], *Handbook for Travellers in Central Italy* (London 1843 and many later editions); Karl Baedeker, *Italy, Handbook for Travellers, Second Part: Central Italy and Rome* (Coblenz 1861 and many later editions).
40 H. H. Milman, *Life of Horace* (London 1849) 108f.

41 John Cam Hobhouse, *Historical Illustrations of the Fourth Canto of 'Childe Harold'* (London 1818) 42f, alluding to Bertrand Capmartin de Chaupy, *Découverte de la maison de campagne d'Horace*, 3 vols. (Rome 1769).
42 See *The Turner Collection in the Clore Gallery* 60f.
43 W. E. Gladstone, *Tu modo dux, tu comes, Uxor, esses* (1859), in Lord Lytton and W. E. Gladstone, *Translations* (London 1861) 147–51.
44 G. O. Trevelyan, *Interludes in Verse and Prose* (1905) (London 1924) 97. A 'lac' or 'lakh' (Hindustani) is a large quantity (usually 100,000), particularly of rupees.
45 Tyrrell, *Latin Poetry* 189–91.
46 Thomas Hood, *Works* vol.v (London 1871) 302.
47 *Further Extracts from the Note-Books of Samuel Butler* 124.
48 Thomas Hardy, *Jude the Obscure* (1895) Book I, chapter 5.

11 HORACE'S KIPLING

Kipling's Medici Press *Horace* (edited by E. G. Wickham, 1910), the illuminations cut from his smaller *Horace* (with Conington's translation, George Bell, 1908), his letters to C. R. L. Fletcher, Charles Graves' and A. B. Ramsey's letters to him, and Charles Carrington's notes from Mrs Kipling's destroyed journal, are in the collection of Kipling's papers deposited by the National Trust in the Library of the University of Sussex, and are identified throughout as 'Sussex'. I am grateful to Bet Inglis and Helen Bickerstaff with their assistants for guidance through these, and to the National Trust for persmission to quote from them.

Mrs Kipling gave the Medici Press *Horace*, shortly after her husband's death, to her daughter's husband, Captain George Bambridge, who wrote saying that there was no memorial he would value more, because of his memories of reading Horace with Rudyard Kipling. The annotations in it were printed by Charles Carrington, with a genial though somewhat careless commentary, as *Kipling's Horace* (London 1978). Slightly different versions of twelve of them, with one on *Odes* 3.16 which had nothing corresponding in the Medici Press book, and is not printed by Carrington, were printed in the *Magdalene College Magazine* in June 1932, and have several times been reprinted privately, notably in R. Harbord, *The Reader's Guide to Rudyard Kipling's Works* (8 vols., Canterbury and Bournemouth 1961–72). Neither they, nor Kipling's boyhood translation of *Donec gratus eram* are included in Rudyard Kipling's verse (London 1940 often reprinted). It is much to be wished that they could be more easily obtained.

1 R. Kipling, 'The Bull that Thought', *Debits and Credits* (London 1926).
2 T. S. Eliot, *A Choice of Kipling's Verse* (London 1941) 14.
3 R. Kipling, *Many Inventions* (London 1893).
4 *Choice of Kipling's Verse* 14.
5 R. Kipling, *Early Verse by Rudyard Kipling*, ed. A. Rutherford (Oxford 1986) 138.

6 R. Kipling, *Traffics and Discoveries* (London 1904).
7 R. Kipling, *A Diversity of Creatures* (London 1917).
8 Actually the 37th of the First. A secretarial error?
9 R. Kipling, *Something of Myself* (London 1937) 32–3.
10 G. Murray, *An Unfinished Autobiography* (London 1960) 78–9.
11 *United Services College Chronicle*, 24 July 1982: Early Verse 160–1: Kipling's Horace 3.
12 R. Kipling, *Land and Sea Tales for Scouts and Guides* (London 1923) 268.
13 R. Kipling 'The Uses of Reading', *A Book of Words* (London 1928) 90.
14 Kipling, *Diversity of Creatures* 262. S. Treggiari, 'Kipling's Classics', *Kipling Journal* xxxix (181) 7 records some of these tags.
15 Kipling, *Book of Words* 89–90.
16 R. Kipling, *Stalky & Co.* (London 1899) ix.
17 'The Last Term', *Stalky & Co.* 230.
18 C. Carrington *Rudyard Kipling His Life and Work* (rev. edn London 1978) 323.
19 R. Kipling, *Departmental Ditties and other Verses* (16th edn London 1904) 175–6.
20 Kipling, *Book of Words* 91–2.
21 Kipling, *Something of Myself* 39.
22 First printed in the Bombay edition of Kipling's Works vol. xxv (London 1919): included in *Kipling's Verse*.
23 See n. 61.
24 Letter to Fletcher. See n. 61.
25 Carrington, *Rudyard Kipling* 188.
26 Kipling, *Something of Myself* 185. Kipling had thought of some such story in 1897 (Carrington, *Rudyard Kipling* 441) and again in 1902 (D. Wilson, *Gilbert Murray* (Oxford 1987) 96).
27 Mrs Kipling's journal (Sussex): R. L. Green, 'Kipling and Horace', *Kipling Journal* xxiv (124) 8 suggests the connection.
28 Eliot, *Choice of Kipling's Verse* 3.
29 R. Kipling, *Puck of Pook's Hill* (London 1906) 156.
30 Kipling, *Many Inventions*.
31 Kipling, *Puck of Pook's Hill* 139.
32 W. E. Gladstone's version, *The Odes of Horace . . . translated . . .* (1895), but cited from S. A. Courtauld's excellent *The Odes and Epodes of Horace: Metrical Translations by various authors* (2nd edn London 1916).
33 Sussex. See the illustration in this book, p. 222.
34 Kipling, *Puck of Pook's Hill* 163.
35 Kipling, *Puck of Pook's Hill* 154.
36 Kipling, *Something of Myself* 190.
37 R. Kipling, *Rewards and Fairies* (London 1910) 319.
38 Kipling, *Diversity of Creatures*.
39 Mrs Kipling's Journal (Sussex).
40 Kipling, *Book of Words* 90–1.
41 Kipling, *Something of Myself* 32.

42 Kipling, *Diversity* 248.
43 Kipling, *Diversity* 260.
44 Kipling, *Diversity* 262.
45 Kipling, *Diversity* 252.
46 Kipling, *Diversity* 252.
47 Kipling, *Diversity* 356: he uses Horace similarly at 336 and 339.
48 Kipling, *Diversity* 214. This verse by itself is attached to *Odes* 4.3 in the Medici Press *Horace*, and appeared as the epigraph to 'The Village that voted the Earth was Flat' when that was first published independently in 1913. Carrington, *Kipling's Horace* 85, does not notice that it is partly translated from the *Ode*.
49 Carrington, *Kipling's Horace* 1: Carrington does not notice that this gloss paraphrases the *Ode*.
50 Kipling, *Diversity* 250–1. For further comments on the poem, see A. D. Nuttall's essay above: for Kipling's concern with work, C. S. Lewis, 'Kipling's World', in *They Asked for a Paper* (London 1962) 75–7 – an otherwise rather unfair essay.
51 E. Pound, *Ripostes* (London 1912).
52 Kipling, *Book of Words* 90.
53 Kipling, *Book of Words* 90.
54 Carrington, *Kipling's Horace* 75.
55 R. Kipling, *Just So Stories* (London 1902) 169.
56 Letter to C. R. L. Fletcher, 21 April 1917 (Sussex).
57 To Fletcher, 24, 27 and 29 April 1917 (Sussex).
58 To Fletcher, 29 April and 18 December 1917 (Sussex).
59 To Fletcher, 18 and 25 December 1917 (Sussex).
60 To Fletcher, 2 January 1918 (Sussex).
61 To Fletcher, 2 January and (with 'The Pro-Consuls') 12 January 1918 (Sussex).
62 See Norman Vance's essay, above. To Fletcher, 17 February 1918 (Sussex).
63 Carrington, *Kipling's Horace* 91, 99.
64 W. Wallace, *Harry Lauder in the Limelight* (Lewes 1988) 49: Carrington, *Kipling's Horace* xx.
65 Carrington, *Kipling's Horace* 100.
66 *King Lear* III.vi.85 (numbering as in *Riverside Shakespeare*, Boston 1974).
67 C. R. L. Fletcher to Kipling, n.d., in answer to Kipling's letter, 24 March, and referring to an earlier letter (Sussex).
68 To Fletcher, 24 March 1918 (Sussex).
69 R. Kipling, *The Years Between* (London 1919).
70 C. L. Graves to Kipling, 6 November 1920 (Sussex).
71 C. L. Graves to Kipling, 6 November 1920 (Sussex).
72 A. D. Godley, R. Kipling and C. Graves, *Q. Horati Flacci Carminum Liber Quintus* (Oxford 1920) 3, 5.
73 To Fletcher, 12 July 1918 (Sussex).
74 E. I. Fripp, *Shakespeare Man and Artist* (London 1938) vol. I, 146.

75 'The Craftsman', in Kipling, *The Years Between*.
76 Carrington, *Kipling's Horace* 67.
77 Carrington, *Kipling's Horace* 35.
78 Carrington, *Kipling's Horace* 33.
79 Carrington, *Kipling's Horace* 37.
80 Carrington, *Kipling's Horace* 19.
81 Kipling, *Debits and Credits*, as n. 1.
82 Carrington, *Kipling's Horace* 39, 13, P. E. Easterling. 'Carrington on Kipling on Horace', *Kipling Journal* lvi (224) 31 thinks Kipling unfair to Horace.
83 Carrington, *Kipling's Horace* 19.
84 Kipling, *Book of Words* 92.
85 Kipling, *Many Inventions* 105.
86 To Fletcher, 21 September 1925 (Sussex).
87 Typed draft (Sussex).
88 Kipling, *Debits and Credits*.
89 H. Waddell, *Peter Abelard* (London 1933) 13–15.
90 Carrington, *Kipling's Horace* 73.
91 Carrington, *Kipling's Horace* 83.
92 Kipling to Harris, 6 December 1895; *The Letters of Rudyard Kipling*, ed. T. Pinney (London 1991) 217.
93 Kipling, *Debits and Credits*.
94 Kipling, *Debits and Credits*: cf. S. Medcalf, 'Virgil at the Turn of Time', in C. Martindale, ed., *Virgil and his Influence* (Bristol 1984) 215–44.
95 R. Kipling, *Limits and Renewals* (London 1932).
96 Kipling, *Limits* 94.
97 Kipling, *Limits* 89.
98 Kipling, *Limits* 103.
99 Acts 11:5–10; John 6:9.
100 Kipling, *Limits* 103.
101 Kipling, *Limits* 103.
102 Kipling, *Limits* 109–10.
103 Kipling, *Limits* 113.
104 Kipling, *Limits* 251.
105 Kipling, *Limits* 251.
106 *The Morning Post*, 23 May 1932.
107 A. B. Ramsay to Kipling 18 March 1932 (Sussex).
108 Mrs Kipling's Journal (Sussex).
109 Carrington, *Kipling's Horace* 29.
110 In the collected verse it is renamed 'Samuel Pepys'.
111 R. Kipling *Letters of Travel* (London 1920) 257–9. There is an illustrated account of Menna's tomb in A. Mekhitarian, *Egyptian Painting* (Lausanne 1954) 72–95.
112 Kipling, *Something of Myself* 33.

12 SOME ASPECTS OF HORACE IN THE TWENTIETH CENTURY

1 Robert Pinsky, *An Explanation of America* (Princeton 1979).
2 Reuben Brower, *The Poetry of Robert Frost* (Oxford 1963) chapter 3.
3 Friedrich Nietzsche, *Beyond Good and Evil*, trs. Helen Zimmern (Edinburgh and London 1907) 216–17.
4 Friedrich Nietzsche, *The Case of Wagner, Nietzsche Contra Wagner, The Twilight of the Idols, The Antichrist*, trans. Thomas Common (London 1899) 233–4. I have emended one or two awkwardnesses and touches of late Victorian rapture.
5 D. M. Hooley, *The Classics in Paraphrase* (Susquehanna 1988) 109.
6 Frank Stack, *Pope and Horace* (Cambridge 1985) 103–4.
7 C. Smart, *The Works of Horace Translated Literally into English Prose* (London 1752) vol. I.
8 Ezra Pound, 'Horace', *The Criterion* 9 (1929–30) 217–18.
9 Basil Bunting, 'An Interview with Basil Bunting', *Scripsi* (Summer/Autumn 1982) 30.
10 D. S. Carne-Ross, 'Jocasta's Divine Head', *Arion* Third Series vol. 1 No. 1 (1990) 135–6.
11 J. V. Cunningham, *The Helmsman and The Quest of the Opal* (The Colt Press, San Francisco 1942 and Alan Swallow, Denver 1950, bound together and issued, unpaginated, presumably by Alan Swallow).
12 Donald Davie, *Collected Poems* (Manchester 1990) 447–8.
13 Basil Bunting, recorded interview (the New York Center for Visual History 1984).
14 David Gordon, 'A Northumbrian Sabine' *Paideuma* vol. 9 No. 1 (1980) 83, 85.
15 Richard Johnson, *Man's Place, an Essay on Auden* (Ithaca 1973) 92.
16 D. M. Hooley, *The Classics in Paraphrase* 121.

POSTSCRIPT: IMAGES OF HORACE IN TWENTIETH-CENTURY SCHOLARSHIP

1 There are useful bibliographies to Horace in the *Cambridge History of Latin Literature* ed. E. J. Kenney and W. V. Clausen (Cambridge 1982) 850–1, and in volume II, 31.3 of *Aufstieg und Niedergang der römischen Welt* (Berlin and New York 1981) 1408–1558, 1674–1788, 1866–1920: see also *Bollettino di Studi Latini* 20 (1990) 47–83 (Horace and Greek epigram).
2 D. Kennedy rev. S. J. Harrison, *Oxford Readings in Vergil's Aeneid*, *Hermathena* forthcoming.
3 Quoted from the version printed in *New Studies of a Great Inheritance* (London 1921) 44–65. Footnote 1 on p. 44 gives there the history of the piece: 'Given as a public lecture first at Cardiff (to the Frogs Society) in November, 1903, and frequently elsewhere since then; first printed by the Leeds Branch of

the Classical Association in January, 1917 (in a volume called *Uvae Falernae*) and subsequently, with some changes, in the *Transactions of the Plymouth Institution* under the title "The Power of Poetry in History."' The version printed in *Falernian Grapes* (edited by W. Rhys Roberts, Cambridge 1917: *Uvae Falernae* in the subtitle) is prefaced by a short address congratulating Leeds on its contribution to 'extending the old culture to the newly enfranchised generation' at a time when 'the best friends of popular education, especially the representatives of Labour, are demanding that everyone shall have access, not merely to the outworks, but to the central treasures of the higher education so long enjoyed, and on the whole so splendidly used, by the governing classes of this country'.

4 *A Toast to Horace* (Cambridge, Mass. 1937) 31.

5 Rand unconsciously echoes Ezra Pound (see above, p. 1) cf. also Lionel Trilling in *Arion* 9.2–3 (1970) 131.

6 J. Perret, *Horace* (Paris 1959). There is an English translation by B. Humez (New York 1974). Nisbet's review is in *JRS* 50 (1960) 279–80.

7 *Gnomon* 44 (1972) 347–56 at 351. It is instructive to contrast La Penna's reading of the Nisbet and Hubbard commentary (*A Commentary on Horace: Odes Bk I*, Oxford 1970) with that of Kenneth Quinn, one of the pioneers of New Criticism in classical studies. Writing in *Arion* 9 in 1970 (264–73) he makes fun of the massive erudition of the volume, but bizarrely claims that it would suit only 'the Patrick Wilkinson audience (the school-master, the civil-servant on Sunday, the country parson on Monday, the don who has specialised in another department of the Classics)' (271). It is easier to see the volume of Nisbet and Hubbard and its successor on *Odes* Book 2 published in 1978, with their stress on the need to document the conventions and codes of ancient literature before interpretation can take place and their insistence that even apparently obvious and natural 'facts' like the whiteness of swans (see on *Odes* 2.20.10) must be shown to be culturally acknowledged, as testimonies rather to the growing importance of structuralism: see below p. 274.

8 'The Old Lie: Dulce et decorum est' *Omnibus* 15, 16–17. Nisbet suggested *dulci decorum est pro patria mori* (though he now has doubts).

9 Compare D. Armstrong, *Horace* (New Haven and London 1989) 1, 'If his public is smaller now, perhaps both scholars and poets appreciate him more vividly and in better ways than in Victorian and Edwardian times, when Horace served more as an author read in the original by "every schoolboy" than as a source of inspiration and literary imitation.' But Armstrong's elision of the difference between scholars and poets is a comforting piece of academic self-deception: it would be hard to argue that Horace's influence on contemporary English literature has been greater than it was in Victorian and Edwardian times.

10 American classical studies had from their beginnings been influenced by German professionalism: see e.g. Paul Shorey's 'Fifty Years of American Classical Scholarship', *TAPA* 50 (1919) 33–61, a brilliant and largely persuasive case for American scholarship as the *via media* between English

amateurism and German pedantry (see especially 56–7). Shorey's own commentary on the *Odes* and *Epodes* (first edn Chicago 1898; revised edn 1910) remains of value and continues to be kept in print by reprint houses.

11 Quoted from the translation of Wilamowitz's 'Zukunftsphilologie!' in S. Nimis, 'Fussnoten: das Fundament der Wissenschaft', *Arethusa* 17 (1984) 105–34 at 109. The original piece, with the other documents of the controversy, can be found in K. Gründer, *Der Streit um Nietzsches 'Geburt des Tragödie'* (Hildesheim 1969): for an excellent discussion of Wilamowitz's strengths and weaknesses, see M. S. Silk and J. P. Stern, *Nietzsche on Tragedy* (Cambridge 1981) 95–105.

12 Cambridge 1945: edn 2 1951, edn 3 1968.

13 *TLS* 15 November 1957, 688. I do not know who the reviewer was: in a letter in a subsequent issue (773) his reply to the accusation made by F. W. Bateson of being a 'clever amateur' suggests that he was not a professional classicist.

14 See especially H. D. Weinbrot, *Augustus Caesar in 'Augustan' England: the Decline of a Classical Norm* (Princeton 1978), H. Erskine-Hill, *The Augustan Idea in English Literature* (London 1983).

15 R. Syme, *The Roman Revolution* (Oxford 1939).

16 London 1947, 9.

17 *JRS* 36 (1946) 185–9, at 186.

18 C. O. Brink, *Horace on Poetry* III: *Epistles Book* II: *the Letters to Augustus and Florus* (Cambridge 1982) 524.

19 D. Armstrong, 'Second Thoughts on Fraenkel's Horace', *Arion* 3 (1964) 116–28.

20 Three volumes, Oxford 1950.

21 *JRS* 48 (1958) 170–8, as 171.

22 cf. H. Glaser, *The Cultural Roots of National Socialism*, trans. E. A. Menze (London 1978).

23 Berlin 1926, discussed in A. La Penna, *Orazio e l'ideologia del Principato* (Turin 1963) 19.

24 Fraenkel, *Horace* 443 n. 1.

25 Fraenkel, *Horace* 26.

26 Coleridge's famous dictum that 'nothing can permanently please which does not contain in itself the reason why it is so, and not otherwise' (*Biographia Literaria* ch. 14, ed. J. Engell and W. Jackson Bate, Princeton 1983, 2.12) takes us back to German romantic criticism: see N. Frumann *Coleridge, The Damaged Archangel* (New York 1971) 191, quoting A. W. Schlegel, *Lectures on Dramatic Art and Literature* trs. J. Black, revised A. J. W. Morrison (London 1846) 416.

27 *Princeps Aeolium carmen ad Italos / deduxisse modos.* But even here the ambiguities multiply: Horace is proud to be the *princeps*, and *deduxisse* is the word used of bringing a defeated enemy home to a triumph (Nisbet–Hubbard on *Odes* 1.37.31), but it is also a word used for drawing off water from a larger body for irrigation or drainage (cf. Virgil *Georgics* 1.269, Manilius 2.10: *modos* 'measures' joins in the ambiguity) and since Virgil's *deductum dicere carmen* in *Eclogue* 6.5 it had become the *vox propria* for expressing the

Hellenistic ideal of small-scale, polished poetry, Callimachus' *mousa leptalee*, 'slender Muse'. Is the Roman achievement triumphal or derivative, a principled refusal to thunder in bombastic epic or an inability to rise to such heights?

28 See especially Jasper Griffin's review of the Nisbet and Hubbard commentary on *Odes* 2, in *JRS* 70 (1980) 182–5, with Nisbet's review of *Latin Poets and Roman Life* in *JRS* 87 (1987) 184–90.

29 G. Pasquali, *Orazio Lirico* (Florence 1920, reprinted with an important introduction by A. La Penna, Florence 1964). There is a brief biography (with further bibliography) of Pasquali by the Italian Marxist scholar (and friend of Fraenkel) L. Canfora in W. W. Briggs and W. M. Calder III, *Classical Scholarship: a Biographical Encyclopedia* (New York and London 1990) 367–75.

30 See especially the bitter review by Corrado Barbagallo, 'Un libro sbagliato sulla poesia di Orazio', first published in *Nuova Rivista Storica* for 1922 and then reprinted with some omissions in *Athenaeum* 1 (1923) 59–68: cf. Canfora in *Classical Scholarship*. On the background to the antipathy to Germany in scholarly circles, see especially Canfora's 'Sciovinismo e studi classici nella "grande guerra": Vitelli e le correnti nazionaliste in Italia', reprinted in his *Ideologie del classicismo* (Turin 1980) 39–56.

31 See Canfora's 'Cultura classica e fascismo in Italia' in *Ideologie del Classicismo* 76–103 at 83–90, with S. Timpanaro's introduction to the reprint of G. Pasquali *La preistoria della poesia Romana* (Florence 1981) 47–8, 54–9. In general on Horace in Fascist Italy, see G. Bandinelli 'Le letture minate' in *Lo Spazio Letterario di Roma Antica* vol. 4 eds. G. Cavallo, P. Fedeli, and A. Giardina (Rome 1991) 361–97, at 394–7 (with excellent bibliography).

32 Brink, *Horace on Poetry* 523.

33 Wilkinson, *Horace and his Lyric Poetry* 5.

34 See most notoriously John Henderson's brilliant attempt to bring alive a sense of disgust at *Epode* 8 in 'Suck it and See', *Homo Viator: Classical Essays for John Bramble*, ed. M. Whitby, P. Hardie and M. Whitby (Bristol 1987) 105–18, with the oppositionalist feminist reply by E. Oliensis, 'Canidia, Canicula, and the Decorum of Horace's *Epodes*', *Arethusa* 24 (1991) 107–38 (Henderson 'leaves Horace on top').

35 I import the metaphor of the poet as Orpheus or Pentheus, torn apart by his interpreters (cf. of course *S* 1.4.62) from Numenius on Plato's treatment at the hands of later philosophers: fr. 24 des Places, with his note. The myth of a Socratic unity-in-irony which the later schools (Academics, Stoics, Cynics) shattered is important for Horace's ethical 'eclecticism': compare the motifs of Colin Macleod's celebrated attempts to rehabilitate Horace as a serious moralist (above p. 20: *Collected Essays*, Oxford 1983, 218–91).

36 P. Shorey, *Horace Odes and Epodes* 479.

37 C. Beckenhaupt 'Horatius Travestitus. Un pastiche allemand' in *Etudes Horatiennes, Travaux de la Faculté de Philosophie et Lettres de l'Université de Bruxelles*, vol. VII (Brussels 1937) 11–34 at 15. On the concept of Romantic Irony in relation to classical literature, see *Materiali e discussioni per l'analisi*

dei testi classici 22 (1989) 75–122 at 109–113, A. Schmitt, 'Ironie und Humor bei Theokrit', *Würzburger Jahrbücher für die Altertumswissenschaft*, NF 15 (1989) 107–18.

38 H. Walter, *The Age of Tennyson* (London 1897) 239.
39 I am grateful for comments and corrections to the editors, and to R. O. A. M. Lyne and R. G. M. Nisbet. The last offers me an epigraph: 'if the pendulum stops swinging, the clock will stop ticking'.

BIBLIOGRAPHY

What follows is a selective list of secondary material relating specifically to the translation, imitation, reception and interpretation of Horace by British writers. Incidental discussion of Horace will, of course, also be found in many general studies of poetic genres (satire, verse-epistle, ode), or particular periods of English literature, and of individual writers.

Many of the English translations of Horace are listed in:

Gillespie, Stuart, 'A Checklist of Restoration English Translations and Adaptations of Classical Greek and Latin Poetry, 1660–1700', *Translation and Literature* 1 (1991) 52–67

Palmer, H. R., *A List of English Editions and Translations of Greek and Latin Classics Printed before 1641* (London 1911)

Watson, George, ed., *The New Cambridge Bibliography of English Literature* (5 vols., Cambridge 1969–77) I. 2170–1; II. 1497–8

Further suggestions on primary and secondary reading will be found in :

Brown, Huntingdon, 'The Classical Tradition in English Literature: A Bibliography', *Harvard Studies and Notes in Philology and Literature* 18 (1935) 7–46

Carlsen, Hanne, *A Bibliography to the Classical Tradition in English Literature* (Copenhagen 1985)

Highet, Gilbert, *The Classical Tradition: Greek and Roman Influences on Western Literature* (Oxford 1949)

Kallendorf, Craig, *Latin Influences on English Literature from the Middle Ages to the Eighteenth Century: an Annotated Bibliography of Scholarship, 1945–79* (New York and London 1982)

Aden, John M., *Something Like Horace: Studies in the Art and Allusion of Pope's Horatian Satires* (Kingsport, 1969)

Armour, E. D., *Echoes from Horace in English Verse* (Toronto 1922)

Baldwin, T. W., *Shakespeare's Small Latine and Lesse Greeke* (2 vols., Urbana 1944) II.497–525 on Shakespeare and Horace

Benham, Allen R., 'Horace and his 'Ars Poetica' in English: a Bibliography', *Classical World* 49 (1956) 1–5

Brower, Reuben, *Alexander Pope : the Poetry of Allusion* (Oxford 1959) chap. 9 on Pope and Horace

Clifford, Frederick B., *Horace in the Imitations of Alexander Pope* (Lexington 1954)
Coolidge, John S., 'Marvell and Horace', *Modern Philology* 63 (1965) 111–20
Dixon, Peter, *The World of Pope's Satires: an Introduction to the Epistles and Imitations of Horace* (London 1968)
Edden, Valerie, 'The Best of Lyrick Poets', in C. D. N. Costa, ed., *Horace* (London 1973) 135–60, English translations of Horace before 1670.
Ellis, A. M., 'Horace's Influence on Dryden', *Philological Quarterly* 4 (1925) 39–60
Erskine-Hill, Howard, *The Augustan Idea in English Literature* (London 1983) Horace and English 'Augustanism'.
Finley, John H., Jnr, 'Milton and Horace: a Study of Milton's Sonnets', *Harvard Studies in Classical Philology* 48 (1937) 29–73
Fuller, John, 'Carving Trifles: William King's Imitation of Horace', *Proceedings of the British Academy* 62 (1976) 269–91
Gillespie, Stuart, 'Dryden's *Sylvae*: a Study of Dryden's Translations from the Latin in the Second Tonson Miscellany, 1685' (unpublished Cambridge Ph.D. thesis, 1988)
Goad, Caroline, *Horace in the English Literature of the Eighteenth Century* (New Haven 1918)
Haight, Elizabeth Hazelton, 'Robert Herrick : the English Horace', *Classical Weekly* 4 (1911) 178–81, 186–9
Hammond, Paul, *John Oldham and the Renewal of Classical Culture* (Cambridge 1983) chap. 4 on Oldham's Horace.
Herrick, Marvin T., *The Fusion of Horatian and Aristotelian Literary Criticism 1531–55* (Urbana 1946)
Hooley, Daniel M., *The Classics in Paraphrast: Ezra Pound and Modern Translators of Latin Poetry* (London and Toronto 1988) chap. 4 on translations of Horace.
Hughes, R. E., 'Pope's *Imitations of Horace* and the Ethical Focus', *Modern Language Notes* 71 (1956) 569–74
Hunter, G. K., 'The "Romanticism" of Pope's Horace', *Essays in Criticism* 10 (1960) 390–404
Janoff, Ronald W., 'Eliot and Horace – Aspects of the Intrinsic Classicist', *Cithara* 5 (1965) 31–44
Jiriczek, Otto L., 'Der Elizabethanische Horaz', *Shakespeare-Jahrbuch* 47 (1911) 42–63
Kupersmith, William, 'Pope, Horace and the Critics: Some Reconsiderations', *Arion* 9 (1970) 205–19
  Roman Satirists in the Seventeenth Century (Lincoln, Nebr. 1985)
Leishman, J. B., *Translating Horace* (Oxford 1956)
Levi, Peter, 'Horace', in *The Art of Poetry: the Oxford Lectures, 1984–9* (New Haven and London 1991) 47–66
Lord, Louis E., 'Two Imperial Poets – Horace and Kipling', *Classical Journal* 52 (1956) 67–76

Maresca, Thomas E., *Pope's Horatian Poems* (Columbus 1966)
Martindale, Charles, 'Unlocking the Word-hoard: In Praise of Metaphrase', *Comparative Criticism* 6 (1984), 47–72 translations of *Odes* 1.5.
Martindale, Joanna, 'The Response to Horace in the Seventeenth Century' (unpublished Oxford D. Phil. thesis, 1977)
Mason, H. A., 'Horace's Ode to Pyrrha', *Cambridge Quarterly* 7 (1976) 27–62 translations of *Odes* 1.5.
   'Dryden's Dream of Happiness', *Cambridge Quarterly* 8 (1978) 11–55; 9 (1980) 218–71 Dryden's translation of *Epod.* 2.
   'Living in the Present : Is Dryden's "Horat. Ode 29. Book 3" an Example of "Creative Translation"?' *Cambridge Quarterly* 10 (1981) 91–129
   'The Hallowed Hearth : Some Reflections on Dryden's Version of the Ninth Ode in Horace's First Book', *Cambridge Quarterly* 14 (1985) 205–39
Miner, Earl, *The Cavalier Mode from Jonson to Cotton* (Princeton 1971) chaps. 2, 3, 6 on Horace and the Cavalier poets.
Mustard, W.P., *Classical Echoes in Tennyson* (New York, 1904) chap. 9 on Tennyson and Horace.
Nitchie, Elizabeth, 'Horace and Thackeray', *Classical Journal* 13 (1918) 393–410
Nügel, B., *A New English Horace: die Übersetzungen der Horazischen 'Ars Poetica' in der Restaurationzeit* (Frankfurt 1971)
Ogilvie, Robert M., 'Horace and the Eighteenth Century', in *Latin and Greek: a History of the Influence of the Classics on English Life from 1600 to 1918* (London 1964) 34–73
   'Translations of Horace in the 17th and 18th Centuries', in Walther Killy, ed., *Geschichte des Textverständnisses am Beispiel von Pindar und Horaz* (Munich 1981) 71–80
Papajewski, Helmut, 'Die Bedeutung der *Ars Poetica* für den Englischen Neoclassizismus', *Anglia* 79 (1961) 405–39
Pierce, Robert B., 'Ben Jonson's Horace and Horace's Ben Jonson', *Studies in Philology* 78 (1981) 20–31
Pound, Ezra, 'Horace', *Criterion* 9 (1930) 217–27
Pritchard, J. P., 'Aristotle, Horace and Wordsworth', *Transactions of the American Philological Association* 74 (1943) 72–91
Quiller-Couch, Sir Arthur, 'The Horatian Model in English Verse', in *Studies in Literature, First Series* (Cambridge 1919) 51–75
Regenos, Graydon W., 'The Influence of Horace on Robert Herrick', *Philological Quarterly* 26 (1947) 268–84
Røstvig, Maren-Sophie, *The Happy Man: Studies in the Metamorphoses of a Classical Ideal* (2nd edn, 2 vols., Oslo 1962) translation, influence and reception of *Epod.* 2.
Rudd, Niall, 'Dryden on Horace and Juvenal', *University of Toronto Quarterly*, 32 (1963) 155–9 (reprinted in *The Satires of Horace* (Cambridge 1966))
   'Pope and Horace on Not Writing Poetry: a Study of *Epistles* II.2', in Claude Rawson, ed., *English Satire and the Satiric Tradition* (Oxford 1984) 167–82
   'Variation and Inversion in Pope's *Epistle to Dr Arbuthnot*', *Essays in*

Criticism 34 (1984) 216–28 Pope's use of Horatian epistolary models.
'Horace *Odes* 3.29 and Tennyson's "To the Rev. F.D. Maurice",' *Hermathena* 150 (1991) 5–19.
Ruggles, Melville J., 'Horace and Herrick', *Classical Journal* 31 (1936) 223–34
Saitonge, P. F., Burgevin, G. and Griffith, H., *Horace: Three Phases of his Influence* (Chicago 1936)
Sherbo, Arthur, ed., *Christopher Smart's Verse Translation of Horace's 'Odes'* (Victoria, BC 1979) contains very full introduction on Horace in the eighteenth century.
Showerman, Grant, *Horace and his Influence* (Boston 1922)
Stack, Frank, *Pope and Horace: Studies in Imitation* (Cambridge 1985)
Steiger, Richard, 'Pope's Augustan Horace', *Arethusa* 10 (1977) 321–52
Storrs, Ronald, ed., *Ad Pyrrham: a Polygot Collection of Translations of Horace's Ode to Pyrrha (Book 1, Ode 5)* (London 1959)
Syfret, Rosemary, 'Marvell's Horatian Ode', *Review of English Studies*, NS 12 (1961) 160–72
Thayer, Mary Rebecca, *The Influence of Horace on the Chief English Poets of the Nineteenth Century* (New Haven 1916)
Weinbrot, Howard D., *Augustus Caesar in 'Augustan' England: the Decline of a Classical Norm* (Princeton 1978) Horace and English 'Augustanism' and 'Anti-Augustanism'.
Alexander Pope and the Tradition of Formal Verse Satire (Princeton 1982) Pope and the Horatian satirical tradition.
Eighteenth-Century Satire (Cambridge 1988) chap. 2 on Horace and English 'Augustanism'; chap. 5 on Rochester and Horace; chaps. 8–9 on Pope and Horace.
White, H. M. O., 'Orazio nella Letterature Inglese', in *Orazio nella Letteratura Mondiale* (Rome 1936) 95–111
Willkinson, L. P., *Horace and his Lyric Poetry* (2nd edn, Cambridge 1951) chap. 6 on translations of Horace.
Williams, Aubrey L., 'Pope and Horace: *The Second Epistle of the Second Book*' in Carroll Camden, ed., *Restoration and Eighteenth-Century Literature : Essays in Honor of Alan Dugald McKillop* (Chicago 1963) 309–21
Wilson, A. J. N., 'Andrew Marvell: *An Horatian Ode upon Cromwell's Return from Ireland*: the Thread of the Poem and its Use of Classical Allusion', *Critical Quarterly* 11 (1969) 325–41
Wrenn, C. L., 'Chaucer's Knowledge of Horace', *Modern Language Review* 18 (1923) 286–92

INDEX OF HORATIAN PASSAGES

Ars Poetica 255, 261–2
23: 141
24–5: 146
29f: 6
30: 175
47–8: 137, 139
52–3: 138
53–8: 138
58–63: 182
70: 171
70–2: 134–5, 182
72: 139
73–4: 173
86–7: 161
90–1: 133
124: 183
131–5: 170
133–4: 146
133–5: 162
151–2: 133
156–7: 180
179–88: 134
189: 128
231: 133
240: 133
263: 140
267: 182
268–9: 161
285–91: 162
309–10: 163
334: 141
338: 136
343: 129, 147
343–4: 164, 178
343–50: 129
351–3: 127
372–3: 182
408–11: 144

416–18: 140
494–7: 164
555–8: 164

Epistles
1.1
  (14): 15
  (66): 201
1.2: 115
1.4: 62
  (6–11): 143
  (15–16): 99
1.6
  (1–2): 12
  (58): 206
  (111ff): 14
1.7: 31–2
  (10–12): 37
  (29–36): 31
  (44–5): 83
  (46ff): 14
1.10 (32–3): 79
1.11 (29–30): 43
1.14 (10–13): 43
1.16: 241
1.17 (10): 83
1.18: 38
  (103): 83, 174
1.19: 38
  (19): 147
1.20: 62
  (24–5): 99
2.1: 12
  (34–5): 131
  (76–7): 131
  (156): 199
  (250): 164
  (251): 169

INDEX OF HORATIAN PASSAGES

2.2
  (51): 12
  (55): 10
  (58–64): 275
  (88–91): 142
  (109–10): 182
2.7 (28ff): 14

Epodes
1.2: 29–30, 30–1
2: 15, 72, 76–7, 147, 216, 265–7, 275
6: 5
8: 5
12: 5
13: 5

Odes 208, 255–6, 259–60
1.1: 4, 96, 227
1.2: 6
  (9) 236
1.3: 66, 147, 209
1.4: 76, 77–8, 81
  (1): 81, 209
  (1–4): 69
  (4): 81
  (15): 205
1.5: 4, 204, 240, 262–3, 264
  (5): 75, 233
1.6: 14–15
1.7: 3, 80
1.9: 23, 71, 74, 75, 76, 147, 202, 209
  (1): 233
  (5): 75
  (9): 117
  (12): 233
1.11: 4, 67, 75–6, 113
  (7–8): 67
  (8): 205
1.13: 246, 250
1.14: 212, 236
  (20): 212
1.17: 206
1.19: 232
1.22: 3, 211
  (1): 225
1.23: 5
1.24: 202, 235
1.27: 202
1.31: 255–6
1.33: 24

1.34: 15
1.35: 200
1.37: 4, 23, 90, 91–2, 248
  (12): 229
  (21–3): 92
  (29–32): 91
  (32): 90
1.38: 204–5, 208
  (2–5): 233
2.1: 26
2.3: 5, 80, 113
  (6) 208
  (26): 80
2.5: 5, 6, 23
2.6: 3
2.7
  (5–8): 235
  (6f): 208
  (9–10): 202
2.8: 72
2.9: 24, 80, 82
  (6–8): 81
2.10: 69, 260
  (1–4): 52–3
  (5): 7
  (13–20): 80–1
  (15–17): 81
2.11: 3, 113
  (1–4): 206
  (35): 215
2.14: 77–8, 80, 250–1
  (1–2): 78
2.15: 260
2.16: 72
  (13–14): 79
  (14): 75
2.17: 234
  (5–9): 209
  (21): 209
2.18: 62–3, 66, 79, 83
  (1–2): 199
  (14): 66
2.19: 232
2.20: 6
3.1
  (1): 143, 201
  (16): 80
  (40): 202, 204
3.2 (13): 201, 213
3.3: 21, 52, 56, 60, 63, 275

INDEX OF HORATIAN PASSAGES

(1–8): 50, 50–1
(12): 6
(49): 216
3.4: 21, 215
  (24): 215
  (53–8): 59
  (58–64): 203
3.5: 212–13, 224, 225
  (2–3): 19
  (53–6): 89–90
3.6: 224
3.7: 215
  (29–30): 233
3.9: 15, 72, 218
3.12: 250
  (3): 235
3.13: 24–6, 89, 208, 234
3.14: 21, 95
3.16: 212
  (31): 212
3.17: 234
  (10): 233
3.18 (7–8): 233
3.19: 232
3.21: 232
3.25: 12, 232
  (10): 233
3.27: 218
3.28: 237
  (16): 236
3.29: 72, 80, 147, 148–58, 240
  (12): 209
  (32–41): 151
  (40–56): 155–6
  (41–8): 153
  (42–8): 76
  (61): 157
3.30: 18, 94–5, 255–6, 274
4.1: 4, 6, 15, 62, 64–5, 67, 72, 99–101, 245
  (1–8): 245
  (3–4): 205
  (4–7): 65
  (29–40): 65
4.2: 14
4.3: 10, 226
4.4 (57–60): 221
4.5: 20, 273
  (9ff): 21
4.6: 229
4.7: 77–8, 81, 97, 97–8, 224, 228

(1–2): 81
4.8: 87–9
4.10: 75
4.11: 12, 232
  (31–4): 23
4.12: 114
  (28): 201
4.13: 5, 229
4.15: 20
4.23: 74

Sermones
1.1 (120): 55
1.2: 7, 9, 206
1.3 (11–17): 14
  (107–8): 9
  (139): 55
1.4: 55, 57
  (13–16): 55
  (34–8): 55–6
  (39–44): 169
  (42): 147
  (81–5): 56
1.5: 10, 34
1.6 (110ff): 12
1.8: 206
1.9: 55, 147, 167
1.10: 55, 144
  (4): 143
  (9–14): 164–5
  (14–15): 166
  (56–8): 167
  (68): 132
  (68–70): 142
  (78–91): 55
  (90–1): 145–6
2.1: 29, 36
  (1–4): 29
  (68): 57
  (82–3): 57
2.2 (129–35): 67
2.3 (61): 207
  (325): 12
2.5: 44–8
  (1–5): 44
2.6: 30, 39–42, 77, 103–26, 186–91
  (1): 30, 83
  (17): 169
  (20–4): 187
  (60): 216

INDEX OF HORATIAN PASSAGES

(63): 79
(93): 189
(93–7): 114
(97): 114, 189
(100–1): 189
(116): 189

2.7: 29, 30, 58, 63
 (2): 208
 (28–9): 30
 (45): 55
 (83–8): 60

GENERAL INDEX

NOTE: references in italics denote illustrations.

Actium, battle of 10
Addison, Joseph 7, 10, 20, 164, 180; and Dobson 206, 207–8
Aesop's Fables 74, 121; Caxton's edition 49
agelasts 185, 186
Agrippa, M. Vipsanius 14–15
Alamanni, Luigi 35–7, 39
Alcaeus 3, 97, 202
Aldus Manutius 267
Anacreon 74, 79, 84, 95–6, 202, 256
Apostles, The (Cambridge University) 209
Archilochus 202
Ariosto, Ludovico 32–4, 39, 45
Aristippus of Cyrene 111
Aristotle 128, 130, 159, 160
Armstrong, David 13, 272
Arnold, Matthew 184–5, 200, 203, 204, 206, 210–11
Ars Poetica: André Dacier's edition (1691) *Pl. 6b*; Dryden and 127–47; translations, (Jonson) 130, 262, (Roscommon) 161–2, 178, 182, (Sisson) 255, 261–2; *see also* Index of Horatian Passages
Ashmore, John 72
ataraxia 109–10, 114, 174
Athena 66
Auden, W.H. 2, 17, 21, 242, 252–4
Augustine, St 14, 204
Augustus: ambivalence in English attitudes to 271, 272; Horace's relationship with 10, 12, 18–20, 26, 63, 172; myths associated with cult of 63; reforms 21
Ausonius, pseudo- 76
Austin, Alfred 211–12
autobiographical writing, Horace's 9, 11–18, 82
Aytoun, W.E. 213

Baedeker's guidebooks 214
Baiae 215
Bakhtin, Mikhail 185–6, 189, 191, 198
Bandusia, spring at 24–5, 89, 214
Barrett, Elizabeth 199
Barthes, Roland 11
beans, Pythagorean 107, 108
Beaumont, Francis 121, 122
Behn, Mrs Aphra 240
Benjamin, Walter 22
Bentley, Richard *Frontispiece*, 8, 9, 177
Béranger, Jean-Pierre 204
Betjeman, John 14
Bewick, Thomas *126*, *Pl.8a*
Bible 82, 113
biographical criticism 11–13, 17
Blackett, John 210
Bloom, Harold 8
Boileau, Nicholas Despréaux 160, 161, 162, 172, 175, 194
Bolingbroke, Henry St John, 1st Viscount Bolingbroke 165–6, 171
Botticelli, Sandro *Pl. 1*
Bowra, C.M. 97
Braden, Gordon 84
brevity 164–5
Brian, Sir Francis 44–6, 48
Brink, C. O. 272
Brontë, Branwell 199
Brontë sisters 199
Brophy, Brigid 23
Brower, Reuben 242, 243
Brown, Tom 76
Browning, Robert 227
Bunting, Basil 242, 244, 246, 247, 248, 250–2, 257
Butler, Samuel 201, 216

321

GENERAL INDEX

Byron, George Gordon, 6th Baron 200, 213, 214

Callimachus 5, 25
Calverley, C.S. 202, 209
Cambridge University 208–9, 237
Campbell, A.Y. 25
Campbell, Thomas 213
Campion, Thomas 263
Caracci, Agostino 267
Carew, Thomas 54, 68–9, 70
Carmen Saeculare: Fraenkel on 272; Hardy on 216; Kipling's parody 220, 229; Sisson's translation 254, 260–1
Carne-Ross, D.S. 247
carpe diem theme 67, 78, 113–14; Arnold 210; Dryden 148; Herrick 67, 75–6, 77–80, 84; Jonson 67; Lovelace 67, 74–5, 76
Carrington, Charles 219
Catullus 3, 19, 154, 202, 258, 259
Caxton, William 49
Censure of the Rota pamphlets 136
Chamberlain, Joseph 211
Charles I, King of Great Britain 51, 64, 90, 91
Charles II, King of Great Britain 53, 130; *see also* Restoration
Charles V, Holy Roman Emperor 34, 47
Charleton, Walter 110–11, 111–12, 117, 119
Chatham, William Pitt, 1st Earl of 200
Chaucer, Geoffrey 140
Chesterfield, Philip Dormer Stanhope, 4th Earl of 200
Christianity 11, 113
Churchill, Lord Randolph 199
Cibber, Colley 181
Cicero 54
city life 43, 114–16; *see also* mice
civitas, use of poetry in 161, 176, 178–9, 179–80
Clare, John 215
classic quality of Horace 8–10
Cleopatra 4, 23, 90, 91–2, 218, 248
Clough, Arthur Hugh 203, 213–14, 216, 255
coarseness, Horace's 5, 67, 206
Cockayne, Sir William 64
Coiro, Anne Baynes 83–4
Coleridge, Hartley 199
Coleridge, Samuel Taylor 208

Commager, Steele 154, 157
Commonwealth period 22, 52, 91, 92, 93
Congreve, William 76, 103
Conington, J.C. 201–2, 221
Connor, Peter 154, 155
conservatism 21
contentment 43–4, 106–7, 153–4
Conway, R.S. 269
Cotton, Charles 26
country life 29–30, 43–4, 215–16; city life contrasted 43, 114–16; Herrick on 11, 54, 76–7, 82–3; *see also* mice
Cowley, Abraham 103–26, 164, 191; *Anacreontics* 116; on city life 114–16; and Dryden 152; English analogues for Roman details 122–3; and Epicureanism 109–13, 117–19, 126; and *Epodes* 30–1, 108; *Essays* 10, 21, 54, 103–26; 'The Garden' 112; 'Of Liberty' 106, 112–13; mock-heroic style 122; paraphrase 109; successors 72; and town and country mouse story 21, 103–26, (daring) 107, 108–9, (personal implication) 125–6; translations (Anacreon) 256, (*Odes* 1.5) 263, (*Sermones* 2.6) 103–5, 109; and Virgil 108; wit 119, 116–17
Cowper, William 103, 202
Crabbe, George 215
Creech, Thomas 54, 116, 146
criticism, literary: biographical 11–13, 17; Dryden 127–47; Pope 159–83; *see also* *Ars Poetica*; New Criticism
Crofts, William 218, 219
Croke, Sir George 51–2
Cromwell, Oliver 22, 52, 91, 92, 93
Cromwell, Thomas 37, 38
Cruquius (Jacob de Crusque) 139
Cunningham, J.V. 247–8
Cyrenaics 111
Czartoryski, Prince Adam 213

Dacier, André 53, 185, 186, 190, 191; *Ars Poetica* (1691) Pl. 6b
Dante Alighieri 6, 27, 90
Davie, Donald 248–9, 255
deconstruction 16
Dekker, Thomas 55, 58, 61
Denham, Sir John 51–2
Derrida, Jacques 16–17
Dickens, Charles 199

GENERAL INDEX

différance 16–17
diplomats, sixteenth-century 32, 47
disproportion, deliberate 23
Dobson, Austin 206, 207–8
Donne, John 93, 99, 167–70
Dorset, Charles Sackville, 6th Earl of 131
Dowson, Ernest 205–6, 216
drama, Horace on 176
Drant, Thomas 27–8, 31, 34, 38, 121
Dryden, John: and Aristotle 128, 130; on Chaucer 140; and Cowley 106, 152; criticism 127–47; on Horace 184, (good humour) 23, 53, 185, (metaphor) 136, 139, (politics) 19, 167, (on *Sermones* 1.9) 22, 55, (*see also* translations *below*); and Jonson 130, 138–9, 140, 141, 142, 143; and Juvenal 154, 184; language 134, 135–40; on licence 136; and Longinus 128, 130, 136; and Lucretius 152, 256; on Martial 136; on Milton 140; and Ovid 136, 140, 146, 256; Pope on 172, 175, 181; quotation of Horace, erroneous 127–8, 131; and Rochester 146; and Sedley 143; and Shadwell 140–4, 147; on Shakespeare 130, 137, 138; on Spenser 140; translations 259, (Horace *Odes* 1.9) 76, (Horace *Odes* 3.29) 72, 118, 148–58, 240, (Juvenal) 154, (Lucretius) 152, 256, (Ovid) 256, (Persius) 20, (theory) 146–7, 149; and Virgil 136, 137, 138, 156
  WORKS: *All for Love* 55, (Preface) 145–6; *Annus Mirabilis* 137; *The Assignation* 143; *Astraea Redux* 130; *The Author's Apology for Heroic Poetry and Poetic Licence* 136; *The Conquest of Granada, Part II* 138–9; *Defence of An Essay of Dramatic Poesy* 135–6; *Defence of the Epilogue* 139, 141–2; *To the Earl of Roscommon* 146; *Essay of Dramatic Poesy* 128, 131–5, 138; *Mac Flecknoe* 140, 144; Preface to *Ovid's Epistles* 146; *Religio Laici* 147; *Sylvae* 53; *Troilus and Cressida* 134
Du Bartas, Guillaume de Salluste, Seigneur 69, 136
Du Bellay, Joachim 34, 45
Dufferin and Ava, Frederick Blackwood, 1st Marquis of 219, 269
Dunkin, William 117, 118, 121
Du Quesnay, Ian 13

Eagleton, Terry 20
ecphrasis 88–9
Edwards, Michael 149
Eliot, George 199, 201
Eliot, T. S.: on Kipling 217, 221, 231; on Marvell 24; 'the mind of Europe' 23; on Pound 247; on recognition 83; on translation 126; on wit 24
Elton, G.R. 36
emblem poems 74, 219
Emerson, Ralph Waldo 242
English language, fluidity of 134
Ennius 176
epic poetry 176: mock– 122, 123–4, 193–4; *see also* Homer
Epicureanism 53–4: *ataraxia* 109–10, 114, 174; Charleton on 110–11, 111–12, 117, 119; Cowley and 109–13, 117–19, 126; hedonism 76, 80, 110; Horace's 'conversion' to theism from 15; Kipling and 237; *lathe biosas* 174; mortalism 110; 19th century perception 204
Epicurus 76, 80
epigrams, Herrick's 83
Epistles 6, 42, 164, 202; 16th century and 27, 42; 17th century and 72; 18th century and 9–10; Pinsky and 241–2; *see also* Index of Horatian Passages
Epodes: alleged 'immaturity' 5; Cowley and 108; Sisson's translation 265–7; 20th century and 275; *see also* Index of Horatian Passages
Erasmus, Desiderius 160, 166
Erskine-Hill, Howard 64, 72
Escher 93
Este, Ippolito d' 32
Euripides 14, 91

Fanshawe, Sir Richard 72, 73, 121, 240, 263–4
Fascism 270, 271, 272–3, 274
father, Horace's 18
Fawkes, Francis 107–8, 116
feminism 270
Fifth Book of Odes 229–31, 232, 237
flattery in Restoration criticism 130
Flecknoe, Richard 144, 147
Fletcher, C.R.L. 229, 230, 232
Flood, great 6
florilegia, Renaissance 2

323

GENERAL INDEX

Fortune 155–6, 158
Foucault, Michel 19, 20
fox in grain bin 31, 32
Fraenkel, Eduard 11–13, 270, 271–4;
  biographical criticism 11–13, 17; on
  'immaturity' in *Epodes* 5; on *Odes* 3.29
  150–1; on *Sermones* 2.6 186–7
France: classicism 160–1, 180–1; 19th
  century 200
Francis I, King of France 47
Frost, Robert 242–4, 246
Frye, Northrop 22

Games, Secular (17 BC) 10
garden, Pope's 174
Gassendi, Pierre 110, 113, 117
Gautier, Théophile 207
Gay, John; *Beggar's Opera* 195
Gentile, Giovanni 274
Germany: Jewish exodus from Nazi 270–1;
  romanticism 273
Gladstone, William Ewart 200, 201, 210,
  215
glosses, Renaissance 128, 129
Godley, A.D. 232
Goeree, Jan *Frontispiece*, 8
Goethe, Johann Wolfgang von 200
Goldsmith, Oliver 192, 195, 197
Gordon, Charles George 213
Gordon, David 252
Gosse, Edmund 207
Graves, Charles 201, 211, 216, 229, 230, 231
Gray, Thomas 195–8, 200
Greece: Horace and culture of 199, 274,
  (and lyric poetry) 3, 94, 95–7, 162–3, 178,
  202; language 96; 19th century
  nationalism 213
Greene, Thomas M. 67–8
Grüninger, Otto *Pl. 3a*
guidebooks, 19th century 214

Hallam, Arthur 208–9
Hamlett, Katharine 231
Hammond, Paul 155
Hampden, John 51
Handel, George Frederic 7–8
Hardy, Thomas 215, 216, 252
Harington, Sir John 48–9
Harris, Joel Chandler 234
Harrison, Bernard 17

Harvard College, Massachusetts 269
Heath-Stubbs, John 2
Heber, Reginald 215
hedonism 76, 80, 110, 111, 113–14
Heine, Heinrich 258, 275
Heinsius, Daniel 53, 142
Henry VIII, King of England: and diplomats
  34, 45, 46–7; Treason Act (1534) 36–7,
  38–9, 40
hermeneutic approach 7
Herrick, Robert 76–85; and Anacreontic
  tradition 79, 84; and pseudo-Ausonius 76;
  carpe diem theme 67, 75–6, 77–80, 84;
  and Civil War 81, 82, 84; on country life
  11, 54, 76–7, 82–3; epigrams 83; irony 83;
  Jonson's influence 54; and Martial 82, 83,
  84; and *Odes* 3.3 51; and Sabine farm
  poems 11, 83; on simple life 79; on
  transience 80–2
  WORKS: 'A Country Life' 54, 76–7;
  'Farewell Frost' 81–2; 'Gather ye
  Rosebuds' 76, 78; *Hesperides* 76–85; 'His
  Age' 73, 77–9; 'A Panegyric to Sir Lewis
  Pemberton' 76, 77
Herzen, Alexander 186
historicism 11, 270–4; New 13
Hobhouse, John Cam 214
Hofman-Peerlkamp, Petrus 203
Holkham MS 318 *Pl. 2b*
Homer 88, 115, 122, 133, 188, 199; Pope
  and 123, 170, 172, 193–4, 195
Hood, Tom 216
Hooley, D.M. 244, 245, 256
Horace *see individual aspects throughout
  index*
Housman, A.E. 6–7, 97–8, 209
Hovenden, R.M. 206
Howard, Frances 64
Howard, Sir Robert 131, 132
Hubbard, M. 15, 268, 270, 274
Hugo, Hermann 93
Hugo, Victor 200
humour, Horace's 23–4, 148, 184–98, 264–5;
  Cowley and 116–17, 119, 120–2; Dryden
  on Horace's good 23, 153, 185; town and
  country mice 186–91, 264–5

idiomatic language in lyric metre 95
imagery, Horace's 5, 23, 51
Imagists 232

GENERAL INDEX

imitations 3–4, 74, 170–1, 201–2
India 215, 219–20, 269
interlinguistic poetry, Marvell's 94, 97
invitation poems 61, 76, 209–10
Ireland 211
irony: Herrick 83; Horace 14–15, 23, 30–1, 108; Romantic 275
Italy, 19th century interest in 213–15

James I and VI, King of England and Scotland 64
Jennens, Charles 7–8
Johnson, Richard 253
Johnson, Samuel: on bustle 186–7; on classical quotation 19; on Cowley 106; on Gray 197, 198; and Horace 10, 15, 19; and Juvenal 254; on Pope 18, 194
Jones, David 254
Jones, Inigo 60, 64
Jonson, Ben 54–67; allusiveness 67; *carpe diem* theme 67; and Cicero 54; confidence in imitating classical authors 67, 69; defence of satire 55–8; Dryden and 130, 138–9, 140, 141, 142, 143; editions of Horace owned by 64; ethical approach to satire 52, 57, 62–4, 166; and Horace's style 64–5, 65–7; and Inigo Jones 60; invitation poems 61; and Juvenal 54, 58, 59; and Machiavelli 64; and Martial 54, 57, 68; and Persius 54; politics 57, 64; and Sabine farm poems 11; self-portraiture 62; and Seneca 54; and Shadwell 140, 141, 143; on Shakespeare 181; 'sons' 67–85; and Tacitus 54; on toil in art 57, 58, 181; translations of Horace, (*Ars Poetica*) 130, 262, (*Epodes 2*) 72, (*Odes 3.9*) 72, (*Odes 4.1*) 4, 62, 72, 245
  WORKS: *Catiline* 51; *The Devil is an Ass* 64, 67; *Discoveries* 1, 132; 'An Epistle Answering to One that Asked to be Sealed of the Tribe of Ben' 59–61, 61–2; 'If men and times were now' 58–9, 61; odes to friends 61–2; odes to himself 58–9, 60–1, 65, 78; *Poetaster* 50–1, 54–8, 59, 60, 61, 64; *The New Inn* ode 59, 61, 72; 'To Penshurst' 11, 54, 62–3, 65–6; 'To Sir Robert Wroth' 54, 72, 76, 77; 'To Sir Thomas Roe' 60; 'On the Town's Honest Man' 60; 'Where dost thou careless lie?' 58–9, 61, 65, 78

Juvenal: contrast with Horace 166–7, 184; Dryden and 154, 184; Johnson's use 254; Jonson and 54, 58, 59; Pope and 175

Keats, John 88
Keble, John 203
Kent, William *Pl. 6a*
Kermode, Frank 253
King's College, London 209
Kipling, Carrie 220
Kipling, John 219, 229, 236
Kipling, Rudyard 217–39; Cambridge fellowship 237; on Cleopatra Ode 218; Daemon 217–18, 230, 231, 238; and Epicureanism 237; grief 229, 230–1, 239; illuminations for the *Odes* 221, 222, 223; and India 219–20; Medici Press *Horace* owned by 221, 227, 228, 229, 234, 238; and Sabine farm poems 11; on Shakespeare 231; translation of *Odes* 4, 218; Wellington College talk 219, 224–5, 228
  WORKS: 'Carmen Circulare' 220, 229; 'The Church that was at Antioch' 235–6, 239; 'To the Companions' (1926) 234; 'To the Companions' (1933) 237–9; *Debits and Credits* 233–4; *Departmental Ditties; L'Envoi* 219; *A Diversity of Creatures* 226, 227, 229, ('Regulus') 212, 218, 219, 224–5, 227; 'The Finest Story in the World' 217, 220, 232; 'Horace, Bk.V, Ode 3' 4, 96; *Kim* 220, 221; 'The Last Ode' 234–5; *Limits and Renewals* 235–6; 'Lollius' 229, 234; *The Muse among the Motors* 220; 'The Pro-Consuls' 220, 229; *Puck of Pook's Hill* 220–2, 223; 'A Recantation' 229–30; 'Recessional' 219; *Rewards and Fairies* 223–4; *Something of Myself* 218, 239; *Stalky & Co* 224; 'The Storm Cone' 236–7; 'The Survival' 233–4; 'A Translation' 226–8, 229; 'The Tree of Justice' 223–4, 228, 238–9; *The Years Between* 230; 'Wireless' 217, 225, 231
Klinger, F. 272
Knox, Ronald 19
Kynaston, Edward 207

La Penna, A. 270, 273
Laelius 173

GENERAL INDEX

Lambinus 55
Lang, Andrew 203–4, 207, 213
language, poetic 96, 134, 135–40
Lauder, Sir Harry 230
Lawes, Henry 206
Lawrence, Edward 209
Leavis, F. R. 2
Leishman, J.B. 75
Lewis, C.S. 10
licence, poetic 136
Lippert, Philippe Daniel *Pl. 2a*
Lloyd, Charles 208
Lloyd George, David, 1st Earl Lloyd-George 229
local references, substitution of 260–1
London University; King's College 209
Longinus 128, 130, 136
Loutherbourg, Philip James de, RA *Pl. 7*
Lovelace, Richard 26, 54, 74; 'Advice to my Best Brother' 69–71; *carpe diem* theme 67, 74–5, 76; 'The Grasshopper' 26, 73–5
Lubinus 128
Lucan 93
Lucilius: Horace on 142, 143, 167, 171, 172, 174; Pope and 175
Lucretius 9, 76, 146, 152, 256

Machiavelli, Niccolo 64, 92
Macleane, A.J. 263, 264, 265
Macleod, Colin 20
Maecenas: at Actium 10; Horace and 12, 18, 31–2, 107, 164, 186–7; Tennyson on 209
Maidwell, Lewis 134
male friendship 199, 206–10, 269
Manicelli 265
Marston, John 55
Martial: Dryden on 136; Herrick and 82, 83, 84; Jonson and 54, 57, 68; obscenity 5
Martin, Richard 57
Martin, Sir Theodore 206–7
Marvell, Andrew 86–102; on Charles I 90, 91; on Cromwell 22, 52, 91, 92, 93; Eliot on 24; Horace compared with 86–102; interlinguistic effects 94, 97; and Lucan 93; modulation of tone 98; and Tacitus 93
  WORKS: 'The First Anniversary' 52–3; 'The Garden' 86–7, 89; 'To His Coy Mistress' 75, 98; 'An Horatian Ode' 22,
52, 73, 90–3, 248; 'The Mower against Gardens' 87; 'The Picture of Little T.C. in a Prospect of Flowers' 75; 'Tom May's Death' 50–1, 52, 53
Mason, H.A. 187, 188, 189
Matthew, Gospel of 113
Maurice, F.D. 209–10
Mazzini, Giuseppe 213
mean, golden 7–8, 172–3
Medici Press *Horace*, Kipling's copy of 221, 227, 228, 229, 234, 238
melancholy 10, 23, 78, 97–8, 113–14
men, society of 199, 206–10, 269
Messalla Corvinus, M. Valerius 20
metaphor 136, 139
metres: Dobson and old French 207–8; 19th century translations 202; quantitative 242–3, 245, 246–7; 20th century poets 242–3, 245, 246–8, 250, 252–3
mice, town and country: Bewick's illustrations *126, Pl. 8*; Cowley's version 103–26; humour 186–91, 264–5; Wyatt's version 39–42
Michie, James 93–4, 245
Millet, Jean François 215–16
Milner, Alfred, 1st Viscount Milner 220
Milton, John: anger in 6; collocations of words 65; on Cowley 106; Dryden on 140; Handel's settings of 7–8; Pope on 177; Sonnets 73, 206, 209; translations of *Odes* 1.5 3–4, 65, 262–3
Miner, Earl 74
mock-heroic style 122, 123–4, 193–4
moderation 7–8, 172–3
modernism, literary 270
modernization in translations 260–1
Montagu, Lady Mary Wortley 240
Montaigne, Michel Eyquem de 106–7, 164
Moore, Marianne 247, 249–50, 252
Moore, Thomas 203, 205
Morley, John 211
'mosaic of words' 244–5, 251
Mulgrave, John Sheffield, 3rd Earl of 161, 162
Murray, Gilbert 218
Murray, John; guidebooks 214
Musset, Alfred de 207
mythology: Augustan 63; Ovid and 11

nationalism, 19th century 213–14

GENERAL INDEX

New Criticism 11, 16, 270, 273
Newcastle, William Cavendish, Duke of 143
Nietzsche, Friedrich Wilhelm 244–5, 270
nineteenth century 199–216
Nisbet, R.G.M. 15, 19, 268, 270, 274
Noah's Ark 82
Nomentanus 172
non semper theme *see* transience
Norbrook, David 63–4, 92
Norden, Eduard 272
nostalgia for youth 23
Noyes, Alfred 271–2

obscenity 5, 9
Odes: 17th century and 61, 65–7, 72; 19th century and 202; 20th century view 5–6, 242, 275; Fifth Book 229–31, 232, 237; original reception 3–4
Odysseus 44–5
Ogilby, John 121
Oldham, John 146, 147, 164–5, 240, 262
Orellius (John Gaspar Orelli) 88, 89
otium 20, 174
Otway, Thomas 54, 72
Ovid 6, 11, 94, 275; Dryden and 136, 140, 146, 256
Oxford University 208, 212, 270, 273
oxymoron 3, 5, 6, 7, 65

Pantabolus 172
paradox 3, 5, 6, 7
Partenio, Bernardino 64, 66
particles, Greek 96
Pasquali, Giorgio 268, 274
patronage: Restoration 130; *see also* Augustus (Horace's relationship)
Peel, Sir Robert 200
Pepys, Samuel 237, 238, 239
periodicals, 18th century 20; *see also* Addison, Joseph; *Spectator*
Perret, J. 270
Persius 19–20, 54, 167, 175
persona 14, 16, 62, 99–101
Petrarch 11
Petronius Arbiter 93
Philippi, battle of 10, 241
Philips, Ambrose 9–10
Pindar 3
Pinsky, Robert 241–2
place, sense of 34, 48, 49, 214–16

Plautus 134, 176
pleasure doctrine *see* hedonism
Plommer, John 38
Pointz, John 38–9, 40
Pole, Reginald, Cardinal 34
Polish nationalism 213
politics, Horace's 18–22, 23, 93–4, 269, 271; 16th century use of 32–49; 19th century view 210–14; Dryden on 19, 22, 167; Fraenkel on 271–3; Jonson and 57, 64; pragmatism 63–4; public/private distinction 21–2; retirement from 215–16 (*see also* country life); *see also* state
Pollio, Vedius 12, 79
Ponsard, François 202–3
Pope, Alexander 159–83; on Aristotle 159; and Bentley 9; Byron and 200; concision 165; on Cowley 106; on criticism 159–60; on Dryden 172, 175, 181; epic, mock- 193–4; grotto *Pl. 6a*, 173–4; humanity 6; humour 162, 163, 192, 193–5; identification with Horace 240; and imitation 170–1; and king 179; moral aim 171; on obscenity in Horace 9; and Sabine farm poems 11; self-conscious virtuosity 23, 121–2, 123, 124; self-presentation 18, 101; translation of Homer 123, 170, 172, 195; translations of Horace 170–1, 259, (*Epistles*) 175–82, 183, (*Odes* 4.1) 62, 245, (*Sermones* 2.6) 121–2, 123, 124
    WORKS: *Dunciad* 175, 181; *Epilogue to his Satires* 175; *Epistle to Dr Arbuthnot* 101, 163, 175, 180; *Epistle to Miss Blount* 101; *An Essay on Criticism* 159–61, 162–3, 165, 175–6, 183, 191; *An Essay on Man* 163, 165–6; ethical epistles 163, 166; *Horatian Imitations* 167–71, 175; *Imitation of Horace* 18; *Rape of the Lock* 193–5; 'Sober Advice from Horace' 9
postmodernism 276
post-romanticism 203
Post-structuralism 11
Potter, Beatrix *Pl. 8b*
Pound, Ezra 1, 254; and Horace's style 246–7; and metre 246–7, 250, 252; and *Odes* 242, 244, (translations) 4, 255–7; 'Seafarer' 227–8; and syntax 251
poverty, Horace's claims to 13, 156–7
power, Foucault on 19

327

GENERAL INDEX

Poynter, Ambrose 220
pragmatism, Horace's 63–4
Priapea 5
printing: first illustrated edition of Horace (1498) *Pl. 3a*
Prior, Matthew 75
private/public distinction 21–2
Prometheus 66

questions, Horace's use of 66
quietude 43–4
quotation of Horace, erroneous 127–8, 147

Rabelais, François 185–6
Ramsay, A.B. 230, 237
Rand, E.K. 269
Randolph, Thomas 66
Raphael *Pl. 3b*
Reason 20
reception theory 1
recusatio 14
Regulus 89–90, 212–13, 224, 225
religion: Horace 203, 204; Virgil 203
Renaissance texts 2, 127–8, 129
Restoration 53, 106, 130; *see also* individual poets
restraint, lack of 4–6
retirement 215–16
Rhodes, Cecil 212
Ricks, Christopher 92
river, description of 151–2
Rochester, John Wilmot, 2nd Earl of 76, 144–6, 166
Romanticism 198, 273
Ronsard, Pierre de 69
Roscommon, Wentworth Dillon, 4th Earl of 146, 147, 163; *Essay on Translated Verse* 161, 162; translation of *Ars Poetica* 161–2, 178, 182
Rudd, Niall xx, 44

Sabine Hills, Horace's farm in 11, 31, 83, 214
Saltonstall, Wye 119
Sappho 3
Sarbiewski, Casimir 74
Scaliger, Joseph Justus 184
scepticism, Ovid's 11
scholarship: Renaissance 2, 127–8, 129; 19th century 203; 20th century 268–76; *see also* individual scholars

Schrevelius, Cornelius 129, 134
Scipio, Publius Cornelius 173
Scriblerus club 195
Sedley, Sir Charles 72, 132–3, 143
self-consciousness, Horace's 217, 231, 232
self-presentation of poet 14, 16, 62, 99–101
Sellar, William 150
Seneca 14, 54, 204
Sermones: 16th-century view 27–9, 42, 44–5, 55, 61; 17th century 72; 20th century 275; autobiography 8–9; humour 186–91; morality 164; as Pope's model 159
Seward, Anna 240
sexuality, Horace on 5, 7, 11, 12–13, 206
Shadwell, Thomas 140–4, 147
Shaftesbury, Anthony Ashley Cooper, 3rd Earl of 19, 191
Shakespeare, William: Dryden on 130, 137, 138; Jonson on 181; Kipling and 230, 231; 19th century and 207; Pope on 123, 177, 178; Victor Hugo on 200
  WORKS: *Hamlet* 231; *A Midsummer Night's Dream* 200; *Richard III* 157–8; *Romeo and Juliet* 123
shield, loss of 202
Sidney, Sir Philip 56, 136, 240, 269
Simonides 98
Sisson, C.H. 21, 254–5, 258–67; translations: *Ars Poetica* 255, 261–2; *Carmen Saeculare* 254, 260–1; *Epode 2* 15, 265–7
sixteenth century 27–49
Skinner, Cyriac 206
Smart, Christopher 116–17, 118, 245, 248
Smith, James and Horace 201
Smith, W.H. 199
South Africa, Gladstone and 211, 212
Southey, Robert 208
Spectator 7, 9–10, 211; *see also* Addison, Joseph
Spenser, Edmund 140
Stack, Frank 18, 245
Stanley, Thomas 110–11
state, function of art in 161, 176, 178–9, 179–80
Steele, Sir Richard 206, 207–8
Stevenson, Robert Louis 200–1
Stoicism 54, 63, 107, 204
storm, Horace on 51, 157, *Pl. 7*
structure of Horace's poems 23
style, Horace's: Dryden on 152–3, 169;

328

Horace's prescription for *sermo* 167;
  Jonson and 65–7; 'mosaic of words'
  244–5, 251; possible strangeness to
  original readers 3–4
Suetonius 12
Surrey, Henry Howard, Earl of 240
Swift, Jonathan 6, 10, 121, 180, 195
Swinburne, Algernon Charles 250
Syfret, R.H. 93
Sylvester, Joshua 69, 136
Syme, Sir Ronald 11–12, 19–20, 271

Tacitus 19, 54, 93
Talbert, E.W. 56
Talleyrand-Périgord, Charles Maurice de 206
taste, lack of good 6–7
Tatler 10
Teiresias 44–5
Tennyson, Alfred, 1st Baron Tennyson 11, 208–9, 209–10, 215, 247–8
textual criticism: Renaissance 127–8, 129; 19th century 203
textuality 11, 16–17
Thackeray, William Makepeace 200, 204–5, 207
Tiber, description of 151–2
Tibullus 20, 143
Tomlinson, Charles 263
Tonson, Jacob 146, 240
topoi 23
transience, theme of 67, 80–2, 97–8, 113–14, 202, 203–6
transitions, Horace's 65, 108, 248
translation: 17th century 72, 76, 107–8, 121, 263–4; 19th century 200, 201–2; of Catullus 258, 259; English analogues for Roman details 122–3; and Horace's style 3–4; local references, substitution of 260–1; modernization 260–1; *see also under* Cowley, Abraham; Dryden, John; Jonson, Ben; Kipling, Rudyard; Milton, John; Pope, Alexander; Pound, Ezra; Roscommon, Earl of; Sisson, C. H.
transpositions 94–5
Treason Act (1534) 36–7, 38–9, 40
Trevelyan, G.O. 201, 202, 208, 215
Turner, J.M.W. 212–13, 215
twentieth century: poetry 240–57; scholarship 268–76

Tyndale, William 38
Tyrrell, R.Y. 203

Vaenius, Otto Pls. 4, 5a
Varius 176
Vaughan, Henry 54, 71–2
Vietnam War 241
villanelle 207, 208
Virgil: Carew and 69; and Christianity 11; Cowley and 108; Dryden and 136, 137, 138, 156; *Eclogues* 5, 235; *Georgics* 108, 117; on growth and decay of cities 221; Horace on 176; Kipling and 235; 19th-century view 199–200; pastoral poetry 5, 69, 108, 117, 235; politics 167; on Roman imperium 179; reception of 11; religiosity 11, 203; Tennyson and 215; translations 258, 259
virtus 156–7
Vives, Juan Luis 132

Waddell, Helen 233
Wagner, Richard 244
Wallace, John M. 53
Waller, Edmund 75
Walpole, Sir Robert 172
Walsh, William 163
war 210–14
War, English Civil 51, 70, 71, 72, 81, 82, 84
War, first Punic 176
War, First World 229
War, Second World 270–1
War, Vietnam 241
War of the Theatres 55, 58
water imagery of poetry 25
Weinbrot, Howard 16
Wellington, Arthur Wellesley, 1st Duke of 200
Wellington College, Kipling's talk at 219, 224–5, 228
West, David 25
Wickham, E.C. 265
Wicksted 19
Wilamowitz-Moellendorf, Ulrich von 270, 274
Wilkes, John 19
Wilkinson, L.P. 271, 272, 275
Williams, Gordon 5–6, 15, 22, 25, 273–4
Wilson, A.J.N. 87
wit *see* humour

Wither, George *Pl. 5b*
women: attitudes to Horace 199, 270;
  Horace's attitude to 4–5, 6, 9, 23
Wordsworth, William 25, 106, 200, 208
Wotton, Sir Henry 34, 47
Wroth, Sir Robert 68, 72
Wyatt, Sir Thomas 22, 34–49; Satires 35–46, 49

Yeats, W.B. 101
Young, Edward 195
youth, nostalgia for lost 23

Zukofsky, Louis 246